Deviance, Conformity, and Social Control in Canada

Deviance, Conformity, and Social Control in Canada

Fifth Edition

Tami M. Bereska
MacEwan University

 Pearson

Toronto

VICE PRESIDENT, EDITORIAL: Anne Williams
ACQUISITIONS EDITOR: Keriann McGoogan
MARKETING MANAGER: Euan White
CONTENT MANAGER: Madhu Ranadive
PROJECT MANAGER: Christina Veeren and
Colleen Wormald
CONTENT DEVELOPER: Alanna Ferguson
MEDIA EDITOR: Alanna Ferguson
MEDIA DEVELOPER: Bogdan Kosenko
PRODUCTION SERVICES: iEnergizerAptara®, Ltd
PERMISSIONS PROJECT MANAGERS: Tanvi Bhatia
and Anjali Singh

PHOTO PERMISSIONS RESEARCH:
iEnergizerAptara®, Ltd
TEXT PERMISSIONS RESEARCH:
iEnergizerAptara®, Ltd
INTERIOR DESIGNER: iEnergizerAptara®, Ltd
COVER DESIGNER: iEnergizerAptara®, Ltd
COVER IMAGE: Marcos Calvo Mesa/123RF
VICE-PRESIDENT, CROSS MEDIA AND PUBLISHING
SERVICES: Gary Bennett

Pearson Canada Inc., 26 Prince Andrew Place, North York, Ontario M3C 2H4.

ISBN 978-0-13-4301068

Library and Archives Canada Cataloguing in Publication

Bereska, Tami M. (Tami Marie), 1968–, author
      Deviance, conformity, and social control in Canada / Tami
M. Bereska. — Fifth edition.

ISBN 978-0-13-430106-8 (hardcover)

      1. Deviant behavior—Textbooks. 2. Conformity—Textbooks.
3. Social control—Textbooks. 4. Canada—Social conditions—
Textbooks. 5. Textbooks. I. Title.

HM511.B47 2017   302.5'420971   C2017-904839-2

4 2019

Brief Contents

Contents

Preface

INTRODUCTION

The sociology of deviance is a diverse field of study, and this diversity is reflected in the content of Canadian textbooks that are available. Some books are based on theory, with separate chapters on each category of deviance theory and specific deviance examples to illustrate components of those theories. These books provide a thorough description and critical analysis of a wide range of theories, but if there is one way to make a fascinating subject like deviance rather dull in the eyes of students (as they have repeatedly pointed out to me), it is to bombard them with theory for the sake of theory. In contrast, this textbook reviews theories of deviance in two chapters, but the remaining chapters focus on substantive issues, bringing in relevant theories when doing so can meaningfully contribute to the overall "story" being told within a particular section of the chapter and within the chapter as a whole.

While some books address mainly theory, others have a criminological focus, containing extensive discussions of topics like violent crime, property crime, white-collar crime, police deviance, cybercrime, and sexual assault. These are all very important topics for students to be familiar with. However, students who take separate courses in criminology and in deviance frequently experience too much overlap between the course materials. In contrast, this textbook is specifically intended for courses in deviance or social control. There will still be a small amount of overlap for students taking both criminology courses and deviance courses, but that overlap is minimal. Furthermore, the material that might overlap is presented in a context very different from that in a student's criminology course.

Some textbooks contain collections of readings that are based on a similar theoretical approach, such as social constructionism. These collections have the benefit of providing students with original readings; however, they lack a cohesive context to enhance student learning. This book is the kind of single-authored textbook that many professors and students prefer.

Finally, some books are characterized by what Ben-Yehuda (1990, p. 5) calls "radical phenomenalism," where countless numbers of isolated, specific phenomena (e.g., call girls, transsexualism, and marijuana use) are described in tremendous detail but without reference to a broader social and historical structure. These phenomena are usually quite interesting to read about, but without a wider context the logic of including the various specific phenomena is unclear. To the reader, it can feel somewhat like randomly grabbing items in an all-you-can-eat buffet rather than sitting down to a four-course meal with different courses designed to complement each other. In contrast, in this textbook there is a method to the madness: the specific topics and issues addressed in each chapter have been selected as parts of a cohesive whole. Each individual topic covered is placed within a sociocultural context and contributes to a bigger picture.

WHAT'S NEW

In addition to updated statistics and research throughout the text, listed below are key changes integrated into each chapter of the fifth edition.

Chapter 1: Determining Deviance

- The introductory sections of the chapter are revised to be more concise and student centred. The chapter begins with a new *Ask Yourself* exercise that presents students with a list of behaviours, and then directs them to determine which of those behaviours they consider to be deviant. The chapter then further draws upon student responses to the exercise to create a foundation for understanding the objective/subjective dichotomy, the varying definitions of deviance, and the "deviance dance." Other parts of the chapter then refer back to that exercise to create a cohesive narrative.

- A new box explores how definitions of conformity (or normality) are intertwined with each of the varying definitions of deviance presented in the chapter.

- The levels of social construction are expanded from four to five: individual; interactional; institutional; sociocultural; and global (in terms of processes associated with globalization).

- A new *Exercise Your Mind* activity asks students to explore the notion of "positive deviance" using each of the various definitions of deviance addressed in the chapter.

Chapter 2: Explaining Deviance: The Act

- Robert Agnew's general strain theory is currently the most widely-used positivist theory of deviance. The discussion of general strain theory is expanded to include the different coping strategies identified by the theory and their consequences, as well as current research that applies general strain theory to criminal and non-criminal forms of deviance.

- The section of the chapter that addresses the critiques of functionalism is reorganized for better structure and clarity, highlighting critiques of logic, critiques of ideology, and critiques of bias.

- The discussion of Durkheim's notion of anomie highlights his emphasis on anomie being inherent in trade and commerce, and goes on to explore how that is related to processes of globalization today.

- Techniques of neutralization used by parents who spank their children and by university officials who covered up Jerry Sandusky's sexual abuse of children are addressed.

Chapter 3: Explaining Deviance: The Perception, Reaction, and Power

- Updated examples are used to illustrate key points, including the emergence of the #BlackLivesMatter movement, racial profiling by law enforcement, and debates over the Quebec Charter of Values (and its successors).
- The discussion of stigmatization is expanded to explore, in greater detail, the nature and forms of stigma, as well as the implications of using specific stigma management strategies.
- A new box looks at a community program that teaches formerly-incarcerated men how to manage their impressions in order to obtain stable employment.
- More material is included on the ways that structural components are integrated into interpretive theories, such as Sheldon Stryker's theorizing and empirical research on how the effects of stigmatization vary by race.
- Research examines public restrooms as sites of surveillance, and the implications for gender-variant persons.

Chapter 4: Deviance 2.0: The Role of the Media

- New data on patterns of media use compares 2001 and 2015, and highlights simulmedia, variations across age groups, youth as digital natives, and the favourite websites of Canadian children in grades 4 through 11.
- The implications of media framing are explored in greater detail. This includes the following: the way video gamers are framed in the media and its connection to the #Gamergate scandal, which revealed the ridicule and harassment faced by women in the gaming industry; contemporary examples of whitewashing in Hollywood films; and the implications of media framing for studying deviance.
- There is new material on resistance to media framing, such as social media campaigns (#whitewashedOUT; #OscarsSoWhite).
- A new box looks at the Truth and Reconciliation Commission's calls to action regarding media as an illustration of resistance to media framing and its implications.
- In the section "Using Media for Deviance," there is new material on the ways that some deviant actions include both online and offline components, such as "Internet banging" among gangs and school shooters' use of media to ensure their acts are interpreted correctly.

- Recent examples of cyberterrorism and cyberespionage include the Sony hack (2014), the Yahoo hack of 1 billion user accounts (discovered in 2016), and allegations that the Russian government interfered with the American and German elections.
- In the section on "Media and the Deviance Dance," there is a new box on the Dark Net, as well as new examples including Creep Catchers and social media videos of police shootings of unarmed black men.

Chapter 5: "Deviant" and "Normal" Sexuality

- The section on Indigenous sexualities is further contextualized by pointing out that the regulation of Indigenous sexualities was part of the larger project of colonization, with implications for landholdings, territoriality, and governance.
- There is material on how the legalization of same-sex marriage in the United States in 2015 led to resistance in the form of anti-LGBTQ laws (such as refusal of service) in more than 20 states.
- In the section on exotic dancing, a new paragraph addresses the varied effects of exotic dancing on the self-concepts of dancers, comparing women who dance for men and men who dance for women. These differences emerge, in part, from the ways that women are, to a greater extent, sexualized and objectified throughout society.

Chapter 6: The Troubling and Troubled World of Youth

- There are updated statistics (and related figures) on youth crime, gangs, and substance use.
- The material on the relationship between parenting styles and youth crime is replaced with material looking at the relative influences of family, school, and peer variables.
- There is new material that highlights how individual and collective trauma contribute to youth crime, and emphasizes the corresponding need for the youth justice system to evolve. For Indigenous youth in particular, this requires not only cultural resources to be integrated into the youth justice system, but also broader processes of reconciliation in society at large.
- A new box on cyberbullying links the experience of cyberbullying to outcomes such as depression, suicide, and substance abuse.
- There is new material on the Master Settlement Agreement with tobacco companies and the industry's efforts to market tobacco products to youth.

- The influence of tobacco images in youth-rated movies on youth attitudes and smoking behaviour is explored, as are associated measures of social control by various groups (such as the World Health Organization).
- The section on "alcopops" is expanded to address Diageo's strategy to access the underage alcohol market by developing Smirnoff Ice and marketing it in youth-oriented media venues—a strategy that included hiring a former executive from the tobacco industry.

Chapter 7: Looking Deviant: Physical Appearance

- In the section on voluntary and involuntary physical appearance, new examples include school dress codes (for revealing clothing and gang colours) and debates over cultural appropriation (such as Indigenous headdresses at music festivals).
- In the section on subjectivist approaches to studying body modification, narrative approaches are introduced and the section is re-framed in terms of "stories of gender" (e.g. skank flanks), "stories of work" (e.g., occupational identities; acceptance of body modification in the workplace), and "stories of interpersonal relationships" (e.g., memorial tattoos).
- Social media is discussed as a site of fat-shaming and thin-shaming; as a site of resistance to deviantization; and as a causal factor in body dissatisfaction for all ages and sexes.
- New research examines the stigmatization of very thin people and the coping strategies they use.
- Updated examples of government and community strategies for healthier weights and fitness are presented, such as the Honour Your Health Challenge in Indigenous communities across British Columbia.

Chapter 8: Mental Disorders

- There is new material on mental illness across diverse social groups (e.g., immigrants, refugees, LGBTQ individuals, Indigenous communities), and the corresponding need for mental health initiatives to address the distinct needs of those groups.
- There is an expanded section on media framing of mental illness and the consequences of those portrayals.
- New research is presented on the effects of economic recession on mental health.
- There are updated examples and illustrations, such as states of emergency declared in several Indigenous communities due to suicides among youth.

Chapter 9: What Do You Believe? Religion, Science, and Deviance

- The concept of sects as "churches of the disinherited" is introduced.

- There is new material on how the framing of cults in the media has evolved since the 1950s, and the frames that comprise the "cult narrative" in contemporary fictional entertainment media.

- The discussion of resistance by deviantized religious groups is expanded to include the use of litigation in response to criticism, the recruitment of celebrities, and the use of media (such as art and music) to communicate their ideologies.

- The section on the witch persecutions includes a discussion of how such persecutions continue into the present day in some parts of the world.

- There are updated examples of scientific misconduct, such as social psychologist Diederick Stapel, who built his entire career on misconduct.

- New research is presented on the following topics: retracted journal articles as indicators of scientific misconduct; macro-level factors that contribute to misconduct; the varied reasons for scientific misconduct, depending on the individual's role (e.g., senior researcher versus support staff); misconduct among fieldworkers due to moral challenges and declining morale.

Chapter 10: The "Deviance Dance" Continues

- Updated examples of the core concepts, ideas, and themes of the text drawn from previous chapters.

- A series of new *Exercise Your Mind* boxes ask students to think about additional examples of the objective–subjective continuum, social typing, social control, power, and the deviance dance.

FEATURES

The features of this textbook include the following:

- *Pedagogical aids for students* appear throughout every chapter. Students are asked to engage with the material as they read it. *Ask Yourself* sections direct students to think about certain questions, their own lives, or their own points of view. *Exercise Your Mind* sections ask to explore particular issues in more detail. *Time to Review* sections present students with review questions at regular intervals throughout the chapters. Although formulated as pedagogical aids for students, many instructors report that they make use of these features as class activities or assignments or to stimulate class discussion.

- *Objective and subjective approaches* to deviance are integrated in the textbook, rather than only one or the other being focused on. They are also presented as complementary (rather than contradictory) approaches.

- *Two theory chapters* review those theories that are used in more objective approaches (Chapter 2) and more subjective approaches (Chapter 3).

- The topics of the substantive chapters are *relevant to students' lives*—media, sexuality, youth, voluntary and involuntary physical appearance, mental disorders, religious belief systems, and scientific belief systems. The topics illustrate that deviance is not a characteristic of particular Others, but rather a set of processes that students themselves are subjected to and participate in each day.

- Each of the substantive chapters incorporates material on *social typing* and *social control*.

- Each of the substantive chapters reveals the *"deviance dance."* That is, each chapter demonstrates how the social typing of deviance is not a uniform process but is characterized by *disagreement, debate,* and *resistance.*

- Each of the substantive chapters *tells a cohesive story.* Students are not bombarded with an assortment of cafeteria-style facts and theories; rather, they learn about the sociocultural context within which particular forms of deviance are socially typed and socially controlled.

- In the narrative of each chapter, both *criminal* and *non-criminal* forms of deviance are explored in relation to the topic at hand.

- The vital role of *power* in determining and controlling deviance is discussed in each chapter.

- In this fifth edition, more than 300 new references are included.

STUDENT SUPPLEMENTS

Companion Website (www.pearsoncanada.ca/bereska)   The updated companion website is organized by textbook chapter and features chapter learning objectives, quizzes, recommended readings, and additional multi-media content.

INSTRUCTOR SUPPLEMENTS

These instructor supplements are available for download from a password-protected section of Pearson Canada's online catalogue (www.pearsoncanada.ca/highered). Navigate to your book's catalogue page to view a list of those supplements that are available. Speak to your local Pearson sales representative for details and access.

Computerized Test Bank   Pearson's computerized test banks allow instructors to filter and select questions to create quizzes, tests or homework. Instructors can revise questions or add their own, and may be able to choose print or online options. These questions are also available in Microsoft Word format.

Instructor's Resource Manual   Each of the chapters in this manual includes a lecture outline, teaching suggestions for active learning, video suggestions, and website suggestions.

PowerPoint Slides   The PowerPoint slides offer over 25 slides per chapter and highlight key concepts featured in the text to assist instructors.

Learning Solutions Managers   Pearson's Learning Solutions Managers work with faculty and campus course designers to ensure that Pearson technology products, assessment tools, and online course materials are tailored to meet your specific needs. This highly qualified team is dedicated to helping schools take full advantage of a wide range of educational resources, by assisting in the integration of a variety of instructional materials and media formats. Your local Pearson Canada sales representative can provide you with more details on this service program.

Acknowledgments

There are many people to thank for this work. Special thanks must go to those who choose to work with academics, despite our peculiarities. The entire editorial team at Pearson Canada provided welcome instruction, guidance, and tolerance.

The most special of thanks goes to my students, who continue to inspire me with their thought-provoking ideas. It is the students who must ultimately read the books they are assigned—I have written this book for them.

Author Biography

Tami Bereska received her PhD in Sociology from the University of Alberta. Having a passion for teaching undergraduate students, she currently teaches a variety of classes at MacEwan University, including Introductory Sociology, Deviance and Conformity, Social Psychology, Advanced Topics in Deviance, and Advanced Topics in Youth. She is the author of multiple textbooks, instructor's resource manuals, and student resources. In this work, she focuses on creating materials that both facilitate student learning and show students that the sociological imagination is a tool not only for the classroom, but also for their everyday lives.

Chapter 1

Determining Deviance

Learning Objectives

After reading this chapter, you should be able to

1   Describe the objective/subjective dichotomy.

2   Provide four definitions of deviance traditionally associated with the objective side of the objective/subjective dichotomy and explain their limitations.

3   Describe the definitions of deviance traditionally associated with the subjective side of the objective/subjective dichotomy and summarize the concept of social construction.

4 Explain why it is more appropriate to refer to an objective–subjective continuum rather than an objective/subjective dichotomy.

5 Explain how the study of deviance is influenced by how the researcher defines it. Depict the role of change, negotiation, opposition, and diversity in the "deviance dance" in Canadian society.

6 Outline the three components of the social typing process through which someone is defined as "deviant."

What comes to mind when you think of deviance, or in contrast, conformity? Actress Gemma Arterton (Wiseman, 2016) states, "It's easier to conform and shut up." This suggests that our lives will run more smoothly if we conform; however, it also makes the claim that we may have to silence a part of ourselves to do so. Television producer David Lee (n.d.) goes a step further, saying that "You have to be deviant if you're going to do anything new." According to this claim, acting or thinking in a novel way is necessarily deviant, and although "thinking outside the box" is a popular business phrase, Lee suggests that only "deviants" will do so.

The claims made in these quotations raise questions about deviance and conformity. Who are the conformists in our society and in our world? Is life easier for them? Who are the deviants? Are they the innovators of our world, or do they represent some sort of problem that we need to control? How can we distinguish between a "deviant" and a "conformist"?

Ask Yourself

Which of the following people do you consider deviant: a person with green hair; someone who smokes; an individual convicted of a crime; a member of a white supremacist group? Once you have made your selections, consider another set of questions. How did you come to know that the people you selected are deviant? Where did that knowledge come from and how was it transmitted to you?

Who Is Deviant?

The earlier quotation by David Lee equates deviance with innovation. However, our own implicit assumptions about deviance can stand in stark contrast. Think about the times when you have heard someone use the word "deviant." More often than not, the term refers to a person, characteristic, or behaviour that is considered strange, inappropriate, or immoral—in need of some form of social control. A quick online search using the term *deviance* reinforces this view, and highlights criminal activity and sexual fetishes. Traditionally, deviance textbooks have also reflected this view, focusing attention on "nuts, sluts, and perverts" (Liazos, 1972, p. 103). The *Ask Yourself* exercise will have you reflect on your own views of deviance.

In the first part of the *Ask Yourself* exercise, you may have identified the person with green hair as deviant, because most people do not have green hair. Or perhaps the person who smokes, an activity that causes physical harm to oneself as well as to other people nearby. Maybe you selected the individual convicted of a crime, because he or she has violated important norms in our society. Perhaps you included the member of a white supremacist group, whose beliefs are condemned by most Canadians.

The second part of the *Ask Yourself* exercise highlights the construction of knowledge. Your own social interactions may have led you to conclude that people with green hair are few and far between. Medical science identifies smoking as harmful, knowledge conveyed to you through the media and perhaps in your elementary or middle school curriculum. The law, embodied in the *Criminal Code* of Canada, tells you that certain behaviours are so unacceptable, they may even lead to incarceration; your parents or the religious system you are affiliated with may have also socialized you to believe that some of those behaviours (e.g., stealing) are wrong. By observing people's negative reactions to racism in a wide range of settings—including public protests and social media campaigns—you may have concluded that most Canadians disapprove of racist beliefs.

If you compared your responses to the *Ask Yourself* exercise to other people's responses, you might note some differences, such as disagreements over whether a certain behaviour is deviant or not. Your parents or grandparents might consider green hair deviant, while you see it as an innocuous style choice. You might identify members of white supremacist groups as deviant, while others claim they have a right to free speech. In addition to the ways that your responses might differ from those of other people, you might have also noted a plurality of viewpoints within your own responses. Maybe you consider someone convicted of assault to be deviant, but not someone convicted of marijuana trafficking. Perhaps you argue that people with green hair are not deviant, but acknowledge that they are often treated as such. You might have even thought about how the same behaviour can be viewed very differently at various points in time. For example, although medical science today emphasizes the harms of smoking, a half century ago doctors sometimes promoted smoking (e.g., as a tool for weight loss), and smoking was even permitted in hospital rooms.

Taken together, the questions in the *Ask Yourself* exercise draw our attention to both the qualities of deviance (e.g., harm; violation of norms) and the processes by which we come to view certain people, behaviours, or characteristics as being deviant (and how those views can vary across people and over time). In the sociology of deviance, some scholars focus more on the former, while others emphasize the latter. These different approaches reflect the **objective/subjective dichotomy** (Rubington & Weinberg, 2008).

The Objective/Subjective Dichotomy

A dichotomy is characterized by two oppositional and mutually exclusive categories. These categories are analogous to the two sides of a coin that, when tossed, will show either heads or tails, but not both. Deviance scholars who are more interested in the qualities of deviant acts represent the objective side of the objective/subjective dichotomy. Scholars primarily interested in the processes by which we come to perceive certain acts as being deviant (and how those perceptions can vary) represent the subjective side of the dichotomy. The two sides of this dichotomy have their foundation in contrasting views of the definition of **deviance** itself and, as you will see in the remainder of the textbook, have implications for the knowledge that scholars generate and the social practices that emerge from that knowledge.

Objectivism: Deviance as an Act

The **objective** side of the dichotomy makes the assumption that there is a quality inherent in a person, behaviour, or characteristic that is necessarily deviant—much as you might have argued that smoking is harmful or that people convicted of crimes have violated norms (Rubington & Weinberg, 2008). However, the precise nature of that essential quality is a matter of debate. While some objectivists identify statistical rarity as the quality that makes a person, behaviour, or characteristic necessarily deviant, other objectivists claim that it is harm, normative violation, or a negative reaction by society's masses (Sacco, 1992). Thus, there is not a singular definition of deviance agreed upon by scholars on this side of the dichotomy, but rather four divergent ones. Because underlying definitions of deviance have implications for knowledge creation and for subsequent social practices, it is important to look at not only each definition, but their limitations as well.

Statistical Rarity. According to some objectivists, deviance is defined as people, behaviours, or characteristics that are statistically rare in a population. Thus, according to this definition, because only 21.4 percent of males and 14.8 percent of females smoke, smoking is deviant in contemporary Canada (Statistics Canada, 2015). Similarly, convicted criminals are deviant because most people have not been convicted of crimes. People with green hair are deviant because very few people have green hair. Members of white supremacist groups are deviant because only a minority of people belong to such groups.

This definition of deviance is often used in settings outside of academia, but is not commonly used by deviance scholars because of the nature of its limitations. First, quantifying "rare" presents a problem. Is a behaviour rare if its prevalence is less than 50 percent? Or does it have to be less than 30 percent? The Ontario Student Drug Use and Health Survey finds that 46 percent of students in grades 9 to 12 have consumed alcohol within the past month (Boak, Hamilton, Adlaf, & Mann, 2015). Is this behaviour rare? The difficulty in determining the criteria for rarity illustrates one of the limitations of this definition of deviance.

This definition of deviance is also criticized because of its failure to correspond to our tacit understandings of deviance as behaviours that are strange, inappropriate, or immoral—in need of social control. On one hand, some behaviours are statistically common but may still be considered unacceptable in the larger society and are subjected to control efforts. For instance, 72 percent of youth in grade 12 have consumed alcohol within the past year (Boak, Hamilton, Adlaf, & Mann, 2015). Thus, alcohol consumption is statistically *common* rather than rare for that group, and yet extensive efforts to prevent this behaviour are found in the school curriculum, community programs, and families, and the behaviour is, in fact, prohibited by law for those under the age of 18 or 19 (depending on the province in question). On the other hand, there are also many uncommon behaviours or characteristics that are widely accepted in Canadian society. Left-handed people are statistically rare, but they are not treated as deviant (although they were seen that way historically) (Barsley, 1967). Sports prodigies (like Connor McDavid or Sidney Crosby) are few and far between but are respected and envied. Only 2 percent of adolescent girls meet the recommended daily requirements for physical activity (Statistics Canada, 2013), but few of us would say that girls who are physically active are considered deviant in our society.

The nature of these limitations suggests that there is something more than just the statistical number of people who engage in a specific behaviour that determines what is considered deviant in our society. Some deviance scholars propose that the important factor is harmfulness.

Harm.   The second definition of deviance associated with the objective side of the objective/subjective dichotomy is based on the concept of **harm**. That is, deviance is defined as those people, behaviours, or characteristics that cause harm. The most obvious type of harm is *physical harm*. Thus, if someone harms someone else—for example, through assault, drunk driving, or exposing others to secondhand smoke—then the perpetrator of that harm is deviant. Physical harm can also be done to oneself, for example through self-mutilation or drug abuse. *Emotional harm* can be done to others (e.g., by acts of racism) and to oneself (e.g., through negative self-talk) as well.

Harm may also be directed not at a human being but at society itself—certain behaviours or people may constitute *social harm*, because they interfere with the smooth running of society. Criminal activity threatens the safety of the population at large as well as the social order. In fact, implicit in criminal law is the assumption that certain acts must be prohibited because of their harmfulness. In Canada, *all* crimes are considered to harm society itself; the court case is between the Crown (i.e., the state) and the defendant, not the victim and the defendant. As another example, obesity and physical inactivity carry considerable economic costs for society (such as through health care costs), with global estimates of up to $2 trillion annually (Dobbs et al., 2014).

Finally, in some cases *ontological harm* can occur when there is a threat to the fundamental ways we understand the world and our place in it. Historically, religious belief systems have frequently provided us with this means of abstract understanding on a large scale. Even in contemporary societies, religious belief systems provide many people with a fundamental way of understanding existence. When new religious belief systems emerge (or are imposed) to displace older ones, or conflicts emerge between individuals or groups with different religious beliefs, or people with strong religious beliefs find themselves confronted with an increasingly secular world, there can be threats to the fundamental ways that people understand the world and their places in it. The *Exercise Your Mind* activity asks you to apply these different dimensions of harm to a specific example, terrorist acts.

Exercise Your Mind

In 2014, Warrant Officer Patrice Vincent was killed in a Quebec parking lot, and Corporal Nathan Cirillo was killed at the National War Memorial in Ottawa. Both incidents were labelled acts of terrorism. Within the context of harm, these incidents can be perceived as causing all four types of harm and in multiple ways. Identify the ways that terrorism causes (a) physical harm, (b) emotional harm, (c) harm to the social order and the smooth running of society, and (d) harm to the way people understand the world and their place in it.

At first glance, notions of physical or emotional harm to someone, harm to the social order, and harm to abstract worldviews appear to be useful in recognizing and defining deviance. Many different forms of deviance, from criminal acts to smoking to religious conflicts, can be considered to cause various types of harm. And perceptions of harm frequently do galvanize social action, such as the creation of non-smoking bylaws and anti-terrorism legislation. However, a more critical look at the idea of harm is useful.

The very idea of physical harm is not as clear as it might initially appear, and it has sometimes changed. Claims of physical harm can be and have been disputed. For many years, the tobacco industry claimed that smoking did not cause the harm that anti-smoking activists argued it did. In the past, some claims of physical harm were also greatly exaggerated. A century ago, doctors argued that masturbation caused hairy palms, acne, and outright insanity. For example, look at the following excerpt from a lecture by nineteenth-century health reformer Sylvester Graham: "This general mental decay ... continues with the continued abuses [of masturbation], till the wretched transgressor sinks into a miserable fatuity, and finally becomes a confirmed and degraded idiot, whose deeply sunken and vacant glassy eye, and livid, shriveled countenance, and ulcerous, toothless gums, and fetid breath, and feeble broken voice, and emaciated and dwarfish and crooked body, and almost hairless head—covered, perhaps, with suppurating blisters and running sores—denote a premature old age—a blighted body—and a mined soul" (cited in Whorton, 2001, p. 3).

Elaborate measures were taken to curb children's masturbation in orphanages, hospitals, boarding schools, and middle-class homes. This included behavioural controls such as cold baths, intense exercise, sleeping on hard beds, and moderate eating

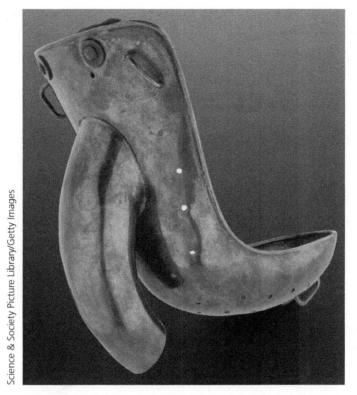

A variety of anti-masturbation devices were used on children during the Victorian era and the early twentieth century because of the harm that the behaviour was thought to cause.

(Hunt, 1998). It also included a wide range of anti-masturbation devices: Bondage would prevent children from touching themselves at night; the Stephenson Spermatic Truss prevented erections from occurring; the Bowen Device would pull on the wearer's pubic hair if an erection occurred; steel armour was padlocked shut at night, and a key was required to allow trips to the bathroom; and penis-cooling devices splashed cold water on the genitals if an erection occurred (Hunt, 1998).

Exaggerated claims about the dangers of marijuana use were also common in the past. In the years leading up to the criminalization of marijuana in 1923, social activists, community leaders, and law enforcement officials spoke out about the physical harm it caused. As can be seen in Box 1.1, marijuana use was alleged to cause horrific violent crimes, murder, idiocy, and ultimately complete insanity and even death. Today, such claims are perceived as greatly exaggerated; however, debates over the physical harm caused by marijuana use continue, as do debates over the physical *benefits* for medical purposes, both of which have been fundamental to debates over decriminalization and legalization in Canada and elsewhere.

Emily Murphy's Marijuana Campaign

Emily Murphy, the first female judge in the British Empire and a leading Canadian suffragist in the early twentieth century, was dismayed at what she saw as the horrors of Canada's drug trade. After interviewing both drug users and law enforcement officials from across North America, in 1922 she wrote *The Black Candle*, a book about drug use. One chapter focuses specifically on the harms caused by marijuana use, quoting police officials: "[Marijuana] has the effect of driving the [user] completely insane. The addict loses all sense of moral responsibility. Addicts to this drug, while under its influence, are immune to pain... While in this condition they become raving maniacs and are liable to kill or indulge in any form of violence to other persons, using the most savage methods of cruelty.... They are dispossessed of their natural and normal will power, and their mentality is that of idiots. If this drug is indulged in to any great extent, it ends in the untimely death of its addict" (Murphy, 1973 [1922], pp. 332–333). These types of claims are somewhat humorous to today's reader, but they had a significant influence on changing drug laws at the time.

When it comes to the idea of interfering with the current social order or threatening a belief system or worldview, the limitations of defining deviance by virtue of harm become more evident. First, whether society or a belief system is being *harmed* can be subjective. For instance, historically, Christian nuns wore a garment known as a habit. It was considered an essential component of membership in a religious order, in part symbolizing the discarding of the worldly individual and becoming part of a communal whole, a sign of one's dedication to God. Although it is relatively uncommon to see a nun wearing a habit today, there remain some religious orders that consider this change to be a threat to the larger religious belief system (Kuhns, 2003).

During the twentieth century, there were several times when women in North America were accused of harming the social order or abstract belief systems or both. Early feminists who fought for the right of women to vote faced such accusations, as did later groups of women in the 1960s and 1970s when they questioned the "natural" role of women as homemakers and moved outside the home into paid employment. Were these women causing harm to society or to beliefs? Because the word *harm* implies a negative impact, many would say that these women were not *harming* society—they were simply changing society. Others would say that by *changing* society they were having a negative impact on the social order of the time, and thus were technically causing harm, but that it was a social order that needed to be changed.

Ask Yourself

What are some of the controversial or hotly debated issues that are occurring in your community or in the larger society now? Are claims of "harm" being made in any of these debates? In those instances, is harm (a) *actually* present, (b) a perception on the part of some groups of people but not others, or (c) merely being used as a justification for implementing particular actions?

Indeed, there are times when the reactions cause more overt harm than the initial behaviours, characteristics, or people themselves. For instance, in 2007 Polish immigrant Robert Dziekanski arrived at the Vancouver airport. His mother was supposed to pick him up; however, due to a series of procedural problems, he ended up wandering through the airport for 10 hours, unable to speak English. He became increasingly disoriented and his behaviour came to be perceived as potentially problematic. The RCMP were called, and following a confrontation in which officers say Dziekanski raised a stapler to them in an aggressive manner they tasered him five times, which resulted in his death. Certainly, in this case, the measures to control Dziekanski's behaviour were far more harmful than his behaviour was. Similarly, the criminalization of marijuana in the early twentieth century, as well as other drugs since that time, points to the harms caused by their use. However, proponents of decriminalization or legalization counter argue that drug prohibition fuels organized crime, and organized crime causes immeasurable harms that range from identity theft to the illegal weapons trade to human trafficking.

All of the above limitations of defining deviance on the basis of harm illustrate that the idea of harm, in and of itself, is inadequate as the defining characteristic of deviance. Despite its limitations, this definition of deviance underlies a great deal of social activism and social policy.

Lianos (with Douglas, 2000) proposes that what is most significant to the study of deviance is not whether someone actually causes harm or is actually dangerous, but rather whether someone *seems* dangerous. Deviance specialists from the subjective side of the objective/subjective dichotomy suggest we look at the social processes that result in someone being perceived as potentially dangerous and not consider whether that person actually *is* dangerous. The *Ask Yourself* exercise has you further explore the concept of harm within the context of contemporary social debates.

Societal Reaction. The third definition of deviance that is associated with the objective side of the objective/subjective dichotomy is based on the nature of societal reaction. That is, deviance refers to those people, characteristics, or behaviours that society's "masses" respond to negatively with dislike, anger, fear, distrust, or disapproval. On that basis we could say that members of white supremacists are deviant because most Canadians condemn racist beliefs.

However, focusing on a **negative societal reaction** as the defining characteristic of deviance raises many questions. Why does society react with disapproval to some actions, characteristics, or people and not others? By focusing on the reaction itself, rather than the factors that contributed to that reaction, this definition of deviance leaves that question unanswered.

How many individual negative reactions must exist before we can say that society's "masses" are reacting negatively? Like the challenges associated with determining the point at which a given behaviour can be considered "rare," this definition is challenged by questions of the point at which society's masses are considered to be reacting negatively: Must 50.1 percent of the population react to a given behaviour with dislike in order for it to be considered deviant? Or must that proportion be much higher?

Surveys of public opinion reveal diverse points of view on any topic—just as in the *Ask Yourself* exercise at the beginning of the chapter, some of you may have felt dislike toward the person who smokes while others did not. Societal reactions are not uniform, and different groups of people react in various ways to the same behaviour or issue. That leads to the question of whose reactions are the ones that are most likely to be acted upon within our social institutions. Is my reaction as a social scientist more likely to have an impact on society than your reaction as a student? Is the prime minister's reaction more likely to have an impact than mine? Indeed, an examination of our political system reveals that there are times when public opinion appears to matter much less than other factors, such as political ideologies or the opinions held by political figures. Although we could explore that idea within the context of any political party in power, two contrasting cases from the tenure of the Conservative Party of Canada under Prime Minister Stephen Harper (2006–2015) are especially illustrative.

For many years before and after the Conservative Party of Canada was elected in 2006, Canadian surveys consistently revealed that "a strong majority ... favour[ed] a limited fine as the maximum penalty for cannabis possession" (i.e., decriminalization) (Fischer, Ala-Leppilampi, Single, & Robins, 2003, p. 277), and 57 percent support[ed] full legalization (Angus-Reid, 2012). Despite this consistent data on societal reaction, during its time in power the Party's official platform stated that they would "prevent the decriminalization of marijuana" (Conservative Party of Canada, 2006, p. 25). That remained true even at the time that the party lost the election in 2015.

In contrast, the Conservative government's position on same-sex marriage was that it would "hold a truly free vote on the definition of marriage, [and] ... if the resolution is passed, the government [would] introduce legislation to restore the traditional definition of marriage" (Conservative Party of Canada, 2006, p. 33). On December 7, 2006, parliamentarians voted on a motion against same-sex marriage; the motion failed 175 votes to 123 votes. Elected officials in Parliament presumably consider a free vote representative of Canadian public opinion—that is, a proxy for societal reaction. The comparison of these two issues shows that the reaction toward one issue (i.e., same-sex marriage) was based on a representation of societal reaction, while the reaction toward another issue (i.e., the decriminalization of marijuana) was independent of societal reaction and appeared to directly oppose public opinion. These inconsistencies reveal that determinations of who or what is deviant in Canadian society are based upon processes that go beyond societal reaction.

Normative Violation.   Finally, the last group of objectivists define deviance not in terms of rarity, harm, or societal reaction, but rather **normative violation**. That is, deviance refers to people, behaviours, or characteristics that violate society's norms. In fact, even the Merriam Webster (2017a) defines deviance in this way. Early objectivists used an "absolutist" conception of normative violation, wherein certain behaviours or characteristics were perceived as being inherently and universally deviant (Adler & Adler, 2016, p. 2). According to this view, there are certain immutable norms and values that should be held in all cultures and at all times—norms and values that emerge from the word of God, the laws of nature, or some other unchangeable source. Because of that absolute moral order, what is considered wrong in one place should be considered wrong everywhere; cross-cultural and trans-historical norms prohibiting incest, murder, and lying are perceived as evidence of this absolute moral order.

The simplistic view of norms in the absolutist view led many objectivists to abandon it. Today most objectivists perceive norms as being culturally specific rather than universal—that is, based on a given society's moral code rather than on any type of absolute moral order. From birth, we are socialized into the norms that govern the society we live in, and we learn its standards and expectations. In Canadian society, we are taught as we grow up to share with others, to be polite, to work hard, to listen to our teachers—in essence, most of us are taught by our parents, teachers, community leaders, and religious leaders to follow the rules. We learn what behaviours are expected of us (like arriving at work on time) and what behaviours are not (like having green hair, smoking, or breaking the law). Knowing these expectations, if we then go on to violate the norms, we are "deviant." The *Ask Yourself* exercise requires you to take a closer look at some of the norms in Canadian society.

Ask Yourself

List the norms that are being violated by each of the following people: an obese person; a student who plagiarizes by purchasing a term paper online; someone on social assistance; a drug addict or alcoholic; a thief. Remember, norms refer to standards or expectations of behaviour, so ask yourself what expectations each of these people is not living up to.

Looking at the examples in the *Ask Yourself* exercise, one can see that not all norms are the same. While violating some norms may result in prison (as for the thief), violating other norms has different (and some might say less severe) consequences. The obese person, alcoholic, social assistance recipient, and plagiarizing student will not be arrested for their normative violations. These differential outcomes of normative violation emerge from the existence of various types of norms, ranging from *folkways* to *mores* to *laws* (Sumner, 1906).

Norms, as standards or expectations of behaviour, can refer to informal, everyday behaviours such as rules of etiquette, choice of clothing, and behaviour in the university classroom. These kinds of informal norms are called **folkways**, and if you violate these norms you might be considered odd or rude. Other norms are taken more seriously. **Mores** are those standards that are often seen as the foundation of morality in a culture, such as prohibitions against certain sexual practices. If you violate these norms you may be thought of as immoral. Finally, some norms are considered so central to the smooth running of society that they are enshrined within the legal system—for example, in Canada's *Criminal Code*. If you violate the *Criminal Code* you will be thought of as a criminal. At times, the legal system integrates mores (e.g., different sexual practices are criminalized in various countries); however, other acts that are not perceived as the foundation for morality (e.g., drug possession) may also be integrated into the legal system.

The way that norms are integrated into objectivist definitions of deviance presumes a certain level of consensus (Rubington & Weinberg, 2008). Although cross-cultural variations in norms are acknowledged, it is assumed that, in each society, most citizens agree upon the norms. However, this assumption must be looked at critically. There are countless numbers of groups in society having innumerable different sets of rules; even a single individual belongs to multiple groups having varying sets of expectations. In your own life, you can think of the various ways you are expected to look and act when in the presence of different groups of people (e.g., your friends versus your grandparents). Given the multiplicity of individuals, groups, and sets of expectations that coexist in a society, normative consensus is difficult to determine (Adler & Adler, 2016; Becker, 1963). In fact, given these different sets of expectations that exist in society simultaneously, which expectations are the ones that constitute society's "norms" and are then used to judge deviance and normality?

In response to these critiques, some objectivists have elected to focus on those norms that they suggest are characterized by some consensus and are reflected in a society's laws. This **consensual view** of law views the law as arising out of social consensus and then equally applied to all (Siegel & McCormick, 2016). However, some **criminologists** (i.e., deviance scholars who focus their studies on criminal activity) draw our attention to the fact that law creation is a political activity, wherein those norms that are embodied in law reflect the behavioural expectations of only some of its citizens (Des Rosiers & Bittle, 2004).

Critiques of the consensual view of law point to conflict and interactionist views. Criminologists who use the **conflict view** perceive the law as a tool used by the ruling class to serve its own interests (Siegel & McCormick, 2016). They believe that the law is more likely to be applied to members of the powerless classes in society. For example, Howard Becker (1963), one of the first deviance specialists to critique objectivist views of deviance, suggested that even when lower-class and middle-class youth engage in similar minor forms of law-breaking, police are more likely to enter the former into the justice system while letting middle-class youth go with a warning or into their parents' custody. More recently, Siegel and McCormick (2016) point out that as of 2016, "the financial institutions and their agents responsible for the 2008 [worldwide] economic melt-down have yet to face any penalties at all" (p. 18).

Another view of crime, the **interactionist view**, also presents a nonconsensual view of criminal law. This view suggests that society's powerful define the law at the behest of interest groups who appeal to those with power to rectify a perceived social ill (Siegel & McCormick, 2016). Again, criminal law is not seen as emerging out of consensus, but rather out of the interests of certain groups in society. Looking at these different views, we can see that criminal law is based on more than a simple consensus about what society's norms are.

The normative objectivity of the law has also been critiqued on the question of the situational applicability of broad social norms. For example, in a rather objective fashion we might say that legal prohibitions against murder reflect normative clarity in society—we know that murder is wrong. However, some deviance specialists point out the many situational characteristics that can modify this abstract norm. Depending on the laws of a country, self-defence, capital punishment, military action in wartime, and doctor-assisted death are all circumstances in which taking a human life may be considered acceptable.

So, is taking another human life deviant? Looking at the above, we see that the answer to this question is that taking another human life is deviant in some situations but not others. In fact, in situations where taking another human life is considered acceptable, the behaviour is not called "murder." For example, during wartime, the death of innocent civilians is not "murder," but "collateral damage."

Some deviance scholars step into this debate over the degree of consensus involved in social norms by proposing that some norms do have higher levels of consensus. For example, despite the situational variations in prohibitions against taking another human life, it is likely that most Canadians expect individuals to refrain from doing so; the same can also likely be said for auto theft, sexual assault, and break-and-enter. Thio (1983) uses the concepts of **high-consensus deviance** and **low-consensus deviance** to distinguish between forms of deviance that have differential levels of support in the broader society. The norms reflected in criminal law are characterized by relatively more consensus than are society's non-legislative norms (such as norms governing physical appearance). And within the law, certain laws are characterized by relatively more consensus than are others.

Although the dictionary defines deviance based on normative violation, the limitations of that definition make it problematic. In fact, limitations are associated with each of the objective definitions of deviance—not only normative violation, but also statistical rarity, harm, and a negative societal reaction. These limitations are emphasized by subjectivist deviance scholars, who hold very different views of deviance.

Learning Objective 1

■ What is the objective/subjective dichotomy?

■ What do the objective and subjective sides of the dichotomy focus their attention on?

Learning Objective 2

■ What is the core assumption underlying the objective side of the objective/subjective dichotomy, and why do four different objective definitions of deviance exist?

■ What are the four different objective definitions of deviance? Provide examples of each.

■ What are the limitations of each of the objective definitions of deviance? Provide examples of each.

■ According to those who define deviance based on harm, what are the different types of harm that can occur?

■ How has the objectivist notion of normative violation changed over time?

■ What are the different views of the role of consensus in the development of criminal law?

Subjectivism: Deviance as a Label

Having looked at the objective side of the traditional objective/subjective dichotomy, we now turn our attention to the subjective side. From this point of view, there is a very different view of deviance. While objectivists define deviance in terms of a specific quality (e.g., harm), subjectivists fundamentally disagree. Because of the limitations associated with each of the qualities highlighted by various objectivists, subjectivists argue that it is not a *quality* that lies at the core of deviance, but rather a *process*. That is, groups with some influence on society have told us that certain people, behaviours, or characteristics are deviant (Becker, 1963).

The foundation for this process lies in the **dominant moral codes** (Goode & Ben-Yehuda, 2009, p. 114) that serve as the foundation for determining who or what is deviant in society. There are multiple moral codes that exist simultaneously, corresponding to the variety of social groups that comprise society at any given time—much like the way some of your grandparents might consider a person with green hair to be deviant, while you do not. These moral codes dictate the people, behaviours, and characteristics that are right/wrong, appropriate/inappropriate, moral/immoral, or good/bad. Although multiple moral codes co-exist, only certain moral codes are reflected in the society's institutions (e.g., the criminal justice system, the mainstream media, and the education system). Thus, certain moral codes attain positions of dominance in society. Groups that hold some level of power are in the best position to have their own moral codes become dominant.

For instance, scientists were able to influence perceptions of smoking, and political figures can decide what behaviours will be prohibited by legislation. Consequently, from a subjective perspective deviance is defined as those people, behaviours, and characteristics that society's dominant moral codes deem to be unacceptable and in need of control.

However, subjective deviance specialists point to the complex nature of power relations. Social processes involve far more than simply the control and oppression of the powerless by the powerful. The use and legitimization of power interacts with negotiations about moral boundaries—negotiations in which less powerful groups in society are also able to participate. Consequently, powerless groups can resist and act in their own interests, rather than simply be at the mercy of the interests of the powerful. Continual negotiations are occurring, such that the social construction of deviance and normality/conformity is in a constant state of flux (Goode & Ben-Yehuda, 2009). For example, for many years the tobacco industry resisted the claims of medical science with counterclaims from their own scientists, and in many countries today the industry continues to resist legislative restrictions by launching lawsuits against national governments.

Subjectivity and the "Social Construction" of Deviance

Referring to the subjective nature of deviance means focusing on deviance as a *social construction*. **Social constructionism** refers to the perspective proposing that social characteristics (e.g., "thin," "delinquent") are creations or artifacts of a certain society at a specific time in history, just as objects (e.g., houses, cars) are artifacts of that society. Consequently, a person, behaviour, or characteristic that is constructed as "deviant" within a society's dominant moral code may be constructed as "normal" within another society's dominant moral code (or even within subordinate moral codes that exist in that same society).

Social constructionism has become a dominant force in the study of deviance today. In fact, more than two decades ago Erich Goode (1997) suggested that "most deviance specialists are *constructionists*" (p. 35). However, there are different levels or different types of constructionism. One type of constructionism is labelled **radical** (Goode, 1997) or **strict** (Best, cited in Rubington & Weinberg, 2002); the other type is labelled **soft** or **contextual** (Best, cited in Rubington & Weinberg, 2002).

Radical constructionists postulate a distinct theoretical perspective claiming that the world is characterized by endless relativism, that "there is no essential reality to the social world at all, that if everything and anything is simply looked at in a certain way, that is the way it is" (Goode, 1997, p. 35). However, "most [contemporary deviance specialists] are not *radical* constructionists. What I mean by this is that most do *not* believe that *everything* is a matter of definition, that there is *no* essential reality to the social world at all.... Rather, most sociologists of deviance believe that there are limits to social constructionism" (Goode, 1997, p. 35). Consequently, sociologists who are soft or contextual constructionists emphasize the pathways by which certain

Figure 1.1 Levels of Social Construction

social phenomena come to be perceived and reacted to in particular ways in a given society at a specific time in history.

Viewing social constructionism as a process implies that what is of sociological significance is not the individual behaviour or characteristic itself, but rather (1) its place in the social order, (2) the roles assigned to people who exhibit that behaviour or characteristic, and (3) the meanings attached to that behaviour or characteristic. For example, homosexuality is "universal" in the sense that it has existed across the world and throughout history. What varies is the way that homosexuality is perceived and reacted to in specific societies; thus, while homosexuality is a part of nature, and therefore "biological," it is also "socially constructed." Deviance is constructed by processes that occur at multiple levels (Nelson, 2010). These processes range from our own personal identities at the micro level to processes of globalization at the macro level (see Figure 1.1).

The first processes to consider are at the *individual* level: at this level our own identities, conceptions of self, and ways of understanding our own existence in the world affect the path of social construction. The second set of processes are at the *interactional* level: our interactions with other people influence the way we think and feel about others, thereby determining the role that each of us plays in social construction. The third set of processes are at the *institutional* level: the structures of our society, such as government, the education system, and religion (among others) that affect social construction. The fourth set of processes are at the *sociocultural* level: beliefs, ideologies, values, and systems of meaning have an influence on the path of social construction. The final set of processes are at the *global* level as part of **globalization,** which refers to processes that create "tight global economic, political, cultural, and environmental interconnections and flows that make most current borders and boundaries irrelevant" (Steger, 2013, p. 9). The growing interconnectedness of the world that emerges from globalization touches every aspect of our lives, from the way we think about ourselves, to the range of people we can communicate with using digital technologies, to the food we eat, to the systems of meaning that guide our everyday lives.

The two sides of the objective/subjective dichotomy have different definitions of deviance as their foundations. Objectivists claim that there is a specific quality that necessarily makes a person, behaviour, or characteristic deviant. Statistical rarity, harm, a negative societal reaction, and normative violation have each been identified as that quality (whether by scholars, laypersons, social activists, or politicians). In contrast, subjectivists claim that there is no underlying quality that is inherently deviant; instead, a person, behaviour, or characteristic is deviant if enough important people say so. Through the processes of social construction, which are influenced by power, dominant moral codes emerge that then serve as the standard against which deviance and normality are judged. Just as the two sides of the dichotomy are based on different definitions of deviance, they are based on varying definitions of conformity or normality as well (see Box 1.2).

The implications arising from the specific definitions of deviance and normality being used are significant. Those behaviours or characteristics that are viewed as deviant are subjected to measures of social control—which you will learn more about at a later point in the chapter.

The Objective–Subjective Continuum

Although objective and subjective have traditionally been addressed as a dichotomy, a closer analysis questions this dualistic view and points to the ways that objective and subjective perspectives are integrated in a variety of ways. We have already seen some evidence of this in the previous discussions of the objective/subjective dualism. For example, we have seen that, over time, objectivists have changed their conceptions of norms from that of an absolute moral order to that of a culturally specific moral order. Similarly, over time, subjectivists have come to use the concept of norms but refer to expectations that are socially constructed and determined by processes of power.

For example, Tittle and Paternoster (2000) propose that group-specific normative systems *can* be identified, such as the normative system of middle-class America. They

Box 1.2

Defining Normality (or Conformity)

In the sociology of deviance, the terms *normality* and *conformity* are often used interchangeably, as the converse of the term *deviance*. While the class you are taking may be labelled "deviance and conformity," the dictionary lists the term "normal" as an antonym to the term "deviant" (Merriam Webster, 2017a). From a social psychological perspective, conformity refers to changes in our attitudes or behaviours to be in accordance with those of people around us. Sometimes we conform because we believe the attitudes or behaviours of people around us to be correct, while at other times we conform because we want to fit in and be socially accepted (Aronson, Wilson, Fehr, & Akert, 2017). In either case, conforming makes us normal and failing to conform makes us deviant. Because deviance and normality (or conformity) exist only in relation to each other, the definition of normality is tied to one's location on the objective/subjective dichotomy and the precise definition of deviance being used (Bereska, 2014; Freud, 1999). That means if deviance is defined as behaviours or characteristics that are statistically rare, then normality refers to those that are statistically common. If deviance is defined as behaviours or characteristics

that cause harm, then normality refers to those that are harmless. If deviance is defined as behaviours or characteristics that society's masses respond to negatively (e.g., dislike, anger, disapproval), then normality refers to those that society's masses respond to positively (e.g., pleasure, joy). If deviance is defined as behaviours or characteristics that violate society's norms, then normality refers to behaviours or characteristics that correspond to society's norms. If deviance is defined as behaviours or characteristics that are socially constructed as unacceptable within society's dominant moral codes (which are influenced by power), then normality refers to those that are socially constructed as acceptable within society's dominant moral codes (Bereska, 2014). Behaviours or characteristics that are deemed to be normal according to one definition may be considered deviant according to another. For example, having green hair may be considered normal in that there is no obvious harm being caused, and yet could also be considered deviant in that having green hair is statistically rare. You might be able to think of additional examples that illustrate such contradictions.

suggest that, although this is only one of countless numbers of normative systems in society, it is the one that has come to dominate American society as a whole through the power that the middle-class holds in processes of social construction: "[T]he middle class dominates U.S. society, both by imposing its standards through the schools, the mass media, and the law and by enjoying a degree of natural hegemony in behaviour styles and thinking that flows from the admiration and emulation of those with higher status" (p. 29).

The boundaries of objective and subjective become further blurred when looking at the extent to which the qualities highlighted by objectivists are used within processes of social construction. For instance, interest groups that are opposed to same-sex rights sometimes argue that homosexuality is statistically rare, a violation of the laws of nature or the word of God, or a threat to "the family" and to any children being raised by gay or lesbian parents. People who work toward toughening young offender legislation bring arguments of harm into their work. Those trying to decriminalize marijuana possession often refer to changing public attitudes that reflect a positive societal reaction to the issue of marijuana use. These groups are involved in the process of social construction in that they are attempting to influence the meanings attached to a behaviour, its place in the larger social order, and the roles assigned to individuals who engage in that behaviour. Yet they also draw upon objectivist concepts as a foundation for their arguments, so that objectivist traits are embedded within the subjectivist process of social construction.

Examining the complexities of the work of both past and present deviance specialists indicates that perhaps the traditional objective/subjective dichotomy that has served as the foundation for discussing definitions of deviance in the field has always been an oversimplification. The actual nature of the work done by sociologists of deviance frequently transcends the dichotomy, blending aspects of both objective and subjective. Rather than being embedded in a dichotomy, definitions of deviance and research on deviance fall along more of a continuum, with more objective assumptions lying at one end of the continuum and more subjective assumptions lying at the other (see Figure 1.2).

At the extreme objective end of the continuum are those who adhere to the absolutist view of norms as the standard for determining deviance; at the extreme subjective end are the most radical constructionists, who suggest that there is no reality outside of perception. The definitions and analyses of any individual view of deviance falls somewhere along this continuum, with some being more objective in nature and some being more subjective in nature. Deviance scholars who lean toward objectivism may be more likely to study those forms of deviance that Thio (1983) referred to as high-consensus forms of deviance, such as homicide, gang membership, white-collar crime, and police corruption. Those who lean toward subjectivism may be more likely to study those forms of deviance that Thio referred to as low-consensus forms of deviance, such as marijuana use, pornography, sexual fetish

Figure 1.2 The Objective–Subjective Continuum

communities, gambling, and aspects of physical appearance (e.g., tattoos, body piercing, hair colour).

TIME TO REVIEW

Learning Objective 3

- What is the core assumption of definitions of deviance on the subjective side of the objective/subjective dichotomy?

- What are the roles of *power* and *dominant moral codes* according to subjective definitions of deviance?

- What does it mean when we say that deviance and normality are socially constructed?

- What are the two types of social constructionism, and how do they differ?

- What are the five levels at which the social construction of deviance and normality occurs?

- In what way are definitions of normality or conformity intertwined with definitions of deviance?

Learning Objective 4

- Why is it more appropriate to think of objective and subjective as existing on a continuum rather than as a dichotomy?

Studying Deviance

The way that deviance is defined along the objective–subjective continuum has implications for the way deviance is studied. That is, deviance specialists who lean more toward objectivism will study deviance in ways that those who lean more toward subjectivism will not (and vice versa).

Studying the Act: Why People Behave the Way They Do

Those who lean toward the more objective end of the objective–subjective continuum shine their analytical spotlight on a certain act or characteristic. The deviant nature of these behaviours/characteristics is, to some extent, taken for granted (because, after all, they *are* violating norms, or *are* causing harm, etc.); then the details of the deviance are studied—who the people are, how they became deviant, what their lives are like (Adler & Adler, 2016; Rubington & Weinberg, 2008). In essence, the interest lies in explaining the person, behaviour, or characteristic in question. For instance, if people know that smoking causes physical harm, then why do they smoke? Similarly, if people know that most Canadians condemn racist beliefs, then why do some join white supremacist groups?

Studying Social Processes:
The "Deviance Dance"

Deviance specialists who lean toward the more subjective end of the continuum are less interested in shining their analytical spotlight on the act itself and more interested in shining it on society and social processes—the perceptions of and reactions to the act as well as the role of power in those perceptions and reactions. For example, what processes led smoking to be viewed as an unacceptable behaviour in need of prevention and control? Which specific individuals and groups were involved in that process? What were the arguments and counterarguments involved? How have smokers' perceptions of themselves evolved over this time?

The focus of this type of analysis becomes the "**deviance dance**"—the interactions, negotiations, and debates among groups with different perceptions of whether a behaviour or characteristic is deviant and needs to be socially controlled and, if so, how. The participants in this "dance" each take certain "steps" to move the dance in the direction they desire, whether that direction is the creation of a new law, the legalization of a behaviour that was previously illegal, achieving public recognition of a new social problem or one previously ignored, or changing public perceptions that will reduce the stigma faced by certain groups.

In some cases, this "dance" may be characterized by considerable cooperation among the participants in achieving a consensual goal—analogous to a country line dance in which everyone does precisely the same steps. In other cases, it is characterized by participants taking opposing steps, but still moving together in their negotiation over the outcome—analogous to a waltz, where one partner moves backward and the other forward as they set their joint course across the dance floor. And in some cases the "dance" may look more like a mosh pit at a heavy metal or punk rock concert—with each participant moving independently of the others and in varying and often opposing directions, intentionally pushing, shoving, and ramming into other participants to move in his or her own individually desired direction.

The centrality of interactions, negotiations, debates, and resistance in the social construction and social control of deviance is illustrated by Hier (2002). In 1999, three young adults died at rave dances in Toronto following the consumption of the drug ecstasy. With widespread media attention, Toronto city council and rave organizers (i.e., the Toronto Dance Safety Committee, or TDSC) joined together in an effort to improve safety at raves; at the TDSC's request, Toronto city council passed legislation governing various safety-related measures at raves. However, as media attention continued over the next several months, some members of city council adopted a new goal—banning raves altogether. The deviance dance was played out within the media, as those in favour of banning raves used mainstream newspapers to win public favour and achieve their goal, while rave organizers, who were more concerned about threats to safety that would emerge if raves were driven underground, used a wide range of media outlets (including MuchMusic) to communicate their message to the public. What began as a cooperative effort quickly became an antagonistic debate between opposing sides.

Studying struggles and debates over deviance requires going beyond the problem of "radical phenomenalism" (Ben-Yehuda, 1990, p. 5) that some researchers see as plaguing the sociology of deviance, wherein countless numbers of specific phenomena (e.g., call girls, drug users, swingers) have been studied in tremendous detail without any attention being paid to larger social structures. Ben-Yehuda (1990) suggests that the "study of deviance should be reframed ... within general societal processes [of change and stability], in a dynamic historical and political perspective" (p. 5). In this vein, understanding an act of deviance requires understanding its larger context in a society's value system and understanding the configuration of power relationships that influence the negotiation of moral boundaries among different groups of people.

Exercise Your Mind

List some current examples of each of these types of "dances": (a) groups who agree that a particular behaviour is deviant and work together to control that behaviour (a "country line dance"); (b) groups whose perceptions are somewhat different (although they may agree that a behaviour is deviant, they disagree as to how to best control it) but who still cooperate in some way (a "waltz"); and (c) groups who have completely different perceptions (they disagree as to whether a behaviour is deviant at all) and try to impose those perceptions on others (a "mosh pit").

Studying Acts and Social Processes

Ask Yourself

Make a list of groups of people that you are aware of who try to influence society's dominant moral codes by seeking to influence our notions of right/ wrong, bad/good, deviant/normal, acceptable/unacceptable. At its simplest level, these are groups that you feel are trying to change people's perceptions of a certain behaviour or group of people.

Both the more objective and the more subjective approaches help our understanding of deviance. The most comprehensive knowledge emerges from combining an analysis of the social processes involved in the "deviance dance" with an explication of the act or characteristic in question. For example, information about why people become overweight can be combined with knowledge of the processes by which certain people come to be perceived as "too fat" and are then made subject to various measures of social control.

Similarly, an understanding of the factors that contribute to youth smoking can be combined with knowledge of the processes by which smoking was perceived as acceptable (and even sophisticated) in the past, while in contemporary society smoking (and smokers) are subjected to widespread social control efforts. Each of these levels of understanding paints an important part of the picture of deviance that will be integrated into this text. At various points we will analyze acts/characteristics, perceptions of and reactions to those acts, and the role played by power in these perceptions and reactions.

The Role of Powerful People

Who are the "important" people who can influence the dominant moral codes of society, from which emerge standards of deviance and normality? In Canadian society, some of the most powerful groups involved in this process are politicians/government, scientists, religious institutions, the media, and commercial enterprise. Each of these groups of people may act as or have a relationship with **moral entrepreneurs** (Becker, 1963), those who "manufacture public morality" first by bringing a problem to public awareness and second by facilitating "moral conversion" (Adler & Adler, 2006, p. 136). For example, participants in the temperance movement, the abolitionist movement, and the "child-savers" movement all acted as moral entrepreneurs who worked to influence the development and enforcement of society's moral codes during the Victorian era.

In the temperance movement, members of church-based groups (frequently women's groups) throughout North America and Great Britain declared the "demon liquor" a social evil and agitated for reduced alcohol consumption ("temperance"). In Canada and the United States, groups of people acting as moral entrepreneurs sought abolition (the eradication of slavery under the law) and demanded voting rights for women. And throughout North America and Western Europe, the "child-savers"

Bettmann/Getty Images

With a hatchet in one hand and a Bible in the other, prohibitionist Carry A. Nation would enter saloons and greet the bartender by saying, "Good morning, destroyer of men's souls."

influenced child labour laws, sought the criminalization of child abuse and neglect, and encouraged compulsory education for children. During the 1950s and 1960s, North America's civil rights activists acted as moral entrepreneurs in their efforts to end segregation and gain rights for black Canadians and Americans. These groups had an influence on society's dominant moral codes, and thereby on perceptions of what was considered deviant and normal. In contemporary society, we continue to see groups of moral entrepreneurs, as illustrated in the *Ask Yourself* exercise.

Perhaps the most central group in society that acts as or has a relationship with moral entrepreneurs is composed of *politicians*. Politicians are the people in whom ultimate power has been vested in modern state systems—they have powers to invoke, revoke, and determine the enforcement of legislation and social policy. Interest groups, acting as moral entrepreneurs who have identified a social ill that they think must be solved in some way, often lobby the government to initiate change.

A second group, composed of *scientists*, is able to effectively make claims that influence society's moral codes. The claims made by scientists are backed by the domain that is granted perhaps the highest level of credibility in our society—that of science. As we will see in the chapter on religious and scientific belief systems later in this text, when scientists proclaim truths, many of us will believe those claims simply because scientists say so. When scientists tell us that smoking is harmful, or that having sex too frequently indicates an addiction, or that hearing voices indicates mental illness, they have a persuasive impact on what we see as "normal." When making such claims, scientists themselves may be acting as moral entrepreneurs; in addition, the claims made by scientists may be used as convincing support for the efforts of other moral entrepreneurs, such as anti-smoking activists.

Religious institutions have also played a central role in the creation of the dominant moral codes that determine deviance and normality. For example, during the Middle Ages and into the early Renaissance, the Christian church was the instigator of witch persecutions and the Spanish Inquisition, both of which resulted in countless numbers of people being tortured and killed for their deviance. In the present day, the power of religious institutions can be seen in the many nations in which religious-based governments are the source of social order. For instance, ISIS-controlled areas of the Middle East impose an extremist interpretation of Islamic beliefs on the people living there. Contemporary Canadian society is characterized by a separation of church and state; however, the influence of religion on perceptions of deviance and normality maintains its presence in many ways. Canadian society itself is built upon a Judeo-Christian foundation. Two of our national statutory holidays are Christian holidays—Christmas Day and Easter. Our criminal law is based on the Judeo-Christian ethic of free will—we are responsible for our own actions, and redemption can occur through punishment (Caputo & Linden, 2016).

At a more individual level, many Canadians adhere to various religious belief systems. Their belief systems provide them with moral codes that subsequently affect the role individuals play in larger social processes. The Victorian prohibitionists, abolitionists, and child-savers described earlier were typically members of various Christian church-based groups.

In our twenty-first-century world, the *media* serves as the central battleground in the struggles over moral codes. The media is a powerful tool used by a wide range of moral entrepreneurs. When politicians, medical doctors, or interest groups endeavour to raise awareness of an issue or sway public opinion, they turn to the media. Public service announcements, press conferences, and issue-driven advertisements all appear in the media. However, the media is not just a tool used by moral entrepreneurs; it also acts as a moral entrepreneur itself in terms of the choices made about what will and will not be included on a program or in a commercial segment. For example, when a television news program features child molesters being captured through sting operations, it contributes to the construction of pedophilia as a deviant (and criminal) activity.

Finally, in a modern capitalist economy, *commercial enterprise* has a significant level of power as well, frequently in conjunction with the use of the media; in fact, most components of the media itself are commercial enterprises driven by a profit motive. Advertisements, commercials, magazines, television programs, and movies tell us how we are and are not supposed to look: punk rock characters in a movie are the butt of the movie's jokes; magazine articles tell us we will be happier if we can just lose those 10 pounds by Labour Day; personalities on the newest popular reality TV show model the right clothes to wear. The media also tells us how we are supposed to act: beer commercials show us that drinking is the best way to have fun with friends; a fictional television show tells us that "potheads" are losers; and a nighttime news program tells us that joining a cult is problematic.

Commercial enterprise has power outside of the media as well. For example, Giesbrecht (2000) discusses the power of the alcohol industry over the content and form of alcohol policies created by government. The manner in which alcohol production, marketing, and consumption is controlled in both Canada and the United States is determined, in part, by the influence of the alcohol industry itself. A similar example can be seen in the historical development of the institution of law in modern state systems. It is the law that delineates those actions considered to require the greatest level of control by society; historically, English law developed on the basis of merchant and commercial interests. With the end of feudalism, kings had much to gain from the wealth of merchants involved in international trade. Feudal lords no longer had the means to finance the nation's warfare and colonial expansion, but merchants did. It was in the best financial interests of the king, as he oversaw the development and growth of a centralized state, to form it in accordance with commercial interests. These origins serve as the foundation for modern Canadian law, wherein most legal infractions by those involved in commercial enterprise are dealt with under the more lenient civil law rather than the more punitive criminal law (Kueneman & Bowness, 2016).

This brief discussion of politicians, scientists, religion, the media, and commercial enterprise demonstrates the complexity of the notion of power. People are powerful for many different reasons, and their power operates in diverse ways. The moral entrepreneurship of one group of powerful people may contradict or even oppose the moral entrepreneurship of another group of powerful people; for instance, the efforts of commercial enterprise might oppose the efforts of members of a religious-based group. But whether one group's involvement in social construction contradicts or, conversely, coincides with another group's involvement in social construction, the process through which they operate is the same—that of social typing.

The Social Typing Process

As moral entrepreneurs influence the content and enforcement of society's dominant moral codes, the foundation is laid for the standards that subsequently determine deviance and normality. A closer look at the process by which some people come to be seen as deviant and others come to be seen as normal reveals what Rubington and Weinberg (2008) label **social typing**. This three-component process has the result of changing the way society treats people who are typed or categorized as deviant (see Figure 1.3).

The first component of the social typing process is **description**, wherein a label is placed on an individual because of an observed or presumed behaviour or characteristic. You may find it helpful to think of it as a noun. The exact nature of the label that is applied depends on the culture in question (Rubington & Weinberg, 2008). For example, in contemporary Canada we are more likely to label someone a "terrorist" than a "heretic"; in contrast, in Europe during the sixteenth century, people were more likely to be labelled "heretics" than "terrorists." Terrorism is a social phenomenon that has become an integral part of our worldview in the twenty-first century, while the concept of heresy reflected the religious foundations of the European worldview in the sixteenth century.

The second component of the social typing process is **evaluation**. This occurs when a judgment is attached to the individual by virtue of the label that was previously given or the category that individual was placed in under the description component. If someone is socially typed as deviant, this judgment is characteristically negative in nature. You may find it helpful to think of it as an adjective. For instance, if someone has been labelled a "terrorist" in the first step of the social typing process, then a corresponding judgment might be "dangerous."

The third component of the social typing process is **prescription**. This is where the processes of social control or regulation emerge. Because of the label that has been given and the resulting judgment that occurs, the individual is treated in a specific way—a way she or he would not be treated if the initial label had not been applied. In other words, individuals are subjected to a range of social treatments

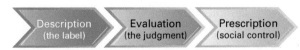

Figure 1.3 The Social Typing Process

designed to regulate or control their deviance. For example, someone who is a "terrorist" and therefore "dangerous" may face arrest and imprisonment. Just as the larger culture determines the initial label that is used, it also shapes the nature of the prescription that is used. For example, a Canadian woman who violates standards of female dress is likely to be teased or stared at rather than made subject to stoning, as several women have been in ISIS-controlled regions of the Middle East.

Exercise Your Mind

Go through the three components of the social typing process, using the example of one of the people listed in the *Ask Yourself* exercise at the beginning of the chapter who you considered to be deviant: a person with green hair, someone who smokes, an individual convicted of a crime, or a member of a white supremacist group. What description or label is given to this person? What judgments or evaluations are attached to this person because of the label you have just given him or her? Finally, how is this person treated or socially controlled?

Forms of Social Control

As Newman (2008) points out, "all societies have ways of keeping deviants under control.... The ancient Greeks killed them; nineteenth-century societies hid them in their closets and attics, and twentieth-century societies rationalized this solution by building large institutions in which they were hidden" (p. xi). In contemporary society, we can see the regulation or social control of a person who has been subjected to the social typing process takes a variety of forms: formal or informal; retroactive or preventative; and control of others or self-regulation. First, social control may be *formal* or *informal* in nature (Becker, 1963; Edwards, 1988; Rubington & Weinberg, 2002). The informal aspect of the prescription component emerges at the level of patterns of informal social interaction—patterns of interaction with diverse people, such as family members, friends, acquaintances, colleagues, or strangers. As you go about your day seeing many different people, you react to them and interact with them in various ways. You may smile at, frown at, stare at, tease, laugh at, agree with, disagree with, talk to, avoid, ignore, criticize, applaud them, and more. These are all means by which **informal regulation** or **informal social control** can occur.

You can see one example if you think back to your adolescent years. Perhaps as you were leaving the house, your parents saw what you were wearing and clearly disapproved. They may have asked, "What do you think you're wearing?" They may have said, "In those baggy pants you look like a bum!" Or they may have even sent you back to your room to change. That is informal regulation. Alternatively, you may have noticed people staring at you and laughing or frowning when you walked down the street. Informal regulation comprises much of our daily lives today, and prior to industrialization it served as the dominant way that deviance was controlled (Spector, 1981).

As a student at the university you attend, how is your behaviour or appearance informally controlled? In other words, how is your behaviour or appearance controlled at the level of everyday social interaction? How is it formally regulated at an organizational or institutional level?

Formal regulation or **formal social control** involves processing at some type of an organizational or institutional level. Prior to industrialization in the Western world, church prohibitions served as the central means of formal social control. With industrialization and the creation of a centralized government, there was a dramatic increase in organizations and agencies involved in regulation and social control (Spector, 1981). A wide range of types of formal regulation can serve as controls for deviant behaviour—a nation's laws (such as Canada's *Criminal Code*), a school or work dress code, regulations governing driver's licences or hunting permits, school policies that govern student misconduct, or the psychiatrists' handbook that lists the symptoms of various forms of mental illness. Take a moment to look at the *Ask Yourself* exercise and consider how informal and formal social control affects your life.

In answering the *Ask Yourself* questions, you may have referred to informal social controls such as peer pressure—the desire to fit in with your classmates might influence the clothes you wear to class, the way you style your hair, or whether you go to the library versus the bar after class. Maybe you recall a time when you were whispering to a friend during class and two of your classmates gave you a dirty look or even asked you to keep it down. When you first became a post-secondary student, perhaps an older sibling gave you advice on what it would be like and how you should act. These are all examples of informal control. You may have also listed various formal social controls, like registration requirements—you are permitted to take Class B only if you have already passed Class A. You might have referred to the regulations governing student conduct at your university—what behaviours are considered unacceptable and what are the consequences for those behaviours? Perhaps you referred to a course syllabus, which tells you what exams and assignments you must complete to pass a course. Maybe you attend a university that has a student dress code. After an outburst in class, possibly the chair of the department gave you a reprimand or made you see a student counsellor. These are all examples of formal regulation.

Social control may be either **retroactive** (treating a known deviant in a certain way) or **preventative** (trying to prevent deviance in the first place—through socialization, for example) (Edwards, 1988). Social control may be directed at an individual by someone else (e.g., a doctor, a parent, a judge), or may occur at the level of **self-regulation** or **self-control**, where people regulate their own behaviours (such as by dieting to try and conform to an idealized body image, joining a self-help group to treat substance abuse, or hiding characteristics for which they know they will be criticized) (Foucault, 1995; Gottfredson & Hirschi, 1990).

Of course, because the social construction of deviance and normality are embedded within a bigger "dance," it means that a specific behaviour, characteristic, or person is not subjected to only one social typing process at any given moment. Multiple processes of social construction may be going on simultaneously, processes that may even contradict each other. One segment of society may socially type someone as "deviant," while another segment of society may claim that same person is "normal." In some areas of society, for example, someone who is perceived as overweight is labelled "too fat," has negative judgments attached to him or her, and is then treated in certain ways as a result; however, in other areas of society that person may be seen as "normal" or "healthy."

Even if there is some agreement that a person, behaviour, or characteristic is deviant, there may be differing views on what the appropriate forms of social control are. For example, while some people suggest that addiction is a disease and should be medically regulated, other people disagree and argue that substance abuse should be controlled in other ways, such as through the criminal justice system. Thus, within these multiple social typing processes, the claims made by one group often must compete with the claims made by another; claims-makers compete with other claims-makers "in a [deviance] marketplace" (Richardson, Best, & Bromley, 1991, p. 5). But the principal role of power in this process ultimately means that some people's claims count more than other people's, and that some people's claims have a greater bearing on the society at large—its expectations, its structure, its institutions, and its people.

The consequences of the social typing process, whereby a person, behaviour, or characteristic becomes typed as deviant or is **deviantized**, are far-reaching. Through this process "description becomes prescription, which is then transformed into a desirable standard of normal behaviour to be upheld and maintained by the educational system, the religious system, the legal system, and of course the psychotherapeutic system, and to which every section of the population has to measure up or be found deficient" (Freud, 1999, p. 2). Some people become **criminalized** (when the context for the social typing process is the criminal justice system), some are **medicalized** (when the context for the social typing process is medical or psychiatric science), and others are deviantized in a variety of additional ways.

Exercise Your Mind

Does "positive deviance" exist? A quick online search reveals a number of practical initiatives that highlight positive deviance, especially in health care and business. However, the answer to that question will vary depending on the definition of deviance being used. Try to answer that question yourself using each of the definitions of deviance addressed in this chapter.

The introduction to the sociology of deviance in this chapter has corresponded to our tacit understandings of deviance as behaviours that are considered strange, inappropriate, or immoral—in need of social control. Some people question whether deviance can be positive; if it can refer to certain behaviours that are viewed positively as well. The *Exercise Your Mind* activity asks you to address this question. Once again, you will see that one's location on the objective–subjective continuum, along with the specific definition of deviance being used, gives rise to a variety of different views.

Our Journey through This Book

Reflecting various points along the objective-subjective continuum, many questions will serve as a guide in the remaining chapters of this book:

■ What is the source of a specific act or characteristic, and what is its nature?

■ What is the nature of the social typing process? What are the descriptions, evaluations, and prescriptions that are being applied to this person, behaviour, or characteristic?

■ Who has done the social typing?

■ What is the foundation for their arguments?

■ Who benefits from the deviantizing of this behaviour, characteristic, or person?

■ What larger social conditions support the social typing process?

■ How is the "deviance dance" evident?

These kinds of questions will guide us in our understanding of deviance in relation to media, sexuality, youth, physical appearance, mental illness, religion, and science. The choice of these topics is intended to provide you with critical insight into some of the core processes that make up the foundation of our society. Such critical insight will be based on both specific structures and processes of deviance as described in the particular topics above, as well as at a level of theoretical understanding and explanations of deviance more generally.

By the end of this book, you will see that deviance is not a characteristic ascribed to only certain groups of people living in the periphery of society. Instead, you will see that the processes by which deviance and normality are constructed are a part of your own everyday life. You contribute to the processes that deviantize others and, at the same time, are subjected to those processes yourself.

CHAPTER SUMMARY

Numbers in parentheses indicate the corresponding learning objective.

- The study of deviance is characterized by disagreement about how deviance should be defined. Some deviance specialists suggest that there has been a general shift from *objective* to *subjective* definitions, drawing upon the notion of an objective/subjective dualism or dichotomy. (1)

- The *objective* side of the dualism defines deviance in terms of a single quality that makes certain behaviours or characteristics inherently deviant. The four different defining traits that laypersons, social activists, politicians, or academics have mentioned are *statistical rarity*, *harm*, *negative societal reaction*, and *normative violation*. (2)

- According to the *subjective* side of the dichotomy, deviance is not determined by any inherent quality. Instead, deviance refers to behaviours or characteristics that are deemed to be unacceptable by the *dominant moral codes* in society. In other words, deviance is a *social construction*. (3)

- Looking at deviance from a social constructionist point of view, what is of interest are a behaviour's place in the social order, the roles assigned to people who exhibit that behaviour, and the societal meanings attached to it. (3)

- Recent work in the study of deviance integrates both objective and subjective components. Thus, objectivism and subjectivism may be thought of as existing along a continuum rather than as a dichotomy. (4)

- The way that deviance is defined has implications for the way it is studied. Researchers who lean toward the objective end of the objective–subjective continuum focus their analyses on the act itself, assuming that it can be classified as a form of deviance. Researchers who lean toward the subjective end of the continuum highlight the processes that create our perceptions of and reactions to the act; they also recognize the plurality of perceptions and reactions (i.e., the *deviance dance*). (5)

- The perceptions of *powerful groups* play a central role in the creation of the *dominant moral codes* that underlie the construction of deviance. In our society, powerful groups include politicians, religious institutions, scientists, the media, and commercial enterprise. (6)

- Central to issues of deviance are the processes of *social typing*, wherein someone is labelled in a particular way, judged on the basis of that label, and subjected to measures of social control. Such treatment can occur through various forms of regulation or social control—formal or informal, retroactive or preventative, and control of others or self-regulation. (6)

> To learn more about the topics discussed in this chapter and to complete chapter quizzes, visit the Companion Website for *Deviance, Conformity, and Social Control in Canada*.

Chapter 2
Explaining Deviance: The Act

Learning Objectives

After reading this chapter, you should be able to

1   Explain why different theories correspond to objective and subjective views of deviance, and describe the focus of positivist, interpretive, and critical theories.

2   Describe the core motivations of positivist theories, as well as how deviance is explained by the three types of positivist theories presented in this chapter.

3   Describe the core assumptions of functionalist theories, as well as how deviance is explained by (1) Durkheim's anomie theory, (2) Merton's anomie and strain theories, (3) differential opportunity theory, (4) general strain theory, and (5) Cohen's theory of status frustration. Outline the criticisms that have been directed at functionalist theories and identify any responses to those criticisms.

4   Describe the core assumptions of learning theories, as well as how deviance is explained by (1) differential association theory, (2) neutralization theory, and (3) social learning theory. Outline the criticisms that have been directed at learning theories and identify any responses to those criticisms.

5   Describe how Hirschi's social bonds theory explains deviance and its absence. Describe Gottfredson and Hirschi's more recent self-control theory. Outline the criticisms that have been directed at social control theories and identify any responses to those criticisms.

Theorizing Deviance

"Theory" is sometimes perceived as the flip side of the coin from "practice"; it is seen as isolated from the "real world." But in fact, "there is nothing more practical than a good theory" (Brezhnev, 2006). Theory and practice are intimately intertwined, in that "theory is the central tool used in science to organize accumulated knowledge" (Hay & Meldrum, 2010). It is through theory that we come to understand the world we live in. It is through past developments in theory that those of us living in the twenty-first century can understand gravity, nuclear power, and child development. Similarly, it is through theory that we are able to try to understand the way society works, the reasons why people commit crimes, why people get tattoos, and how an underweight female body has somehow come to represent the North American cultural ideal. That is, theory provides us with the central means of explaining and understanding deviance—what could be more practical than that?

Scientific theories of crime have existed for a century. The scientific study of criminality is recognized as beginning in the early twentieth century with the work of Cesare Lombroso, who explained criminality on the basis of evolution. He suggested that criminals were **atavists**—evolutionary throwbacks whose biology prevented them from conforming to society's rules (Lombroso, 1911). Other biological theories of crime soon followed, many of which explained criminality on the basis of heredity. According to those theories, just as the colour of one's eyes is biologically inherited, so is social behaviour like criminality (e.g., Goring, 1919). By mid-century, *social* theories of crime had largely replaced biological theories, and theorizing about non-criminal forms of deviance gained prominence as well.

Deviance specialists, whether they focus on criminal or non-criminal forms of deviance, use a wide range of theories: general sociological theories (e.g., conflict theory), specific criminological theories (e.g., strain theory), and interdisciplinary theories (e.g., feminist theories). Numerous theories exist simultaneously in the social sciences, unlike in the natural sciences where more accurate theories replace older theories that have been disproven. The poem "The Blind Men and the Elephant" serves as an interesting analogy for this characteristic of sociological theory (see Box 2.1).

Box 2.1

The Blind Men and the Elephant

A Hindu Fable

It was six men of Indostan
To learning much inclined
Who went to see the Elephant
(Though all of them were blind),
That each by observation
Might satisfy his mind.

The *First* approached the Elephant
And happening to fall
Against his broad sturdy side
At once began to bawl:
"God bless me! but the Elephant
Is very like a wall!"

The *Second*, feeling of the tusk,
Cried, "Ho! What have we here
So very round and smooth and sharp?
To me 'tis mighty clear
This wonder of an Elephant
Is very like a spear!"

The *Third* approached the animal,
And happening to take
The squirming trunk within his hands
Thus boldly up and spake:
"I see," quoth he, "the Elephant
Is very like a snake!"

The *Fourth* reached out his eager hand,
And felt about the knee.
"What most this wondrous beast is like
Is mighty plain," quoth he; "'Tis clear

enough the Elephant
Is very like a tree!"

The *Fifth*, who chanced to touch the ear,
Said: "E'en the blindest man
Can tell what this resembles most;
Deny the fact who can,
This marvel of an Elephant
Is very like a fan!"

The *Sixth* no sooner had begun
About the beast to grope,
Then, seizing on the swinging tail
That fell within his scope,
"I see," quoth he, "the Elephant
Is very like a rope."

And so these men of Indostan
Disputed loud and long.
Each in his own opinion
Exceeding stiff and strong,
Though each was partly in the right,
And all were in the wrong!

MORAL
So oft in theologic wars,
The disputants, I ween,
Rail on in utter ignorance
Of what each other mean,
And prate about an Elephant
Not one of them has seen!

—John Godfrey Saxe (1816–1887)
(Saxe, 1873)

When American poet John Godfrey Saxe wrote this poem based on a Hindu fable more than a century ago, would he have predicted what a useful analogy it would be for sociological theory? What do blind men and elephants have to do with understanding society and explaining deviance?

Just as the blind men's explanations of the nature of the elephant depended on what part of the elephant each focused on, sociologists' explanations of the nature of society depend on what aspect of society each theory focuses on. There are diverse ways of looking at the world around us, and each theoretical perspective has a different view. Each of these ways of looking at society shines a spotlight on a different aspect of the social order—some theories focus on the stability of society, some focus on conflict, some focus on interaction. But when a spotlight is directed at one particular location, all other areas necessarily fall into the shadows, just as each blind man's hands resting on one part of the elephant mean that the rest of the elephant's body is going untouched. In other words, an area of focus within each sociological theory may be easily explainable, but areas outside of the focal range are explained to a lesser extent, if at all.

Because each theory's way of looking at the world affects its focus, the explanations provided take a particular form. Thus, certain theories may be more useful than others in coming to understand a given issue or aspect of deviance. If you are interested in deviant *acts* (as those deviance specialists who lean toward the objective side of the objective–subjective continuum are), some theories of deviance will be more useful to you than others. In contrast, if you are more interested in the *perceptions* of and *reactions* to particular acts, as well as the role that power plays in those perceptions and reactions (as those deviance specialists who lean toward the subjective side of the objective–subjective continuum are), other theories will be of more use to you.

In Chapter 1, more objective ways of recognizing deviance were addressed, including views based on normative violation, statistical rarity, harm, and societal reaction. Each of these definitions of deviance suggests that there is a trait that all deviant people share that differentiates deviants from those who are normal. Emerging from this core idea is an interest in finding out *why* people become deviant—why they violate norms, or engage in behaviours that are atypical, or cause harm, or act in ways that result in a negative societal reaction. This way of looking at deviance is intimately linked with theories of deviance that are labelled **positivist** (Ashley & Orenstein, 2001). Positivist theories will be the focus of the remainder of this chapter.

The more subjective ways of looking at deviance, which will be examined in Chapter 3, suggest that the only characteristic all deviant people have in common is that enough important people have said they are deviant. Emerging from this core idea is an interest in exploring the social typing process—the process through which deviance and normality are socially constructed. Who becomes typed as deviant, how are they treated, and what rationales are offered? In what way does power influence societal perceptions of and reactions to particular behaviours? This way of looking at deviance is intimately linked with theories that are labelled **interpretive** and **critical** (Ashley & Orenstein, 2001). Interpretive and critical theories will be the focus of Chapter 3. Because an exhaustive analysis of theories of deviance would require a virtual library of books, this text will focus on the core assumptions of the theories that have been the most commonly used or have had the greatest impact in the sociology of deviance.

Although positivist, interpretive, and critical theories will be discussed separately, a significant trend in theorizing is that of theoretical integration—combining aspects of different theories to explain a particular phenomenon. Consequently, positivist, interpretive, and critical theories may be integrated in multiple combinations (Ashley & Orenstein, 2001). Theoretical integration is not an entirely new phenomenon; even elements of positivist Émile Durkheim's work of more than a century ago have served as a foundation for some early interpretive and critical work. However, it is a growing trend in the sociology of deviance (Kubrin, Stucky, & Krohn, 2009). As you progress through the chapter, you will see some examples of how aspects of various theories have been combined to better explain a particular phenomenon.

Why Do People Become Deviant?

Using Positivist Theories

Positivist sociological theories are fundamentally interested in explaining why people act in particular ways. They are modelled after approaches to theorizing in the natural sciences, which "seek generalizable, universally applicable laws" (Ashley & Orenstein, 2001, p. 30) that govern the environment. In pursuing the rules that govern the *social* environment, positivist sociologists seek cause-and-effect relationships in the form of statistical relationships—they look for those variables that are associated with a particular behaviour or outcome (Ashley & Orenstein, 2001). Both positivist sociological theories and theories in the natural sciences are based on a technical interest in the mastery of the environment; in the case of positivist sociological theories, this technical interest is in pursuit of planning for a better society (Ashley & Orenstein, 2001).

Thus, seeking to understand why deviant people act that way triggers subsequent attempts to prevent other people from becoming deviant. Positivist explanations of deviance are inevitably coupled with efforts at social control, efforts you might personally agree with (such as with violent crime) or disagree with (such as with homosexuality). Individual theorists may not personally seek more effective social control of particular behaviours; their interest may lie solely in explaining the variability in people's behaviours. However, positivist theorizing lays the groundwork for those individuals who are seeking more effective social control or improvement of society (Ashley & Orenstein, 2001).

The remainder of this chapter will review some of the positivist theories that have been commonly used to explain deviant acts and that have had significant influences on the sociology of deviance as a discipline. These include functionalist theories, learning theories, and theories of social control.

TIME TO REVIEW

Learning Objective 1

■ Why do multiple theories coexist in the sociology of deviance, and how can each theory be both "partly in the right" and "partly in the wrong"?

■ What is the nature of the link between particular types of theorizing

(i.e., positivist, interpretive, and critical) and the objective–subjective continuum?

Learning Objective 2

■ What are the central motivations of positivist theories?

Functionalist Theories: The Social Structure Creates Deviance

Functionalist theories, which in the past were also called *structural functionalist theories*, have their origins in the birth of the discipline of sociology itself; in fact, this theoretical perspective dominated the discipline until the mid-twentieth century. In this perspective, society is seen as comprising various structures (e.g., the family, the education system, the political system), each of which fulfills necessary functions for the smooth running of the social order. Some are **manifest functions**, which are intended and recognized; others are **latent functions**, which are unintentional and unrecognized. For example, a manifest function of post-secondary education is to train young adults for employment, but post-secondary education does more than this: its latent functions may include providing individuals with social networks and facilitating the formation of romantic relationships. The *Ask Yourself* exercise addresses manifest and latent functions in the context of your own life.

Analogous to this functionalist view of society is a pyramidal stack of cans on display in the supermarket; each can is necessary for the display as a whole to keep standing. You may be afraid of selecting one of those cans to place in your shopping cart, because if you move the wrong can, or if one of the cans is not perfectly in position, the entire display may collapse. Similarly, the smooth running of society is threatened if one of its structures has a poor fit with the other structures that make up society.

One of the core concerns in the functionalist perspective is the maintenance of the social order. This conservative focus is inherent in the perspective because of the assumption that the rules that make up the social order are consensual; in other words, the rules exist because we agree that they should exist. And we agree they should exist because they serve a useful function for society. Thus, if the rules are typically functional, and if rules exist because we agree they should, we need to figure out why some people do not follow those rules. It may be that a part of the structure of society has become dysfunctional, which is causing people to break the rules.

Within these broad functionalist assumptions, individual theorists have taken different paths in applying the assumptions to the study of deviance. In the remainder of this section we will look at the different ways that Émile Durkheim, Robert Merton, collaborators Richard Cloward and Lloyd Ohlin, Robert Agnew, and Albert Cohen have applied functionalist assumptions to an understanding of deviance.

Anomie Theory: The Problem of Too Much Social Change

Not only is Émile Durkheim (1933, 1951) recognized as one of the founders of the discipline of sociology, his work also defined the structural functionalist perspective

> ## Ask Yourself
> One of the functions of families is the socialization of children, which is accomplished, in part, by parents providing their children with specific rules. Consider an example all of us are likely familiar with—a parent requiring you to clean your room. The intended purpose of this rule (i.e., its manifest function) may be to keep the house looking nice. But what else were you learning by virtue of having to clean your room (i.e., latent functions)?

itself. In his theory, the notion of deviance is addressed in two ways. First, Durkheim suggested that a certain level of deviance is actually functional for society: deviance serves a useful purpose in helping maintain society's balance or equilibrium. Second, Durkheim addressed deviance in the context of dysfunctional levels of deviance that occur when society changes too quickly and **anomie** (normlessness) emerges.

Deviance is functional in that seeing someone break the rules leads the rest of us to realize how important the rules are and the necessity of following the rules. A certain level of deviance thereby enhances social order and *increases social solidarity* among those of us who join together to fight back against those people who break the rules. Deviance is also functional in that it is through observing behaviour and its consequences that *a society determines what its moral boundaries are*, what its rules should be, and what is considered acceptable and unacceptable. Deviance can be functional in that it *tests society's boundaries* and may demonstrate when certain rules no longer work and need to be changed. Finally, deviance serves as a way of *reducing societal tensions*, which it can do in two ways. First, societal tensions can be reduced when there is some sort of scapegoat that can be blamed for a social problem, since blaming a scapegoat takes the pressure off society at large. The second way that societal tensions can be defused is when individuals engage in small acts of minor deviance that act as a safety valve and let off some steam.

Parsons and Smelser (1956) elaborate on this last function, suggesting that letting off steam through minor acts of deviance subsequently activates social processes that return deviant actors to their acceptable roles in society. Social processes that accomplish this include *socialization* (wherein deviant actors who are letting off steam have internalized society's rules sufficiently that they return to their legitimate social roles), *profit* (which teaches citizens that there is a payoff or benefit accorded to those who conform to society's rules), *persuasion* (through advertising, the sermons of religious leaders, psychologists' advice, etc.), and *coercion* (punishment for those who do not return to their legitimate social roles).

Several researchers have explored the functionality of deviance. Kai Erikson's (1966) classic analysis of the Puritans of the Massachusetts Bay Colony reveals that acts of deviance helped to reinforce the moral boundaries of their community. As the needs of the community changed over time, the system of crimes and punishments changed as well, illustrating to citizens, for example, the power of the church (through the punishment of witchcraft) or the value of private property (through the punishment of theft). The nature of these punishments also reminded citizens of the norms and values that were considered important by authorities in that community. For example, when resident Anne Hutchinson began using Bible study classes held in her home as a forum for criticizing the minister's Sunday sermons, she was charged with heresy and disobedience to the church fathers. Her "crimes" under civil and religious law caused her to be banished from the colony and excommunicated from the Puritan church. Hutchinson's deviance reminded others of what the rules were; the severe consequences she faced by breaking those rules pointed to the importance of those rules. The entire situation reinforced the power of the civil and religious authorities in the community.

The role of deviance in testing society's boundaries and facilitating changes in outdated rules can be seen historically: Anne Hutchinson eventually came to be seen as a champion of women's rights and religious freedom (and in the 1980s the governor of Massachusetts granted her a posthumous pardon). More recently, the actions of activists on behalf of civil rights, women's rights, transgender rights, and disabled rights certainly changed society in significant ways. Their efforts demonstrated to the rest of society that some of its norms were outdated and needed to be changed. That is, certain norms had become dysfunctional for society and had to be modified to maintain social order.

Does deviance increase social solidarity? Hawdon, Ryan, and Agnich (2010) had a unique opportunity to explore this question. In 2006, they conducted a comprehensive survey of students at Virginia Polytechnic Institute in the United States. The survey included questions on social solidarity. For example, students were asked the extent to which they agreed with statements such as, "People at Virginia Tech share the same values," "I trust the students/faculty/staff at Virginia Tech," and "I am proud to be a member of the Virginia Tech community." Less than a year later, in April 2007, the most deadly school shooting in American history occurred on that campus. Twenty-seven students and five faculty members were killed, and another 23 were wounded. Hawdon, Ryan, and Agnich were given the opportunity to survey the students again to see if social solidarity had changed since the previous year. They re-surveyed the students five months, nine months, and one year following the tragedy. They found that solidarity had increased significantly at five months, showed some decline at nine months, and showed even further decline at one year. However, even after one year, social solidarity remained higher than it had been prior to the tragedy.

Joejune/Shutterstock

The candlelight vigils that follow tragic events reflect social solidarity.

Hawdon, Ryan, and Agnich found evidence of social solidarity in the results of their surveys. We can also see social solidarity reflected in practice following such tragic events, such as in memorial services, YouTube video tributes to victims, and in physical memorials, such as the Peace Garden at Dawson College in Montreal, Quebec.

Although Durkheim (1933, 1951) proposed that deviance is functional for society, he pointed out that it remains functional only up to a point. Beyond a certain level, deviance no longer enhances the social order but rather interferes with it. Living in nineteenth-century Europe, Durkheim observed that the processes of industrialization and urbanization, with their growing emphasis on individuality, were causing more deviance—wherein deviance exceeded a functional level. He noted, for example, that suicide rates were higher in more individualistic communities characterized by less **social integration** (i.e., cohesion or social bonds) and lower levels of **moral regulation** (i.e., the enforcement of society's norms).

In explaining this apparent increase in deviance, Durkheim (1933, 1951) focused on the ways that society's structures had changed with industrialization and the impact this had on people's behaviour, including deviant behaviour. Before industrialization, he theorized, society's structure was held together by **mechanical solidarity**—that is, society was bonded together by *likeness* or by a collective commitment to conformity. These societies were characterized by minimal specialization in the division of labour; people produced whatever they needed for their survival. Interactions between individuals in this type of society were quite personal and often kin-based; everyone knew and had a personal relationship with everyone else. Each person in this society had much in common with every other person.

With industrialization, the bonding mechanism for social structure was transformed into one of **organic solidarity**—society was bonded together by *difference* or interdependence through a highly specialized division of labour. In industrial society, the tasks that keep society running smoothly are divided among different institutions. The education system fulfills certain tasks while the political system and the medical system fulfill other tasks. Interactions among people in this type of society are somewhat impersonal, based primarily on our dependence on others because of the degree of specialization in the division of labour. A collective way of thinking and interacting is replaced by individualism.

Under conditions of both mechanical and organic solidarity, social integration and moral regulation have the potential to keep deviance at a functional level and facilitate the degree of conformity necessary to maintain social order. However, when social change occurs at too rapid a pace, individualism gets out of control, and bonds between people become weaker than is necessary for the well-being of society. Traditional norms and means of social control deteriorate, creating a situation of *anomie*. The presence of anomie in modern societies opens the door for greater levels of deviance beyond the degree that is functional for society. Thus, the structure of society itself and its impact on individuals contributes to harmful levels of deviance in society.

Durkheim highlights the economic structure of society in particular, noting that anomie is inherent in the economic advancements and economic crises that characterize trade and commerce. Not only does this apply to the period of industrialization that he studied, but also more recent economic advancements and crises that other scholars have analyzed. For example, Walberg and colleagues (cited in McKee, 2002) found that in the decade following the dissolution of the Soviet Union, Russian communities with the most rapid and extensive socioeconomic change had the highest crime rates and the largest decreases in life expectancy, in large part due to alcohol abuse. The anomic disorder created by the swift transition from communism to capitalism facilitated greater demand for alcohol and other substances because of weakened social cohesion; in addition, it improved the supply of such substances because of diminished moral regulation in the form of police and government corruption (McKee, 2002). In those communities where people lived more traditional lifestyles and had stronger family and social networks (e.g., rural areas and areas with large Muslim populations), addiction-related problems were less common (Walberg et al., cited in McKee, 2002). Other scholars argue that anomic disorder now exists on a global scale, due to the economic changes associated with globalization. Some recent research supports this assertion. Levchak (2015) finds that those nations on the receiving end of more foreign investments and ownership (one of the measures of globalization) have higher homicide rates; the United States and Mexico are examples of these nations, while Japan is an example of a nation with low foreign investments and a low homicide rate.

Here we have seen one theorist's application of functionalist ideas to an explanation of why deviance occurs. Durkheim's approach exemplifies the central concern of both objective ways of defining deviance and the related positivist theoretical perspectives. Robert Merton, a twentieth-century functionalist theorist, both built upon and moved away from Durkheim's ideas. Looking at Merton's theory shows us another way that functionalist assumptions have been applied to the study of deviance.

TIME TO REVIEW

Learning Objective 3

- According to Durkheim's anomie theory, in what way is deviance functional?

- According to Durkheim's anomie theory, why does deviance reach dysfunctional levels?

- What historical and contemporary evidence supports Durkheim's claims?

Merton's Anomie and Strain Theories: The (North) American Dream Gone Awry

Robert Merton (1938, 1968) applied functionalist assumptions to the study of deviance in different ways, but he is best known for applying functionalist assumptions in the form of his anomie and strain theories (often labelled *classic strain theory*), which dominated "the area of deviance from the early 1950s until about 1970" (Collins, cited in Pfohl, 1994, p. 279). In fact, Merton's theory of the link between anomie and strain "has been heralded as among the most significant of all major sociological theories" (Featherstone & Deflam, 2003, p. 471). Merton suggested that deviance originates not only from the individual, but also from the structure of society, which propels some people into deviance. What is it about the structure of society that creates a greater likelihood that some people, more than others, will become deviant? The *Ask Yourself* exercise will bring you closer to an answer to this question.

The *Ask Yourself* exercise asks you to think about what Merton referred to as **institutionalized goals**. In contemporary capitalist society, these are the goals that are culturally exalted, the ones that we are taught we are *supposed* to want to achieve. Merton said that in North America, the goals we are to aspire to include *wealth*, *status/power*, and *prestige*—the qualities that make up "success" or the "(North) American Dream." Almost everywhere we look we encounter the message that these qualities are what we should try to achieve in life. Who are the people who are admired and envied in society? We admire the wealthy: people who drive a Porsche, Jaguar, or BMW, who live in houses with indoor swimming pools, and who travel to expensive and exotic places. We admire powerful people, like the late Steve Jobs. We admire professional athletes (such as Sidney Crosby or Stephen Curry), famous actors (such as Ryan Reynolds, Leonardo DiCaprio, or Tina Fey), and famous singers and musicians (such as Beyoncé, Pharrell, or Adele)—people with prestige. Our society rewards those who attain wealth, power, or prestige; they have the nicest "toys," they win awards (such as a Grammy, an Oscar, or a Playoff MVP), they are interviewed endlessly to share their secrets for success, and they have countless numbers of people following their every move in daily sports reports, in the business news, or on Twitter. Of course, some of you might not personally admire people who are wealthy or famous, and you might aspire to other goals. However, even if your personal goals differ from the institutionalized goals to which Merton referred, the larger issue is that our society is structured in a way that gives benefit to or rewards those who have attained these institutionalized goals.

> ## Ask Yourself
> In Canada today, what types of achievements are necessary in order to be perceived as "successful"? What do you see in the society around you that reinforces your belief that these are, indeed, the criteria for success?

Merton suggested that just as our culture is characterized by institutionalized goals, it is also characterized by **legitimate means** of attaining those goals. What are recognized as the legitimate ways of attaining wealth, power, and prestige? We are supposed to get a good education, find a high-paying job, and work hard; alternatively, perhaps you inherited wealth or were born into a powerful family. However, Merton pointed out that both *anomie* and *strain* have come to characterize American society (and presumably, North America more generally). A context of **anomie** has emerged that Merton describes as an imbalance between culturally prescribed goals and legitimate means, whereby society's emphasis on the goals of wealth, power, and prestige exceeds the emphasis on the means of achieving those goals.

This has resulted in a "deinstitutionalization of the means" (Featherstone & Deflam, 2003, p. 478). That is, simply attaining the institutionalized goals has become more important than *how* one attains them. In their *institutional anomie theory*, Messner and Rosenfeld (2013) propose that it is because of the dominance of economic institutions (with their emphasis on competition and success) that anomie characterizes North American society: as economic institutions come to dominate other institutions (e.g., family, religion), economic values come to infiltrate those institutions as well.

In addition to this cultural context of anomie in which we all live, there are also structural constraints for some people. The normative social order is such that not everyone has equal access to legitimate opportunities. A child growing up in a middle- or upper-class neighbourhood—with the best teachers and well-equipped schools, a wide range of extracurricular activities available, a home in a safe community, and middle- or upper-class parents—is likely to have assured access to the legitimate means of achieving institutionalized goals. However, consider a child growing up in an impoverished neighbourhood. The dilapidated schools, devoid of library books, have trouble attracting teachers and offer few extracurricular activities. Home is a run-down house in a disordered community. The parents live in poverty or are chronically on social assistance. Although we often perceive Canadian society as a place of equal opportunity, does this child truly have the same access to legitimate opportunities in life as the middle-class child?

The blocked opportunities that exist in some parts of the social structure create a **strain** between the goals and the means for people who live there. With this structural gap between institutionalized goals and the legitimate means of achieving those goals, individuals must find ways to adapt. According to Merton, people can adapt to the gap between goals and means in five different ways, some of which result in deviance.

The first possible mode of adaptation is **conformity**. The individual continues to accept both society's institutionalized goals and the legitimate means; this person keeps pursuing wealth, power, or prestige by going to school, finding a good job, and working hard.

The second possible mode of adaptation, **innovation**, can result in deviance. The individual accepts the institutionalized goals but rejects the legitimate means and instead seeks alternative means of achieving those goals. For example, if you want to become wealthy, you can do so in a conforming way by pursuing a higher education and training for a high-paying career, or you can do so in an innovative way by selling drugs.

The third possible mode of adaptation is **ritualism**. The person engaging in ritualism has given up on or at least reduced the institutionalized goals but continues to engage in the legitimate means. This is someone who thinks he or she will never get anywhere in life, but still keeps going through the motions—for example, never missing a day of work. With this mode of adaptation, people are unlikely to be looked upon as deviant because, to the outside world, they appear to reliably follow the rules.

Merton's fourth mode of adaptation is **retreatism**, wherein people reject both the institutionalized goals and the legitimate means. These are people who have given up on

Louis Riel was executed for his "rebellion" but later came to be recognized as an initiator of important social change.

the goals, do not even go through the motions anymore, and instead retreat into their own isolated worlds, sometimes characterized by alcohol abuse or drug addiction.

The last mode of adaptation is **rebellion**. As with retreatism, people engaged in rebellion also reject both institutionalized goals and legitimate means; however, unlike retreatists, they substitute new goals and new means. These are people who have a "vision" of a different world and act to bring that vision to life.

For example, Louis Riel had a vision of a nation that would include Métis rights and culture; he fought for that vision in the Red River Rebellion (1869–1870) and the North West Rebellion (1885), eventually being executed for high treason. In his famous "I Have a Dream" speech, American civil rights leader Martin Luther King Jr. described his dream for a society based on equality for all races, religions, and creeds; King was shot and killed by a man who did not share that vision. Nelson Mandela had a vision of a different South African society, one free of apartheid, and he fought for more than 20 years for that vision. In the 1960s and 1970s, the hippie counterculture envisioned a society in which everyone would give up material wealth—including money—and instead seek peace and love. In pursuit of these goals, many hippies stopped working, "made love, not war," consumed a wide range of mind-altering drugs, and moved into various types of commune-like settings.

These examples illustrate how Merton's five modes of adaptation allow people to adapt to the gap between institutionalized goals and legitimate means and how some people are led into deviance—whether through rebellion, retreatism, or innovation. According to Merton, the current structure of society creates this gap, more so for some groups of people in society than for others. This is why some people engage in deviance.

Thus far, we have seen two diverse and highly influential ways that functionalist assumptions have been used to explain why people engage in deviance. As functionalist theories, both Durkheim's and Merton's approaches suggest that parts of the structure of society may become dysfunctional in some way and result in deviant behaviour on the part of some people. The next functionalist theories we will discuss are from collaborators Richard Cloward and Lloyd Ohlin, who also consider that the structure of society may lead to deviance for some people.

Differential Opportunity Theory: Access to the Illegitimate World

Cloward and Ohlin's (1960) theory extends aspects of Merton's strain theory; although their theory has received relatively little empirical attention, it has served as a foundation for social action and policy (Kubrin, Stucky, & Krohn, 2009). Like Merton, they suggest that the way society is structured results in differential access to legitimate opportunities. However, Cloward and Ohlin go on to propose that the way society is structured also results in differential access to illegitimate opportunities—some people have more access to illegitimate opportunities than other people do by living in neighbourhoods that may have street gangs, drug dealers, or sex-trade workers.

Due to the differential access to both legitimate and illegitimate opportunities that is created by the structure of society, Cloward and Ohlin suggest that some people are more likely to become participants in deviant subcultures. Some people in lower-class neighbourhoods may become part of **criminal gangs**, in which criminal behaviour is akin to a small business (e.g., the Fresh Off the Boat, or FOB, gang in Calgary, which formed in the late 1990s for the purpose of selling drugs). Other people may become part of **retreatist gangs**, which, reflecting Merton's concept of the retreatist mode of adaptation, consist of groups of people who retreat into substantial drug or alcohol use. Finally, people in these neighbourhoods may join **conflict gangs**, which fight for status and power in the neighbourhood via the use of violence against competitive gangs. For instance, although FOB formed as a criminal gang in the 1990s, a falling out among some of its members led to the creation of a new gang, the Fresh Off the Boat Killers (FK); extreme violence has now broken out between the two groups, "motivated not by battles over drug turf, but mutual hatred" (Van Rassel, 2009), resulting in dozens of deaths since 2002.

All three of these instances are a consequence of the opportunities that are available in the community. As children grow up in these neighbourhoods, they may see people making their livings through criminal involvement with similar others, people drinking and taking drugs to excess (and perhaps even trying to sell drugs and alcohol to neighbourhood children), or gang violence. Being a part of this environment makes certain illegitimate opportunities easily available.

As with Durkheim's and Merton's theories, Cloward and Ohlin see society's structure as the impetus for deviant behaviour. Robert Agnew, the next theorist to be addressed, also focuses on the roles played by structure and strain in creating deviance, but suggests that they interact with social psychological factors.

Agnew's General Strain Theory: The Effect of Negative Emotions

Robert Agnew (1992, 2001, 2006) has also expanded upon Merton's strain theory, developing a general strain theory that is one of the most commonly used positivist theories in the study of deviance today. First, he extends the notion of strain by identifying a number of possible sources. Merton stated that strain emerges when the social structure places limitations on people's access to the means of achieving positively valued goals. However, Agnew proposes that strain can be produced by a variety of processes. While it can occur when we are unable to achieve goals (e.g., failing a course), it may also arise when valued stimuli are removed (the loss of a job or the dissolution of a marriage) or when negative stimuli are presented (being teased at school or living in a conflict-ridden family). Research by Moon, Hays, & Blurton (2009) illustrates the multifaceted nature of strain, finding that goal blockage, being harassed or embarrassed by teachers, and racial discrimination each have a direct effect on a wide range of violent and non-violent, criminal and non-criminal behaviours among university students.

Second, Agnew (1992, 2001, 2006) argues that strain is not sufficient in itself to produce deviance; there are many people who experience strain who do not engage in deviant behaviour. Instead, strain creates **negative affect** (negative emotions) such as anger, depression, or anxiety. Strain is especially likely to create negative affect if it is perceived as unjust, if it is severe, and if the individual lacks control over the situation (Agnew, 2001).

Individuals will attempt to ameliorate these negative emotions and may use one (or more) of three different strategies; in some cases, these strategies result in deviance, while at other times they do not (Agnew, 1992, 2006). Some people may use **cognitive coping strategies** that transform the way they think about the strain. For example, rather than thinking about one poor exam mark as the end of the world, they may instead see it as an important learning experience. By reinterpreting the experience, they are able to reduce the negative emotions and pre-empt any deviant outcomes. **Emotional coping strategies** may also be used to reduce the negative emotions caused by strain. These strategies may be deviant or conforming in nature; someone who feels anxious, angry, or fearful because of a poor exam mark might try to numb those emotions through drugs or alcohol, or dispel them by talking to a friend or going for a run. Other people may attempt to eliminate the strain itself by using **behavioural coping strategies** that may also be deviant or non-deviant in nature. For instance, in the face of a poor exam mark, some students may register for a study skills workshop while others plagiarize a term paper in order to increase their grade in the course.

A variety of individual and environmental factors influence the experience of strain and people's responses to it (Agnew, 2006). Thus, a person with a close family or friendship network is in a better position to talk to someone as an emotional coping strategy, compared to an individual who lacks those networks. Someone who has used tobacco or alcohol in the past is more likely to use those substances as a form of behavioural coping than is someone who has never smoked or consumed alcohol. Cognitive reinterpretations may come more easily to some people than others.

The social structure also plays an important role (Agnew, 2006). First, people having certain locations in the social structure are more likely to experience particular forms of strain, such as the economic strains associated with poverty. In fact, some locations in the social structure may be characterized by not just one person, but rather a multiplicity of people experiencing similar strains. For example, a neighbourhood may have a large number of people who are living in poverty, or many children who have experienced parental divorce. Second, those social locations also influence the coping resources that may or may not be available. Vacations, massage therapy, gym memberships, psychological counselling, and academic tutoring can provide constructive means of coping—but they are not equally available to all groups in society.

Empirical research shows that the role of emotions as a mediating factor between strain and deviance is more complicated than initially theorized. Negative emotions have been found to play a part in a variety of forms of deviance, including young women's purging behaviour (Sharp et al., 2001), university student's use of stimulants as "homework drugs" (Ford & Schroeder, 2009), and men's hiring of prostitutes (Bucher, Manasse, & Milton, 2015). However, most research finds that negative emotions only partially account for deviance. For instance, in a study of youth victimized by bullying, negative emotions accounted for 24 to 44 percent of the variation in self-harming behaviours and suicidal thoughts; the experience of being bullied itself still had a direct effect, independent of negative emotions (Hay & Meldrum 2010). Similarly, Bucher, Manasse, and Milton (2015) find negative emotions do not mediate the relationship between economic strain and prostitution. That is, most of the women they interviewed entered the sex trade for purely economic reasons—they needed money, or at least needed more money than they currently had. But participating in the sex trade created negative emotions like humiliation, fear, anxiety, and anger, which in many of the women resulted in drug abuse as an emotional coping strategy.

Although general strain theory introduces social psychological factors (such as negative emotions), it is still a functionalist theory in that it argues society is structured in a way that facilitates differential experiences and consequences of strain among people in various social locations. The last functionalist theory we will address is status frustration theory, which also highlights the way that the social structure determines the experiences of different groups.

Status Frustration Theory: The Middle-Class Classroom

Albert Cohen (1955) claims that inequalities in the structure of society are reproduced in the classroom, resulting in delinquent subcultures among lower-class boys. Just as middle-class norms dominate in society in general, they also dominate the structure and functioning of school classrooms. This creates a **middle-class measuring rod** that lower-class boys find difficult to live up to. The school's emphasis on delayed gratification, politeness, and the value of hard work does not correspond well with the lives of lower-class boys. In their homes and communities, delaying gratification may result in the object of the gratification disappearing or being taken away. Politeness may compromise safety, and toughness is emphasized instead. They may see their own parents working very hard, perhaps at two or three jobs, and yet not making any progress; thus, the value of hard work may be unapparent.

When they are unable to succeed according to the standards in the classroom, they experience a situation similar to strain—**status frustration**. As a result, they join together with other lower-class boys who are having the same experience (**mutual conversion**) and develop a set of oppositional standards at which they are able to succeed (**reaction formation**). If the middle-class standard is to delay gratification, the oppositional standard is to be hedonistic. Non-utilitarian, malicious, negativistic youth gangs are the result. In support of Cohen's theory, many empirical studies have found poor school performance or early school leaving to be associated with criminal behaviour (e.g., Gomme, 1985).

TIME TO REVIEW

Learning Objective 3

- According to Merton's concepts of anomie and strain, why does deviance emerge, and what are the different modes of adaptation to strain?

- According to Cloward and Ohlin's differential opportunity theory, how does the structure of society contribute to deviance, and what different forms does deviance take?

- According to Agnew's general strain theory, what causes strain, what role do emotions play, and how do people cope with those emotions?

- According to Cohen's theory of status frustration, why do lower-class boys become deviant, and what form does their deviance take?

Limitations of Functionalist Theories of Deviance

Émile Durkheim, Robert Merton, collaborators Richard Cloward and Lloyd Ohlin, Robert Agnew, and Albert Cohen have each applied functionalist assumptions to an explanation of deviance, although in slightly different ways. Durkheim's theory of society includes discussions of how deviance can be functional for society but can reach dysfunctional levels when social change occurs too rapidly and anomie is created. Merton's theory, which focuses more explicitly on explaining deviance, describes with greater specificity what it is about the normative social order that leads some people into deviance. For Merton, this is the gap between institutionalized goals and legitimate means of achieving those goals, which is experienced more by people located in certain parts of the social structure. Like Merton, Cloward and Ohlin suggest that the structure of society creates differential access to legitimate opportunities, but they extend the notion of differential access in showing how it applies to illegitimate opportunities as well. Agnew goes a step further by saying that strain creates negative emotions, and it is the coping strategies used to deal with those emotions that may result in deviance. Finally, Cohen suggests the reproduction of structured inequalities in the school system serves as the impetus for deviance among groups of lower-class boys.

Despite the slightly different paths that are taken by these various theorists, they all make use of functionalist assumptions—that society comprises structures which fulfill important functions for the maintenance of the social order, that the structure of society contributes to deviance in some way, and that deviance is a threat to society's equilibrium (at least at certain levels).

Functionalist theories have been subject to considerable criticism (Downes & Rock, 2011; Ritzer & Stepnisky, 2014). In fact, Martins (1974) states that "every Autumn term . . . [functionalism] is ritually executed for introductory teaching purposes . . . the demolition of functionalism is almost an initiation rite of passage into sociological adulthood" (p. 247). Functionalism has been criticized, in part, on the basis of its logic, its ideology and political implications, and its biases.

Critiques of Functionalist Logic.   The core assumptions of the functionalist perspective have been criticized as teleological and tautological (Turner & Maryanski, 1979). They are **teleological** (i.e., related to goals) in that the emergence of social institutions is explained in terms of the functions they serve. Functionalism proposes that since society has specific needs, particular institutions are created to meet those needs. For example, because society requires that children be socialized, the institution of family emerged—the existence of family is explained in terms of the functions it fulfills. However, critics argue that functionalism is not able to explain *why* that specific institution, at the exclusion of others, is required to achieve particular societal goals. *Why* is family required for the socialization of children, when there are other institutions (such as the education system) that socialize children as well? If other institutions are able to fulfill that same function, then functionalism really has not explained the need for the family at all. Functionalist arguments are also criticized as **tautological** (i.e., circular), where the whole is described in terms of its parts, and the parts are described in terms of the whole (Turner & Maryanski, 1979). In a tautological argument, we would say that because we see families socializing children, the socialization of children is one of the functions of the family. Similarly, because we see children learning to read in schools, teaching children to read is one of the functions of the education system. The latter part of the argument merely restates the information in the former part of the argument.

Critiques of Functionalist Ideology.   The functionalist perspective is also criticized at an ideological or political level. Critics claim that by determining the functions of almost any aspect of social life, functionalists ignore the social and historical circumstances from which those aspects emerge—such as the sociohistorical circumstances that give rise to specific family forms or particular educational curricula. The presumption of functionality (the idea that society's structure is somehow useful) also contributes to the critique of functionalism's conservative bias (Huaco, 1986). Racial inequalities, gender inequalities, and low wages for the working class can all be justified on the basis of being "functional" for society in some way. For example, strain theorists point out that society is structured in a way that results in differential opportunities and resources for people located in various parts of the social structure, but they do not identify an unequal structure as being problematic or in need of reform. By not critiquing those inequalities, functionalism is inherently supportive of the status quo.

Critiques of Functionalist Bias.   In addition to the basic logical and ideological assumptions of the functionalist perspective being criticized, specific functionalist theories have been critiqued on the basis of a variety of biases related to social class, an overemphasis on criminal behaviour, and lack of attention to gender. It is these particular critiques that functionalist scholars have addressed to the greatest extent over the past two decades.

Merton's theory of anomie and strain, Cloward and Ohlin's differential opportunity theory, and Cohen's theory of status frustration have all traditionally focused attention on criminal behaviour, relying on official crime statistics. Because official crime statistics under-represent the extent of criminal activity in the middle and upper classes, these theories have historically been criticized for identifying deviance and criminality as lower-class phenomena. If criminal behaviour is acknowledged to be a middle- and upper-class phenomenon as well, and non-criminal forms of deviance are also analyzed (e.g., self-harm), then the assumption that deviance originates from differentially structured opportunities comes into question (Downes & Rock, 2011).

For some time now, functionalist scholars have been responding to these traditional critiques. Earlier in the chapter we saw that Agnew's general strain theory addresses the social structure as only *one* of the factors that shapes experiences of strain but points out that there are many different sources of strain (beyond economic), that social psychological factors are also important, and that only certain coping strategies result in deviance (Agnew, 1992, 2001, 2006). General strain theory acknowledges a wide range of forms that deviance can take as well, both criminal and non-criminal. Although Messner and Rosenfeld's institutional anomie theory (2013) continues to be applied primarily in analyses of criminal behaviour, some recent research has extended applications of the theory into non-criminal forms of deviance. For example, Hövermann, Groß, Zick, and Messner (2015) find that individuals with a strong marketized mentality (wherein they prioritize financial success) have higher levels of prejudice toward social groups that they perceive as an economic burden to society—immigrants, the unemployed, and people who are homeless. Scholars have also applied Merton's theory of anomie and strain to a variety of non-criminal behaviours. One of the most interesting studies is one in which the pursuit of fame and celebrity is analyzed (Parnaby & Sacco, 2004) (see Box 2.2).

In addition to biases related to social class and an overemphasis on criminal behaviour, critics have also drawn attention to the **androcentric bias** that has traditionally characterized many functionalist theories. In other words, functionalist theorizing was largely developed on the basis of the male experience; female experiences were either ignored or presumed to be similar. In response to this criticism, there is a growing body of functionalist work that takes gender into consideration, particularly in the case of Agnew's general strain theory.

Box 2.2

The "Strain" of Fame and Celebrity

Although Merton initially emphasized material or economic success in his theory of the relationship between anomie and strain, his later work uses the broader concept of *opportunity structures*, which can be generalized to goals outside of the economic realm (Merton, 1995). Using Merton's revised theoretical formulation, Parnaby and Sacco (2004) suggested that in a media-saturated world, the pursuit of fame has become an institutionalized goal. This idea takes on even greater prominence in the present day when we consider that the social media we now take for granted in our everyday lives (such as Facebook, Twitter, Instagram, and YouTube) did not exist at the time Parnaby and Sacco conducted their research. Legitimate means of achieving fame include "individual struggle (or hard work), personal accomplishment and/or a rare talent, and ... 'dumb luck' " (Parnaby & Sacco, 2004, p. 5). However, the opportunity structure is such that not everyone has equal access to these legitimate means. Thus, individuals who experience the strain between goals and means may use one of the four deviant *modes of adaptation* proposed by Merton.

Innovation involves continuing to pursue institutionalized goals but rejecting the legitimate means of doing so. Innovative means of pursuing fame or celebrity include the gangster celebrities of the past (e.g., Al Capone) and their contemporary equivalents—hip hop artists living the "gangsta lifestyle" (p. 13). The merging of fame and criminal behaviour is also evident in the news media's creation of the "killer as celebrity" (p. 14), whose picture is placed on the front page of every newspaper and news magazine and whose life is dissected and sometimes emulated. Graffiti artists use the innovative mode of adaptation as well, wherein their "tagging" is intended to both bring them recognition as artists and mark their territories.

Ritualism brings a diminishing of goals but an adherence to legitimate means. The ritualistic pursuit of celebrity is found in the workers who dress up as characters at amusement parks and people who detail every aspect of their daily lives on blogs and social media sites. Ritualism is also evident in "the struggling actor ... who abandons his or her dreams of mainstream Hollywood for the pornography industry" and "the cover band that dedicates itself to the remaking of songs when the multi-million dollar record deal becomes more fiction than fact ..." (p. 16).

Retreatism leads individuals to reject both goals and means and retreat into isolation. Although somewhat difficult to apply to those in the public eye, Parnaby and Sacco suggest that this mode of adaptation is evident in those who experience extreme stage fright and people who have already achieved fame yet avoid all of its trappings by leading relatively isolated lives (e.g., Marlon Brando; Johnny Depp).

Rebellion involves replacing existing goals and means with a new vision. "Culture jamming" (Adbusters, cited in Parnaby & Sacco, 2004, p. 20) works toward changing the way that the culture and consumer industries set their agendas. It is linked with critiques of globalization and resistance to corporate-driven global inequality and exploitation.

A number of empirical studies that apply general strain theory have found that there are gender differences in the types of strain experienced, the nature of negative emotions, and the resulting forms of deviance. For instance, a study of more than 12 000 adolescents in grades 7 through 12 found that girls were more likely to have experienced the suicide of a friend or family member, while boys were more likely to have experienced violent victimization. Boys and girls were equally likely to feel anger as a negative emotion, but girls were more likely to experience depressive symptoms. There were gender differences in patterns of deviance as well. Girls were more likely to have had suicidal thoughts and to have run away from home at some point; boys were more likely to engage in weekly drinking and violent behaviour (Kaufman, 2009).

A retrospective analysis of civil rights riots in the 1960s also finds gender differences in strain to be a key factor in explaining why people participate in riots (Santoro & Broidy, 2014). Divergent forms of strain were evident in the people interviewed: Black men were more likely to have experienced strain in the form of police mistreatment, while black women were more likely to have experienced strain in the form of dissatisfaction with housing conditions. Because the former type of strain was a primary motivator for participation in riots, more men than women became involved.

Although a number of studies find a relationship between strain, emotions, and gender, other studies do not. Keith and colleagues (2015) ask the question of whether gender identity may be of greater significance than biological sex. Their research reveals that, among both males and females, those who identify with high levels of masculinity are more likely to experience anger in response to strain while those who identify with high levels of femininity are less likely to experience anger in response to strain.

Functionalist theories dominated the study of deviance in the mid-twentieth century, but their popularity waned in the face of growing critiques. However, because more recent scholars have addressed those critiques in their theoretical reformulations and their empirical analyses, functionalist theories are currently experiencing a resurgence—particularly Agnew's general strain theory (1992, 2001, 2006) and Messner and Rosenfeld's institutional anomie theory (2013).

In addition to functionalist theories, other perspectives originate from a positivist understanding of why people act in deviant ways. The next set of positivist theories we will be addressing are learning theories.

TIME TO REVIEW

Learning Objective 3

- In what ways has functionalist logic been critiqued?

- In what ways has functionalist ideology been critiqued?

- What biases have historically existed in functionalist theories, and how has more recent research responded to critiques of these biases?

Learning Theories: People Learn to Be Deviant

Learning theories, like functionalist theories, have been widely used as explanations of deviance. As the label suggests, these theories explain deviant behaviour as a result of learning processes. In other words, people *learn* to be deviant. The precise nature of this learning process is outlined in various learning theories. In this section, we will focus on differential association theory, neutralization theory, and social learning theory—all of which have had considerable influence on the way deviance has been understood over the last several decades.

Differential Association Theory: Learning from Friends and Family

Our exploration of learning theories begins with an influential theorist whose work is recognized by some people as one of the dominant explanations of deviance today (Cullen & Agnew, 1998; Erickson, Crosnoe, & Dornbusch, 2000). Edwin Sutherland (1947), beginning with the assumption that deviant behaviour is learned, developed a theory that focuses on explaining the nature of the learning process—a process he labelled **differential association**.

Ask Yourself

Think about the various groups that you interacted with as a child or adolescent. For each group, consider the types of techniques and motives you were exposed to. Did you learn ways to engage in what might be seen as deviant behaviour? What were your reasons for doing so? Did you learn ways to engage in conforming behaviour? What were your reasons for doing so? If you consider your childhood and adolescence as a whole, do you think you were exposed to more deviant definitions than conforming definitions, or vice versa?

Although Sutherland's theory was initially proposed as a theory of crime, it has since been successfully applied to other forms of deviance, particularly adolescent substance use (Aseltine, 1995; Elliot, Huizinga, & Ageton, 1985). Sutherland proposed that deviant behaviour is learned through the same process by which conforming behaviour is learned. Central to the learning process is the direct interaction and communication that occurs in small, intimate groups.

Deviant people act that way because that is what they learn through communication within the intimate groups of which they are a part. Intimacy is crucial to the learning of deviance, such that impersonal agents like music, television, and movies are relatively inconsequential. Within these personal groups, individuals learn both **techniques** (skills) and **motives** (reasons) for particular kinds of behaviour. If people are exposed to more deviant definitions than conforming definitions overall, they are likely to become deviant themselves; in other words, if they are learning techniques for how to engage in deviance and motives for engaging in deviance more than they are learning techniques for how to conform and motives for conforming, they are more likely to engage in deviant behaviour.

Research finds that it is the definitions provided by *in-group* members that are especially important in influencing behaviour. Piquero, Tibbets, and Blankenship (2005) presented MBA students with a vignette in which they were responsible for making a decision as to whether the company for which they worked would continue to distribute a drug discovered to be harmful. They were also asked the extent to which they believed their co-workers, friends, business professors, and board of directors would support that decision. Some support for differential association theory was found in that the employees' decisions were associated with the corporate climate—that is, the extent to which they believed the board of directors and their closest co-workers would support that decision. Their decisions were also *negatively* associated with the extent to which they believed their business professors and friends would support those decisions. The researchers concluded that it is "somewhat disturbing" that "many of the respondents ... essentially reported that they would take actions that would lead to injuring or killing innocent people, while knowingly disregarding the ethical responsibilities they learned from their professors and defying moral values of their closest friends" (p. 181). In this case, "the corporate environment can subvert the other associations and normative values that the individual has learned [in life]" (p. 181).

This differential exposure to deviant and conforming definitions is further complicated by the fact that not all group interactions have the same impact on our learning processes. First, the extent of group influence varies by *frequency*, in that those groups we interact with more frequently will have more of an influence on our learning. Second, interactions that are of longer *duration* have more of an influence than those of shorter duration. Third, there is a *priority* to our small group interactions; those intimate groups with which we interact earlier in life have a greater influence on our learning. Finally, interactions vary in *intensity* or in how important a particular group is to us—the more important a particular group is to us, the greater its influence on our learning processes. The frequency, duration, priority, and intensity of exposure to group interactions determine how influential the definitions of behaviour are on our learning processes.

In an analysis of the jamband subculture, Hunt (2010) finds that some of these characteristics may have more of an influence than others. The jamband subculture originated with the Grateful Dead and its fans ("Deadheads"). Musical artists considered to be "jamband" perform a blend of folk, rock, and blues and are known for improvisational jamming in their performances; this makes each individual performance completely unique. They encourage members of the audience to record their performances and share those recordings with others. Members of the jamband subculture follow bands on tour and set up temporary communities in the parking lots outside of concert venues. In these communities, the core values of the subculture are expressed: sharing, pooling resources, trading recordings, and bartering resources such as concert tickets, rides, food, and water. These prosocial behaviours are labelled "kynd" (p. 521), while threatening someone or talking down to them is labelled "unkynd." Well-established members of the subculture consistently adhere to these norms, but those who are less integrated frequently misunderstand or violate the norms. Hunt's analysis revealed that positive evaluations of kynd norms were associated with frequency (how often an individual participates in the subculture), intensity (the extent to which an individual has close friends within the subculture), and priority (the age at which an individual was first socialized into the subculture). However, duration (the length of time an individual had been a part of the subculture) had no impact on support for kynd norms.

Sutherland's explanation of the learning process that leads to deviance had a substantial impact on subsequent theorizing about deviance. Gresham Sykes and David Matza's neutralization theory later highlighted and expanded upon one aspect of differential association theory.

Neutralization Theory: Rationalizing Deviance

Sykes and Matza (1957), like Sutherland, focused on criminal behaviour in the formulation of their theory, which was later appropriated for understanding the broader issue of deviance. They agreed with Edwin Sutherland's suggestion that deviance emerges as the result of a learning process in group interactions. However, the particular focus of their theory is on the nature of some of the *motives* that Sutherland referred to. According to Sykes and Matza, the most important motives that are learned, which subsequently open the door for deviant behaviour, are **techniques of neutralization**. Part of what deviant people learn are the rationalizations for the behaviour they engage in; by rationalizing their behaviour, they can convince themselves that what they are doing is not *really* wrong.

One of the techniques of neutralization is the **denial of responsibility**, which shifts the blame or responsibility off the individual and directs it elsewhere. The blame may be directed at other people, situations, or environments. The second technique of neutralization is the **denial of injury**. In this situation, the accused deviants express the perception that what they have done hurts or harms no one. The **denial of the victim** is the third neutralization technique, where the perception is that the victim of the deviant's behaviour was somehow deserving of her or his fate. The fourth neutralization technique that Sykes and Matza refer to is **condemnation of the condemners**. This technique shifts the focus from the deviant's own behaviour to the deviant behaviour of others, especially people from the social groups that have pointed to this person's deviance. The condemners are accused of being hypocrites who are engaging in other forms of deviance, perhaps secretly. The final technique of neutralization is **appealing to higher loyalties**, where the deviant behaviour is justified as serving a higher purpose. In this situation, people acknowledge that they have violated norms, but in service of other more important norms, values, or principles.

These five techniques of neutralization (since expanded to include a number of additional techniques), adopted through the kind of learning processes described earlier in differential association theory, are central to explaining why people engage in deviance. Only by being able to rationalize their actions do people become deviant. Techniques of neutralization have been explored in a variety of contexts. Heinonen (2015) finds that in Finland, where disciplinary violence (such as spanking) is prohibited by law, parents who have come to the attention of authorities for that behaviour use a variety of techniques of neutralization. They *deny responsibility* by stating that they momentarily

Cyclists who compete in events such as the Tour de France have long faced accusations of using performance-enhancing drugs. In 2012, Lance Armstrong was stripped of seven Tour de France titles for that reason.

lost control or had no other option. Furthermore, they *deny the victim* by claiming that the child's behaviour provoked them. Parents *appeal to higher loyalties*, indicating that their religious belief system or their ethnic culture approves of this behaviour, or even requires it. By arguing that no harm was done to the child, the parents *deny injury*.

Techniques of neutralization are common among numerous other groups as well, such as digital pirates (Steinmetz & Tunnell, 2013), "keener" students (Shoenberger, Heckert, & Heckert, 2012), university students who misuse prescription pain medication (Bennett et al., 2014), and competitive cyclists who use performance-enhancing drugs (Sefiha, 2012).

These techniques have also been highlighted in relation to specific events. For instance, in 2011 the Defensive Coordinator for the Penn State University football team, Jerry Sandusky, was discovered to have been sexually abusing children for a period of more than a decade—sometimes even using university facilities to commit those crimes. In an analysis of court records, Klein and Tolson (2015) found that techniques of neutralization motivated university officials to cover up Sandusky's misdeeds: *denying responsibility* by saying they did not realize the extent of what was going on; *denying injury* by referring to Sandusky's interactions with children as just "horsing around" (p. 483) that would not create any harm; and *appealing to higher loyalties* in their statement about the importance of protecting the university's reputation and its football program (which brought millions of dollars to the university).

Social Learning Theory: Rewards, Punishments, and Imitation

Social learning theory highlights the role of learning processes not only in deviant behaviour but in behaviour more generally. According to these theorists (e.g., Akers, 1998; Bandura, 1986; Burgess & Akers, 1966), all of our behaviours can be explained in the same way.

In social learning theory, it is suggested that all behaviour is the result of *definitions* (attitudes about the acceptability of specific behaviours), *differential association* (with whom one associates), *imitation*, and *differential reinforcement* (rewards and punishments). It is related to the behaviourist theory of *instrumental conditioning*, which suggests that we are more likely to engage in behaviours that we have been rewarded for (or that have been reinforced) in the past, and we are less likely to engage in behaviours that we have not been rewarded for or that we have been punished for in the past. Deviance first emerges from differential association and imitation and then continues (or not) through differential reinforcement and definitions.

> **Ask Yourself**
>
> As a child, how did your parents respond when you broke the rules, like when you stole a cookie from the cookie jar before dinner or broke curfew as a teenager? How did they respond when you did something they approved of, like cleaning your room or receiving a high grade on a report card?

We can see principles of instrumental conditioning being used in parenting all the time: a child who misbehaves is spanked, is given a time out, has telephone privileges taken away, or is grounded, while a child who acts in accordance with the parents' wishes is given praise, attention, or perhaps an increase in allowance. In school, children are rewarded for behaving well and studying by getting good grades and perhaps special privileges (such as getting to help the teacher with special tasks after school).

Social learning theory goes a step further by saying that not only are our behaviours influenced by what we personally have been rewarded and punished for in the past, they are influenced by what we see other people being rewarded and punished for through the process of imitation or modelling. For example, if we hear Dad make a racist joke and see his friends laugh and show approval, we are more likely to act in similar ways and develop similar views. If Mom is bulimic and we see her rewarded with compliments on how beautiful she is, we are more likely to act in similar ways. Thus, people engage in deviance because they either have been rewarded for it in the past or have seen other people being rewarded for it (Akers, 1977; Bandura, 1986).

The role of social learning has been found with a wide range of deviant behaviours, including adolescent cocaine and ecstasy use (Norman & Ford, 2015; Schaefer et al., 2015), academic dishonesty among university students (Vowell & Chen, 2004), and cyberbullying (Li, Holt, Bossler, & May, 2016). Most empirical research has directed its attention to these relatively minor acts of deviance and crime; research on more severe behaviours (e.g., violent crime) is less common and more inconsistent (Kubrin, Stucky, & Krohn, 2009). Earlier research suggested that differential reinforcement was particularly significant. However, a meta-analysis of more than 100 empirical studies of social learning finds that the effects of differential association and definitions are stronger and more consistent than the effects of differential reinforcement and imitation (Pratt et al., 2010).

Akers (1998, 2000, 2006) has recently modified his version of social learning theory to integrate structural factors as well—factors that learning theorists have been criticized for ignoring. He suggests that dimensions of the social structure create the differential contexts in which learning occurs for different people. These dimensions include *differential social organization* (a community's demographic characteristics), *differential location in the social structure* (an individual's defining characteristics such as ethnicity, gender, and educational attainment), *theoretically defined structural variables* (e.g., anomie, conflict, social disorganization), and *differential social location* (an individual's membership in different social groups, such as peer groups). He goes a step further, stating that social learning theory should be integrated with other theories that focus primarily on structural factors.

Limitations of Learning Theories

The principles of social learning theory appeal to most of us at a common sense level; it is fairly easy for us to see reinforcement, punishment, and modelling everywhere around us and in our own lives. Like neutralization theory and differential association theory, social learning theory draws attention to processes of learning as key to explaining why people engage in deviance. Despite the differences in the way each of these theories explains the learning process that leads to deviance, they all point to learning as the answer to the question of why people act the way they do— why people become deviant.

However, learning theories have also been subjected to critique. Methodological criticisms have been directed at differential association theory, with critics pointing to the difficulties in arriving at a "tally" of the number of deviant and non-deviant associations in an individual's life. Furthermore, critics suggest that the theory includes so many qualifications that it is difficult to apply or test (Downes & Rock, 2011). Priority, intensity, frequency, and duration each have an influence on deviant or conforming outcomes. But which takes precedence—the parenting an individual received in early childhood (i.e., priority), which may have involved more "conforming" definitions, or the emotional attachment that a police officer has to the police subculture in which "deviant" definitions may contribute to police misconduct (Chappell & Piquero, 2004)?

Neutralization theory has been criticized for what it *hasn't* explored—how techniques of neutralization may vary across different types of deviant behaviours or across different normative contexts. Research using neutralization theory has responded to these critiques. For instance, Buzzell (2005) compared the use of specific techniques of neutralization among two groups of people purchasing fireworks for Independence Day in the United States. One group lived in an area where fireworks were legal, and a second group lived in an area where fireworks were recently banned. Those living in the area where fireworks had been banned were more likely to agree with statements like "most fireworks people use really don't hurt anyone" (denial of injury) and "if people in my neighborhood are worried about noise or harm from fireworks they should take responsibility to protect themselves or be out of town that evening" (p. 35) (denial of the victim).

Neutralization theory has also been critiqued on the basis of its reasoning and methodology. Although the theory states that techniques of neutralization are used *prior* to committing an act, most research has looked at the techniques being used by people *after* an act has occurred (e.g., convicted shoplifters). Thus, the only conclusions that can be legitimately made are that these are post-act techniques of justification rather than techniques of neutralization that contribute to the act in the first place (Piquero, Tibbets, & Blankenship, 2005). However, Hirschi (cited in Cromwell & Thurman, 2003) suggests that a post-act technique of justification may become a pre-act technique of neutralization in the future, such that the two are not necessarily mutually exclusive. Other research attempts to overcome this critique using a vignette design: participants read about a hypothetical situation and then identify how they would act in that situation and why. For example, MBA students referred to several neutralization techniques when explaining why they would take a particular action in a hypothetical situation that involved distributing/recalling a drug being investigated by the FDA for causing harm to consumers (Piquero, Tibbets, & Blankenship, 2005). Participants who said they would continue to distribute that drug claimed that the government exaggerates the dangers (denial of injury), suggested that government regulations impede business (condemnation of the condemners), and subscribed to the expression "let the buyer beware" (denial of the victim).

The final set of positivist theories that have frequently been used to explain deviance—*social control theories*—provide yet another way of understanding the origins of deviance based on the objectivist conceptualization of the nature of deviance.

TIME TO REVIEW

Learning Objective 4

- What are the core assumptions of learning theories?

- How is deviance learned according to (1) differential association theory, (2) neutralization theory, and (3) social learning theory?

- What type of empirical support exists for each of the learning theories?

- What criticisms have been directed at Sutherland's differential association theory and Sykes and Matza's neutralization theory?

- How have empirical researchers using these theories responded to critiques?

Social Control Theories: What Restrains Most of Us from Deviance?

Social control theories focus on a different type of question. While other positivist theorists direct their attention to why some people become deviant, social control theorists direct their attention to why not all people become deviant. They suggest that deviant behaviour is inherently attractive, exciting, and appealing. Given the appeal of deviant behaviour, it is only through higher levels of social control that some of us do not become deviant.

Social Bonds Theory: Social Bonds Restrain Us

The most widely used social control theory in explanations of deviance has been Travis Hirschi's (1969) social bonds theory. His argument is that four different types of social bonds rein most of us in, restraining us from deviance.

The first bond is that of **attachment** to parents, teachers, and peers. Hirschi suggests that the greater our level of emotional attachment to others, the more bound we are to conformity. Conversely, a lack of emotional attachments leaves us freer to engage in deviance. The *type* of person to whom we are attached is not important; rather, it is the mere fact of having an emotional attachment itself that restrains us from deviance.

The second bond is **commitment** to conformity. Being committed to conventional activities like school, work, organized sports, or childrearing gives us more of a stake in the conventional world; if we were to engage in deviance, we would threaten our investments in conventionality and have too much to lose. In contrast, people who have little invested in conventional activities have less to lose by engaging in deviance.

The third social bond is **involvement** in conventional activities. In other words, people who are highly involved in such activities in terms of time simply do not have any extra time for deviance. People who have substantial unused time on their hands are more likely to be drawn to the appeal of deviance—"idle hands are the devil's workshop."

The last bond is **belief** in the norms, values, and assumptions that compose the conventional world. Holding such beliefs bonds people to the conventional world, while not holding such beliefs loosens the restraints from deviance. The interaction of these four types of social bonds determines the extent to which individuals will be restrained, or fail to be restrained, from the appeal of the deviant world.

Social bonds theory was initially applied to the study of delinquency. However, it has been successfully applied to other behaviours as well, such as driving while impaired (Bouffard & Petkovsek, 2014) and attitudes toward the police (Wu, Lake, & Cao, 2015). Life trajectories can change the nature and extent of social bonds.

> ### Ask Yourself
> Try to apply social bonds theory to your own life. How many people would you say you have an emotional attachment to? What might you lose from your life if you engaged in deviance? How much of your time is spent engaging in conventional activities?

As one makes the transition from adolescence to adulthood, different types of social bonds can emerge, which may further restrain individuals from deviance. A study of adults in their 20s finds that social bonds are significantly related to a lack of criminality (Salvatore & Taniguchi, 2012). Attachment, commitment, and belief were especially important. Religious participation, attachment to parents, property ownership, marriage, parenthood, and job satisfaction were all associated with lower rates of criminality. However, although job satisfaction was important, the number of hours worked per week (as a measure of involvement) was not significant.

Self-Control Theory: We Restrain Ourselves

Although Hirschi initially focused on the relationship between social bonds and deviance, more recently he has collaborated with Michael Gottfredson on what was initially called the *general theory of crime* (Gottfredson & Hirschi, 1990). Here they suggest that **self-control** is central to explaining why some people are predisposed to deviant acts while others are not.

Low self-control is characterized by impulsivity, a preference for simple tasks, risk-seeking, a preference for physical tasks, self-centredness, and a quick temper (Grasmick, Tittle, Bursik, & Arneklev, 1993). It is the result of ineffective parenting—an absence of attachment, weak supervision, and a lack of discipline when deviant behaviours occur. Although it may be ameliorated to some extent by other influences in a child's life, it remains relatively stable throughout life. Whether in childhood, adolescence, or mid-adulthood, individuals with low self-control are more likely to engage in deviant behaviours when the opportunity presents itself than are individuals with higher levels of self-control.

Although self-control theory is relatively recent, a considerable amount of research has been done testing its propositions. Research has directed its attention primarily to criminal behaviours, as well as "analogous behaviours" (Kubrin, Stucky, & Krohn, 2009) such as substance use, texting while driving, and adolescent sexual activity (Hope & Chapple, 2005; Koeppel, Bouffard, & Koeppel-Ullrich, 2015; Quisenberry, 2015; Schaefer et al., 2015; Stylianou, 2002). However, some empirical research expands its focus to other types of behaviours, such as binging/purging, relational aggression (e.g., spreading rumours about someone), suicidal tendencies, and criminal victimization (Harrison, Jones, & Sullivan, 2008; Nofziger & Callanan, 2016; Schreck, Stewart, & Fisher, 2006).

Jones and Quisenberry (2004) found that low self-control is related not only to a wide range of anti-social deviant behaviours connected to risky driving and risky sex, but also to behaviours that are unlikely to be deviantized in society (such as adventure-seeking activities like rock climbing, skydiving, and whitewater rafting). However, they found that the same individuals did not engage in both anti-social deviant behaviours *and* adventure-seeking behaviours. Rather, low self-control led some people into risky driving and risky sex but led others into socially acceptable forms of risk taking, which the theory is unable to explain. Jones and Quisenberry suggest that it is necessary to integrate self-control theory with other theories to explain this phenomenon. For example, certain social bonds, such as attachment to family or commitment to conventionality, may translate low self-control into socially acceptable forms of thrill-seeking behaviour.

Other research has also integrated self-control theory with social bonds theory. Higgins, Wolfe, and Marcum (2008) found that both social bonds (in terms of commitment to school and attachment to parents) and self-control were associated with the illegal downloading of music and software among university students. Self-control has also been integrated with general strain theory. Although most research shows that self-control is not associated with deviant responses to strain in the Western world, among high school students in Hong Kong, higher levels of self-control mediate the effects of strain on a wide range of deviant behaviours—breaking curfew, truancy, smoking, drinking, gambling, property damage, gang activity, and robbery (Wai Ting Cheung & Cheung, 2010).

Limitations of Social Control Theories

Social control theories, by asking why we do not all engage in deviance instead of asking only why some people do engage in deviance, provide us with a unique standpoint from which to study deviance. However, social control theories have been subject to criticism.

Self-control theory has been criticized for the manner in which self-control is defined and measured. First, it is perceived as tautological (Akers, 1991). The origins of the tautology lie within the development of the concept itself. That is, in defining low self-control, Gottfredson and Hirschi (1990) looked to the characteristics of criminal behaviour. For instance, because they considered most criminal acts to be impulsive and resulting in some type of gain for the criminal, they concluded that low self-control includes impulsivity and self-centredness. Particular pieces of research have since been critiqued for tautology at the empirical level as well, by measuring self-control behaviourally. In one study that applied self-control theory to impaired driving (a form of "risky" driving), self-control was measured by the occurrence of other forms of risky driving (driving without a seatbelt, having driven after drinking in the past). They found that people who engage in other forms of risky driving (and who therefore are low in self-control) are more likely to drive while impaired; risky driving behaviours are treated as both the cause and the effect (Keane, Maxim, & Teevan, cited in Kubrin, Stucky, & Krohn, 2009).

In response to these perceived problems in measurement, others have measured self-control psychologically. Using this approach, low self-control is treated as a personality trait and is determined via personality inventories (e.g., Grasmick, Tittle, Bursik, & Arneklev, 1993). This has become the dominant means of defining and measuring self-control in contemporary research, although Hirschi has expressed objections about the movement away from a sociological paradigm toward a more psychological paradigm. However, the results of research applying self-control theory are similar, regardless of which type of measure is used (Kubrin, Stucky, & Krohn, 2009).

Both self-control theory and social bonds theory have been criticized for ignoring the role of peer associations in deviant outcomes. Looking at peer associations within the context of self-control theory, Jones and Quisenberry (2004) suggest that associating with deviant peers may explain why some people with low self-control commit anti-social acts (e.g., risky driving), while others engage in adventure-seeking behaviours (e.g., skydiving). Longshore, Chang, Hsieh, and Messina (2004) propose a more complex relationship between self-control, social bonds, peer associations, and drug use among adults. In their final model, they conclude that low self-control results in associations with deviant peers and weakened social bonds, which result in drug use.

Although social bonds theory and self-control theory have been subjected to critique, research that integrates these theories with each other or with additional theories (e.g., general strain theory) has had some explanatory success, illustrating the role that theoretical integration can play in better explaining deviant behaviour and enhancing our understanding of deviance.

TIME TO REVIEW

Learning Objective 5

■ What are the core assumptions of Hirschi's social bonds theory, and what type of support does it have?

■ What are the core assumptions of Gottfredson and Hirschi's self-control

theory, and what type of support does it have?

■ What criticisms have been directed at social control theories, and how have researchers responded?

The diverse positivist theories of deviance that have been addressed in this chapter share one goal: trying to explain why people act in particular ways. Functionalist theories, such as Durkheim's anomie theory, Merton's strain theory, Cloward and Ohlin's differential opportunity theory, Agnew's general strain theory, and Cohen's status frustration theory, direct their attention to the role that the structure of society itself plays in the emergence of deviance. Learning theories, such as Sutherland's differential association theory, Sykes and Matza's neutralization theory, and social learning theory, point to the centrality of learning processes in the emergence of deviance. In other words, people learn to be deviant from others around them. Social control theories, like Hirschi's social bonds theory, explain why not all of us become deviant. They point to social bonds that restrain us from giving in to the appeal of deviance. Gottfredson and Hirschi's self-control theory addresses the influence that parenting patterns have on the development of self-control.

Functional, learning, and social control theories each shine a light on a particular aspect of social life in their efforts to explain deviance. Despite their differential areas of focus, and despite the diversity within each of these theories, there is a commonality: they are all positivist theories that seek to explain why some people act in deviant ways and others do not.

Positivist theories dominated academic understandings of deviance for many years. However, as more subjective views of deviance developed and become more widespread, different types of theories became useful. Just as certain types of theory correspond with more objective views of deviance, other kinds of theory correspond with more subjective ways of looking at deviance—that is, interpretive and critical theories. These theories will be addressed in Chapter 3.

Exercise Your Mind

How would each of the theories in this chapter explain deviance or conformity as it exists in your own life (or the life of someone you know)? What facets of your experience are left unexplained by each theory? If you had to select the one theory that best explains deviance or conformity in your own life, which would it be? Why?

CHAPTER SUMMARY

- Many different theories are used in the sociology of deviance, corresponding to the various ways one can look at deviance. Each theory shines a spotlight on a particular aspect of deviance and provides one way of understanding it. (1)

- People with more *objective* views of deviance, who are interested in why deviant people become that way, find *positivist* theories to be the most useful. Positivist sociological theories are modelled after theories in the natural sciences as tools for mastering the natural or social environment. (1, 2)

- People with more *subjective* views of deviance find *interpretive* and *critical* theories to be the most useful for understanding societal perceptions of and reactions to particular acts, as well as the role played by power in these perceptions and reactions. (1)

- *Functionalist theories* dominated positivist understandings of deviance for many years, suggesting that problems with the social structure cause some people to become deviant. Durkheim directed his attention to *anomie* as the root cause of deviance; Merton suggested a strain between *institutionalized goals* and *legitimate means* as the cause; Cloward and Ohlin pointed to differential access to *legitimate* and *illegitimate opportunities*; Robert Agnew emphasized the relationship between strain and *negative affect*; and Albert Cohen focused on *status frustration*. (3)

- Functionalist theories have been criticized for their logic, conservative ideology, and biases. Empirical and theoretical research has responded to these criticisms, exploring non-criminal forms of deviance across classes and analyzing gender and gender identity in a variety of situations. (3)

- *Learning theories* explain deviance as a result of individual learning processes. *Differential association theory* suggests that we learn techniques and motives within intimate groups that lead us either into deviance or into conformity. According to *neutralization theory*, the key process is the learning of rationalizations that enable people to think that what they are doing is not really wrong. *Social learning theory* points to the importance of differential reinforcement in particular. (4)

- Some empirical research supports learning theories, and the principles of learning theories are easily visible to the layperson. However, learning theories have been critiqued as well. Methodological critiques are the most common, but recent empirical and theoretical research has responded to these criticisms, particularly with neutralization theory. (4)

- *Social control theories* include Hirschi's *social bonds theory*, which asks why not all of us become deviant rather than why some people do become deviant. He suggests that people with strong social bonds are restrained from deviant behaviour. Gottfredson and Hirschi's *general theory of crime* or *self-control theory* emphasizes the role of ineffective parenting in the development of low levels of *self-control*. (5)

- As the most recently developed social control theory, self-control theory has been subjected to the most criticism. It has been criticized for its measurement of self-control and its assumption that self-control remains stable throughout life. Both control theories have been criticized for ignoring the importance of peer associations, but recent research has responded to this critique by integrating social control theories with learning theories. (5)

To learn more about the topics discussed in this chapter and to complete chapter quizzes, visit the Companion Website for *Deviance, Conformity, and Social Control in Canada*.

Chapter 3
Explaining Deviance: The Perception, Reaction, and Power

Learning Objectives

After reading this chapter, you should be able to

1 Explain how interpretive theories approach the topic of deviance, and describe how symbolic interactionism gives rise to other interpretive theories of deviance.

2 Describe such concepts as labelling, stigmatization, transition from primary to secondary deviance, the dramatization of evil, deviance as a master status, and the deviant career.

3 Identify the limitations of interpretive theories and the theoretical/empirical responses to those limitations.

4   Explain how critical theories approach the topic of deviance.

5   Describe critical theories like conflict theories, power-reflexive theories, feminist theories, and postmodern theories.

6   Identify the limitations of critical theories, and the theoretical/empirical responses to those limitations.

Nonpositivist Theorizing

Philosopher Friedrich Nietzsche (2004 [1886]) claimed that "there are no moral phenomenon [*sic*], but only a moral interpretation of phenomena." This claim emphasizes *interpretation* as the source of understanding, suggesting that moral codes emerge from a process of interpretation rather than from any type of absolute morality. This signals a substantial shift away from the positivist approach to theorizing that was addressed in Chapter 2. Positivist theories shine their spotlight on the actor or the act and try to explain why some people behave in deviant ways while others do not. Affiliated with more objective ways of understanding deviance, positivist theories are based on the assumption that deviance can be identified in some clear-cut way and, once identified, an explanation for that outcome can be sought. The strengths of positivist theories of deviance lie in their search for causation, which facilitates identification of the most effective means of achieving fixed ends (Ashley & Orenstein, 2001). For instance, preventing youth crime or treating alcoholism is most effective when based on an understanding of how people enter criminal activity or begin to abuse alcohol.

However, more subjective views of deviance claim that we cannot know deviance when we see it and instead must be told that a behaviour or characteristic is deviant. Consequently, the associated theories do not look at the violation of social expectations, but rather at the nature of the social expectations themselves (McCaghy, Capron, & Jamieson, 2003). The interest is not in the act, but in the perceptions of and reactions to the act as well as in the role of power in influencing these perceptions and reactions. Deviance is seen as constructed through the social typing process, whereby people have descriptive labels attached to them, are evaluated or judged on the basis of those labels, and then are treated in certain ways because of prior descriptions and evaluations (Rubington & Weinberg, 2008). When society, rather than deviant people, is held under a microscope—when the interest is in understanding social processes rather than specific people—the positivist interest in explaining the acquisition of deviant behaviour becomes less relevant. In its place, those theories that are often categorized as *interpretive* or *critical* are the ones that can best explain the social construction of deviance.

Interpretive theories stand in contrast to positivist theories that seek to identify generalizable, immutable laws that govern the environment. Interpretive theorists claim that the only "reality" is that which emerges through reciprocal, intersubjective understanding between people, and as such these theorists focus on the meanings that emerge from interactions between people who are engaged in symbolic dialogue. In other words, interpretive theories emphasize how people develop understandings of the world around them, other people, and themselves. **Critical theories** have a self-reflective value-orienting foundation (Ashley & Orenstein, 2001), that is, an underlying interest in emancipation and working toward social justice. Their focus is on the power relations that underlie the creation of social rules. Taken together, critical and interpretive theories are useful in explaining those aspects of deviance that more subjective-oriented deviance specialists are interested in: the social construction of deviance.

Interpretive Theories: Understandings of "Deviance" and "Normality"

A wide range of specific theories are used to explain the social construction of deviance and normality. In the remainder of this chapter, the interpretive and critical theories that will be reviewed are those most commonly used to explain the construction of deviance and those that have had significant influences on the sociology of deviance as a discipline.

Symbolic Interactionism: Communication Creates Understanding

Symbolic interactionism, or what some people simply refer to as "interactionism," is the foundation for the range of interpretive theories used to study deviance. This section of the chapter will begin with a broad discussion of the core assumptions of symbolic interactionism and will then progress to some of the more specific interpretive theories of deviance: labelling theories and the theory of the deviant career.

From a symbolic interactionist perspective, social action emerges from meaning, and meaning is "continuously created and recreated through interpreting processes during interactions with others" (Carter & Fuller, 2016, p. 2). Thus, according to Herbert Blumer (1986), society is not a structure, but rather a process. The foundation for our interactions with others is communication through symbols. In other words, society is made up of people in constant communication with each other, and this is the source of all meaning and understanding. All communication is symbolic in nature. The symbols that constitute the English alphabet serve as the foundation for written and verbal communication in English. For example, in English, we use the symbols C-A-T to refer to a small furry creature that meows and grabs your toes under the covers when you are trying to sleep. Nonverbal communication, through avenues such as gestures and facial expressions, is symbolic as well. For example, when you have cut someone off in traffic and you are subsequently shown that person's middle finger, you know precisely what message that person is communicating to you. Clothing serves as a form of symbolic communication as well. For instance, when you are going to a job interview, do you wear sweatpants and a stained T-shirt? Why not? You probably think that would communicate the wrong message to the interviewer. All of these forms of symbolic communication constitute the basic foundation of society, according to symbolic interactionists.

Barton's (2015) research on how self-identified lesbians and gay men say they recognize similar others illustrates the centrality of symbolic communication in social life. Participants used the term "gaydar" (p. 1615) to describe this process of recognition. When asked what activates their gaydar, they pointed to a range of physical, conversational, and interactional cues. *Physical cues* include aspects of physical appearance, such as hair, clothing, grooming, posture, and walk. Physical cues can also involve individuals' personal environments, such as an absence of family photos on their desk at work. *Conversational cues* consist of both the manner of speaking (e.g., vocal inflection, tone of voice) and the content of conversations (e.g., avoiding the pronouns "he" or "she" when talking about their intimate partners, men who do not make comments about attractive women). Most frequently, references to *interactional cues* focused on eye contact—participants used terms such as "double look," "broken stare," "direct stare," and "gaydar gaze" (p. 1629). Participants emphasized the importance of using symbolic cues to identify similar others, not only as a means of expanding their social networks of individuals with shared identities and experiences, but also as a way to avoid being deviantized by non-similar others.

Via these avenues of communication, we create meaning in our lives and an understanding of the world around us, of other people, and of ourselves. Because each of us has a distinct set of interactions during the course of our lives, the way each of us understands the world varies to some extent. For example, one study found that people tend to equate the concept of "violence" with actions that cause harm, are intentional, and occur without a "good" reason. However, there are varied perceptions of precisely when those criteria are met. Research participants read a vignette asking them to imagine that as they leave the supermarket, they observe two people (who know each other, as they call each other by name) having an argument; soon, one person slaps the other's face. Although the majority of participants considered the act to involve some level of violence, (as rated on a scale of 1–10), a small proportion (approximately 2 percent) rated the incident as "not at all violent," and 26 percent stated that there could be a "good reason" for it (Triplett, Payne, Collins, & Tapp, 2016).

Various processes contribute to the meanings and understandings each of us creates. One of these processes is that of **role taking**. By vicariously placing ourselves in the roles of others, we try to see the world from their respective points of view and determine our own attitudes and actions accordingly. In that regard, when you are going for a job interview, you try to imagine the position of the interviewers and what they are looking for in a job candidate when you are deciding what to wear and how to answer their questions. Similarly, an analysis of homeless men finds that they evaluate their routines, lifestyle practices, and use of their bodies from the perspective of law enforcement so that they are better able to avoid unpleasant encounters with authorities (Stuart, 2014).

A second process that contributes to the way we develop meaning is through the role of the **looking-glass self**. When determining how to look or act and how we feel about ourselves, we imagine how we appear to other people and what they think of that appearance. What we imagine other people think of us influences what we think about ourselves and how we look or act. These "Others" may be *significant others* or a *generalized other*. **Significant others** are those people who are important to us—whose perceptions and reactions matter to us. What these significant others think about you has a substantial impact on your actions—you might think, "What would my grandmother/husband/boss/favourite professor say if I did that?!" The **generalized other** refers to "other people" more generally, almost as a generic person, developed through our ability to integrate the views of multiple people simultaneously: "What would people think if I dressed like that?!"

Through the influences of role taking, the looking-glass self, significant others, and the generalized other, we come to understand the world in particular ways, understand our places in that world, and choose our appearances and actions. The *Ask Yourself* exercise further explores these processes.

Ask Yourself

Think for a few moments about the roles that these processes have played in your own life. In what situations have you tried to understand the world from someone else's point of view? Have there been times when other people's opinions of you have affected your own opinion about yourself? Who are the specific people in your life whose opinions matter the most to you? How much does what others think about you matter to you?

As applied to the concepts of deviance and normality, these processes contribute to our understanding of the "rules" in society, our perceptions of and reactions to ourselves and others on the basis of those rules, and whether we identify ourselves as followers of those rules or as rule breakers. It is also through these processes that individuals who share similar perceptions come together and form groups based on those shared perceptions (Moon, 2012). These groups may then attempt to influence the perceptions of deviance and normality held by others, and may even take the form of large-scale social movements (Carter & Fuller, 2016). And because meanings and understandings vary among people based on their own interactions and communications, the "deviance dance" emerges—some individuals or groups will try to socially type certain people as deviant, while other individuals or groups will argue that those same people are normal.

Deviance specialists who hold interactionist views may focus on many different aspects of this deviance dance. What sociocultural and individual forces influence people's understandings of deviance? What leads some people to join groups that consist of others with similar understandings? How do participants in the deviance dance understand and attribute meaning to their roles in the social construction process? How do people and groups try to influence the perceptions of other people and groups? The specific questions that can be asked from within this approach are almost endless. However, what they have in common is the foundational assumption of the symbolic interactionist perspective: We develop understanding and attribute meaning to the world around us and to ourselves on the basis of interactions we have had with other people in our lives.

Labelling Theories: Becoming an Outsider

Arising from the core assumptions of symbolic interactionism are a number of specific concepts and theories used to understand the social construction of deviance. **Labelling theories** all address the very same process but use slightly different language. The process they analyze is that of being labelled deviant and the consequences of that label. When individuals are given a deviant label, people start to treat them differently, in a way that corresponds to that label. Over time, being treated differently has an impact on how those labelled individuals perceive themselves. Finally, as their identities change, their subsequent behaviours and life choices are affected as well.

Tannenbaum (1938) was one of the first scholars to analyze this process, in terms of the role that **tagging** plays in the **dramatization of evil**. He suggested that as observers in society, we may initially identify a particular act as deviant or evil ("tagging") but soon come to generalize that judgment to the person as a whole ("dramatization of evil")—in other words, it is no longer just the initial act that is considered evil, but rather the person is considered evil. This process results in changes in that person's self-image and identity, whereby the identity comes to be built around the label and subsequent behaviours correspond to that label and new identity.

Edwin Lemert (1951) used the term "labelling" rather than "tagging" in what is perhaps the most well-known version of labelling theory. Lemert distinguished between **primary deviance** and **secondary deviance**. He suggested that we all engage in little acts of rule breaking that are seldom noticed and rarely caught by others (primary deviance). Even though we all engage in occasional rule breaking, few of us build a lifestyle around it (secondary deviance). Getting caught sets into motion a series of processes that result in the transition from primary deviance to secondary deviance. Someone who is not caught in an act of deviance may eventually just move on.

For instance, as a child or a teenager you may have shoplifted an item of low value from a neighbourhood convenience store, but it is likely that most of you did that only once or twice and eventually grew out of that "phase." However, Lemert suggested that the mere act of being caught changes the way others see you and subsequently changes the way you see yourself. That is, if you were caught shoplifting and then arrested, the police saw you as a "thief." If convicted in youth court, you were officially labelled a "criminal." Your parents may have then considered you to be a "troublemaker." As a result of this process of labelling, you come to understand and identify yourself in the same way—as a troublemaker who commits crimes.

Howard Becker (1963) elaborated on the processes involved in the transition to secondary deviance. He suggested that once a person is labelled deviant, that label becomes that person's master status. A **master status** is a core characteristic by which others identify you, one that overrides other characteristics you might have. For example, you may immediately identify others on the basis of age ("teenager"), sex ("girl"), or class ("rich"). A deviant label assumes the level of master status; for instance, if you smoke cigarettes, others may see you, first and foremost, as a "smoker."

Once a deviant label becomes a master status, implications for a person's daily life emerge. Certain life opportunities will be blocked, in that the legitimate, "normal" world will be less accepting. If you smoke, you are prohibited from engaging in that behaviour in many physical spaces. But even more significantly, once people perceive you as a "smoker," they may see you differently. The person you ask out on a date may decline because he doesn't date "smokers." During a break at work or between classes, your peers may avoid spending time with you because they do not want to be around cigarette smoke. They might not invite you to join them for a workout at lunch or at the end of the day, because they know you will need to stop for a cigarette first or they assume you are probably out of shape. Your employer may not ask you to work on a special project because (as a reflection of the *evaluation* stage in the social typing process described in Chapter 1) she assumes that you lack self-control or are unintelligent. Soon, you began to feel like an "outsider" (which happens to be the title of Becker's 1963 book).

At that point, it may be that only fellow smokers are willing to spend time with you, and the smoking area located on the periphery of your campus or your workplace becomes the only space where you feel accepted. And before long, you no longer see yourself as a person who smokes an occasional cigarette, but rather as a "smoker." You develop a shared identity with your fellow smokers, and start to spend every break with them in the designated smoking area. Now you find yourself smoking a half pack of cigarettes each day, instead of the three or four cigarettes that you previously consumed. This process of exclusion from the conforming world and acceptance in the deviant world is what Becker suggested led to a lifestyle built around deviance—and what Lemert (1951) called *secondary deviance*.

Other deviance specialists have referred to this process of exclusion, of becoming an outsider, as **stigmatization** (Goffman, 1963). Goffman stated that there are three different types of stigma: physical stigma; moral stigma; and group stigma. We may be stigmatized for certain physical characteristics, such as clothing, hair style, or weight. Research has found that people with physical illnesses, such as celiac disease, often face stigmatization as well (Schroeder & Mowen, 2014; Smith, 2012; Smith & Hughes, 2014; Stringer & Baker, 2015; Wagner, McShane, Hart, & Margolese, 2016). We can be stigmatized for perceived moral failings, such as substance abuse (DePierre, Puhl, & Luedicke, 2014), criminal activity (Moore, Stuewig, & Tangney, 2016), sex work (Armstrong, 2016), or financial problems (Keene, Cowan, & Castro-Baker, 2015). We may be stigmatized because of our association with certain social groups, for instance, those based on religion (Sohrabi & Farquharson, 2016) or sexual and gender identity or expression (Bender-Baird, 2016; Duguay, 2016). We can even face stigmatization for the actions of others—known as **courtesy stigma** (Goffman, 1963) or **stigma by association** (Pryor & Reeder, 2011). For example, an analysis of media coverage of two high school mass shooting incidents reveals the way that family members (and especially mothers) of the shooters are blamed for the incidents (Melendez, Lichtenstein, & Dolliver, 2016).

A proponent of the sociological school of thought known as **dramaturgy**, Goffman (1959) suggested that social life is analogous to being in the theatre. In our lives, we are all assigned or assume particular "roles" to play—university student, daughter, soccer player, smoker. When we are in front of certain groups of people, we play our roles in certain ways; we control the images that we present and the messages that we convey to the audience by bringing out our **front-stage selves**. When we leave the front stage and retreat with select groups of people who are a part of our private lives, we allow our **back-stage selves** to emerge; that is, we no longer feel like we have to play a particular role, but instead can be our true selves. If the role we have assumed is one that incurs stigma, managing how our audience's perceive us is that much more difficult—we risk having a **spoiled identity**.

When on the front stage, we all use techniques to control the impressions that our audiences have of us (i.e., engage in **identity management** or **impression management**). Consider, as an example, the role you play in the workplace. You dress, act, and speak in certain ways (especially when your boss or customers and clients are present)—ways that may be distinct from when you are at home. Rosengren (2015) finds that your use of time is also part of your front-stage self as a worker. The extent to which you respond to work-related emails on evenings or days off, or voluntarily stay late at work, may determine your co-workers' or employer's impressions of you. As one senior-level manager states, "'I can do this job in fewer hours. But it will be seen as not giving the commitment.... You are noticed more by being here at 10 at night than by consistently producing a good product'" (Rutherford, cited in Rosengren, 2015, p. 8).

Although we all perform our roles in controlled ways when on the front stage of the workplace, now imagine that you have a characteristic that is stigmatized, such that managing your impressions at work also entails **stigma management**. Research finds that this adds another layer of complexity to performing our roles at work. For example, Galvin-White & O'Neal (2016) find that female police officers who self-identify as lesbian carefully control with whom they do or do not disclose that information in the workplace. For some groups of people, stigma management can be especially challenging in terms of even being hired for a job in the first place (see Box 3.1).

Ask Yourself

In your own life, has there ever been anything about yourself that you have tried to hide from the outside world because of your fear of stigmatization (such as a criminal past, substance abuse problem, or learning disability)? Have you ever restricted your interactions to people you knew would be accepting of you, people you knew would be able to understand you? Have you ever proudly displayed an aspect of yourself that you know many people in society consider to be deviant? What are the implications of these different approaches to stigma management?

Box 3.1

Learning "Work Wisdom"

Stigma management in the workplace is particularly difficult for individuals who have spent time in prison. Halushka (2015) analyzes a community program for formerly incarcerated men who are seeking employment. In this program, clients learn the "work wisdom" (p. 73) needed to manage their impressions in a way that will enable them to find stable employment.

First, they learn how to selectively disclose their criminal histories during job interviews. They are taught to "hit it and quit it" (p. 73), that is, be up front with their criminal records but then carefully steer the conversation back to the job at hand and the skills they have developed. They learn to re-narrate their criminal histories in order to frame their backgrounds in particular ways. For instance, they will state that they served a 12-year prison sentence, rather than saying they were sentenced to 8 to 12 years; the latter statement could potentially lead to questions in the interviewer's mind about why the offender was unable to be released after 8 years. These brief statements about their criminal histories stand in contrast to the ways that they might spend extended periods of time discussing the details of their incarceration when interacting with similar others.

Second, the facial expressions and physical demeanours that kept them safe in prison are ones that can make employers and co-workers "nervous" (p. 81). Thus, clients learn to modify them. The "smile and a handshake" exercise teaches them to replace their "prison yard face" (p. 81) with one that employers and co-workers will be more comfortable with. Because their "prison bodies" (p. 81) (i.e., muscular, with broad shoulders and large biceps) may intimidate others, they learn to adapt their posture to appear less confrontational. However, clients' living environments were sometimes such that when they returned home at the end of the workday, it was in their best interests to revert back to that tough demeanour.

Third, the men learn "code switching" (p. 82), or how to "conceal discrediting aspects of their race and class" (p. 81) while at work. They might speak African American Vernacular English (AAVE) at home (e.g., saying "nah" instead of "no"), but they were told to switch to Standard American English (SAE) in the workplace. While in the program, clients would be stopped whenever they slipped into AAVE, and have to correct their vocabulary. They might wear baggy pants, tank tops, and do-rags at home, but that attire would be considered unacceptable at work. At the beginning of the program, clients had to pull up their pants and remove do-rags and hats upon entering the program building. As the program progressed, they had to switch to full "interview attire" (p. 83).

Fourth, clients are taught to leave street culture behind and adopt appropriate workplace behaviour norms. For instance, they learn that authority figures should be trusted and obeyed, that they should appear humble, and that it is important to resolve conflicts in non-aggressive ways.

Finally, the program teaches clients to think of themselves in positive and holistic ways rather than letting their criminal histories define them. By raising the men's self-confidence, they develop resolve and are able to maintain a positive view of themselves in the face of the workplace challenges they are likely to encounter.

Stigma management techniques have been studied in a variety of other contexts and populations as well, including male sex workers (Kong, 2009), leaders of Muslim communities (Sohrabi & Farquharson, 2016), people of Middle-Eastern descent (Marvasti, 2008), LGBTQ individuals in the Facebook environment (Duguay, 2016), and professional poker players (Vines & Linders, 2016). A stigma must be managed on a daily basis, and different individuals in varying contexts will use diverse techniques to do so.

There are implications for the specific stigma management strategies that individuals use (Link et al., 1989). Those who are up front about their stigma and attempt to educate others potentially expose themselves to discrimination. Individuals who try to hide their stigma through secrecy may develop feelings of shame. Those who withdraw from social interactions become isolated from potential social support networks. For example, secrecy and withdrawal contribute to poor mental health in people with financial problems (Keene, Cowan, & Castro-Baker, 2015) and a failure to pursue treatment in individuals with substance abuse disorders (Stringer & Baker, 2015).

Although Goffman's work on stigmatization emphasizes the negative impact of stigma, there are potentially positive consequences of stigmatization in certain situations. Braithwaite (2000) postulates that unlike **disintegrative shaming** (wherein deviantized persons are rejected by the community), **reintegrative shaming** is an effective treatment for criminal behaviour. With reintegrative shaming, the criminal is stigmatized, or shamed, for the criminal act, but it is a temporary stigma; the criminal is shown that leaving criminality behind will result in being fully accepted back into the community. Research with individuals who have severe mental disorders has also found that being labelled can have a wide range of positive consequences, including expanding their support networks and exempting such individuals from some of the demands and responsibilities of daily life (Perry, 2011).

Early interactionists, and particularly early labelling theorists, frequently painted a picture of the labelled deviant as a powerless, passive recipient of a socially constructed label that subsequently had irreversible consequences for the deviant's life. However, some deviance specialists have emphasized the possibility of resistance to a deviant label. Kitsuse (1980) refers to **tertiary deviance** as a stage that can potentially emerge after the transition from primary to secondary deviance. Some people who have been labelled and who then develop an identity and a lifestyle based on that label may resist the idea that the label is a "deviant" one. They may go on to try to change social norms, to show society that the behaviour they have engaged in or the characteristic they have is not "deviant" at all. They seek to redefine "normal" to include that act or characteristic. For example, some stigmatized individuals may join together in large-scale social movements (Fuist, 2014).

Whether we use the terminology of "the dramatization of evil," "tagging," "labelling," or "stigmatization," the processes of deviance being referred to are similar. Being perceived as "deviant" affects the way people treat us, which affects the way we see ourselves, which then affects the way we act in the future. But in addition to studying these particular processes, some interpretive theorists are also interested in the process of living a deviant life—the deviant career.

The Deviant Career: Progressing through Deviance

In addition to the work already discussed, Howard Becker (1963) used the concept of the **deviant career** to study deviance. He postulated that deviance emerges, progresses, and changes over time, and there are stages to involvement in deviance just as there are stages in the development of a career. Thus, the concept of the "deviant career" refers not to those who make a living out of deviance, but rather to the way that deviance unfolds in people's lives. Just as in the traditional notion of a "career," people enter deviance, manage their experiences of deviance, and may quit (or exit) deviance, all of which are intertwined with changes in their identities and understandings of self. Becker illustrated this sequential model of deviance with marijuana users, exploring the stages of meaning and understanding by which they became marijuana users, acted as marijuana users, and stopped using marijuana at some point. He identified three "stages" in this career: the beginner user, the occasional user, and the regular user.

A number of factors are involved in "becoming a marijuana user," such as having access to the drug, learning how to smoke correctly, and coming to perceive the effects of the drug as pleasurable. Various **career contingencies**, or what may be seen as significant *turning points*, influence the directions that people take at various points in the deviant career. For example, a lack of access to a steady supply of marijuana may lead some people to drop the habit while leading others into associations with organized groups that have a stable supply of the drug.

While Becker applied the deviant career to marijuana users, other deviance specialists have used the concept to analyze followers of anti-establishment political parties (Kemmers, van der Waal, & Aupers, 2015), women entering the workplace after being paroled from prison (Opsal, 2012), small-scale marijuana growers (Maggard & Boylstein, 2014), methamphetamine users (Kerley et al., 2014), and male clients of compensated dating (Chu & Laidler, 2016). Particular deviance specialists may focus specifically on the entrance phases, management phases, or exit phases of the deviant career. The interactionist concepts and assumptions discussed earlier, such as role taking, meaning, understanding, and communication, lie at the core of the processes involved in deviant careers.

i believe i can fly

Why do some people become part of cannabis subcultures, while others remain casual smokers or do not use marijuana at all?

Limitations of Interpretive Theories

Interpretive theories focus on the construction of meaning and understanding in interpersonal interactions, as well as the consequences of people's understandings for how they treat others and how they perceive themselves. These theories draw our attention to various aspects of deviance. They shine a spotlight on how someone's lifestyle and identity may come to be based on deviance, on the different ways that individuals may react once they are identified as deviant by others, and on how some people may exit deviance. They give us insight into the emergence of the "deviance dance," wherein some people will say that Group X is deviant and can be fixed in a certain way, other people will agree that Group X is deviant but can be fixed in a different way, and other people will say that Group X is not deviant at all.

The primary criticism of interpretive theories has been that they fail to address the social structure and its role in the processes surrounding deviance and normality (Dennis & Martin, 2005; Downes & Rock, 2011). This may be true of Blumer's (1986) approach to symbolic interactionism, which argued that meanings are constantly changing, so all events are unique and unrepeatable. However, later theorists have recognized the relevance of the social structure for interactions. Sheldon Stryker highlights a reciprocal relationship between the individual and the social structure. He proposes that "meanings and interactions lead to relatively stable patterns that create and uphold social structures" (p. 6). The statuses and roles that comprise those social structures then give rise to "symbolic cues that shape individuals' interpretations and actions" (cited in Carter & Fuller, 2016, p. 6).

Empirical research has also integrated structural components into interactionist analyses. For example, interactionist research has demonstrated that anticipated stigma (i.e., the belief that one will personally be discriminated against) has negative effects for individuals. However, a longitudinal study of criminal offenders' adjustment to the community following release from prison finds that the effects of anticipated stigma vary by race (Moore, Stuewig, & Tangney, 2016). Controlling for their level of anticipated stigma prior to release from prison, members of visible minority groups had more positive adjustment to the community (as measured by employment, volunteer work, home ownership, raising children, and obtaining a driver's licence) than did offenders who were not visible minorities. The researchers concluded that because of their structural location, members of visible minority groups face ongoing stigmatization on that basis. The coping strategies they develop as a result are able to lessen the effects of the anticipated stigma stemming from other sources, such as a criminal record.

Lemert's (1951) version of labelling theory in particular has faced a number of criticisms as well. Just as interpretive theories have been criticized for ignoring the role of the social structure, so has his labelling theory. But in addition to that overarching critique, three other specific criticisms have also been made. First, Lemert's labelling theory has been criticized for focusing most of its attention on adolescents at one point in time and not exploring the long-term effects of labelling. Second, much of the research has looked only at those who have been formally labelled in some way (e.g., through the criminal justice system), rather than comparing those who have been labelled with those who have not. Third, the specific processes involved in the transition from primary to secondary deviance have not been sufficiently addressed.

Research by Restivo and Lanier (2005) takes these criticisms into account in their longitudinal analysis of youth crime. Over a three-year period of time, they followed a group of adolescents enrolled in a Children-At-Risk program, where risk was defined in terms of a variety of neighbourhood, school, and family factors. Controlling for demographic factors and pre-existing levels/forms of delinquency, those who experienced formal labelling by being arrested went on to engage in higher levels of subsequent delinquency. That outcome was partially mediated by three variables: negative self-concept, low educational and occupational expectations, and association with delinquent peers. The effect of delinquent peers was particularly strong, which

Learning Objective 1

- Why are interpretive and critical theories particularly useful to more subjectivist deviance specialists?

- How can the processes described in the symbolic interactionist approach help us understand our perceptions of and reactions to particular behaviours and people?

Learning Objective 2

- What are the core assumptions of labelling theories? What are some of the different ways that various interpretive deviance specialists have discussed the process of labelling and responses to being labelled?

- What do the concepts of "dramaturgy" and the "deviant career" add to our understanding of deviance?

Learning Objective 3

- What criticisms have been directed at interpretive theories, and what have been the theoretical or empirical responses to these criticisms?

demonstrates the ways that integrating labelling theories with some of the positivist theories you learned about in Chapter 2 (such as differential association theory) can enhance scholars' abilities to explain social phenomena.

Although interpretive assumptions provide insight into how our perceptions of and reactions to particular acts develop (including our self-perceptions and identity formation), they do not help us understand how some people are more able than others to influence what will and will not be labelled as deviant in a particular society at a particular time in history. Some interpretive theorists (e.g., Becker, 1963) have pointed out that the meanings and understandings held by some groups may be imposed on others. However, interpretive theories do not explain the precise mechanisms by which some people are more able than others to determine the direction that the "deviance dance" will take. Although different people will have varying perceptions of deviance and normality, some people's perceptions have more of an impact on the larger society; in other words, some people's perceptions count more than others. This is where critical theories of deviance step in—exploring the role of *power* in the social construction of deviance.

Critical Theories: Power Relations and Social Justice

The range of theories that have been categorized as **critical theories** of deviance is quite substantial—Marxist theories, non-Marxist conflict theories, non-conflict critical theories, feminist theories, postmodernist theories, discourse theories, anarchist theories, peacemaking theories, radical multicultural theories, and more (Kubrin, Stucky, & Krohn, 2009).

These theories are all both theoretical and practical in nature. At a theoretical level, they analyze the centrality of structures and processes of power in the creation of societal expectations and rules, and people's everyday experiences within them. At a practical level, these are all theories that have an emancipatory interest—that is, an interest in working toward social justice for society's powerless. In fact, conflict theorist Karl Marx stated that social scientists have a *responsibility* to use their work in pursuit of practical, emancipatory goals, which he referred to as **praxis**. It is only by revealing the structures and processes of power at work that they can be dismantled, and positive social change made possible. In the remainder of this chapter, a range of critical theories that have been definitive for the study of deviance will be reviewed: conflict theories, power-reflexive theories, feminist theories, and postmodern theories.

Conflict Theories: Rules Serve the Interests of the Powerful

Although **conflict theories** themselves are of considerable diversity, they do share some core assumptions regarding analyses of deviance (McCaghy, Capron, & Jamieson, 2003). First, they presume that social rules do not emerge out of consensus but rather out of conflict and serve the interests of the most influential groups in society. Second, they suggest that members of powerful groups are less likely to break the rules because the rules were created to serve their interests in the first place. Third, conflict theories propose that members of less powerful groups are more likely to act in ways that violate social rules, either because (1) their sense of oppression and alienation causes them to act out in rule-breaking ways or (2) social rules have defined the acts of the powerless as deviant in the first place. Precisely which groups are perceived as being in conflict varies among specific conflict theories, but all conflict theories integrate propositions about the structures of societal inequality with views about the ideologies that are used to maintain the status quo and reproduce the existing structures of inequality.

The origins of conflict theory are typically attributed to Karl Marx, who proposed that society consists of a small group of powerful people at the top and a large group of powerless people at the bottom. He ascribed these power differentials to economic factors, specifically the relationship to the means of production. Society's powerful (the **bourgeoisie**) are those who own the means of production; society's powerless (the **proletariat**) are the wage earners who work for the people who own the means of production. The sense of alienation experienced by the proletariat because of their working conditions gives rise to deviant behaviour among some people.

Later Marxists fell into two general camps, **instrumental Marxists** and **structural Marxists**. Instrumental Marxists (e.g., Quinney, 1977) propose that institutionalized social rules, such as the law, are created by the powerful to serve the interests of the powerful—the owners of the means of production. A deviant label thereby becomes an instrument used to control the proletariat and maintain the economic structure in society. Structural Marxists (e.g., Chambliss & Seidman, 1982) propose that institutionalized social rules are created by the powerful to protect the capitalist economic system rather than to protect individual capitalists. The need to maintain the power of the economic system as a whole means that even members of the bourgeoisie may be subject to a deviant label if their behaviour threatens the fundamental principles of capitalism.

Although Marxist conflict theories are based on the presumption of economic structures of inequality, other conflict theories claim that power is based on noneconomic factors as well. *Pluralist conflict theory* focuses on multiple axes of inequality that make up the structure of society based on conflicts between various economic, religious, ethnic, political, and social groups. *Culture conflict theory* claims that in societies having multiple, diverse cultural groups, there will be multiple sets of norms that may conflict with each other (Sellin, 1938). Dominant cultural groups have the power to impose the norms that compose their culture on all other cultural groups in society, labelling the norms of conflicting cultural groups as "deviant" and in need of measures of social control.

For example, in 2013 the Quebec government introduced a new bill, the Quebec Charter of Values. As part of the bill, public employees would be banned from wearing religious symbols—but not all religious symbols, only those deemed by the government to be "conspicuous" (*CBC News*, 2013, September 10). In a public education campaign, examples of acceptable and unacceptable religious symbols were provided. Debate and outrage ensued, in that the examples constructed a distinction between not only religious symbols, but religious beliefs themselves. Individuals adhering to Christian belief systems were relatively unaffected as the dominant religious symbol (a cross or crucifix) remained acceptable, provided that it was not too large. In contrast, the bill would prohibit many non-Christians from displaying any religious symbols at all. Many followers of non-Christian religions wear some type of headcovering as a reflection of their beliefs—for instance, the kippah and tichel (Judaism), the turban (Sikhism), the hijab and niqab (Islam), and many others. The Quebec Charter of Values deemed all religious headcoverings to be "conspicuous," and therefore prohibited. This prioritizing of certain religious beliefs over others within law is a clear illustration of culture conflict theory. Because the government in power lost the next election before the bill could be voted upon, it never became law. However, other bills would subsequently be introduced in Quebec that sought similar ends.

In *group conflict theory*, George Vold (1958) extended conflict assumptions beyond cultural groups to a wide range of other groups as well. He suggested that multiple groups are always manoeuvring for more power in society and clash with each other as a result of their simultaneous struggles for power. The norms or social rules of certain groups gain more legitimacy in society because these groups are able to get authorities on their side more effectively. In situations of conflict, crime and deviance emerge because people will commit acts they do not normally engage in (e.g., vandalism, assault) in pursuit of their higher goal—trying to attain more power for their social groups.

Austin Turk (1969) stated that the core struggle in society is more broadly between *those who are in positions of authority* and *those who are subject to authority*. Those who are in authority try to maintain their authority by convincing society's less powerful groups of the validity of the existing social rules using as much coercion as necessary if the less powerful groups refuse to be "convinced." Socially typing the norms or actions of conflicting groups as deviant is one way that positions of authority can be maintained.

Whether referring to Marxist theories, other conflict theories described above, or one of the many additional criminological conflict theories that have been proposed (e.g., Richard Quinney's radical conflict theory or Left Realism), the *theoretical* interest in exploring the struggle for power and its role in defining social norms and the *practical* interest in emancipation together define critical theories of deviance. In essence, the various conflict theories postulate that different groups in society have varied interests and perceptions of what the rules should be; however, having more power and resources enables groups to pursue their own interests more effectively. Thus, the "rules" as perceived by powerful groups are imposed on all of the groups that make up society as a whole.

In this regard, it is society's powerful who are able to construct the dominant moral code by which deviance and normality are defined. Powerful groups are able to maintain their power by socially typing the interests and the perceptions of other social groups as deviant—they are able to quash the competition simply by creating rules that deviantize competitors' behaviours. For example, in an analysis of midwifery in New Orleans, Frailing and Harper (2010) point out that during the course of the 1930s, abortions (performed by midwives) became safer and more women were surviving the procedure. As more women turned to midwives instead of to physicians, the medicalization of pregnancy and childbirth was threatened. Over the course of the next two decades, midwifery was increasingly criminalized; the more powerful medical establishment was able to deviantize midwifery and thereby increase its own market share.

Sometimes it is not the interests and perceptions of non-dominant social groups that are deviantized, but rather the social groups themselves. One of the areas where this may be reflected is in policing, wherein the position of marginalized groups in society results in them being perceived by some as "police property" (Reiner, 2013). Once this perception is in place, the stage is set for acts of racial profiling. An analysis of more than 3000 high school students living in Toronto reveals that black youth were significantly more likely than white youth to have been stopped and searched by the police—multiple times—even when other demographic characteristics, behavioural patterns, and histories of deviance were controlled for (Hayle, Wortley, & Tanner, 2016).

Of course, in contemporary democratic societies the effectiveness of power exercised in oppressive or authoritarian ways is limited, in that it is likely to result in open resistance. For instance, following a number of cases of police brutality against black Americans that were documented and shared on social media, there emerged widespread demands for social change and the social movement #BlackLivesMatter (http://blacklivesmatter.com). Instead, powerful groups can more effectively maintain their power by convincing enough of the populace that they are responsive to the interests of the people and are working in everyone's best interests. For example, anti-immigration political campaigns may be masked by references to protecting citizens against unemployment, crime, or terrorism. To maintain and legitimize their power, powerful groups must strike a balance between pursuing their own interests, integrating some of the interests of society's masses, and integrating the desires of vocal interest groups. In the end, "deviance" is a label that justifies the control efforts of powerful groups and thereby helps them to maintain their power.

Convincing society's masses that those in positions of authority are working in everyone's best interests involves manufacturing a worldview within which the actions of the powerful seem logical. Marx and other conflict theorists use the term **ideology**, in its broad sense, to refer to the worldview (a way of seeing and understanding the world) held by society's powerful groups—a worldview based on the interests and needs of the powerful.

Because the powerful control society's institutions, such as schools and the media, their ideology is taught to citizens as "common sense" via those institutions, thereby achieving what Antonio Gramsci called **hegemony** (i.e., becoming the dominant way of seeing and understanding the world). However, a later school of critical theorists that grew out of the conflict perspective, the Frankfurt School, explained that society's masses develop a **false consciousness** (originally a Marxian concept). Even though the hegemonic ideology is one that serves the interests and needs of the powerful and is imposed on everyone else through society's institutions, people come to perceive it as rational and acceptable. Consequently, they do not realize that they have been duped and come to believe that they have more freedom than they actually do. The roles of ideology, hegemony, and false consciousness are to render any alternative ways of seeing and understanding the world as outside of the realm of possibility in most people's minds, and thus the dominant view becomes "common sense."

Once a particular worldview is perceived as "common sense" by society's masses, there are implications for the structure and functioning of society. This is illustrated by Kent and Jacobs's (2004) application of conflict theory to a cross-national analysis of police presence. Economic-based conflict theory postulates a relationship between economic stratification and the need for social control. Of course, the most overt form of social control is the criminal justice system, including law enforcement. In a capitalist society, the role of law enforcement is to protect the property of the wealthy; thus, more economic stratification should be associated with greater police presence.

Kent and Jacobs compared the ratio of the number of law enforcement officers to the national population from 1975 to 1994 in 11 countries—Australia, Belgium, Canada, Denmark, France, the Republic of Ireland, Italy, Norway, Sweden, the United Kingdom, and the United States. In accordance with conflict theory, they found that nations with higher levels of economic inequality had a greater number of law enforcement officers per 100 000 people in the population. They also found that countries with higher crime rates had a higher ratio of police officers to national population—but only in recent years, once crime had become more politicized in these nations. Kent and Jacobs concluded that the economically powerful play a central role in the politicization of street crime and the corresponding public demand for more police officers; economic inequality gives "economic elites greater control over public values" (p. 357) through ownership and control of the media.

Despite the rather gloomy picture of power and control that conflict theorists paint, they do suggest that change is possible—and in fact, necessary. That is, there will always be some people in society who are able to see the ideological nature of "common sense" and the hidden interests operating in the institutionalized knowledge of society. The goal of theory and action, they suggest, is to enlighten society's masses so that they too become aware of ideology, false consciousness, or hegemony. Only then can hierarchical structures of power be changed to create social justice.

Power-Reflexive Theories: Knowledge Is Power

Power-reflexive theories (which are also sometimes referred to as *poststructuralist*) are built on a foundation that emphasizes the intertwining of knowledge and power. Within these theories it is proposed that all claims to knowledge are socially situated, embedded within relations of power. Multiple **discourses** (bodies of knowledge, or all that is "known" about a particular phenomenon) coexist in society; relations of power determine which claims to knowledge come to be institutionalized or perceived as "truth" within society as a whole (Foucault, 1980). For example, during the Middle Ages in Europe, the claims made by the Christian church (as a quasi-governing body in most European nations) were seen as the "truth." With the Enlightenment and the related development and growth of science, the claims made by science were accorded more "truth" than the claims of the Christian church. As we will address in Chapter 9, in contemporary society, the claims made by science are granted more legitimacy in the eyes of the public than any other claims to truth being made.

Michel Foucault discussed the linkages between power and knowledge (Foucault, 1980) as well as analyzing mechanisms of social control (Foucault, 1995) through his discussion of the **Panopticon**. Philosopher Jeremy Bentham designed a panoptical prison, a design that enabled guards to observe all prisoners at all times. However, the design did not allow prisoners to know for a fact when they were being observed. They therefore lived in an environment in which they knew that the guards *might* be observing them at any given moment. The potential for constant surveillance eventually led the prisoners to regulate their own behaviour, even when they were not actually being observed.

Foucault proposed that the processes of industrialization and bureaucratization have created a panoptical society as well. He suggested that bureaucratization results in the development of numerous mechanisms of social control that ensure "normal" behaviour and punish or prevent "deviant" behaviour. We accept government-sponsored surveillance because it is presented as being for our own good or for our safety and survival, as with the increased surveillance since 9/11 (Staples, cited in Robinson, 2008).

Because of the pervasiveness of social control in modern society—and of the potential for constant surveillance—most of us do not need to be watched for normative transgressions; we engage in self-surveillance and regulate our own behaviours.

This is what Robinson (2008) refers to as "imprinting the panoptic eye in the consciousness of individuals" (p. 235). The more control becomes internalized in the form of self-control or self-regulation, the more effective it becomes.

For example, discourses within government and gambling industry documents make a distinction between "responsible gambling" and "problem gambling" (Miller, Thomas, Smith, & Robinson, 2015). Responsible gambling is fun and good for the community (because of the funds it generates). In contrast, problem gambling is harmful to individuals, families, and communities, and in need of (medical) intervention. Problem gambling is individualized in terms of the emphasis placed on self-monitoring and self-regulation; individuals are to prevent themselves from becoming problem gamblers in the first place, or at least to recognize and seek help for their problem once it has emerged.

The relationship among power, knowledge, and social control is especially evident in those mundane aspects of everyday life that many of us take for granted—such as using public restrooms. Foucault (1995) pointed out that historically, public school restrooms were designed so that school authorities could appropriately surveil students (because their feet were visible beneath the door of the stall), yet students could not inappropriately watch each other (because the walls between the stalls were too high). In the present day, public restrooms continue to be sites of surveillance, especially within the context of sex and gender. Most public restrooms continue to be identified as specific to males or females. For individuals who are **cisgender** (i.e., those whose gender identity or expression corresponds to their birth sex), the "panoptic eye" has been firmly "imprinted" (Robinson, 2008, p. 235). They do not need to be directed to the appropriate restroom, but rather "check the signs, decide which space is meant for them" (Bender-Baird, 2016, p. 985), and go inside—they have regulated their own behaviours on the basis of dominant discourses governing sex and gender. They are monitoring not only their own behaviours in the choice of a restroom, but that of others as well. They "watch each other, ensuring that the unwritten rules of accessing public restrooms are being followed" (p. 985). Thus, for individuals who are **transgender** or **gender-variant** (i.e., whose gender identity or expression does not correspond to their birth sex), the choice of a public restroom is complex. Regardless of whether they choose a restroom that corresponds to their birth sex or their gender identity/ expression, they run the risk of being deviantized. In response to the surveillance of public restrooms by other users, some individuals who are gender-variant may adjust their expression of gender prior to entering a restroom (such as by borrowing a friend's purse in order to emphasize one's "femaleness"), while others avoid using the restroom altogether when away from home (Bender-Baird, 2016).

However, Foucault pointed out that power always goes hand in hand with resistance. Thus, as a result of the activism of gender-variant individuals and their allies, "all-gender" or "gender-neutral" public restrooms are more prevalent and a growing number of education policies are emphasizing the importance of making such restrooms available (e.g., Alberta Education, 2016).

John Arehart/Shutterstock

On what basis do you determine which public restroom is meant for you?

Feminist Theories: Deviance Is Gendered

Rather than there being a "feminist theory," there are in fact multiple forms of feminist theories and practice, often quite distinct from each other (Nelson, 2010), ranging from those that emphasize women's experiences to those that focus on the negative impacts that patriarchy has had on both women and men. Not only is there a wide range of distinct "feminist theories" (such as radical feminism, cultural feminism, liberal feminism, maternal feminism, and post-colonial feminism), but feminist theorizing is also done from within virtually every theoretical perspective addressed in this book. That is, there are feminist interactionist theories, feminist Marxist theories, feminist functionalist theories, feminist learning theories, and feminist social control theories.

Amidst the diversity in feminist theorizing, there are some shared assumptions (Lengermann & Niebrugge, 2007). First, academic research has traditionally been male-oriented (i.e., **androcentric**), failing to adequately address female experiences. Second, because the structure of society is gendered, so too are people's everyday experiences. Within the context of deviance, this means that the bodies of knowledge and the norms by which we judge deviance and normality vary for women and men. That is, what are considered "normal" behaviours, appearances, or characteristics for women are quite different than for men. For example, a woman who wants to work in a daycare centre will be viewed very differently than a man who wants to work in a daycare centre; she is far more likely to be perceived as "normal" while he is far more likely to be perceived as "deviant." Similarly, a woman who dislikes being around children is more likely to be seen as abnormal than is a man who dislikes being around children. Third, research and theory must be intertwined with, not separated from, social and political practice.

Outside of these shared basic assumptions, the topics addressed in feminist analyses of deviance are varied, ranging from motherhood (e.g., Clevenger, 2016) to women working in male-dominated fields (e.g., Galvin-White & O'Neal, 2016). Analyses of female sex work (i.e., prostitution) are quite common. These analyses reveal contrasting perceptions of female sex workers as victims of patriarchal oppression versus agents of power who make rational choices (Shdaimah & Leon, 2015); you will learn more about these contrasting perceptions in Chapter 5. Feminist research on prostitution also emphasizes that society's devaluation of sex work is influenced by the larger subordination of women in society (Armstrong, 2016) and broader assumptions about the nature of femininity—"social expectations for women, who are not supposed to ... engage in too much sex" (Shdaimah & Leon, 2015).

Feminist theorizing, in its diversity, is becoming fully integrated into the study of deviance as a whole. Despite the fact that feminist theorizing has been incorporated into the positivist and interpretive theories reviewed in this book (as well as into other types of critical theories), feminist theories are often categorized as inherently critical theories. This is because of their foundation in the theoretical interest in exploring power relations in society and the practical interest in emancipation—achieving equality for women in society.

Postmodern Theories: Questioning All Knowledge

If discussing "feminist theories" as a cohesive category is difficult and somewhat artificial, discussing postmodern theories as a cohesive category is perhaps even more so (Downes & Rock, 2011). In fact, there is limited agreement about precisely what constitutes "postmodern" theorizing and whether or not it can be included in the category of "critical theories." For instance, postmodernism is sometimes equated with the power-reflexive theories addressed earlier, such as the work of Foucault. Postmodern theories are broadly based on the notion of *rejection*—rejection of overarching theories of society (such as structural functionalism or symbolic interactionism), rejection of social categorization (e.g., "man," "black," "Christian"), and rejection of the possibility of "truth." **Skeptical postmodernism** (Rosenau, 1992) is solipsistic, postulating that knowledge is not possible and that only chaos and meaninglessness exist. In contrast, **affirmative postmodernism** deconstructs what are seen as master narratives, overarching theories, or "knowledge" and focuses analysis on the local and specific. This form is sometimes associated with social movements like environmental activism.

Postmodernists claim that advanced capitalist societies faced rapid social change following the end of World War II. Such societies can no longer be considered "industrial" societies, because symbols and culture (rather than products) have taken centre stage in the economy. Capitalism now exists primarily "by selling consumers new needs, new experiences, and new forms of meaning, all of which are defined exclusively by the marketplace" (Ashley & Orenstein, 2001, p. 475). Commercialism is the defining feature of society, with people pursuing "style over substance" (p. 475). Even politics has become a commercial activity—people are "consumers" rather than "citizens," becoming politically indifferent, self-absorbed, and hedonistic in their endless pursuit of personal style.

Postmodernists speak of the "end of the individual" for this very reason; the individual is no more than the style or image being pursued at a given moment in time, an image that is disjointed and constantly changing. Any notion of a dominant moral code by which we can judge deviance and normality is gradually being eroded. "The postmodern subject is besieged by an endless jumble of messages, codes, and ideas, most of which are incompatible, inconsistent, and quite infantile. Many people respond to the current cacophony of mostly commercial messages that bombard them daily by abandoning all hope that they ever could attain some kind of rational understanding of the world, [becoming] an empty shell that is incapable of exercising any kind of critical judgment" (Ashley & Orenstein, 2001, p. 476).

Although postmodern assumptions in their skeptical forms are rarely used in analyses of deviance, it is interesting to ponder the implications of the lack of a moral code and the creation of subjects that are incapable of critical judgment. Is "deviance" possible if there is no moral code that serves as the foundation for its

Elena Yakusheva/Shutterstock

How do we determine what constitutes deviance and normality when we are bombarded by "an endless jumble of [contradictory] messages"?

social construction? Can anyone be socially typed as deviant if people become incapable of critical judgment? Is a populace that is incapable of critical judgment simply more susceptible to the interests and whims of those who are in authority?

In the study of deviance, postmodernism raises more questions than it answers, which some people say is the point of postmodern theories. They do not pretend to answer questions—their goal is largely to problematize and raise questions about knowledge creation and human behaviour. It is in that regard that they can be considered "critical" theories.

Limitations of Critical Theories

Critical theories are defined by a theoretical interest in the power struggles by which normative social boundaries are created, as well as a practical interest in the pursuit of social justice. Through their analyses, critical theorists try to determine the processes by which the views of certain groups of people come to be applied to society as a whole—how some people's "rules" become society's "rules" and thereby serve as the standard against which deviance and normality are judged.

Conflict theories focus on social structures that create an opposition between the powerful and the powerless. Power-reflexive theories emphasize the intertwining of power relations and claims to knowledge (including their own). Feminist theories focus on the implications of the gendered structure of society and the gendered nature of people's experiences, especially for women. Postmodern theories, which are still rather amorphous and hard to pin down, focus on the "end of the individual" and a rejection of the possibility of "truth." They represent an important layer of recent theoretical development, although their usefulness for understanding the social construction of deviance is yet to be determined.

Some theorists suggest that conflict, poststructuralist, feminist, and postmodernist assumptions may be more appropriately considered processes, perspectives, or ideologies rather than formal theories with empirically verifiable propositions. Siegel and McCormick (2016) state that research on conflict theories "places less emphasis on testing the hypotheses of a particular theory and instead attempts to show that conflict principles hold up under empirical scrutiny" (p. 238).

Furthermore, in the study of deviance and social control, conflict theories in particular have been characterized by inconsistent empirical support; the results of some studies support conflict principles while the results of other studies do not (Chamlin & Sanders, 2013). More broadly, conflict theories have been criticized for failing to recognize the consensus that does exist in society regarding many laws and rules (e.g., prohibitions against theft and murder) (Hayle, Wortley, & Tanner, 2016). Critics suggest that a more complete theory should be able to deal with both conflict and consensus (Ritzer & Goodman, 2004).

Theoretical integration is quite common with critical theories. Different bodies of critical theory have been integrated, in efforts to enhance explanatory value. For instance, feminist and poststructuralist perspectives were applied in an analysis of Aboriginal women's experiences in Vancouver's downtown Eastside, compared to media representations of their experiences in the drug education film *Through a Blue Lens* (England, 2004). Critical theories have also been combined with interpretive theories. One example of this is found in analyses of the complexities of racial profiling in the criminal justice system. Gabbidon (2003) applies interactionist and conflict theories to shoplifting-related false arrest cases. Gabbidon's finding that members of visible minority groups are less likely than white Americans to obtain clear victories in court illustrates the conflict assumption that the law is a tool used by the powerful to oppress the powerless. Gabbidon's finding that black Americans are more likely to be falsely accused of shoplifting than are members of other visible minority groups illustrates interactionist assumptions about the effects of labelling and stigmatization. Stereotypes associate the master status of "black" with the auxiliary trait of "criminal," hence the greater likelihood of false accusations. Independently, interactionist and conflict theories are unable to explain the complete phenomenon, but when integrated they are able to explain both why black individuals are more likely than other minorities to be falsely accused of shoplifting and why members of minorities as a whole are less likely to secure clear court victories.

Taken together, critical and interpretive theories paint a picture of the social construction of deviance. Interpretive theories address the interactions between people by which diverse and even contradictory understandings of deviance and normality emerge. They also explore what happens to people once they have been labelled deviant and how people who are considered deviant attribute meaning to their own life experiences. Interpretive theories draw our attention to the many steps involved in the deviance dance.

TIME TO REVIEW

Learning Objective 4

- What are the theoretical and practical interests shared among critical theories?

Learning Objective 5

- What are the similarities and differences between the different conflict theories addressed in the chapter?

- What do power-reflexive theories tell us about *knowledge* and *social control*?

- What do feminist theories have in common, and why is it difficult to draw conclusions about what "feminist theory" tells us about deviance?

- What are the core assumptions of postmodern theory, and what questions does the theory raise about the study of deviance?

Learning Objective 6

- What criticisms have been directed at critical theories, and what have been some of the theoretical or empirical responses?

On the other hand, critical theories address the role that power plays in the social construction of deviance, whereby the understandings of deviance held by more powerful groups in society are the understandings that become institutionalized. They draw our attention to the fact that some people, such as those of a particular sex, those with more wealth, those who control the media, or those whom we consider "scientists," are better able to determine the direction of the deviance dance—are allowed to "lead" the dance.

At this point in the text, we have explored what "deviance" is, as well as changing conceptions of deviance. We have also reviewed the dominant theoretical perspectives used by deviance specialists who have more objective understandings of deviance (positivist theories) and by deviance specialists who have more subjective understandings (interpretive and critical theories). Having established this foundation of knowledge about the discipline and how deviance may be studied, in the remainder of the book we will turn our attention to an exploration of several substantive topics of deviance and normality—media, sexuality, youth, physical appearance, mental disorders, science, and religion. As you progress through these substantive topics, the concepts, ideas, and theories that have been reviewed in Chapters 1, 2, and 3—for example, normative violation or social typing—will repeatedly emerge. The application of particular concepts and theories in the discussion of concrete situations will clarify these concepts and theories.

Exercise Your Mind

How would each of the theories in this chapter explain deviance or conformity as it exists in your own life (or the life of someone you know)? What facets of your experience are left unexplained by each theory? If you had to select the one theory that best explains deviance or conformity in your own life, which would it be?

CHAPTER SUMMARY

- Deviance specialists who have more subjective understandings of deviance are interested in the way particular acts are socially constructed and socially typed as deviant. *Interpretive* and *critical* theories are the most useful in understanding the social construction of deviance and normality. (1)

- *Interpretive theories*, with their emphasis on how meaning is created through social interaction and symbolic communication, draw our attention to how each of us comes to understand that certain acts are "deviant" while others are "normal." They also draw our attention to how different people develop contrasting understandings of deviance. (1)

- *Labelling theories* explain how the process of getting caught in a deviant act and subsequently being labelled as "deviant" serve as the impetus for the transition from *primary* to *secondary* deviance. A deviant label becomes a *master status* that limits opportunities in the "normal" world, opens up opportunities in the "deviant" world, and changes a person's self-perception and identity. (2)

■ Different people within diverse contexts may react to being *stigmatized* in various ways, such as by trying to hide the stigma, immersing themselves in a world of similarly stigmatized others, or proudly displaying the stigma. (2)

■ The notion of the *deviant career* is another interpretive strategy for exploring people's entrance into, management of, and possible exit from deviant activities. (2)

■ Interpretive theories have faced a number of criticisms, which have been responded to theoretically and empirically. (3)

■ *Critical theories* share a theoretical interest in the power struggles that define normative social boundaries and a practical interest in emancipation. Diverse critical theories exist, including conflict theories, power-reflexive theories, feminist theories, and postmodern theories. (4)

■ *Conflict theories* originated with the economic deterministic model of Karl Marx but have since expanded to include alternative models of power wherein powerful groups are able to impose their moral order on powerless groups. (5)

■ *Power-reflexive theories* emphasize the intertwining of power relations and claims to knowledge. Some power-reflexive theorists also analyze structures of surveillance and the creation of self-surveillance, by which we regulate our own behaviours even if no one else is doing so. (5)

■ *Feminist theories* suggest that deviance and normality are socially constructed in different ways for males and females in society. (5)

■ *Postmodern theories* represent a recent theoretical development arising out of the social changes following the end of World War II. Their proponents propose the notion of the "end of the individual" and posit that people have become consumers rather than citizens. These theorists reject overarching theories of society and claim that the moral codes that would enable people to rationally understand society have eroded. (5)

■ Critiques of critical theories have been responded to in a number of ways, such as through theoretical integration. (6)

To learn more about the topics discussed in this chapter and to complete chapter quizzes, visit the Companion Website for *Deviance, Conformity, and Social Control in Canada*.

Chapter 4
Deviance 2.0: The Role of the Media

Learning Objectives

After reading this chapter, you should be able to

1 Identify forms of media, both *traditional* and *new* or *emerging*.

2 Explain why it is important for sociologists to study media.

3 Describe patterns of media use and the nature of its impact.

4 Distinguish between *administrative* and *critical* approaches to media studies in terms of what they study and the nature of their findings.

5 Outline five different types of relationships that characterize the media–deviance nexus.

Media researcher and anti-violence educator Jackson Katz (1999) claims that the "media is the single greatest pedagogical force of our time." This suggests that the power of media is not limited to any single sphere of social life, but rather permeates all aspects of life in the Western world. Indeed, it is difficult to imagine what school, work, and leisure time would be like without the media. As Silverstone (2007) claims, "we have become dependent on the media for the conduct of everyday life" (p. 6).

The term **media** refers to any form of communication that targets a mass audience in print or electronic format. Traditional forms of media include print (books, magazines, newspapers, comics), radio, cinema, television, and recordings. More recent forms of media include a broad variety of electronic communications that depend on computer technology, for example, websites, mobile computing, blogs, smartphone apps, Twitter, and digitized forms of traditional media. These are referred to as *new* or *emerging* media.

Chapters 1, 2, and 3 of this book have already brought the role of the media in discussions of deviance to light. Several examples were evident in Chapter 1. For instance, Emily Murphy's book *The Black Candle* (a traditional form of media) had an impact on the criminalization of marijuana. More broadly, the media constitutes one of the five most powerful groups that can influence the dominant moral codes of society; it serves as a tool used by a wide range of moral entrepreneurs in their efforts to change society. Chapter 2 addressed the strain of fame and celebrity, such as the killer-as-celebrity phenomenon in the news, people who blog, and culture jamming. In Chapter 3 we explored the role of media in the deviantization of mothers of school shooters, the use of media to resist oppression (e.g., #BlackLivesMatter), the centrality of media in creating hegemony, and postmodernist claims that in the post–World War II era the media has contributed to the *end of the individual*. The current chapter explores more foundational issues related to the media: why it is important to study the media when trying to understand deviance, conformity, and social control; the different approaches that scholars have taken to studying the media that draw our attention to varying aspects of the media; and the nature of the media–deviance nexus, that is, the diverse ways in which the media and deviance are intertwined.

Why Media Matters

In the quote that opened this chapter, Jackson Katz referred to the media as the "single greatest *pedagogical* force of our time" (emphasis added). By that, he means media provide the primary means by which we learn—about ourselves, about others, about the world around us. Other scholars do not consider the media to be as singularly powerful as Katz does, but rather as "part of the circle of primary and secondary definers and claimsmakers" (Tsoukala, 2008, p. 138). Although there may be some disagreement as to the magnitude of the media's power relative to other agents, there is agreement that media are powerful learning tools.

Why study the media? Your responses to the *Ask Yourself* exercise may have already indicated why it is important for sociologists to do so—because so much of our everyday lives are spent using it! Sociologists also study the media because of what the media *does*—its impact on individuals and society.

Patterns of Media Use

Sociologists study everyday life in terms of the interconnections between the micro-level of individual experiences and choices and the macro-level of broader sociocultural structures and processes. The extent of our media use means that understanding everyday life means understanding our relationship with media.

Media is so much a part of our daily lives that in some respects it is rendered almost invisible. Because it is always there, it can be difficult to see the extent of its pervasiveness. Figure 4.1 illustrates the number of minutes each week that Canadian adults spend using various forms of media, comparing 2001 and 2015 (Interactive Advertising Bureau, 2015). You can see that in 2015, the greatest amount of time was spent watching television and using the Internet. The least amount of time was spent reading newspapers and magazines. At first glance, it appears that media use increased significantly between 2001 and 2015 (from 56 hours per week to 70 hours per week). However, some media use is **simulmedia**, using more than one form of media simultaneously. The Interactive Advertising Bureau measured simulmedia for the first

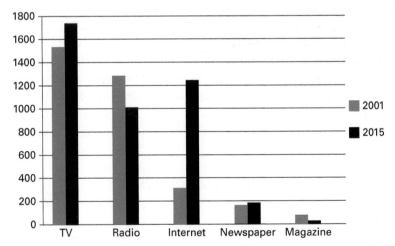

Figure 4.1 Time Spent Using Various Forms of Media among Canadian Adults, 2001 and 2015 (Weekly Minutes per Capita)

Based on Interactive Advertising Bureau of Canada (2015). *Canada's media landscape*. Retrieved from http://www.iabcanada.com.

time in 2015, and found that it is quite common, for example, for people to watch television and use the Internet at the same time. When simulmedia is considered, the total amount of time spent using media remained relatively stable between 2001 and 2015. However, the patterns of media use did change. Use of some forms of media declined over that period, particularly radio and magazines. Use of other forms increased—television and especially the Internet (Interactive Advertising Bureau of Canada, 2015).

Patterns of media use vary across age groups. Among Canadian adults, mobile computing trends younger, while the use of desktop computers trends older (Interactive Advertising Bureau, 2015). Older adults are more likely to engage with traditional versions of television, newspapers, and magazines while younger adults are more likely to engage with digitized versions. As an example, Netflix has its greatest reach among 18- to 34-year-olds, with 50 percent having a subscription (Interactive Advertising Bureau, 2015).

Of note are patterns of use among children and adolescents, who can be considered digital natives. Those born in 2006 or later have never lived in a world without Facebook (launched in 2004), YouTube (launched in 2005), or Twitter (launched in 2006). A survey of more than 5000 Canadian children in grades 4 through 11 reveals that approximately one-quarter of children in grade 4 have their own cellular or smartphones, and that proportion increases to more than 80 percent by grade 11—more than double the proportions of a decade earlier (Steeves, 2014). Social networking services (SNS) play an especially important role in their lives. Three-quarters have a social networking profile or blog, and a list of their top 10 favourite websites is dominated by SNS (see Figure 4.2) (Steeves, 2014).

Although social networking sites are especially important to youth, they play a role in the lives of people in all social groups, including the elderly, recent immigrants, people with disabilities, Indigenous persons, and even the homeless (Taylor, 2011). Social media's primary role is a means to keep in touch with friends and family; in fact, 18 percent of Canadians say they socialize with their friends more online than in the real world (Ipsos-Reid, 2012). However, use of social media is multifaceted, ranging from playing games with others to fighting addiction to political advocacy (Taylor, 2011).

Top 10 Favourite Websites	
1. YouTube	6. Instagram
2. Facebook	7. Minecraft
3. Google	8. Miniclip
4. Twitter	9. Hotmail
5. Tumblr	10. Wikipedia

Figure 4.2 Top 10 Favourite Websites of Canadian Youth, Grade 4 through Grade 11 (2011–2013)

Based on Steeves, V. (2014). *Young Canadians in a wired world: Trends and Recommendations*. Ottawa, ON: MediaSmarts.

Research shows that our use of various forms of media is extensive—well over 50 hours each week on average, and for some people even more! But so what? So what if I watch the next episode of my favourite television show (via cable or Netflix), download a song from iTunes, read the *Globe and Mail* (either in hard copy or online), enter a contest on Facebook, or go see the latest action flick at the theatre? Why does it matter? Scholars suggest that it matters because the media is not innocuous—it is not merely a neutral purveyor of information or entertainment, but rather has an impact on both individuals and society. This point is of relevance to discussions of deviance.

The Impact of Media on Individuals and Society

Part of the media's power is its ability to define. It defines boundaries between groups and communities within those groups, thereby affecting our understandings of "us" and "them." For example, European media coverage of soccer hooliganism makes a clear distinction between irrational, animal-like soccer hooligans and authentic soccer fans (Tsoukala, 2008). The media defines social problems and shapes public debates, indicating which people and issues we should be concerned about and why. As the media is a key site of social inclusion and exclusion, it is through the media (at least in part) that we learn who the "Other" is that we should be concerned about. Within the media, we see morality and ethics in action—the general principles that define good or bad and the application of those principles in action (Silverstone, 2007).

In an important study, Greer and Jewkes (2005) analyzed the "mediated constructions of otherness" (p. 20) in British newspapers. They found that newspapers placed troublesome "Others"—people in need of social control—along a continuum of stigmatized and absolute others. **Stigmatized others** are presented as threats to the way of life of decent people. People on social assistance, single mothers, or those engaged in moderately deviant behaviour "retain a degree of newsworthiness because they form part of a wider, nostalgically reactionary narrative decrying the perceived... collapse of discipline, the lack of respect for authority, the loss of better times, and the wistful (if hopelessly naive) call for a return to the good old days" (p. 23). **Absolute others** are presented as inherently evil and include those who commit exceptional crimes, such as suicide bombers, pedophiles who kill children, and children who commit acts of murder.

Precisely where specific others are located on this continuum is constantly changing in response to shifting public concerns and cultural sensibilities. Thus, stigmatized others can be elevated to absolute others via the media. One instance noted by Greer and Jewkes was the way newspapers came to equate "dole spongers" (people who chronically and unnecessarily rely on welfare) with "terrorists." In covering the story of one woman who was a "dole sponger," a newspaper pointed out several specific cases of Islamic extremists who planned or engaged in terrorist acts while on social assistance: "I'm not saying that every benefit recipient is a terrorist welfare queen. I am saying that the best bet of saving the next generation of [dole spongers] is if the U.S. declares European welfare systems a national security threat" (*The Daily Telegraph*, cited in Greer & Jewkes, 2005, p. 24). In another instance, Greer and Jewkes found that various British newspapers connected the sexual assault and murder of a 12-year-old boy by an illegal immigrant to "the complete breakdown of the immigration system" and an indication of "what can happen when the immigration and asylum system breaks down" (p. 25); "illegal immigrants" come to be equated with "pedophilic killers."

Our extensive media use and its ability to define boundaries, identify social problems, and shape public debate make its study crucial to understanding our everyday lives and the larger society in which we live. But media scholars suggest that such understanding can also be used as a tool to help change people's behaviours, solve some social problems (e.g., violence, eating disorders, premature sexual activity), and enact social change.

Studying the Media

Scholars agree that studying the media is an essential component of understanding contemporary life. However, there are varying approaches to this field of study. In the 1940s, Lazarsfeld (1941) identified a distinction between administrative and critical research in media and communication studies; that distinction has continued to the present day (Hamilton, 2014; Shade, 2014).

Administrative research analyzes the effects of media messages on individuals (Hamilton, 2014). Like deviance scholars who lean more toward the objective end of the objective–subjective continuum, administrative research on media holds the individual under a microscope trying to determine what types of messages will result in certain outcomes in individuals. With its positivist foundation, administrative approaches to the study of media are interested in uncovering cause-and-effect relationships, knowledge that can subsequently be used in the mastery of the social environment—changing the way individuals will act.

Critical research in studies of media analyze processes of social control, structures of power, and the relationship between media and "domination, contradiction, and struggle" (Hamilton, 2014, p. 12). Like deviance scholars who lean toward the more subjective end of the objective–subjective continuum, critical media research holds society, rather than the individual, under a microscope, "revealing how media function in order to reproduce dominant ideology in their given social context" (Hamilton, 2014, p. 11) and how social transformation and collective emancipation can be achieved. While administrative media research largely draws on positivist theories, critical media research primarily uses interpretive and critical theories.

Because of their varying approaches, administrative and critical research may both study the same general topic (e.g., television), but then focus on very different aspects of that topic.

Media and Individuals: Administrative Research

Musician Jim Morrison of the rock band The Doors stated, "Whoever controls the media controls the mind." Administrative research rests on the assumption that the media can affect individuals' thoughts and feelings (i.e., their minds) and their behaviour. The media itself conducts and makes use of administrative research to better influence its users. This is seen most clearly when looking at the efforts of advertisers to influence people's attitudes toward products and thus their actions as consumers. Administrative research is also used by groups and organizations that are attempting to solve social problems that they believe are influenced by the media; one area that has been thoroughly explored is the effect depictions of violence in the media have on the behaviour of those who view it.

Advertising

From commercials on television and radio, to advertisements placed in magazines or on your Facebook page, to product placements in television episodes, movies, and video games, advertising permeates all forms of media. In fact, it can be considered a form of media itself, being found on billboards, the sides of public transit buses, the bulletin boards at your campus, and even inside the doors of bathroom stalls. Advertising is everywhere. It has been estimated that while the average person in North America encountered 500 advertisements and brand exposures daily in the 1970s, now we are seeing more than 5000 each day (with some estimates ranging up to 20 000) (Johnson, 2014).

Ask Yourself
Do you think people
are influenced by
advertising? Do you
think *you* are influenced
by advertising?

Does advertising work? Does it affect people's behaviour as consumers? Research done both inside and outside of laboratory settings finds that, indeed, advertising does work. When people are repeatedly exposed to advertisements, their brand recognition increases, they develop positive associations with those brands, and they subsequently intend to (and do) purchase those specific products (Desmond & Carveth, 2007; Roberts et al., 2016). Of course, given that billions of dollars are spent by companies on advertising each year, this finding may not come as a big surprise; for instance, an estimated $10 billion was spent on advertising in Canada in 2015, and $182 billion in the United States (Statista, 2016).

Advertising's effectiveness lies in its ability to persuade people—that is, to change their attitudes about a product. Research into the process of persuasion studies *who* says *what* to *whom* and with what *effects*. This research finds that characteristics of the source of the communication (e.g., the model featured in an advertisement), the message itself (e.g., the language used in the advertisement), and the audience (e.g., the individual looking at the advertisement) all have an impact on the effectiveness of the attempt at persuasion (Aronson, Wilson, Akert, & Fehr, 2017).

HstrongART/Shutterstock

Research consistently finds that advertising has a significant impact on purchases, including brand alcohol consumption among youth.

Attitudes toward products can also be affected by a subtler form of advertising known as "product placement." This refers to inserting brand-name products into television shows, movies, or video games. For example, the judges on *The Voice* drink from Starbucks cups to raise the profile of that brand, and tobacco companies have paid to have their brands featured in popular movies. A more recent trend has been digitally inserting products into reruns of television shows; this enables different products to be placed in the show in different broadcasts or in different geographical regions. The first instance of digital product placement to reach widespread public attention was when a DVD of the movie *Zookeeper* was placed in a rerun of the television show *How I Met Your Mother*. Sometimes product placement is initiated not by a company spending its advertising dollars to promote a specific product, but rather by the creators of the television show or movie. For instance, during its first season the characters on the television show *Mad Men* were repeatedly shown drinking Canadian Club whisky. Sales for the whisky climbed 8 percent over the next year after many years of a sales plateau (Krashinsky, 2012). The company that owns this brand quickly took advantage of the opportunity, shifting a larger percentage of its advertising dollars to the Canadian Club brand and creating an advertising campaign that dovetailed into the retro nature of the show *Mad Men*: "Damn Right Your Dad Drank It."

Administrative research on the effects of media messages on individuals can provide valuable information to the media itself, enabling it to attract audiences and, in the case of advertising, affect people's behaviour as consumers. But administrative approaches to media research are also of value to groups or organizations that are concerned about the media's potential to contribute to social problems, such as violence in society.

Violence in the Media

Violence permeates the media, whether in the news, movies, the latest video game, children's cartoons, professional sports, or music lyrics. Its pervasiveness has made violence the most-researched topic in media studies. Research in the mid-twentieth century demonstrated that children who witnessed adults (in person) acting aggressively with a doll also behaved more aggressively when they were given the opportunity to play with that doll (Bandura, Ross, & Ross, 1961). The same researchers found similar effects when children watched a film of adults abusing the doll (Bandura, Ross, & Ross, 1963). Does this mean that exposure to violence in the media makes people violent in the real world? Two types of research methods have been used to explore this issue: correlational research and experimental research.

Correlational studies have found a small to moderate relationship between the amount of violent media consumed and people's level of aggressiveness. For example, a meta-analysis of both cross-sectional and longitudinal research finds that media violence is associated with higher levels of aggression among adolescents of all genders and ethnicities (Krahé, 2014). Although the correlation is only small to moderate, it is statistically significant, and in fact is greater than the correlation between exposure to secondhand smoke and the likelihood of developing lung cancer (American Academy of Pediatrics, 2016). However, as you most likely learned in your introductory sociology class, correlational research is not able to determine whether violent television *causes* aggression in viewers; it may be that individuals who are more aggressive to begin with choose to engage with more violent media.

Experimental research attempts to determine causation. In a typical study, individuals are exposed to forms of media with varying levels of violence and are then placed in situations where they can express aggressive attitudes or act aggressively toward someone (e.g., administering a noxious sound). This type of research does find that, at least in the short term, exposure to media violence has several effects, including lower levels of empathy, greater acceptance of aggression as a legitimate means of resolving problems, and higher levels of aggressive behaviour (Krahé, 2014). For example, Fischer and Greitemeyer (2006) had research participants listen to different types of songs. Some contained violent, misogynistic lyrics (e.g., Dr. Dre's "Bitches Ain't Shit") while others were more innocuous pop songs (e.g., Miley Cyrus's "The Climb"). Afterward, when given the opportunity to pour measures of hot sauce that other participants were supposedly going to be forced to drink (although no one did have to drink it), those who listened to the violent songs poured larger amounts of hot sauce, especially when they were pouring it for a female. In another study, boys watched films that either portrayed a bike race or police violence. When playing a floor hockey game after watching the films, the boys who watched the film containing police violence played the game more aggressively as evidenced by behaviours such as body checking, high sticking, and name calling (Josephson, 1987).

Although experimental research does find that exposure to media violence increases aggression in the short term, whether it results in aggression over the long term remains unknown. It may be that media violence affects some individuals more than others. After all, we are all exposed to considerable media violence and yet most of us do not engage in acts of violence. Researchers do find that media violence has a greater effect on people who have higher pre-existing levels of aggression (Gackenbach & Snyder, 2012). Other factors can affect the impact of media violence as well, such as the level of exposure to real-life violence (e.g., family violence; school violence) (Krahé, 2014).

But why is it that violence in the media affects people (or at least some people)? Some scholars suggest the pervasiveness of violence throughout all forms of media desensitizes people, lessening the emotional impact of violent acts and making people more tolerant or accepting of aggression. Indeed, experimental research finds that people who experience more real-life violence and those who consume more violent media report lower levels of anxiety when shown a violent video clip (compared to people who experience less real-life or media violence) (Krahé, 2014; Mrug, Madan, Cook, & Wright, 2015). Desensitization is not just emotional, but physiological as well; individuals who consume more violent media have

Ask Yourself

Do you think different types of media violence have varying effects on people's aggression? Consider, for example, the violence in a children's cartoon compared to a video game (e.g., Call of Duty) or a song.

lower heart rates and blood pressure when viewing a violent video clip, compared to those who consume less violent media.

So does the media control the mind, as musician Jim Morrison claimed? Administrative approaches to media research suggest that in some cases it does. Effective advertising campaigns do affect the way individuals think and feel about specific products and thereby influence their behaviours as consumers. Similarly, the wealth of research on media violence suggests that some type of relationship likely exists between violence in the media and people's levels of aggression, although the precise nature of that relationship and its magnitude remain unclear.

Because of the media's ability to affect individuals' thoughts, feelings, and behaviours—and potentially in negative ways, such as through aggression—administrative research frequently serves as the foundation for demands to change the content or to more stringently regulate various forms of media. Thus, some media becomes deviantized and subjected to measures of social control, a topic that will be addressed later in this chapter.

Media and Society: Critical Research

In the previous section, Jim Morrison stated that the media controls the *mind*. But Allen Ginsberg, a poet and leader of the Beat movement in the 1950s, had a different point of view, claiming that "whoever controls the media, the images, controls the *culture* [emphasis added]." This small difference in their respective statements captures the distinction between administrative and critical approaches to media studies. While administrative research analyzes the effects of media messages on individuals' thoughts, feelings, and behaviours, critical research studies the media's relationship to the broader society—structures of power, processes of social control, and patterns of struggle and resistance. The critical approach to media studies, rather than the administrative approach, "predominates in Canadian research" (Hamilton, 2014; Shade, 2014).

According to critical researchers, the media constructs reality, or at least a portion of it. Media show and tell us the way things are, the way they can be, and the way they should be (Macnamara, 2006). The media doesn't just have an impact on individuals but rather on the entire society—interpersonal relationships, social institutions, societal norms, values, or beliefs, and processes associated with globalization. Thus, critical researchers claim that the media is intertwined with all five levels of social construction (see Chapter 1): individual, interpersonal, institutional, sociocultural, and global. Critical research has emphasized how media socially construct events, issues, and identities, and how those constructions may be affected by changing structures of media ownership.

The Media Frames Society

In media studies, **framing** refers to the way that the media "select some aspects of a perceived reality and make them more salient in a communication text in such a way as to promote a problem definition, causal interpretation, moral evaluation, and/or treatment recommendation" (Entman, 1993, p. 52). In other words, framing refers to the overall way that an issue is depicted in the media, and therefore what we notice about reality. You can think of it as like the framing of a picture. In a selfie, certain parts of reality are seen (e.g., your face), while other parts of reality are hidden (e.g., the dirty dishes in the background). Furthermore, even the parts of reality that are seen in a selfie are portrayed in a certain way; you hold your head at a specific angle when you take your own photo, and afterward may even use a variety of filters to alter the image (e.g., to make your skin look smoother).

Media scholars analyze the aspects of reality that are and are not highlighted in media, and how that reality is portrayed. For example, the news media comprises three generic frames: the **conflict frame**, which emphasizes conflicts between nations, institutions, groups, or individuals; the **human interest frame**, which focuses on human life stories and emotions; and the **economic consequences frame**, which highlights material costs and benefits for countries, regions, groups, or individuals (Price, Tewkesbury, & Powers, 1997). The media frames individuals (such as rival politicians during election time), social issues (such as drug epidemics), health conditions (such as autism or hearing loss), and social groups (such as those based on gender, religion, or ethnicity) (Ahmed & Matthes, 2016; Foss, 2014; Hotton, Farrell, & Fudge, 2014).

Exercise Your Mind

Consider your favourite television shows, movies, or songs. How are various social groups (e.g., based on gender, socioeconomic status, or ethnicity) framed? In other words, which social groups are represented? How are they portrayed? Which social groups are not present? What messages does their absence give consumers of that television show, movie, or song?

Framing Social Groups.   Although the media frames individuals, social issues, social groups, and more, media framing of social groups is especially significant, and central to the social typing process. For instance, the media tends to frame people who play video games as "young, nerdy white guy[s] who like guns and boobs" (Dewey, 2014). From television sitcoms like *Big Bang Theory* and *South Park*, to dramatic series such as *CSI*, *NCIS*, and *Law and Order*, to web-based series like *The Guild*, gamers are not only typically portrayed as male, but more specifically as males who "[frequently] become overweight, ignore basic hygiene requirements, and confine themselves to a basement hideaway" (Bergstrom, Fisher, & Jenson, 2016, p. 239). Data on the demographic profile of the video gaming world stands in stark contrast to these media frames: Females are just as likely as males to play video games, and in fact, adult women are more than twice as likely to play video games as are males between the ages of 10 and 25 (Harwell, 2014). Despite that fact, in large part the gaming industry continues to operate based on the assumption of a young male audience. Characters (and especially lead characters) in video games are much more likely to be male than female, and female leads tend to be portrayed in highly sexualized ways. The #Gamergate scandal in 2014 drew attention to the ridicule, harassment, and even death threats that female video game producers and feminist critics of the androcentric nature of the industry face (Dewey, 2014; Harwell, 2014).

The significance of the media framing of social groups for the social typing process is also evident when considering ethnic minority groups (Ahmed & Matthes, 2016; Fleras & Kunz, 2001). Historically, the media has been characterized by a lack of diversity, presenting primarily people who are white and middle-class. In an analysis of Canadian media, Fleras and Kunz (2001) find that ethnic minorities (and especially visible minorities) tend to be portrayed in one of five interrelated ways. First, they are most typically *invisible*, in that minorities are under-represented in the media. Second, when minorities are represented they are often portrayed in ways that support existing stereotypes; these stereotypes are a foundation for the remaining frames. Third, some minorities are represented as social problems; for example, Jamaican-Canadians are frequently presented as criminals, Asian-Canadians as gangbangers, and Indigenous people as alcoholics. Fourth, some ethnic minorities are represented as adornments, such as the "noble savage" uncorrupted by civilization (e.g., Tonto, the Lone Ranger's loyal companion). Finally, minorities are represented as white-washed, in that their everyday experiences are portrayed as identical to the ethnic majority. White-washing often goes even further, in that the minority characters found in novels are frequently replaced by white actors in film (Hess, 2016). For example, in the movie *Aloha*, Chinese-Hawaiian fighter pilot Allison Ng is played by white actor Emma Stone. Similarly, the film adaptation of the Japanese manga series *Death Note* replaces the character "Light Yagami" with "Light," played by a white actor. There is no shortage of other examples as well: a Korean-American character in the novel *The Martian* becomes a white character in the movie; in another film adaptation of a Japanese manga series, the character Major Motoko Kusangi is played by Scarlett Johansson, wearing a black wig; in the

2013 movie *The Lone Ranger*, the Indigenous character Tonto is played not by an Indigenous actor, but rather by white actor Johnny Depp; the lead character in *The Hunger Games* trilogy, who in the novels has "dark, olive skin" is played by fair-skinned actress Jennifer Lawrence in the films. The framing of ethnic minorities in mainstream Hollywood media has led to resistance. Actors such as Aziz Ansari (*Master of None*), Ming-Na Wen (*Agents of S.H.I.E.L.D.*), Constance Wu (*Fresh off the Boat*), and more have become vocal critics of these media frames, and several social media campaigns were initiated as forms of resistance (e.g., #whitewashedOUT, #OscarsSoWhite) (Hess, 2016).

Critical researchers point out that framing racial and ethnic minorities has implications at the individual, interpersonal, institutional, and sociocultural levels (Jiwani, 2010). First, given the way that media permeates the lives of virtually all people in the developed (and increasingly in the developing) world, when certain communities are not represented in the media they become symbolically annihilated, erased from public consciousness. Second, the media is a public sphere in which important issues are discussed; however, communities must have access to traditional media if their voices are to be heard. Third, well-known media scholar Stuart Hall (2009) pointed out that media representations are not something *outside of* audience members, but rather representations and individuals become intertwined; that is, identity is formed *within* media representations. Thus, the media is an important agent of socialization: the frames used to present minorities may become integrated into the identities of children of those minorities. Finally, media framing has an impact on social policy: "[If] particular groups are consistently under represented, or represented as criminals, as unassailable immigrants, or as simply not belonging, then measures may be enacted that effectively curtail their rights" (Jiwani, 2010, p. 271).

These implications are important to the social construction of deviance and normality. If the voices of a certain social group are not present in traditional media, that means the group's ability to participate in debates over dominant moral codes, or to resist deviantization, is constrained. If people's identities are formed, in part, within media representations, then the processes described by labelling theories (see Chapter 3) come into play. If media framing has an impact on social policy, that means measures of social control that are directed against certain social groups are at risk of being founded on a basis of stereotypes and other biases.

The significance of media framing for Indigenous peoples in particular has been highlighted by the Truth and Reconciliation Commission of Canada (TRC), organized by the parties of the Indian Residential Schools Settlement Agreement (which you will learn more about in Chapter 9). In its final report, the TRC points to the important role of media as part of the reconciliation process (see Box 4.1).

The media frames issues, events, people, and identities in certain ways, which provides us with a cognitive framework by which to understand what we are seeing and places boundaries around what we can (and cannot) see. The media constructs a world for us to see, but at the same time it is also constructed within and by that world (Silverstone, 2007). Media content is shaped by external forces that are

Box 4.1

The Truth and Reconciliation Commission of Canada lists 94 recommendations, referred to as *calls to action*. The following calls to action explicitly draw attention to the media:

84. We call upon the federal government to restore and increase funding to the CBC/Radio-Canada, to enable Canada's national public broadcaster to support reconciliation, and be properly reflective of the diverse cultures, languages, and perspectives of Aboriginal peoples, including, but not limited to:

  i. Increasing Aboriginal programming, including Aboriginal-language speakers.

  ii. Increasing equitable access for Aboriginal peoples to jobs, leadership positions, and professional development within the organization.

  iii. Continuing to provide dedicated news coverage and online public information resources on issues of concern to Aboriginal peoples and all Canadians, including the history and legacy of residential schools and the reconciliation process.

85. We call upon the Aboriginal People's Television Network, as an independent non-profit broadcaster with programming by, for, and about Aboriginal peoples, to support reconciliation, including but not limited to:

  i. Continuing to provide leadership in programming and organizational culture that reflects the diverse cultures, languages, and perspectives of Aboriginal peoples

  ii. Continuing to develop media initiatives that inform and educate the Canadian public, and connect Aboriginal and non-Aboriginal Canadians.

86. We call upon Canadian journalism and media schools to require education for all students on the history of Aboriginal peoples, including the history and legacy of residential schools, the *United Nations Declaration on the Rights of Indigenous Peoples*, Treaties and Aboriginal rights, Indigenous law, and Aboriginal-Crown relations.

Source: Truth and Reconciliation Commission of Canada (2015). *Truth and Reconciliation Commission of Canada: Calls to Action*. Winnipeg, MB: Author. (pp. 13–14).

increasingly global in nature. One of those global forces that critical researchers have paid attention to is the structure of ownership in the media industry.

Media Ownership

In Chapter 3, we saw conflict theorists claim that powerful groups in society can perpetuate a dominant ideology and establish hegemony, thereby controlling how the "masses" think about the world and their place in it. Marxist theorists, in particular, state that power is determined by economic means—by owning the means of production. Critical researchers of media draw our attention to the structure of ownership in the media industry based on this assumption that ownership of the media is intertwined with the nature of the content.

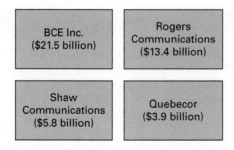

Figure 4.3 Canada's Four Media Giants (with annual revenue for 2015 shown in parentheses)

Of greatest concern within this approach are the trends toward media convergence, conglomeration, and concentration (Shade & Lithgow, 2014). **Convergence** refers to media companies owning multiple forms of media. For instance, a single corporation may own not only several television stations, but also the cable companies that deliver the service; not only websites, but also the Internet service providers. **Conglomeration** refers to the trend toward media companies merging, or some companies purchasing other companies to form large multinational conglomerates—companies own other companies that own yet other companies. Because of convergence and conglomeration, the structure of media ownership is characterized by **concentration**, where a small number of corporations control most media products.

In 1983, approximately 50 companies owned and operated the media in most parts of the world. By 2003, a small fraction of those companies controlled most of the global media (Bagdikian, 2004). Today, five corporations hold most of the power, with combined annual revenues of approximately $US200 billion: Comcast, Walt Disney Corporation, News Corp, Time Warner, and Vivendi; four out of the five are American companies (Shade & Lithgow, 2014). Media convergence, conglomeration, and concentration exist within Canada as well. In fact, Canada "has one of the most consolidated media systems in the world" (Shade & Lithgow, 2014, p. 181). Four companies dominate the media landscape: Bell Canada Enterprises (BCE); Rogers Communications; Shaw Communications; and Quebecor. Bell Canada (BCE) alone controls 30 radio stations, 58 television channels, a wireless network, satellite/digital television infrastructure, and dozens of websites (news, sports, and entertainment), and is a key investor in the Montreal Canadiens hockey team and the Maple Leaf Sports and Entertainment group.

From the perspective of critical researchers, concentration within the structure of media ownership means that "corporate empires control every means by which the population learns of its society" (Bagdikian, 2004, p. 4).

Media Research and Deviance Research

In contemporary society, the media matters more than ever. Administrative research demonstrates that media messages influence the behaviours of individuals, whether through the purchases they make or the acts of aggression they perpetrate. For deviance scholars, this approach to media studies is of greatest value to those who lean toward the more objective end of the objective–subjective continuum. It enables these deviance scholars to analyze the influence that certain media messages may have on specific deviant behaviours, such as crime, gang activity, substance use, premature sexual activity, and eating disorders.

Critical research shows that the impact of media goes beyond the minds of certain individuals whose behaviour may be affected by specific media messages. Media are intertwined with broader structures of power and social control and therefore affect individuals, interpersonal interactions, societal institutions, and cultural norms, values, and beliefs. For deviance scholars, this approach to media studies is of greatest value to those on the more subjective end of the objective–subjective continuum. It enables them to explore the role of media within broader patterns of the social construction of deviance—the role the media plays in our perceptions of and reactions to deviance, and who it is that has the power to determine the nature of that role.

The Media–Deviance Nexus

The components of the media–deviance nexus, or the types of relationships that can exist between the media and deviance, are multifaceted. Five different relationships exist: (1) the media as a cause of deviance, (2) the media as socially constructing deviance and normality, (3) the media as a tool used to commit acts of deviance, (4) the media as a site where the deviance dance is played out—a site of debate, struggle, and resistance—and (5) the media as deviantized itself and subjected to measures of social control.

The Media Causes Deviance

The administrative approach to media studies points to one of the relationships that exists between media and deviance. Administrative research rests on the assumption that the content of media messages influences individuals' thoughts, feelings, and behaviours—although its precise impact may vary across individuals. Thus, specific media messages may propel certain individuals into various forms of deviant behaviour. For example, violence in the media has been found to have an effect on aggressive behaviour in the real world, more so for some people than for others (Gackenbach & Snyder, 2012; Krahé, 2014; Mrug, Madan, Cook, & Wright, 2015).

The view that the media may be a *cause* of deviance, such as aggressive behaviour, is reflected in various areas in the remainder of this book. For example, research on the effects of pornography consumption on youth attitudes and behaviours will be explored in Chapter 5. In Chapter 6, we will see the ways that various forms of advertising affect youth alcohol consumption and the impact of images of smoking in movies on youth tobacco use.

The Media Constructs Deviance and Normality

The critical approach to media studies, which was also presented earlier in this chapter, draws our attention to the second relationship that exists between media and deviance. Critical research rests on the assumption that the media influences the culture (rather than specific individuals) through its power to define boundaries, identify social problems, and shape public debates. For example, the way the media frames various social groups is intertwined with the locations of those social groups in the structure of power, perpetuates those locations, and can be integrated into people's identities. Thus, the media socially constructs deviance and normality, shaping the dominant moral codes that govern what is perceived as acceptable and unacceptable behaviour, characteristics, and people.

The view that the media plays an important role in socially constructing deviance and normality will be put forth throughout the remaining chapters in the book. The role of the sex industry, as well as sexuality within mainstream media (e.g., television), in constructing perceptions of deviant and normal sexuality will be addressed in Chapter 5. In Chapter 6, the way that media portrayals of youth crime and gangs contribute to moral panics is explored. When it comes to aspects of physical appearance, as will be discussed in Chapter 7, the media is central, both in terms of the incorporation of body modification (even in children's media) and in creating the social standards that define certain bodies as "too fat," "too thin," or "ideal." In Chapter 8, we will see that the ongoing stigmatization of mental illness is reflected in television and movies, and those reflections help to perpetuate that stigmatization. Finally, Chapter 9 will explore how the media plays an important role in popular perceptions and stigmatization of specific religious groups as "cults."

Using Media for Deviance

When we think of the relationship between the media and deviance in the twenty-first century, the many ways that the media can be *used* for acts of deviance may first come to mind. The *Ask Yourself* exercise lists some forms of **cyberdeviance** (deviant acts that are committed using computer technology). Some cyberdeviance is unique to the digital world (e.g., creating/spreading viruses and malware or using someone else's wireless signal), while other forms of deviance that occur in the online world can also occur in the offline world (e.g., bullying, watching pornography, selling illegal drugs). Furthermore, because the media is integrated into so much of our everyday lives, in some cases the online and offline components of deviant actions are intertwined. For instance, Paton and Figeac (2015) find that school shooters use various forms of media (such as Facebook posts, email messages, YouTube, and multimedia packages sent to news stations) to both justify their actions to the public and ensure that those actions are correctly interpreted through the frame of "school shooting" rather than as a random act of violence or a result of mental illness. Similarly, Patton and colleagues (2016) find that members of gangs use social media as part of their gang activity, "to brag, post fight videos, and insult and threaten others"—a process known as "internet banging" (p. 2).

Ask Yourself

Have you or anyone you know ever engaged in any of the following acts: visited a pornography website; submitted a term paper that was purchased online; downloaded music or software without paying for it; accessed someone's computer files, email, or social networking profile without their permission; harassed someone via email or social networking sites; used someone else's wireless signal; created/transmitted a computer virus or malware; hacked an organization's computer system; stolen someone's identity with information found online?

Cybercrime

The Internet can be used as a tool for a variety of different criminal activities, including credit card fraud, identity theft, and computer hacking. In the summer of 2012, a two-year undercover investigation known as "Operation Card Shop" resulted in dozens of arrests in 13 countries, including Canada (Canadian Press, 2012; US Attorney's Office, 2012). This organized crime ring used the Internet to buy and sell stolen identities, exploit people's credit cards, create and exchange counterfeit documents, sell hacking tools (including software that enables "cybervoyeurs" to hijack an unsuspecting individual's personal computer camera), and create and spread several computer viruses and malware. More than 400 000 individuals and dozens of businesses were victimized by this cybercrime ring.

One American survey (Holt & Turner, 2012) found that 10 percent of people surveyed reported being victims of identity theft in the previous 12 months. The more time people spent online, the greater the risk of having their identities stolen. Ironically, those at greatest risk were individuals who engaged in various forms of cyberdeviance themselves, such as illegally downloading software or music, cyberbullying, using someone else's wireless signal, accessing someone's computer files without permission, or accessing someone's computer files by guessing their password.

People who access computer systems without authorization and sometimes use that access for malicious purposes are known as **hackers**. Activities can range from hacking celebrity Twitter accounts to plant humorous outgoing messages (Complex Magazine, 2011) to placing viruses in a government's computer system. Computer hacking has significant economic consequences for society, with global economic losses estimated at more than $400 billion each year (and rising rapidly) (Taylor, 2016).

Hackers use computers in two ways: first, as their means of attack, and second, as a way of communicating with other hackers. Holt and Turner (2012) found that a complex hacker subculture exists both online and offline. By analyzing hacker Web forums, interviewing several active hackers, and conducting observations at the annual hacker convention in Las Vegas (DEF CON), the researchers identified five "normative orders" (p. 179) that characterize the hacker subculture: technology, knowledge, commitment, categorization, and law.

- Hackers express a deep overriding interest in understanding and manipulating *technology*, which they report emerging from an early age (sometimes as young as seven). Hackers use Web forums as an important resource for obtaining technical skills, while offline most of the sessions at DEF CON provide a wide range of technical information.

- The continuous quest for *knowledge* is the foundation for hacker identities. Hackers define themselves as people in pursuit of knowledge, and different labels are applied to individuals with varying levels of knowledge. Those with an extensive body of knowledge are considered "hackers," and having a particularly impressive body of knowledge makes one an "elite hacker," also known as "1337" or "'leet" (p. 184). People with little or no knowledge have derogatory labels applied to them and are deviantized within the hacking community. Those who have limited knowledge and whose hacking activities are perceived as simplistic are known as "script kiddies" or "noobs" (p. 184). People who have no hacking knowledge at all and yet still attend the DEF CON convention are labelled "scene whores" (p. 184).

- Pursuing knowledge and using it to master technology requires deep *commitment*. Individuals must be dedicated and willing to persist despite the many obstacles and failures they will inevitably encounter.

- Learning is a process, and as such there are questions about *categorization*. The subculture is characterized by debates over the point at which an individual can be considered an authentic hacker, and there are variations in the point at which individuals integrate "hacker" into their own identities.

- Subcultural debates also revolve around the *law*. These debates revolve around questions about the legality of specific behaviours, as well as what forms of hacking are considered acceptable or unacceptable. Some hackers consider all forms of hacking to be acceptable; others make distinctions between the "normal" hacking community and malicious hackers, who are perceived as "the scum of the earth" (p. 192).

The most malicious hacking, such as using computer viruses and malware to attack businesses or societal infrastructure, is frequently referred to as **cyberterrorism** or **cyberespionage**. In some cases, these acts are state-sponsored. As an example, you may recall a large-scale hack of Sony Pictures in 2014 (because if you had a Sony PlayStation at the time, you were directed to change your password). An FBI investigation into the hack alleges that the government of North Korea was responsible. Malware was placed into computers at Sony, and once that malware was activated, within the one hour it took for authorities to deactivate the malware it stole unmeasurable amounts of data and then "erased everything stored on 3,262 of the company's 6,797 personal computers and 837 of its 1,555 servers" (Elkind, 2015). Some of the stolen data was then publicly released, including confidential emails, employees' social security numbers, and unfinished movie scripts. The largest known hack was discovered in 2016, but had occurred three years earlier when more than 1 billion Yahoo user accounts were hacked; because none of the stolen information was released or sold on the black market, it is suspected that a foreign government was seeking information on specific individuals (Associated Press, 2016). Also in 2016, the CIA alleged that the Russian government sponsored a variety of hacking activities in order to interfere with elections in other countries, including the 2016 American presidential election and the 2017 federal election in Germany (BBC News, 2016).

Digital Piracy

Various forms of cybercrime, such as identity theft, credit card exploitation, malware, and hacking government or military computer systems, can be considered high-consensus forms of deviance—large numbers of people (albeit not everyone) would agree that these behaviours are unacceptable and should face measures of social control. However, there are other types of online activities that, while technically "illegal," could be considered low-consensus forms of deviance—relatively fewer people would agree that those activities are unacceptable and in need of social control. In fact, many people might not even attach the label of "cybercrime" to some of these activities. Digital piracy is one of those activities.

Digital piracy refers to the illegal downloading of music, software, and video. Although some creators make this content available online at no charge, a great deal of digital content is protected by copyright or licensing; to download it without having paid for it is illegal. Although illegal, this activity is widespread. As one active digital pirate states, "it's like jaywalking—everybody does it and no one cares" (Holt & Copes, 2010, p. 637).

Piracy is not unique to the Internet environment. VCRs enabled people to make illegal recordings from television to videocassettes; other pieces of equipment allowed material contained on one videocassette to be transferred to another. The same was true of music cassette tapes. With an inexpensive tape recorder, people could record music from a vinyl record onto a cassette tape, or transfer music from one tape to another. In fact, in the Soviet Union (where music from the West was banned), individuals would smuggle a single copy of a popular album into the country, where it was "pirated" using equipment that imprinted grooves onto discarded X-ray films; these new "albums" were then sold on the black market.

Although pirating is not new, the Internet facilitates piracy through its anonymity, speed of transmission, and "a shift in mindset about ownership given the perception that anything available online is free for others to download with impunity" (Hinduja & Higgins, 2011). The financial impact of digital pirating on creators and artists, companies within the associated industries (e.g., movie studios), and distributors (e.g., retail stores) is of considerable magnitude. It is estimated that digital piracy carries a cost to the global economy of $75 billion annually (Global Intellectual Property Center, 2013). The costs to businesses are then transferred to individual consumers, with higher product costs; because of convergence, conglomeration, and concentration, that means those costs may even be transferred to products outside of music, software, or video (such as the price of cellular phone contracts, cable services, or even hockey tickets).

The nature of digital pirating has changed since the late 1990s. At that time, piracy was technologically complex, so only individuals who had a relatively high level of expertise in computer technology could engage in piracy. However, now the dominant mode of piracy is via peer-to-peer torrent file sharing. With this process, an individual who wants to download a movie or song can "grab" bits and pieces from multiple random computers that are linked into the process, while at the same time allowing other users access to the bits and pieces of digital content on their own computer. This process is fast and easy to use, which means that most pirates no longer need to have any significant expertise in computer technology. Torrent file sharing is also much less vulnerable to detection by authorities, as one instance of sharing may be traced to 10 000 (or even more) nodes in the file-sharing network (Holt & Copes, 2010).

Several sociological theories have been used to explain digital piracy (Hinduja & Higgins, 2011; Holt & Copes, 2010). Using differential association theory (see Chapter 2), researchers analyze the techniques and motives of piracy that are learned in online environments, such as how to recognize files that may contain viruses or malware. Several different techniques of neutralization (Chapter 2) are used by active digital pirates to rationalize their actions. They *deny injury* by stating that corporations in the related industries have more than enough money already; a little bit of downloading won't hurt them. They *condemn the condemners* by claiming that those industries also exploit consumers with high prices. And they *appeal to higher loyalties* by arguing that online material should be free to all so that one's socioeconomic status is not the sole determinant of the media content they can access. Interpretive theories (see Chapter 3) explore processes of identity formation and labelling in digital pirates. For example, Holt and Copes (2010) found that even active digital pirates (people who have downloaded an average of five files per week for the past six months) may identify themselves as "pirates" as a personal identity but do not identify themselves with the online pirating subculture. From this perspective, these researchers also found that there is labelling and stigmatization within the pirating community. Those who sell pirated materials (rather than freely share them) are considered "lowlife shit(s)" (p. 642), and people who download significantly more files than they *seed* (i.e., share) are labelled "leeches" (p. 642).

Although digital piracy is an activity that is subjected to formal measures of social control (through legislation and persecution), it is a common activity in contemporary society and is considered by many to be normal and acceptable. This stands in contrast to perceptions of other forms of cybercrime—such as identity theft and hacking—which are more often perceived as unacceptable and in need of social control.

The Media and the Deviance Dance

The media also serves as a social typer of deviance. Through its framing of issues, events, and identities, it shows us who should be considered deviant, why they should be considered deviant, and what should be done about it. Even though particular frames predominate in the mainstream media, differing points of view, debates, and resistance can also be found. Some parts of the media may socially type a specific person, behaviour, or characteristic as deviant, while other parts of the media contradict or resist that deviant label. One set of media voices may declare a certain solution to a form of deviance, but other media voices may put forth a very different solution. The media may support dominant ideologies and the status quo, yet it may also promote alternative ideologies and provide the means to dismantle the status quo.

The multifaceted nature of the media means that the deviance dance is an inherent part. For instance, smoking is pervasive on fictional television programs and in movies, yet during commercials it is common to see public service announcements about the dangers of smoking. Some music lyrics may promote acts of violence while others extol the virtues of peace. Media images frequently present a narrow vision of the "ideal" body, while at the same time magazine articles and television talk shows may discuss how unrealistic those images are (see Chapter 7).

One of the clearest ways we can see the deviance dance within the media is in the fact that although the media can be used as a tool to commit various deviant acts (hacking, digital piracy), it is also used as a tool to exert measures of social control on deviant acts. For example, Facebook has a technology that scans postings and chats for evidence of criminal activity, such as cyberterrorism and the distribution of child pornography (Menn, 2012). Authorities can scan torrent file-sharing sites for the IP addresses of the heaviest digital pirates. In the United States, this has resulted in several prosecutions (Holt & Copes, 2010). In Canada, many digital pirates have received letters from anti-piracy companies hired by movie studios, demanding large sums of money in order to avoid legal action (Harris, 2016).

Individuals and groups may also use the media as a tool to exert measures of social control on deviant acts. Some people (such as Creep Catchers) use social media to entrap and embarrass suspected pedophiles. Others use social media to draw attention to violent oppression. In that regard, human rights groups train people in closed countries (e.g., Syria) how to take high-quality video on their smartphones so that human rights abuses can be documented. Similarly, videos of American police officers assaulting, and even killing, unarmed black men have become common. In fact, Diamond Reynolds used Facebook Live—in real time—to show her boyfriend dying in their car after being shot by a police officer. Some people claim that these sorts of videos are crucial in raising awareness, holding authorities accountable, and confronting issues of racism and other forms of oppression. However, others argue that there is a risk of desensitizing viewers over time (as with other forms of violence in media), and thereby normalizing these forms of violence even more (CBC News, 2016d).

The media is a tool for resistance to the social typing process as well. Individuals or social groups that face stigmatization or oppression offline—such as people with disabilities, transgendered persons, and members of various lifestyle groups (e.g., rave, straightedge)—can find online communities of support. **Hashtag activism** (i.e., activism using social media) acts to change society's dominant moral codes. For example, #WhyIStayed resists victim-blaming in cases of domestic violence; #sayhername draws attention to the violence faced by black women; #Free_CeCe was an effort to intervene in the case of a black transgender woman who had been arrested and charged with murder after killing her attacker in a racist and homophobic incident (Clark, 2016; Fischer, 2016; Williams, 2016).

The nodal network known as "Anonymous" uses the Internet to resist social typing and change moral codes as well. Even though these people are computer hackers and are committing cybercrimes, they do not perceive themselves as criminals. Instead, they consider themselves to be "hacktivists"—social activists who hack computers to improve society. "Anonymous" hacks computers to expose pedophilia online and to reveal corruption by religious organizations, but it is perhaps most well known for its relationship with WikiLeaks. They hack government computer systems to obtain information that they believe the government is hiding and the public has the right to know. After obtaining this information, they post it online for all to see, such as on the WikiLeaks website.

The deviance dance is an inherent part of media in that it is a site of claims and counterclaims—a site of deviance, deviantizing, and resistance. This is perhaps most evident when we look at the Dark Net, the hidden underworld of the Internet. The Dark Net is simultaneously a tool for committing acts of deviance, a tool *for* resistance, and is inherently a form *of* resistance itself (see Box 4.2).

Box 4.2

The Deviance Dance in the Dark Net

Guteksk7/Shutterstock

As you have already learned in this chapter, the Internet can be used as a tool for committing various acts of deviance, such as digital piracy and identity theft. A quick Google search directs you to numerous sites that you can use to illegally download music, videos, or software. When you engage in everyday activities online, like banking or entering your name and address on a website, you may be at risk of identity theft. However, there are deeper parts of Internet where an even wider range of deviant acts are revealed. Think of the Internet as comprising multiple layers (Weimann, 2016). Standard search engines only access the Internet's surface layer,

gathering information on the connections between various websites to compile a list of search results; sites that have few, or even no, connections to others are not indexed and will not appear in the search results. These hidden layers of the Internet are the Deep Web (Weimann, 2016). The deepest layers of the Deep Web are known as the Dark Web or Dark Net—material that is intentionally hidden and that can only be accessed using specialized software, such as Tor (Eddy, 2015; Weimann, 2016). With the development of Tor by the US Department of Defense in 2003, the Deep Web and the Dark Net were born (Eddy, 2015; Kushner, 2015).

Although the Dark Net was initially developed to protect classified military and government communications, today it is an arena for a wide variety of deviant activities. It includes online communities that normalize the actions of people with anorexia (such as by giving tips for how to continue to lose weight even while hospitalized), give information to those looking

(continued)

for techniques or assistance in committing suicide, provide avenues of communication for neo-Nazi groups planning their next actions, and more (Bartlett, 2015). Criminal enterprises also abound on the Dark Net, such as those involving child pornography, murder-for-hire, human trafficking and slavery, drug sales, money laundering, and the illegal sale of weapons (Martin, 2014; Weimann, 2016). It is estimated that there are approximately 28 illegal black markets on the Dark Net, with more than 10 000 vendors (Kushner, 2015). Because sites are characterized by ongoing migration and displacement—bouncing from one computer or server to another, spanning the globe—policing the Dark Net is extremely challenging. For instance, one illegal black market "claimed that its source code was backed up to 500 locations in 22 countries, so if authorities shut it down, administrators can rebuild it in 15 minutes flat" (Greenberg, 2014).

But wherever there is deviance, there are also efforts at social control. Hacktivist group Anonymous was able to hack Freedom Hosting II, part of the Dark Web infrastructure, and as a result knock one-fifth of the Dark Web offline in a campaign against child pornography (McGoogan, 2017). While the American government were the ones to initially develop the Dark Net, they have also more recently developed a new piece of software (Memex) designed to scour the Dark Net for illegal activity (Kushner, 2015).

The Dark Net is a tool for deviance and corresponding social controls, but it is also a tool for resistance. Various groups who are at risk of harm use it to communicate, including abused women who are seeking refuge or are already in hiding, journalists covering stories in closed countries where they are at risk of imprisonment, and political dissidents and civil rights activists living under oppressive regimes (Kushner, 2015; Weimann, 2016). Governments continue to use the Dark Net as well, to protect classified communications. In fact, Tor receives 60 percent of its funding from the American government.

The Dark Net is a prime example of the deviance dance. Not only is the Dark Net a tool used by various people in their acts of resistance, the technology can be considered a form of resistance as well. Individuals and groups choose to hide in the Dark Net, but the technology itself is also hidden.

Deviantizing the Media

At times, media products themselves are socially typed as deviant and are subject to measures of social control. When the media is deviantized, it might be subjected to formal social control (e.g., censorship or regulation through policy). For instance, in the 1980s a group of wives of American politicians who were concerned about sexually explicit music lyrics formed the Parents Music Resource Center (PMRC). Initially calling for specific songs to be banned, eventually their efforts resulted in the labelling of albums containing explicit lyrics. Given their location in the structure of power, their concerns elicited formal Senate hearings over the issue. Not only did members of the PMRC and various scientific "experts" testify, so did several musicians who were opposed to the PMRC's efforts, such as Frank Zappa and Dee Snider; the full PMRC Senate hearing is available on YouTube. In the present day, we can also see regulation and censorship of media in cases where forms of media are banned by governments in certain countries, whether it is music, movies, or social networking sites such as Twitter and Facebook. As an example, the government of China banned Facebook in 2009 to suppress information about the Urumqi riots, in which 140 people were killed (Thomson Reuters, 2016).

Informal social controls can be exerted as well. Parents may restrict their children's media use, whether by limiting their screen time, setting rules about what types of movies or television programs they can watch, or using software to block certain types of websites. Audiences may boycott media as a form of protest. For example, following several police shootings of unarmed black men in the United States in 2016, NFL quarterback Colin Kaepernick refused to stand for the American national anthem before a game as a statement about racial injustice. Across the NFL and college football leagues, many other players followed suit in the coming weeks. In response, millions of viewers stopped watching NFL football on television because they considered these actions to be unpatriotic (Ozanian, 2016).

Springhall (1999) suggests that youth forms of media are especially likely to be deviantized. Penny theatres and dime novels in the nineteenth century, gangster films of the 1930s and 1940s, American horror comics of the 1950s (which were banned in Great Britain), gangsta rap in the 1990s, and various video games more recently have all stimulated public criticism and attempts at regulation.

One of the reasons why youth media is deviantized is because of its presumed effects on youth. We see this in contemporary debates over violent video games, but we can see it historically as well. For example, in the 1920s it was argued that the rhythms and instrumentation of jazz stimulated the sexual energies of youth and contributed to the "outrageous" style of dancing (e.g., the Charleston), the physical appearance of young women (with short skirts, short hair, and makeup), and behaviours like smoking and drinking (especially in females). Some politicians, along with popular women's magazines, called for an outright ban on jazz music (Fass, 1979).

A second reason why youth media may be deviantized is because of its association with a group of youth who are considered troublesome. Under the Nazi regime in Germany, youth who were part of the swing music subculture were subjected to surveillance by the Gestapo, arrest, expulsion from high school or university, assignment to the front lines during the war, and even imprisonment in concentration camps. These social controls were not imparted because of swing music's perceived effects on youth, but rather because everything about the swing subculture contradicted the social order the Nazis were trying to create. The Nazi government wanted a clean-cut, militaristic, uniform youth culture that supported their social and military goals. In contrast, the "swing kids'" style was English in nature, and the British were Germany's enemy. The boys wore baggy trousers with an English newspaper in the back pocket, trench coats, and a closed umbrella over one arm. They did not listen to German folk music, but rather to English and American music. Their slouching walk was anything but militaristic, and instead of greeting each other with "Heil, Hitler," their greeting was "Swing, heil"—expressing an allegiance to the music rather than to the nation's leader (Wallace & Alt, 2001).

Springhall (1999) states that although the deviantization of youth media is frequently rationalized in terms of its effects on audiences, if we look at all the various forms of youth media that have been deviantized in the past and present, similar motivations are apparent. The process of deviantization is not really about the youth themselves, but rather is indicative of the fear of technological change, the future, and challenges to dominant moral codes in some parts of the adult world.

As one of the central pedagogical forces in the twenty-first century, the media and deviance are intimately intertwined. The media can be analyzed as a cause of deviance, as a site where deviance and normality are socially constructed, as a tool to be used for acts of deviance, as a site for the deviance dance, or in terms of its own deviantization. Although only a limited number of illustrations of the media–deviance relationship have been addressed in this chapter, in the remainder of the book you will continue to see that studying deviance necessarily means studying the media as well.

TIME TO REVIEW

Learning Objective 5

- What are some of the ways that the deviance dance is evident in the media?

- What are some examples of the media being used to socially control online and offline deviance?

- What are some examples of the media being used to resist a deviant label and change society's dominant moral codes?

- In what way is the deviance dance evident on the Dark Net?

- What are some forms of youth media that have been deviantized?

- Why was jazz music deviantized in the 1920s?

- Why was the swing music subculture deviantized in Nazi Germany?

- What forms of youth media are frequently deviantized?

CHAPTER SUMMARY

- It is important for sociologists to study the media because of the amount of time we spend engaged with it and the impact that it has (both on individuals and on society). (2)

- Most time online is spent on social networking sites, although the amount of time spent watching videos online is rapidly increasing. The media has an impact on individuals and society in that it serves as one of the primary definers of boundaries between groups and the communities within, identifies social problems, and shapes public debates. (3)

- *Administrative* approaches to media studies focus on the effect of media messages on individuals. Findings from this type of research can be of value to media itself, such as in creating more effective advertisements. Findings can also be of value to groups who are concerned about the potential role played by the media in creating social problems, such as violence. (4)

- *Critical* approaches to media studies analyze processes of social control, structures of power, and the relationship between the media and hegemony. (4)

- Through *framing*, the media constructs a reality for us to see. The way it frames issues, events, and identities has an impact on individuals, interpersonal interactions, institutions, and larger cultural norms, values, and beliefs. (4)

- Critical scholars claim that framing is influenced, in part, by the structure of media ownership, which is increasingly characterized by convergence and concentration. (4)

- The media–deviance nexus is characterized by five different types of relationships: The media is a potential cause of certain types of deviance (e.g., violence), serves as a site for the social construction of deviance, is a tool used for the commission of acts of deviance (e.g., cybercrime), is a site of the deviance dance (e.g., social control and resistance), and is sometimes deviantized itself (e.g., jazz). (5)

To learn more about the topics discussed in this chapter and to complete chapter quizzes, visit the Companion Website for *Deviance, Conformity, and Social Control in Canada*.

Chapter 5

"Deviant" and "Normal" Sexuality

Inked Pixels/Shutterstock

Learning Objectives

After reading this chapter, you should be able to

1   Contrast the sexual cultures of traditional Indigenous societies with that of the colonizing Europeans, and explain the role that regulating Indigenous peoples' sexualities played in the larger project of colonization.

2   Describe how deviant sexuality was defined and regulated from the seventeenth century through the twentieth century, and explain how the changing sexual cultures reinforced class, gender, and racial hierarchies of the times.

3   Explain how consent, nature of the partner, nature of the act, frequency, and setting serve as criteria by which we judge deviant and normal sexuality.

4   Outline the nature of the deviance dance surrounding the issues of exotic dancing, pornography, and prostitution.

What Is Deviant Sexuality?

Renowned sexuality researcher Alfred Kinsey (1894–1956) (2006) claimed, "the only unnatural sexual act is that which you cannot perform." In contrast, author W. Somerset Maugham (1874–1965) (1998) suggested "there is hardly anyone whose sexual life, if it were broadcast, would not fill the world at large with surprise and horror."

These two quotations demonstrate the complexity of sexuality in human societies and point to the different lenses through which sexuality can be viewed—biological and sociological. Kinsey's view of sexuality draws on biology as the foundation upon which normal and deviant sexuality is defined, and maintains that normal sexuality is simply that which is physically possible. However, Maugham suggests that we all judge people's sexuality, and that most people's sexual lives, if known, would be judged negatively. Evidently, something more than biology plays a role in how sexuality is perceived and in the aspects of sexuality that are defined as deviant or normal. There appears to be a substantial difference between what is biologically possible and what is considered socially acceptable.

Ask Yourself

In Canadian society, what forms of sexuality do you think are perceived as "normal" and "deviant"? What makes you think so? Where do you see messages that reinforce those views?

The *Ask Yourself* exercise asks you to focus attention on the social processes that underlie the dominant moral codes governing sexuality in society. More objective deviance specialists refer to cultural and historical variations in the norms used as the standard against which deviance is judged, and more subjective deviance specialists refer to processes of social construction. Social processes determine who is socially typed as deviant through the processes of *description* (placed in a category because of their sexuality), *evaluation* (judged because of the category into which they have been placed), and *prescription* (made subject to measures of regulation or social control). Thus, although similar sexual activities and characteristics may be found throughout the world, there is variation across cultures and time as to where those characteristics fit within the social hierarchy, the roles assigned to people who exhibit those characteristics, and the meanings attached to those characteristics. Scientific, political, legal, religious, and media discourses of sexuality "shape the ways audience members can imagine organizing their lives" (Moon, 2008, p. 193). **Elite discourses**—that is, the knowledge about sexuality that emerges from positions of authority in society—place limits on "what kinds of persons it is acceptable or even possible to be" (p. 194) at a sociohistorical moment, such that individuals cannot even imagine possibilities that lie outside of those limits.

As you progress through the remainder of this chapter, which addresses the social construction of sexuality cross-culturally, historically, and in contemporary Canadian society, you will see that when we study the social construction of sexuality, we are learning about more than just sexuality. We are also learning about broader sociocultural forces, such as structures and processes of power (e.g., hierarchies of race, ethnicity, class, and gender).

The Cultural and Historical Construction of Sexuality

Even a brief look at cultural and historical variations in sexuality reveals how the perceptions, meanings, and control of sexuality in contemporary Canada represent only a small portion of that which is found throughout the world. Cross-cultural variations in sexuality have been studied for a century, especially by anthropologists. For instance, Herdt's classic (1984) research on the Sambia of New Guinea found ritualized same-sex sexual activities among males during a certain period of life. These activities, required of all males without exception, were intended to reproduce the distinct roles of men and women, the patriarchal structure of society, and the ability of men to be fierce and powerful warriors should the need arise.

Historians and classicists have also drawn attention to cultural and historical variations in sexuality. For example, Arkins (1994) has shown that in Athens during the fifth century BCE, "normal" and "deviant" sexuality were defined based on power. Dominant moral codes governing sexuality highlighted the needs and desires of aristocratic males (the only "citizens" of Athens) and reproduced the existing social structure. Aristocratic males were permitted marital sex for producing male heirs, as well as sexual relationships with other women, slaves, foreigners, and aristocratic adolescent boys for pleasure. However, sexual activity was only acceptable between two persons occupying higher and lower positions on the hierarchy of power in society; sexual activity between two aristocratic men (i.e., two "equals") was considered unacceptable and subjected to measures of social control.

Looking at the sexual cultures of Sambian society, ancient Athens, or any other number of cultures around the world shows us the power of elite discourses of sexuality. Elite discourses place boundaries around what individuals in those cultures perceive as being acceptable, normal, or even possible. At the same time, the elite discourses of sexuality that govern Canadian society in the twenty-first century influence our reactions to the sexual cultures of other societies as well as our own sexual choices. The elite discourses of sexuality in our society today have undergone a long evolution. That evolution begins with traditional Indigenous cultures prior to and following colonization, and continues through considerable social changes from the seventeenth century through today.

Traditional Indigenous Cultures: From Holism to Oppression

The arrival of Europeans in what is now the Americas and their subsequent colonization of that land and Indigenous peoples had a massive impact on all aspects of Indigenous societies. For hundreds of years, various facets of Indigenous cultures were suppressed, facing potential and actual eradication at the hands of political and religious authorities.

Historical evidence points to a stark contrast between the perceptions of sexuality in Indigenous and European cultures (Barman 1997/1998; Windecker, 1997). The different constructions of sexuality were so distinct that sexuality became a nexus of conflict and subsequent social control as colonization progressed (Mandell & Momirov, 2000). Furthermore, colonial discourses of sexuality and race frequently overlapped, such that "racial degeneracy and sexual pathology" were often intertwined (Balestrery, 2012, p. 647). Controls imposed upon Indigenous sexualities (and their surrounding structures of marriage and kinship) were also "a key part of breaking up indigenous landholdings, 'detribalizing' native people, and/or translating native territoriality and governance into the terms of [Eurocentric] liberalism and legal geography" (Rifkin, 2011, pp. 5–6). Controls on sexuality were just some of the tools used for the larger project of colonization (which you will learn more about in Chapter 9).

There was considerable variability across Indigenous cultures in the dominant moral codes governing sexuality. In some cultures, women who engaged in premarital or extramarital sexual activity were subjected to measures of social control, while in others, premarital and extramarital sex were accepted practices and might involve gifts being given to the woman's family (Windecker, 1997). However, amidst these differences a commonality was that sexuality was inextricably interwoven with all other aspects of social life (Newhouse, 1998). Life was viewed as consisting of four components: physical, intellectual, emotional, and spiritual. The physical, intellectual, emotional, and spiritual were considered to be a part of sexuality, and conversely sexuality was thought to enhance these four components in other aspects of a person's life. Sexuality itself was unlikely to be stigmatized. Sexual terms were integrated into some place names, and sexuality was incorporated into myths and stories. For instance, one Anishinaabe story describes how the Creator made sex an act of pleasure so that men and women would come to live together and thereby increase the population (Newhouse, 1998).

Recognizing multiple sex/gender combinations, many cultures perceived a wider range of sexualities as normal and acceptable (Nelson, 2006). Varying combinations in biological males have been recognized in 110 to 150 Indigenous cultures, and varying combinations in biological females in 55 to 75 cultures (Nanda, 2000). For instance, the Inuit used the term *sipiniq* to refer to biological males with a female essence and the Ojibwa used the term *okitcitakwe* to refer to biological females with a male essence (NativeOUT, n.d.). European explorers used the derogatory term **berdaches** ("male prostitutes") to refer to biological males who assumed female roles. To overcome the stigma associated with that Euro-Canadian term, in 1990 the term "Two-Spirited" was adopted by participants in a conference for Indigenous people (Roscoe, 1998).

In some Indigenous cultures, sexual relationships between two people of the same biological sex were acceptable if they were of different genders, while in other Indigenous cultures sexual relationships between people of the same gender were acceptable as well. Not only were people who fell outside of the Eurocentric dualisms of sex, gender, and sexuality accepted in many Indigenous cultures, they were often given specialized roles in the social structure and associated with spiritual power (Newhouse, 1998). For the colonizing European cultures of the time, sexuality had a very different meaning. With their foundation in interpretations of Christian religious doctrine at the time, European sexual cultures were not only heteronormative, but also patriarchal and highly conservative. Sex was for the purpose of reproduction, and even then, notions of pleasure were frowned upon; sexuality was sinful, requiring careful and stringent control. Sexuality was not integrated into social life, but rather isolated from it, almost as a necessary evil, and infused with guilt (D'Emilio & Freedman, 1997; Newhouse, 1998). The only acceptable sexuality was that which occurred between husband and wife, and even then, only if their sole sexual behaviour was intercourse, if it took place in the "missionary" position, and if they did not enjoy it too much or do it too often. The sexuality of women had to be strictly controlled to maintain the purity and sanctity of the home—and to assure paternity (Barman, 1997/1998). Same-sex activities were unacceptable and subject to both informal sanction (e.g., by the community) and formal sanction (e.g., excommunication from the church) (D'Emilio & Freedman, 1997).

Of course, with these considerably divergent sexual cultures, conflict between European and Indigenous peoples became inevitable. The gifts that were given within some sexual relationships in Indigenous cultures were labelled by Europeans as indicative of "prostitution" (Barman, 1997/1998). The sheer variability in sexuality across Indigenous cultures was perceived as problematic. However, during the early years of colonization in Canada, sexual unions between white men and Indigenous women were common because of the relative scarcity of white women as well as the usefulness of Indigenous women's skills in trapping, languages, diplomacy, and other areas (Das Gupta, 2000; Mandell & Momirov, 2000; Razack, 2002). The Indigenous women with whom early European settlers formed relationships were called **les femmes du pays,** or "country wives" (Mandell & Momirov, 2000, p. 22). Such pragmatic concerns led the Hudson's Bay Company to not only allow but encourage these interracial relationships among employees. Even missionaries during the early years did not actively discourage the unions (Razack, 2002). However, as colonization progressed, Indigenous sexuality became one of the things that the emerging authorities felt the need to regulate: "missionaries attempted to eradicate 'devilish' practices such as polygamy and cross-dressing, and condemned the 'heathen friskiness' of the natives" (D'Emilio & Freedman, 1997, p. 6).

Changes in the social perceptions of sexual relationships between Indigenous and Euro-Canadians occurred as settlement progressed and as the fur trade was slowly replaced by agriculture as Canada's primary economic activity. Relationships between Euro-Canadian men and Indigenous women were discouraged as the population of mixed-race women, such as Métis, grew. Being of mixed ancestry, these women were perceived as more acceptable partners (Das Gupta, 2000; Mandell & Momirov, 2000). Even in Western Canada (which was settled considerably later), by the mid-nineteenth century "colonial officials and religious authorities began to fear the consequences of this widespread 'race-mixing'" (Razack, 2002, p. 52). Laws were instituted at various times in various parts of Canada as well as the rest of the Americas prohibiting white–Indigenous relationships.

However, such relationships continued in various forms. For example, during the gold rush of the mid-nineteenth century, men could form sexual relationships with Indigenous women in the many "dance halls" that were found along the west coast; outside of the dance halls, it is estimated that one in ten Indigenous women in British Columbia were cohabiting with a non-Indigenous man during this time. Although many of these relationships were consensual, some were not. Some cases of Indigenous fathers trading their daughters for gold or other resources have been documented (Barman, 1997/1998). In other cases, it is suggested that the "wild west" environment of the gold rush, where women were outnumbered by men by as much as 200:1, placed all women (and especially Indigenous women) at risk of sexual victimization; in these instances, the "choice" to cohabit with a man was less an illustration of free will and more a desire for safety (Barman, 1997/1998; Windecker, 1997).

Thus, over time, we can see Indigenous sexuality being socially typed—it was described as "hypersexualized" (Smith, 2014, p. 89), judged as being "out of control" (Smith, 2014, p. 89), and made subject to a wide range of prescriptions, including Indigenous people being taught by church fathers the "right" way to have sexual intercourse (hence the phrase "missionary position"). With such overt attempts to regulate and control Indigenous sexuality, substantial changes occurred in the sexual cultures of Indigenous societies. Many adopted the dualistic and heteronormative views of Euro-Canadian society (Newhouse, 1998). Others became desexualized, in a desire to avoid the hypersexualized stereotype (Smith, 2014). Indigenous feminist scholars and activists today argue that reclaiming their sexualities is crucial for decolonization—"We are alive, we are sexy, and some of us are queer" (Finley, cited in Smith, 2014, p. 98).

Sexual cultures are composed of dynamic and ever-changing processes, whether we are speaking of Indigenous cultures or other cultures of the world. As cultures continuously evolve and transform, so does sexuality, as we can see by looking at how the meanings and place of sexuality in the social structure have changed in the dominant culture of North America over the last few centuries. It is by looking at trans-historical changes—changes over time in a single society—that the powerful role of social processes in the creation of sexual cultures and sexual identities becomes acutely evident.

North America: The Evolution of Meanings of Sexuality

The past few hundred years have been a time of immense social change in North America. And as economic, religious, familial, scientific, and other cultural changes have occurred, sexuality has changed as well. Looking at social changes in Canadian and American history reveals that the meaning of sexuality, its place in the social order, how it is judged, and the agents of its regulation have all fluctuated over time

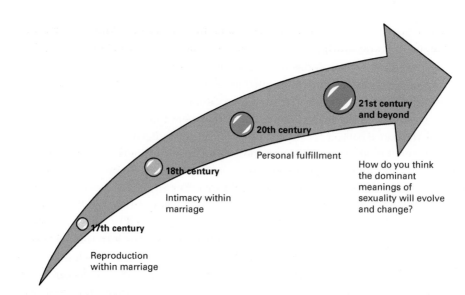

Figure 5.1 Changes in the Dominant Meaning of Sexuality

and been intertwined with assumptions about race, class, and gender, and their associated hierarchies (D'Emilio & Freedman, 1997; Valverde, 1991). Since the seventeenth century, the meaning of sexuality has transformed from being primarily associated with reproduction within a powerful structure of kinship to being primarily associated with emotional intimacy in marriage, and then to being associated with personal fulfillment for individuals (see Figure 5.1).

The seventeenth century in Canada was a time of early exploration and settlement, and economic activities revolved around the fur trade. As described previously, sexual relationships between Indigenous women and white men were common and accepted during this time, despite broad differences between Indigenous and European sexual cultures. Meanwhile, among the small number of European families who had settled in Eastern Canada, ownership of black slaves also sprang up during this era and continued until the early nineteenth century (Das Gupta, 2000). The practice of slavery was closely intertwined with the control of sexuality. Slave owners frequently determined who was permitted to mate with whom (and when) for the purposes of reproduction. Female slaves were valued in part for their reproductive capacities, and certain male slaves were selected as "studs" to impregnate these females (Das Gupta, 2000). Female slaves were also expected to be continually sexually available for male members of the owner's family. Even the sexuality of free blacks came to be socially controlled, as laws were instituted prohibiting black individuals from marrying outside their race (Das Gupta, 2000).

In the more urbanized United States, sexuality during this era was channelled into marriage for the purpose of reproduction, although some sexual activity was tolerated in courtship. Sexuality outside of the arenas of courtship and marriage was considered unacceptable, and sexuality was formally and informally controlled by the local Christian church, the courts, family, and the community. Premarital pregnancy would usually result in marriage being enforced, often at the insistence of the young woman's father. The young couple would respect the father's directive because the kinship system was considered a legitimate regulator of sexuality and reproduction.

The community was also seen as a legitimate regulator of deviance, and it was not uncommon for neighbours to report sexual improprieties to relevant family members or community and church leaders. Individuals could be excommunicated from the local church for deviant sexuality, and in some regions, certain forms of sexual deviance were considered criminal and even punishable by death. However, during this era in the United States, deviating individuals were more often seen as having made an error in judgment—it was the behaviour that was viewed as deviant rather than the person. Thus, some form of punishment for the unacceptable behaviour was dispensed so individuals could learn the error of their ways (e.g., via public whipping or sitting in the stocks) and thereby be accepted back into the family, the community, and the church.

The specific nature of the punishment dispensed depended on the social characteristics of the person involved. The higher the socioeconomic status of the sexual transgressors, the less severe their punishments. In the case of rape, upper-class men were less likely to go to trial and usually received milder penalties if they did, while more severe penalties were dispensed to lower-class men. Women and men also regularly received different types of punishment. Men, who often owned property, were more likely to be fined, while women, who did not own property, were more likely to be physically punished. Women were also more likely than men to be punished for sexual deviance such as adultery, in part because it threatened the husband's patriarchal power and could potentially undermine paternal certainty.

Racial hierarchies embedded in the social structure of the time were also reflected in colonial society's sexual culture and its definition and regulation of deviant sexuality. In many American colonies, black men convicted of raping white women (but not black women) were castrated. In contrast, white men convicted of raping either white or black women were not castrated; in fact, in most regions, it was unlikely that a white man could be considered as having "raped" a black woman.

The various ways that deviant sexuality was controlled and defined revolved around dominant meanings of sexuality during the seventeenth century, meanings that incorporated both pragmatic considerations as well as cultural ideals. In the growing Euro-Canadian and Euro-American cultures, the nature of the definition and control of sexual deviance "served the larger function of reminding the community at large that sexuality belonged in marriage [or in Canada, marriage-like relationships between European men and Indigenous women] for the purpose of producing legitimate children" (D'Emilio & Freedman, 1997, p. 28). The definition and control of sexual deviance also reinforced socioeconomic class, gender, and racial hierarchies through which society was constructed.

Near the end of the eighteenth century and throughout the nineteenth century, Canadian and American society underwent significant changes that affected the way sexuality was perceived (D'Emilio & Freedman, 1997; Valverde, 1991). Urbanization and wage labour outside of the kinship system took hold and progressed at a rapid pace, creating more anonymous lives distanced from extended family members and community surveillance. Religious shifts transferred the responsibility for salvation onto the individual, reducing the role of the church and subsequently the state as regulators of morality. Economically based and arranged marriages declined, people were more likely to be marrying for "love," and more open expression of affection emerged.

Enlightenment ideology within philosophy and science identified nature (including sexuality) as inherently good. These changes permeated the sexual culture of the time, such that the language of sexuality was no longer reproductive but based on *emotional intimacy* in marriage. The role of the church in regulating sexuality declined, as did the role of the state. The family was becoming more of an isolated unit in society, recognized as a *private* realm outside of the surveying gaze of many others. However, the role of other social control agents grew: women, the medical profession, social reformers, and culture industries (D'Emilio & Freedman, 1997; Valverde, 1991).

Women played a larger role in regulating sexuality through their efforts at reducing pregnancy rates. Previously, high infant mortality rates meant that women would have many babies to ensure that enough them survived into childhood to contribute to the maintenance of the family. During the nineteenth century, infant mortality rates declined, but perinatal and postnatal mortality rates of women did not. With the tremendous health risks associated with pregnancy and childbirth, and less need for large numbers of children, middle- and upper-class women acted to reduce pregnancy by abstaining from sex with their husbands for extended periods of time and by using contraception.

The use of contraception was aided by the medical profession, which was growing in size, knowledge, and legitimized power. The medical profession came to have a more encompassing role in the regulation of sexuality by "scientifically" defining sexual deviance (such as the "disease" of sodomy) and by conveying medical knowledge to the broader community. For example, medical knowledge at the time described the body as a closed energy system, wherein overindulgence in any activity (including sexual) could be dangerous to physical health—*self-control* became a dominant theme in the contributions of science to the sexual culture of the time.

Self-control as a means to avoid illness and energy depletion was perceived as particularly important during this era because of its relevance to commercial expansion. The "self-made man" was idealized in politics, religion, and popular culture; to achieve such success in this new industrial and capitalist economy, he had to ensure that he did not waste too much of his bodily energy elsewhere. Controlling his sexual passions would enable him to focus his energies on economic success.

The economic changes that were occurring in society now included the emergence of a powerful culture industry—newspapers, magazines, mass-produced books, and more. On one hand, the culture industry contributed to the sexual culture of the era in terms of the spread of the sex industry, such as in pornography (in the form of stories, books, drawings, burlesque shows, and early photography). But other facets of the culture industry regulated sexual deviance. For example, young women were viewed as being extremely vulnerable to the sexual appetites of unsavoury young men in growing cities. In response to this problem, poems and stories in popular publications warned young women of these dangers, and these stories frequently ended with the untimely death of the young woman who had been led astray.

The **social purity** or **sex hygiene movement** emerged, which equated social purity with sexual purity; sexuality was the heart of morality, which was defined as the cornerstone of society. Social purity activism was well established by the late 1800s in Canada, the northeast United States, and Britain and included several alcohol temperance groups, such as the Woman's Christian Temperance Union, as well as female suffragettes (Valverde, 1991). The concerns of these groups included "prostitution, divorce, illegitimacy, 'Indian and Chinese [male immigrants],' public education, suppression of obscene literature, prevention (of prostitution) and rescue of fallen women, and shelters for women and children" (Valverde, 1991, p. 17). Social

Cyril Jessop/Library and Archives Canada.

Nellie McClung was a suffragette, and also a member of the Woman's Christian Temperance Union.

purity efforts were directed particularly at the lower classes which, by simply being lower class, were presumed to be sexually depraved as well.

The specific ways in which sexual deviance was defined and regulated depended on social characteristics, just as it had in earlier eras. Racial ideologies continued to infuse sexual culture. In the media, black men's sexuality was portrayed as dangerous and uncontrollable, making them liable to rape white women. Chinese men, brought to Canada as labourers to build the railway, were also perceived as a threat to young white women, who might be easily lured by what was perceived as the men's more innocent countenance and by the opium they might supply. It was thought that opium had strong sexual qualities, which would result in "the amazing phenomenon of an educated gentlewoman, reared in a refined atmosphere, consorting with the lowest classes of yellow and black men" (Emily Murphy, cited in Valverde, 1991, p. 184). In the early twentieth century such attitudes would serve as a rationale for the efforts of Emily Murphy (the first female judge in the British Empire and a leading Canadian suffragist) to regulate immigration (Valverde, 1991).

The nineteenth century, then, brought considerable transformation to Western sexual culture. The meaning of sexuality changed, and responsibility for controlling sexual deviance shifted to individuals and their own self-control. The role of the state in regulating sexual deviance declined somewhat in the early part of the nineteenth century. However, as moral entrepreneurs identified and drew attention to sexual "diseases" (e.g., sodomy, homosexuality), the sex industry, and female sexual exploitation, the state's role in controlling sexual deviance and regulating morality grew once again.

With the dawn of the twentieth century, the sexual culture of North American society continued to transform. The dominant meaning of sexuality eventually shifted from a focus on emotional intimacy in marriage to a focus on *personal fulfillment* regardless of marriage (D'Emilio & Freedman, 1997). In other words, sexual activity came to be accepted not only in marriage but also in courtship, casual dating, and even much briefer relationships. Sexuality continues to be controlled in many arenas, including the criminal justice system and the culture industry. In the realm of criminal justice, criminal codes regulate sexual deviance by criminalizing certain aspects of sexuality, such as sexual assault and public indecency.

The culture industry grew rapidly during the twentieth century to become the dominant force it is today. Today, the culture industry, through the sex industry and integration of sexuality into mainstream media (television, movies, music, advertising, etc.), is perhaps

Ask Yourself

Reflecting on what you have learned about the way sexuality was socially constructed in Canadian and American culture during the nineteenth century and into the early twentieth century, consider the following questions: Who was doing the social typing of deviant sexuality? What was the foundation for their arguments—that is, did they type certain sexual behaviours as deviant because they thought those behaviours violated norms, engendered a negative societal reaction, or were statistically rare or harmful? What role did the structure of power in society play? Which groups of people benefitted the most from the social typing that was occurring?

the predominant contributor to sexual culture. At the same time, moral entrepreneurs and special interest groups also use the media as a tool for communicating their positions in the deviance dance. For example, public service campaigns promote "safer sex" in magazines, the pharmaceutical industry creates television commercials for the drug Viagra, and gay rights organizations send out press releases about their organizations' activities.

Exercise Your Mind

For this exercise, watch television, go to the movie theatre, or rent a movie. And yes, you can tell everyone that you are doing this as an exercise for your deviance class. Spending a night watching television or movies is a good way to see the role played by the culture industry in the way sexuality is socially constructed in modern society. As you watch these television shows or movies, think about the broader sexual culture involved. What are these shows or movies saying about sexuality? What meanings of sexuality are they communicating to the audience? What is "acceptable" and "deviant" sexuality according to whatever shows or movies you are watching? Are there conflicting or opposing messages about sexuality being conveyed?

You may want to rent some movies or watch reruns from different time periods to see the ways in which the sexual culture has changed or stayed the same. Movies you might want to choose from include *Gone with the Wind* (1939), *The Philadelphia Story* (1940), *The Graduate* (1967), *Animal House* (1978), *Porky's* (1982), *American Pie* (1999), and *Sausage Party* (2016). Easily found television shows from different eras include *I Love Lucy*, *M*A*S*H*, *Seinfeld*, *Two and a Half Men*, and *How to Get Away with Murder*.

If you have engaged in the *Exercise Your Mind* activity, you now have some additional insight into the media as one facet of sexual culture and into how, even when focusing solely on mass media, there have been considerable changes in the way sexuality has been socially constructed over the past several decades. The way that sexuality is constructed has a tremendous impact on how we, as people living in each society at a precise moment in history, think and act, and how we are treated by others in terms of sexuality. The last few centuries have been characterized by changes in the dominant meanings of sexuality, and as broader social and cultural forces continue to change, our dominant meanings of sexuality will continue to evolve as well. This realization brings us to the present moment and the sexual culture of *our* time. In the following sections of the chapter, we will more closely examine the sexual culture of contemporary Canadian society.

Learning Objective 1

■ How was sexuality embedded in Indigenous views of life, and how did that contrast with the Euro-Canadian view of sexuality?

■ What role did the social control of Indigenous peoples' sexualities play in the project of colonization?

Learning Objective 2

■ How have the dominant meanings of sexuality changed in North America since the seventeenth century, and how has sexual regulation change during that time?

■ How were the meanings of sexuality and its regulation integrated with hierarchies of race, class, and gender from the seventeenth century onward?

Sexual Culture Today

If you participated in the *Exercise Your Mind* activity, you spent some time watching television or movies to learn something about sexuality in contemporary society. In watching television or movies, you observed the construction of deviance and normality in those arenas—what is considered acceptable, what is considered deviant, and what happens to those who are deviant. These are precisely the issues we will direct our attention to in this section of the chapter. We will explore some of the criteria by which sexual deviance and normality are determined in the sexual culture of our time, and some of the contrasting viewpoints in this deviance dance.

Criteria for Determining Deviance

Ask Yourself

How can you determine whether someone's sexuality is "deviant" or "normal"? Make a list of the criteria that you use when you make judgments about other people's sexuality or your own.

A closer look at our contemporary sexual culture reveals several criteria that are used to evaluate sexuality as either "deviant" or "normal." Dimensions that have been explored by other deviance specialists include the degree of consent, nature of the sexual partner, nature of the sexual act, setting, frequency, time, age, and number of partners (Goode, 1997; Wheeler, 1960). We will explore consent, nature of the partner, and nature of the act as core criteria by which we determine "deviant" sexuality, and setting and frequency as two of the more peripheral criteria.

Consent

One criterion we use to determine sexual deviance is that of **consent** (Goode, 1997; Wheeler, 1960), and some researchers (e.g., Mackay, 2000) use the concept of consent as the defining characteristic of "normal" sex. Although the notion of consent is commonly used within legal and social discourses, conceptually there is some disagreement regarding how consent can be defined (Beres, 2007). Is "consent" an attitude (based on the intention to engage in certain sexual activities)? If that is the case, then determining whether consent is present in a situation requires access to a person's thoughts and state of mind. Or is it a behaviour (based on actions)? If that is the case, then determining whether consent is present in a certain situation requires comparing actions that have (or have not) occurred to some type of agreed-upon list of precise behaviours that constitute "consent." Is consent implied by the absence of "no," or is it only present if "yes" is explicitly expressed?

Despite different conceptions of how consent is defined, there is some consensus that at its broadest level, "consent represents some form of agreement to engage in sexual activity" (Beres, 2007, p. 97). Is consent involved in the sexual act in question? Is it even possible for consent to be involved in this act? The most obvious use of this criterion is by the criminal justice system in cases of sexual assault; if there is no consent involved, then the act is a criminal one, making it necessarily deviant.

In fact, the complete lack of consent leads many people to interpret sexual assault as an act of violence rather than a sexual act. In court cases involving "date rape"—that is, a victim sexually assaulted by a date—the issue of consent is usually central to the case. The defence attorney will argue that the victim did consent, or at least that the defendant reasonably thought that consent had been given, and the prosecutor will argue that the victim did not consent. In the courtroom, the way date rape cases are argued elicits the question of whose story is more believable—the defendant's or the victim's.

The question of whether it is possible for consent to be involved is another aspect of this criterion for judging sexual deviance. Beginning in the late 1990s, the use of **date rape drugs** escalated. These drugs, such as Rohypnol (also known as "roofies" or "roopies") and GHB (also known as "G" or "Liquid X"), are odourless and tasteless, and when mixed with alcohol cause intense drowsiness and memory impairment. If one of these drugs is slipped into someone's drink, that person will not know it is there and may not be able to remember anything that happens in the ensuing hours. These drugs are referred to as "date rape drugs" because they have been used to have sex with someone without consent.

Because of the effects of these drugs, they have been labelled as dangerous, and formal and informal regulation has emerged. It is likely that the student services organization at your university has had campaigns to raise people's awareness of these drugs and the way they are used. For example, you may have seen posters displayed on your campus that provide information about how to avoid being a victim. When you and friends go to bars or nightclubs, perhaps you do not accept drinks being brought to you by anyone other than the bar server. The legal system has determined that having sex with someone after giving them these drugs constitutes sexual assault, arguing that in these situations the person is not in a state of mind where giving consent is possible.

Courts have also argued that consent is not possible in situations involving sexual acts between children and adults. Due to the level of cognitive development as well as significant power differentials, a child is not considered capable of giving consent, especially to an adult. Thus, sexual acts between children and adults are defined as crimes on the part of the adult. You can see a description of Canada's age-of-consent laws—and their complexities—in Box 5.1.

What is the age of consent for sexual activity in Canada? The answer to that question is not as straightforward as one might initially think. Canada's age-of-consent laws are multifaceted and complex. Under current legislation, the laws governing sexual behaviour, in which age of consent is an issue, are as follows:

Sexual Assault: A common defence in sexual assault trials is that the accused believed there was consent involved in the sexual activity. However, if the complainant is under the age of 16, the accused cannot make the claim of consent; consent is perceived as not being possible in that instance.

Sexual Interference: This is a crime defined by the sexual touching of a body of someone under the age of 16. The lack of the possibility of consent is what defines this crime.

Invitation to Sexual Touching: This is a crime defined by requesting someone under the age of 16 to sexually touch the accused. Again, the lack of the possibility of consent is what defines this crime.

The above age-of-consent laws are further complicated by the question of the age of the accused. That is, consent

is considered possible regarding the above behaviours if the complainant is 12 or 13, if the accused is no more than two years older than the complainant, *and* if the relationship is not one of trust, authority, dependency, or exploitation. Consent is also considered possible if the complainant is 14 or 15, if the accused is less than five years older, and the relationship is not one of trust, authority, dependency, or exploitation. In these instances, legislation prevents the criminalization of sexual activity between youth of similar ages who are in a dating relationship.

Bestiality in the Presence of a Child: Bestiality (sexual activity with an animal) is itself a crime. However, committing an act of bestiality in front of a child under the age of 16, or inciting a child under the age of 16 to commit an act of bestiality, is a specific subsection of that same law.

Sexual Exploitation: Although the age of 16 is highlighted in the age-of-consent laws described above, sexual exploitation involves sexually touching (or inviting sexual touching from) someone under the age of 18 if there is a relationship of trust, authority, dependency, or exploitation.

Although sexual interaction between adults and children is necessarily deviant because it is forbidden by the *Criminal Code*, social characteristics of the child and the adult may play a role in public perceptions of deviance or normality. The age of the child and the age of the adult may influence public perceptions of whether consent is possible. For example, an 8-year-old may be perceived as much less capable of giving consent than a 13-year-old. And if a 13-year-old is having sex with her 16-year-old boyfriend, in contrast to her 37-year-old boyfriend, the public may view it as a consensual relationship (even if they disapprove of 13-year-olds being sexually active in general). The interaction of gender with age may affect public perceptions of deviance or normality as well. That is, teenage boys are often seen as being more capable of giving consent to adults than teenage girls are. In part, this is because males tend to be perceived as sexual aggressors, while females tend to be viewed as objects of (male) sexual attention—perceptions that are perpetuated and reinforced in a variety of ways, including the framing of women and men in the media (Goffman, 1979; Jhally, 2009; Macnamara, 2006).

Issues of consent are perceived differently across place and time. Although "no means no" even within marriage in Canadian society, in many countries consent is not considered necessary between husband and wife; sexual relations are prescribed as required in the marital relationship. In fact, it was only in 1983 that the Canadian legal system defined sexual assault as being possible in marriage. Similarly, it was only in 1987 that our legal system made sexual assault laws gender-neutral, recognizing that it is possible for a man to be raped by either another man or a woman (Nelson & Robinson, 2002); many societies today continue to define the crime of sexual assault only in terms of a male perpetrator and a female victim.

In the historical section of this chapter, we saw that from the seventeenth century through most of the nineteenth century, black women were expected to be sexually available to white men (Das Gupta, 2000; D'Emilio & Freedman, 1997; Mandell & Momirov, 2000). Because of this expectation, white men were unlikely to be charged with raping black women if there was no consent. In fact, if the black woman was a slave and the white man a member of the slave-owner's family, then consent was a non-issue because she was considered a piece of the family's property, to do with as they pleased.

Today, divergent points of view exist even on the issue of the age at which consent is possible, not only across cultures but within North America itself. The North American Man/Boy Love Association (NAMBLA) argues that teenagers can give consent in sexual relationships with adults, and some members of NAMBLA suggest that even younger children can give consent (NAMBLA, n.d.). Of course, as you may have expected, tremendous opposition exists to NAMBLA's message and to the organization itself. Afraid of being associated with this organization, gay rights organizations have been especially vocal in their opposition, "deploring NAMBLA and everything it advocates which basically amounts to a push to legitimize child molestation," and arguing that the organization "has no legitimate place in society, Queer or Straight" (NAMBLA Controversy, n.d.). Obviously, the debate over age-of-consent laws is a highly contentious one. By challenging one of society's most firmly held beliefs, members of organizations like NAMBLA have been socially typed as deviant—they are described as "pedophiles," evaluated in an extremely negative light, and face intense public opposition (as well as criminalization if they violate age-of-consent laws).

Nature of the Sexual Partner

The historical and cross-cultural variations that were presented earlier in this chapter pointed to the role that the **nature of the sexual partner** plays in determining sexual deviance. In Athens during the fifth century BCE, acceptable sexual partners for aristocratic men included wives, prostitutes, slaves, foreigners, and adolescent males, while men of equal social status were defined as inappropriate sexual partners. In the dominant Europeanized culture of North America from the seventeenth century onward, marriage gradually lost its monopoly as the only legitimate outlet for sexual behaviour, and a wider range of sexual partners came to be deemed appropriate. However, despite this transition to more freedom in the selection of a sexual partner, there still is not *complete* freedom in the choice of a sexual partner in contemporary North America.

Beginning with the law, we can see certain people being defined as unacceptable sexual partners. We already addressed the issue of age-of-consent laws, making individuals who are under the age of consent inappropriate sexual partners. The *Criminal Code* also prohibits sexual relationships between close family members—parents, children, grandparents, grandchildren, siblings, and half-siblings. Violating this prohibition between close family members constitutes the crime of *incest*. Bestiality is a crime in Canada, making animals unacceptable sexual partners. Finally, several sexual laws in the *Criminal Code* (such as "sexual exploitation") define anyone over whom the individual is in a position of trust or authority as an inappropriate sexual partner, or anyone who is in a relationship of dependency with the individual.

The nature of the sexual partner is also controlled outside the legal system. The choice of sexual partners is formally regulated in some places of business, where company policies may prohibit intimate relationships between bosses and employees or between co-workers. Some universities prohibit sexual relationships between professors and students. Within the psychiatric and psychological communities, professional organizations define sexual relationships between therapists and clients as a violation of the professional code of ethics. Additionally, if the sexual partner in question is not a person but an object that is necessary for sexual stimulation to occur, the psychiatric community labels the sexual activity a *fetish*, for which treatment can be obtained.

At an informal level, certain sexual partners may be perceived as socially unacceptable. For example, although the law does not prohibit sexual relations between first cousins, such relations would still push the boundaries of social acceptability (although, in other cultures, it is quite common for marriages to be arranged between first cousins).

And even though many universities do not have policies prohibiting intimate relationships between students and professors, within the cultural climates of those institutions professors who engage in such relationships may still be stigmatized.

At both formal and informal levels, members of the same sex continue to be defined as inappropriate sexual partners to some extent. In 1967, Everett Klippert was sentenced to an indefinite prison term as a dangerous sex offender for having admitted that he was gay, thereby becoming the last person convicted of such a crime in Canada. There have been significant changes in social attitudes regarding homosexuality over the past several decades because of social activism and education, and these changes have increased individual freedom to choose a member of the same sex as a sexual partner.

Philip Scalia/Alamy Stock Photo

The Stonewall Inn, in Greenwich Village, New York City.

In large part, these changes stem from the Stonewall riots in New York's Greenwich Village in 1969, an event that heralded the beginning of the modern gay rights movement. In the early morning hours of June 28, police conducted yet another raid of a gay bar, this one located in the Stonewall Inn. But this time, instead of quietly accepting it, the patrons fought back with several days of riots and protests in the streets of Greenwich Village. The Stonewall Inn was declared a National Historic Landmark in 2000.

During the same year as the Stonewall riots, the Canadian government decriminalized same-sex sexual activities between consenting adults. Then Justice Minister Pierre Trudeau (who would later become prime minister) stated that "There's no place for the state in the bedrooms of the nation" (*CBC News*, 2012). Three years later, homosexuality was removed from the *Diagnostic and Statistical Manual of Mental Disorders*.

Despite the changes that were occurring at that time, the Canadian federal government was still trying to purge homosexuals from the public service, based on the belief that homosexuals had psychological characteristics that made them more vulnerable to Communist influence (Kinsman & Gentile, 2009). Over a period of 30 years (and extending into the 1980s), suspected homosexuals in the public service underwent interrogation, surveillance, and illegal searches by the RCMP. They were tested using a machine that tracked heart rate, eye movements, and sweat reactions while they were shown a series of sexually explicit photos of someone of the same sex. Confessing their sexual orientation was not sufficient; they were also expected to provide a list of names of other homosexuals with whom they associated. Groups that were a part of the gay rights movement were also subjected to RCMP surveillance and later raids throughout the early 1980s.

The continued efforts of LGBTQ (Lesbian, Gay, Bisexual, Transgendered, and Queer) movements have created some significant changes since that time. In 1996, Parliament voted to add sexual orientation to the *Canadian Human Rights Act*. Same-sex common-law couples began to receive the same benefits as opposite-sex common-law couples in 2000, and same-sex couples gained the right to legally marry across Canada in 2005 (*CBC News*, 2007). And in 2016, Prime Minister Justin Trudeau announced that Everett Klippert would be posthumously granted a pardon (*CBC News*, 2016a). However, despite some changes in prevailing social attitudes, gays and lesbians continue to be deviantized in many ways because of the nature of their sexual partners. Of course, the stigmatization experienced by gays and lesbians in Canada may not be as formal as in some other cultures around the world, where homosexuality continues to be criminalized, and may even be punishable by death. But even in the United States, the formal struggles for LGBTQ individuals are ongoing. When same-sex marriage was legalized in that country in 2015, it engendered considerable resistance. More than 20 states implemented a variety of anti-LGBTQ laws, including refusal of service laws (which enable private business owners to refuse service to LGBTQ persons) (Powers, 2016).

In the informal realm of everyday interaction, stigmatization is evident as well. LGBTQ individuals are at greater risk of criminal victimization than the general population and may be subjected to hate crimes in particular. In Canada, approximately 12 percent of all police-reported hate crimes are committed on the basis of sexual orientation, placing it in the top three motivations for hate crimes, following race/ethnicity and religion (Statistics Canada, 2016c). Hate crimes based on sexual orientation are far more likely to be violent in nature compared to hate crimes based on other characteristics (Allen, 2015).

The consequences of stigmatization can be especially severe for LGBTQ youth. LGBTQ students report that they hear anti-gay comments or experience name calling an average of 26 times a day. More than one-quarter are told by their parents to leave home, and as a result LGBTQ youth are at greater risk of becoming homeless (PFLAG Canada, n.d.). They are more likely to be bullied, and in the Internet age bullying is not limited to school but follows them home as well, on their smartphones, in their

Box 5.2

Providing Support Online

New media provide expanded opportunities for stigmatizing LGBTQ youth, such as through cyberbullying. But new media also provide opportunities to resist stigmatization and its potential consequences. Online communities of similar others provide an interactive support network. "Justleftthe-closet" is "a social network, a safe place, and a family for LGBTQ youth and their friends" that can be accessed as a website, or on Facebook and Twitter. Formal and informal YouTube campaigns provide emotional support as well. The "It Gets Better Project" features videos from people from all walks of life (from a young man living in Toronto to well-known celebrities), telling LGBTQ youth that life can get better for them, and suggesting ways to make their own lives better. Several organizations provide a variety of resources online as well. In the United States, "The Trevor Project" was established specifically to provide crisis intervention for suicidal LGBTQ youth. Its website offers resources and a special suicide hotline. PFLAG Canada's website provides information for LGBTQ youth, family members, friends, and educators. It includes a series of video clips featuring LGBTQ individuals of all ages and ethnicities, parents of LGBTQ children, and children being raised by same-sex parents; there is a link for visitors of the site who would like to be chosen to tell their own story in a video clip.

emails, and on their Facebook pages. Stigmatization by strangers, family members, and peers can take its toll. According to PFLAG Canada (n.d.), 43 percent of transgender youth attempt suicide and almost one-third of youth suicides are among those who are LGBTQ. The problem of suicide among LGBTQ youth has resulted in multifaceted efforts to intervene (see Box 5.2).

Overall, Western cultures are characterized by considerably more freedom in the choice of sexual partners today than in the past. However, freedom is not unlimited. The choice of sexual partners is still regulated by the law and other formal processes, as well as informal means like social stigmatization. The nature of the sexual partner is an important criterion in our evaluations of people's sexuality as either deviant or normal (Goode, 1997; Wheeler, 1960). However, even if the sexual partner is considered acceptable and "normal," other criteria become involved in our evaluations as well, such as the nature of the sexual act.

Nature of the Sexual Act

Even if your choice of sexual partner is defined as normal and acceptable, is what you are doing with that partner considered "kinky"? That is, are you engaging in sexual acts that are perceived as acceptable or unacceptable? The answer to that question is both culturally and historically specific and at times can also be tied in with the nature of the partner. For example, following European colonization of the Americas, sexual intercourse between husbands and wives was the only acceptable sexual act and only if in the "missionary" position.

Even over the last century there have been significant changes in the way that sexual acts are perceived as being "deviant" or "normal." For example, in Chapter 1 there was a discussion of the extreme measures taken in the early twentieth century to prevent masturbation in children based on medical discourses of the time, which claimed there was a wide range of physical, mental, and social harms as consequences of masturbation. Now, in the twenty-first century, the same stigma is no longer attached to masturbation. The growing sexual freedom of the last century has allowed a range of sexual acts to be seen as more acceptable. Walk into any bookstore or public library and you will find books that present information on various sexual positions to try and techniques to use. Retail stores (both online and offline) that sell a variety of "sex toys" to incorporate into sexual acts abound, and some sex toys can even be found in your local drug store.

Due to the rapid growth in sexual freedom over the last century, greater subjectivity has emerged in precisely which sexual acts are perceived as "kinky." In other words, what is considered a sexually deviant act is now more in the eye of the beholder than was true in the past. Our sexual culture has come to be infused with an ideology of privacy; if a sexual activity is performed by consenting adults outside the view of others, we define it as being nobody else's business. And although each of us individually might perceive certain sexual acts as "kinky," the ideology of privacy limits contemporary social controls on sexual behaviours, particularly at a formal level. Just as Pierre Trudeau suggested that the government had no place in the bedrooms of adult Canadians, today we also think that none of us as individuals has a place in the bedrooms of others.

The issue of consent, the nature of the sexual partner, and the **nature of the sexual act** are three of the core criteria by which we evaluate sexuality and subsequently judge it as either deviant or normal. In addition to these three core criteria, there are also a few more peripheral criteria that are used for judgment in contemporary sexual culture (Goode, 1997). For example, sexual activities in certain locations are considered deviant.

An episode of the TV show *Seinfeld* highlights the issue of location in determining deviance. In this episode, George Costanza has a sexual encounter with the cleaning lady in his office cubicle. The next day he is called into his boss's office and fired for that encounter, despite his protests that he had never been warned that the company frowned upon having sex in the office. This *Seinfeld* episode points out that the workplace is an inappropriate setting for sexual activity. In Canada, the law defines certain locations (i.e., public places) as unacceptable for sexual activities. People who enjoy having sex in places where others might see them are labelled **exhibitionists**.

The frequency of sex is another one of the more peripheral criteria used to evaluate sexuality. Is someone having sex too often, not often enough, or just the right amount? Those who have sex too frequently may be labelled "nymphomaniacs" or may even be diagnosed with a sexual "addiction." In the recent past, people who had sex too infrequently were often perceived as "frigid." However, in the twenty-first century infrequent sexual activity may be considered a sexual dysfunction. Individuals who identify as asexual (that is, as not having sexual feelings or desires) are "at best viewed as a puzzling aberration," but also sometimes as sexuality-not-yet-emerged or even as pathological (Scott & Dawson, 2015, p. 3).

Contemporary society is one in which sexuality has become highly medicalized (and commercialized). Drugs like Viagra, which were initially marketed to aging men with erectile dysfunction, are now used by increasingly younger men as part of a demonstration of sexual prowess and masculinity (Marshall, 2006; Tiefer, 2006). Low sexual desire in women is now being similarly medicalized, and its solution is found not in changing relationships and gendered responsibilities, but rather in the search to develop the "Pink Viagra" (Marshall, 2006, p. 287). And in the world of email spam, pills, lotions, and gels designed for improved sexual performance are common. In our current "Viagra culture" (Potts & Tiefer, 2006, p. 267), where sexual desire (for women) and sexual prowess (for men) are essential components of the discourses of sexuality, masculinity, and femininity, frequency has assumed a whole new level of importance.

Discussions of frequency, location, nature of the act, nature of the partner, and the issue of consent point to both the increasing freedom that has come to characterize our sexual culture and the formal and informal limitations that continue to be placed on that freedom. As a society, we perceive a narrower range of behaviours as sexually deviant than we did in the past, but using various criteria sexual deviance continues to be defined, identified, and controlled. However, the processes of defining, identifying, and controlling sexual deviance are not uniform; they are part of the "deviance dance."

TIME TO REVIEW

Learning Objective 3

- What roles do *consent*, *nature of the partner*, *nature of the act*, *location*, and *frequency* play in our perceptions of deviant and normal sexuality?

- How do perceptions of *consent* vary based on marital status, gender, race, and age?

- How was the gay rights movement affected by the Stonewall riots?

- How were homosexuals treated by the federal government from the 1950s through the 1980s?

- In what ways have individuals of the same sex come to be seen as more acceptable sexual partners? In what ways do they continue to be perceived as unacceptable sexual partners?

- What role do new media play in stigmatizing LGBTQ youth but also in helping them resist stigmatization?

Sexuality and the "Deviance Dance"

In any given culture at any time in history, certain trends or characteristics can be identified in sexual culture. However, a multiplicity of perceptions, reactions, and social controls are also intertwined with those broader trends. Sexual relationships between aristocratic adult and adolescent males, although common in fifth-century BCE Athens, were not uniformly accepted. Segments of Athenian society were critical of such relationships, and often sought to initiate levels of control for the purposes of protecting these "exploited" adolescent males (Bloch, 2001). The discussion of Canadian and American history presented earlier in this chapter captured some of the diversity entwined within sexual culture, wherein class, race, and gender variations were central to the ways that sexuality was constructed and controlled. During the Victorian era, considerable restrictions on sexual behaviour were countered with the expansion of the sex industry—photographs, books, and sexually oriented live performances (D'Emilio & Freedman, 1997; Ullman, 1997).

In contemporary North America, considerable debate exists over many aspects of sexual culture. The large numbers of shops selling sexual "toys" coexist with organizations that condemn TV programs that include explicit sexual references, such as to masturbation, oral sex, and partial nudity (Parents Television Council, 2017). LGBTQ activist groups and changing human rights legislation coexist with segments of society that continue to stigmatize and condemn homosexual practices. Widespread efforts to eliminate the sexual abuse and exploitation of children even coexist with organizations trying to place limits on those controls, like NAMBLA. Many of the debates surrounding sexuality revolve around issues related to the sex trade, such as exotic dancing, pornography, and prostitution.

Exotic Dancing

Exotic dancing has a long history in North America, with burlesque shows and other forms of "stripping" going back centuries. However, after a period of stagnancy, exotic dancing has gained in popularity over the last decade. This trend has contributed to a rapidly growing body of research, which explores the meanings that dancers attribute to their experiences and the structures of power that underlies those experiences.

There are ongoing debates between radical feminist and sex-radical feminist perspectives: "The former views all sex work as being exploitative of women within the patriarchal structure in which we operate as a society, often taking a view of the sex worker as a *victim*; the latter views sex work as subversive of this structure and maintains that the decision to participate in sex work is a choice that women make, and that they further exercise their agency through the individual negotiations that occur within that context" (Morrow, 2012, pp. 359–360). Some research does find support for the victimization hypothesis: substance abuse, life histories of physical/sexual/emotional abuse, low self-esteem, and backgrounds characterized by risky sexual behaviours are common among exotic dancers (Mestemacher & Roberti, 2004). Furthermore, many women enter the occupation because of financial desperation (Sloan & Wahab, 2004; Wesely, 2003). However, research is somewhat contradictory. In a comparison of female exotic dancers and university students, Pedersen, Champion, Hesse, and Lewis (2015) find that although there are differences in attitudes toward sex and responsible sexual practices, there are no significant differences in personality measures or self-esteem.

Other researchers go beyond the victimization debate and instead explore the everyday experiences of women—and men—involved in the industry. Sloan and Wahab (2004) find that a "continuum of work and life experience" (p. 19) is characteristic of the exotic dancing subculture. They describe four different types of female exotic dancers. First, there are **survivors**, who have extensive histories of childhood abuse and who felt forced into the industry because of few available alternatives. Second, there are **nonconformists**, rebels who come from privileged, educated backgrounds and who have the freedom to enter and leave the industry as they wish. When dancing is no longer "fun," they change careers (by going to medical school, for example). Third, there are **dancers** who have considerable training in dance and who enjoy the artistic and creative expression of the industry. Finally, there are **workers**, women primarily from working-class backgrounds who become exotic dancers because of the money they can earn.

Regardless of the type of exotic dancer, all dancers must negotiate relationships with customers, as well as their own identities, within a structure of power inside the industry. That structure of power is multifaceted, existing at the individual, organizational, and institutional levels (Deshotels, Tinney, & Forsyth, 2012). At the individual level, power manifests itself in the interactions between dancers and customers. The dancers are objects of the customers' desire and must embody the fantasies that brought the customers into the club. That is, the dancers must be whatever or whomever the customers want them to be because their job is to make the customers stay in the club and spend money on drinks. As one dancer says, there are times when she wants to say to the customer, "shit I don't wear these heels at home! I am a regular girl. I wear flannel pajamas and you are ugly!" (Egan, 2003, p. 113).

Even though in some ways the dancers appear to be subjected to the power of customers, they are also active agents of their own power. They perceive their male customers as "lonely and . . . want[ing] somebody to make them feel better" (Egan, 2003, p. 114). The women use their bodies to manipulate customers and earn more money, creating a fantasy relationship based on "counterfeit intimacy" (Mestemacher & Roberti, 2004, p. 49)—an approach that is reinforced by their managers (Stone, 2014). For example, in the fantasy relationship they create, they may secretly "confess" to a customer what their "real" names and life stories are—however, it is all a lie designed to "hook a regular customer" and "keep him coming back" (Egan, 2003, p. 112). Part of the image that dancers create is that of the customer being in control of the interaction (Morrow, 2012).

As dancers negotiate relationships with customers, they must make decisions about personal boundaries—what they will and will not do for money (Kaufman, 2009; Wesely, 2003). Give a lap dance? Go to a private room? Leave the club with a customer if enough money is offered? Dancers' boundaries frequently change over time as they become more embedded in the industry (Wesely, 2003). As the boundaries change and become more flexible, many dancers end up feeling violated, not by customers but by themselves; the gap grows between their *ideal selves* (who they want to be) and their *perceived selves* (who they see themselves as being currently) (Wesely, 2003). Thus, some dancers talk about loosening boundaries in both their work lives and personal lives through exhibitionism and promiscuity: "You've given yourself up to so many situations, it really doesn't matter anymore" (p. 498). One dancer says, "About a year and a half into it, it was hard to separate the stage Julie from the real-life Julie" (p. 499). Others speak of becoming numb and losing their sense of self over time: "There is no real identity there" (p. 500).

On the other hand, Scull (2015) reports that working in the industry can also have positive effects on dancers' self-concepts and self-esteem. Through the process of the looking-glass self (which you learned about in Chapter 3), customers become the lens through which dancers view themselves—in this case, a lens of sexualization, objectification, and/or admiration. Because women are sexualized and objectified in numerous ways in society, women who dance for men (WDM) are faced with further objectification, which can lower their self-esteem and contribute to more fragile self-concepts. But with men who dance for women (MDW), the situation is somewhat different. The exotic dancing industry is one of the few arenas where their bodies are sexualized. Consequently, MDW often report that they feel admired more than objectified—"it's like being a rock star for three hours" (p. 897). This brings with it greater confidence in other areas of life, and higher levels of self-esteem. In fact, many MDW say that although they entered the industry for financial reasons, they remain in the industry because of the way it makes them feel about themselves.

The interactions between dancers and customers within the individual level of the power structure take place within a larger context of the organizational level of the power structure. The organizational level comprises the rules governing customer and dancer behaviour, such as customers being prohibited from touching dancers and dancers having to share tips with servers, bouncers, and bartenders. At first glance, it appears that the clubs' rules exert control over the dancers' actions. However, Deshotels and Forsyth (2008) have found that dancers use the rules to their advantage to make more money and protect themselves. By giving extra tips to the bartender, the dancer receives information about which customers are the big spenders based on how many (and what brand of) drinks they have ordered. The bartender will then also make stronger drinks for those customers, loosening their inhibitions and their wallets. Separate rooms provide a venue for possible rule breaking, and an extra tip to the bouncer in the room makes him look the other way. The stricter the rules governing dancer–customer interactions, the more the dancer can charge a customer for prohibited behaviours. At the same time, dancers can enforce the rules when they wish, if they have made a choice to not give private dances as part of their job, if they don't like a certain customer, or if the customer is not spending enough money. Thus, the "rules of exotic dancing establishments, although regulating behavior at the meso/organizational level, also allow individual [dancers] to control customers, as well as raise their income by supplying forbidden behavior" (Deshotels & Forsyth, 2008, p. 485).

Individual power relations take place within the context of organizational power. Yet both exist within the larger context of institutional power. The exotic dancing industry is affected by the structure of contemporary capitalism and, for female dancers, by cultural ideals of female beauty. Sociologist Max Weber (1946) claimed that in the twentieth century, capitalism became characterized by rationalization. Ritzer (2006) suggests that this is particularly evident in the routinization of activities. He refers to this as the **McDonaldization of society**, which consists of four components: efficiency, predictability, control, and calculability. These four characteristics govern all industries, including the exotic dancing industry. In an analysis of female exotic dancers, Deshotels, Tinney, and Forsyth (2012) find that dancers make efficient use of their time, trying to interact with as many customers as possible during a shift. As one dancer notes, "I realized early on to watch for the cues to see when I had maxed out his wallet" (p. 143). Predictability is reflected in "product specification" (p. 143), where a specific standard of beauty is applied in hiring dancers. The more elite the club, the higher the standard of beauty, with the ideal being "what you would see in *Playboy* magazine" (p. 143). That standard of beauty is enhanced (and enforced) through control by the club owner or manager and the dancer herself—wearing extremely high heels to make the legs look longer, shaving all body hair, and using camouflaging body makeup to hide imperfections. Plastic surgery (e.g., breast implants, buttock implants) is encouraged and sometimes even financially supported by club owners. Control is also evident in the standard set of "characters" that dancers dress as (e.g., schoolgirl), their dance moves, and the lines they use with customers to get more money. Finally, calculability emerges in the dancers' song selection and timing. When on the main stage, dancers select songs of a certain length, just long enough to tease the customers and make them want more (and thereby be willing to pay for a private dance).

Female exotic dancers are active agents of power at the individual and organizational levels. However, their power at those levels is dependent on the extent to which they reproduce dominant ideals of female beauty for the pleasure of male customers within the context of contemporary capitalism—what Deshotels and colleagues (2012) call "McSexy" (p. 140). At the institutional level, dancers' power is also influenced by the nature of ownership within the industry (see Box 5.3).

Are exotic dancers exploited through a patriarchal structure, as radical feminists suggest? In some ways, it appears they are. Are they agents of choice and power within their everyday lives as workers? In other ways, it appears they are. The deviance dance surrounding the issue of exotic dancing is extremely complex.

Box 5.3

Organized Crime and Human Trafficking

The structure of ownership of exotic dancing clubs is an additional dimension of the institutional level of power. The clear majority of clubs build their business around a specific form of exotic dancing —women dancing for male customers. Many (if not most) exotic dancing clubs in Canada are not owned by individual entrepreneurs, but rather by units of organized crime. Historically, the clubs were typically owned by motorcycle gangs, such as the Hells Angels or the Outlaws. Although this continues to be the case in some regions of Canada, a growing proportion of exotic dancing clubs are now controlled by the Russian mafia, various organized crime syndicates originating in countries that used to be part of the Soviet Union. The Russian mafia is known to be involved in **human trafficking** (illegal trade in human beings for the purposes of sexual exploitation, forced labour, or slavery), among other criminal activities. Consequently, a concern arose that some temporary foreign workers employed as exotic dancers may be victims of human trafficking by organized crime syndicates.

Thus, the federal government enacted a National Action Plan to Combat Human Trafficking. As part of this plan, employers in the sex trade (e.g., exotic dancing clubs, escort services, massage parlours) were immediately prohibited from hiring temporary foreign workers, and those currently employed in the sex trade would not have their visas renewed (Human Resources and Skills Development Canada, 2012).

The Adult Entertainment Association argued that the plan would cause their industry undue economic hardship, just as prohibiting temporary foreign workers in Alberta's oil industry would cause that industry a hardship. It would immediately affect approximately 800 (out of an estimated 38 000) exotic dancers in Canada and would cause a labour shortage. The association's efforts to halt the plan were not successful, and it was implemented in July 2012. In response, club owners would now have to attract more Canadian women into the industry. To do this, Godfrey (2012) reports that the Adult Entertainment Association was preparing to recruit high school students in the Toronto area. They were creating brochures to hand out outside of high schools, which assured potential applicants that sexual activity was not a part of the job and claimed "working as a dancer pays well, offers flexible hours, and makes a great part-time job to raise college tuition."

Although the "deviance dance" is evident in many issues related to sexuality, including exotic dancing, it is particularly evident when considering the issue of pornography. Anti-pornography activism exists alongside anti-censorship groups seeking to control the influences of such activism, and the question of whether pornography is "harmful" continues to be a nexus of passionate debate. Even the question of what pornography *is* remains subject to debate.

TIME TO REVIEW

Learning Objective 4

- How is sexuality involved in the "deviance dance"? Give cross-cultural, historical, or contemporary examples.

- What are the four types of exotic dancers?

- In what ways does power manifest itself at the individual level in exotic dancing?

- How does exotic dancing impact dancers' sense of self?

- How do exotic dancers use organizational rules to their advantage?

- In what ways is the "McDonaldization of society" evident in exotic dancing?

- How has the federal government recently intervened in the exotic dancing industry in terms of hiring dancers?

Pornography

What is **pornography**? Is it harmful? Should it be controlled, and if so, how? These questions represent continuing discrepancies of opinion when the topic of pornography arises. Many definitions of pornography incorporate some notion of *explicit sex*, which at the surface seems a commonsense assumption. However, even this assumption is more ambiguous than it may initially appear (Childress, 1991).

A certain level of subjectivity is involved when trying to determine precisely what constitutes "explicit" sex—whether it can be found in mainstream media (like *Fifty Shades of Grey*) or solely in those videos and magazines that only adults may purchase. The often-cited words of United States Supreme Court Justice Potter Stewart (see Childress, 1991) suggest that despite the difficulties in defining pornography, we all know it when we see it. However, as Childress (1991, p. 178) points out, "Although everyone knows hard-core pornography when they see it, they see it in strikingly different places, and so no one really knows it at all."

Academics, politicians, and social activists have tried to define pornography, resulting in several different types of definitions. Some are **functional definitions** that suggest pornography is anything used by an individual for the purposes of sexual arousal (Goode, 1997)—pornography is "in the groin of the beholder" (McKeen, 2002, p. D6). The broad nature of this definition means that the women's undergarment section of the Eaton's catalogue of the early twentieth century (which boys would sneak peeks at), the Victoria's Secret catalogue today (which many boys and men sneak peeks at), and romance novels (e.g., Silhouette Desire) could all be considered "pornography" if they are used by people to become aroused.

Other definitions are **genre definitions** (Goode, 1997), which propose that products created for the purposes of arousing the consumer constitute "pornography." Even the definition of pornography offered in the Merriam-Webster (2017b) adheres to this principle: Pornography is "the depiction of erotic behavior (as in pictures and writing) intended to cause sexual excitement."[*] Of course, this type of definition leads us to try to infer what the producer's intentions were, in some cases. Are Harlequin romance novels trying to cause sexual excitement? How about the publishers of *Maxim* magazine or the *Sports Illustrated* swimsuit issue?

Labelling definitions of pornography focus on community standards—anything that community members deem obscene (Goode, 1997). The notions of obscenity and community standards are central to Canadian law. Section 163 of the *Criminal Code* defines an obscene publication as "any publication a dominant characteristic of which is the undue exploitation of sex, or of sex and any one or more of the following subjects, namely, crime, horror, [or] cruelty and violence." (Criminal Code [R.S.C., 1985, c. C-46], Published by Department of Justice Canada).

Exceptions to this definition include publications that have artistic or literary merit or that are for educational or medical purposes. The "community standards test" has traditionally been one way of determining whether a publication can be considered obscene. Like the objectivist definition of deviance that highlights a negative societal reaction, the question here is what most Canadians would not tolerate other people seeing. More recently, the Supreme Court has moved away from the concept of "community standards" of tolerance in favour of the concept of "harm" when determining whether obscenity laws have been violated.

The legal definition of **child pornography** is considerably clearer. Section 163 of the *Criminal Code* defines child pornography as any representation of someone under the age of 18 engaged in explicit sexual activity or any representation of someone under the age of 18, "the dominant characteristic of which is the depiction, for a sexual purpose, of a sexual organ or the anal region." (Criminal Code [R.S.C., 1985, c. C-46], Published by Department of Justice Canada). Again, materials having artistic or literary merit or those that are for educational or medical purposes are excluded from this definition, as are personal writings that are kept private (such as a diary or short story) and self-photographs that are kept private. However, even though the legal definition of child

Ask Yourself

In 2012, discussion of the *Fifty Shades of Grey* book trilogy filled the media. A story of a woman's sexual life, the books contain extremely explicit descriptions of bondage and sado-masochistic sexual activities. Both celebrated and vilified in the media as "mommy porn," many female readers credited it with saving their marriages. The first book in the trilogy became the fastest-selling paperback book in history, and the trilogy sold more than 25 million copies in the United States alone in only four months. In your opinion, is *Fifty Shades of Grey* "pornography"?

---

[*] By permission. From Merriam-Webster's Collegiate® Dictionary, 11th Edition ©2017 by Merriam-Webster, Inc. [www.Merriam-Webster.com].

pornography has greater clarity than the legal definition of obscenity (not involving children), both have been subject to social and legal debate.

One of the current social and legal debates about child pornography is whether adolescents who text or email nude or partially nude photos of themselves (such as to a boyfriend or girlfriend), or share someone else's **sexting** photos, should be charged with child pornography. Dozens of youth in the United States have been charged with child pornography for doing so. In Canada, fewer cases have been reported, and early social control efforts have leaned toward diversion programs to educate girls about the consequences of sexting in lieu of criminal charges. However, in 2014 a teenage girl was convicted of possession and distribution of child pornography when she shared sexual images of her boyfriend's former girlfriend. In December, 2016 the British Columbia Court of Appeal ordered a new trial based on a constitutional challenge—the argument that youth who face these charges "suffer more harm from the justice system than they cause by sending the images" (Dickson, 2016).

The question of whether pornography that includes only adults is harmful has been a matter of considerable debate as well, both inside and outside the legal realm (Childress, 1991; Davies, 1997; Greco, 1995; Stark, 1997). Some participants in this debate focus on the question of physical harm—whether male consumers of pornography will be driven to sexually victimize women. Other participants in this debate focus on the question of a broader harm to the functioning of society—that is, whether pornography affects attitudes toward and perceptions of women in society. Still other participants direct their attention at questions of ontological harm. Such questions may address religious issues or concerns about the moral fibre of society.

The foundation for the public debates over harm stem from academic research that looks at the effects of media on consumers (see Chapter 4). Just as the Internet has increased the availability of various forms of media content, such as magazines, movies, music, and books, it has also increased the availability of pornography. Now a world of pornography is immediately available, in massive amounts, and frequently free of charge. Given the extent to which youth use the Internet, recent research has focused on the effects of pornography on youth. A recent review of the research (Owens, Behun, Manning, & Reid, 2012) analyzed the relationship between adolescent consumption of pornography and sexual attitudes, sexual behaviours, and self-concept. They found that much of the research is contradictory. Some research finds an association between the consumption of pornography and more permissive sexual attitudes, unrealistic ideas about sex, and a preoccupation with sexual thoughts, but other research does not find this association. Some research finds that greater consumption of pornography is associated with earlier sexual experimentation and riskier sexual behaviours, but other research does not. There are two areas in which research is more consistent. First, there is a correlation between the consumption of violent pornography and sexually aggressive behaviours. Second, pornography appears to affect adolescents' self-concepts. Girls worry about not looking like the women in pornography, while boys worry about not being able to perform sexually like the men in pornography.

More recently, research on pornography has undergone a paradigm shift (Attwood, 2011). A growing number of scholars are stepping outside of the effects-based research and debates over harm that have dominated the discourse. Instead, they provide a more complex analysis of pornography, looking at the consumption and significance of pornography for specific groups and communities. For example, research with undergraduate students finds that pornography use has become normalized, compared to just a decade ago (Beaver & Paul, 2011). The Internet has facilitated normalization. Between 1998 and 2007, the number of sexually explicit websites increased from only 8000 to more than 4 million, many of them "altporn" sites to which people can upload their own personal photos or videos. In addition, one-quarter of search engine requests are pornography related.

Beaver and Paul (2011) found that Internet pornography use among undergraduates cuts across social groups—it does not vary on the basis of family structure, parental supervision during adolescence, parental use of Internet filters, family income, academic achievement, depression, residential status, or religiosity. There is widespread acceptance of Internet pornography, although there are some gender differences. Males are more likely than females to access Internet pornography (although approximately one-third of visitors to pornography sites are women). Two-thirds of males consider pornography use to be completely or somewhat normal, while women are relatively equally divided on whether it is normal or deviant. Males also express more positive attitudes toward pornography: 94 percent of males, compared to 65 percent of females, enjoy it or feel neutral about it.

Pornography use has become more normalized, but at the same time there remains an ambivalence about it. A study of Swedish youth found Internet pornography use to be common (Löfgren-Mårtenson & Månsson, 2010). They access it in groups of peers to laugh at it, joke about it, and critique it. They use it as a source of information about sexuality, sexual activity, and physical appearance. They also use it as a stimulus for sexual arousal. The extent of Internet pornography use among youth shows the pornographic script to be "a frame of reference for young people in relation to physical ideals and sexual performance" (p. 576). And yet the youth recognize that males and females are portrayed unequally in pornography. They realize that "love" is missing from the pornographic equation, and that real relationships are better. Many girls express being disgusted by pornography, even though they are physically aroused by it. And some male users say they are simply tired of it. Pornography use may be considered normal in many ways, and it may serve a variety of functions in youths' lives, but there continues to be some mixed feelings about it. The spectre of "deviance" is still there (Löfgren-Mårtenson & Månsson, 2010).

Learning Objective 4

■ How do functional, genre, and labelling definitions of pornography differ?

■ What is child pornography?

■ What are some of the social and legal debates surrounding child pornography and "obscenity"?

■ What are the effects of pornography on adolescents?

■ In what ways is Internet pornography use among youth characterized by both normalization and ambivalence?

Prostitution

When it comes to the issue of prostitution, the cornerstone for differing views and debates is social policy—what should be done *with* prostitution, what should be done *to* sex workers, and why. However, in debates about prostitution, "it [is] not really prostitution but 'something else' that [is] being discussed" (Ball, 2012, p. 36). Precisely what that "something else" is varies over time (see Figure 5.2).

Ball (2012) has found that over the course of the nineteenth century, Canadian debates over prostitution were about "relationships between women and men in general and between middle-class and upper-class women and men in particular" (p. 27). As the ideals governing relationships between women and men changed during the course of the century, so did perceptions of prostitutes and the social policies targeting them. In the early part of the century, the prostitute was considered a fallen angel, in contrast to the saintly nature of the ideal woman. Discourses of morality first labelled the prostitute herself with moral weakness, but later assigned that weakness to deceitful males who seduced unsuspecting young women. Through this interpretive lens, the solution to prostitution was religious intervention to strengthen morals. As the century progressed, political, medical, and commercial voices guided discussions of prostitution. These discussions integrated public health and commercialism. Prostitution became state regulated to reduce the spread of contagious diseases and to protect male consumers of the trade from "faulty goods" (p. 31).

Figure 5.2 Changing Discourses of Prostitution

Suffragettes voiced a contrasting view of prostitution: They claimed women and men should be equals. Victimization dominated this view. Prostitutes were victims, not of deceitful men who seduced them, but rather of bullies who forced them into prostitution. Politicians, who regulated prostitution but did not criminalize it, were considered "male allies of male bullies" (Ball, 2012, p. 31). Soon, discourses of victimization became more pronounced, and prostitutes were seen as white slaves to highly organized groups. Through this lens, prostitutes needed protection for their own good and against their wills if necessary. Prostitution was finally criminalized in *An Act Respecting Vagrants* in 1869, where punishments were directed at the prostitute herself. Nearing the close of the nineteenth century, legislation continued to criminalize prostitutes but was also extended to male customers who seduced young women between the ages of 12 and 16.

More than a century later, discourses of morality and victimization continue to underlie debates over prostitution. These debates use the "language of work and commerce on one hand and the language of exploitation and victimization on the other" (Davies, 2015, p. 79). The "oppression paradigm" (Weitzer, 2010, p. 15) has dominated media reports and public policy, equating prostitution with the epitome of male violence against women in a patriarchal society—for example, as "rape that's paid for" (Raymond, cited in Weitzer, 2010, p. 17). From this perspective, sex workers are considered incapable of being agents of choice or power. However, Weitzer (2010) is critical of this view, suggesting that it is based not on reliable research evidence but rather on moral rhetoric. First, he is critical of research that is based in the oppression paradigm for discounting "inconvenient findings" (p. 21). When sex workers being interviewed for the research disagree with some aspect of the oppression paradigm, their voices are discounted by the researcher as indicative of their inability to notice their own oppression. Second, research within the oppression paradigm tends to make sweeping generalizations. Individual stories of horrific abuse within the industry are presumed to be representative of the whole. All types of sex workers are considered the same, when other research shows significant differences between the working conditions and experiences of sex workers on the street and sex workers in indoor establishments (e.g., brothels or bawdy houses) (Seib, Fischer, & Najman, 2009; Weitzer, 2010). Weitzer argues that the oppression paradigm should be replaced by a "polymorphous paradigm" (p. 26) that recognizes the varied working conditions and experiences of different groups of sex workers in varying arenas.

Similarly, van der Meulen (2011) calls for discourses of morality and victimization to be replaced by discourses of human/worker rights in policies governing prostitution. Prostitution itself is not illegal; it is various activities surrounding prostitution that are criminalized in the *Criminal Code*, such as seeing clients at a fixed address, sharing a work location, and driving a sex worker to a location used for prostitution. The result is that sex workers are placed in unsafe working conditions, prevented from taking measures that would improve worker safety in a job that is, in itself, legal. After many years of effort by a number of sex workers and the organization Sex Professionals of Canada, in 2011 the Court of Appeal for Ontario agreed, saying that some of these laws "place unconstitutional restrictions on prostitutes' ability to protect themselves" (Humphreys, 2012). In this ruling, soliciting customers on the street remains illegal, as does living off the avails of prostitution in circumstances of exploitation (i.e., by pimps). The law criminalizing brothels or bawdy houses was overturned, and sex workers would be able to hire body guards, drivers, and support staff. In 2013, the Supreme Court of Canada agreed with that ruling, and gave the federal government one year to enact new legislation (or alternatively, to not legislate prostitution at all). In December 2014 the federal government enacted *Bill C-36: The Protection of Communities and Exploited Persons*. Debates surrounding the activities that are (and are not) criminalized in this legislation continue. According to the legislation "...to be paid for sex is to be *prostituted*, which is to be sexually exploited" (Davies, 2015, p. 78), which once again emphasizes victimization. While the law gives certain types of sex workers the opportunity for greater safety and protection, some critics argue that it drives prostitution indoors, where it is more difficult for social workers and police officers to aid underage workers or those needing help to leave the job. Other critics contend that because certain acts are no longer criminalized, it sends a message to children that prostitution is acceptable. Thus, now we see discourses of morality, victimization, and worker rights comingling within the deviance dance surrounding the issue of prostitution.

Sexual culture is of considerable complexity, integrating sexual, scientific, religious, political, family, and popular discourses. What is considered sexually deviant varies among cultures based on these varying discourses. However, all cultures do differentiate between deviant and normal sexuality, and all cultures formally and informally regulate sexuality.

TIME TO REVIEW

Learning Objective 4

- In what way did discourses underlying the issue of prostitution change during the nineteenth century, and how did these changes affect social policy?

- In what ways are nineteenth-century discourses underlying the issue of prostitution still evident today?

- How do the oppression paradigm and polymorphous paradigm differ?

- In what ways are discourses of human/worker rights reflected in recent rulings on prostitution laws?

CHAPTER SUMMARY

- Perceptions of "deviant" and "normal" sexuality vary cross-culturally and historically, but also vary among different social groups in a certain culture at a particular time in history. (1)

- Traditional Indigenous societies had very different sexual cultures than those of the colonizing Europeans. With European colonization, the sexual cultures of Indigenous societies were subjected to significant measures of social control. (2)

- In North America from the seventeenth century to the twentieth century, meanings of sexuality shifted from focusing on *reproductive ideals*, to *intimacy in marriage*, to *personal fulfillment*; agents of social control changed during this time as well. During all eras, hierarchies of race, class, and gender influenced the complexities of sexual culture. (3)

- In North America today, although sexual freedom has increased considerably since previous eras, judgments of "deviant" and "normal" sexuality continue to be made. Criteria we use to make these judgments include *consent, nature of the sexual partner nature of the sexual act, location,* and *frequency.* (4)

- In any given culture at any given time, there is a multiplicity of perceptions, reactions, and social control measures surrounding sexuality. (5)

- In contemporary society, the deviance dance is particularly evident when considering issues related to sex work, such as exotic dancing, pornography, and prostitution. (5)

> **To learn more about the topics discussed in this chapter and to complete chapter quizzes, visit the Companion Website for *Deviance, Conformity, and Social Control in Canada.***

Chapter 6

The Troubling and Troubled World of Youth

Learning Objectives

After reading this chapter, you should be able to

1 Compare popular images of youth crime with statistics on the nature and prevalence of youth crime, and explain why a gap exists between the perceptions and realities.

2 Describe theoretical and empirical research on youth crime and gang involvement.

3 Explain how gangs and youth crime are socially controlled.

4 Describe the extent and patterns of use of tobacco, drugs, and alcohol among youth, as well as how their usage is socially controlled.

5   Explain what the concept of "at-risk youth" means and what the "science of risk" does.

6   Describe how *all* teenagers are perceived as deviant in society, and explain the nature of the generation gap in the past, present, and future.

Ask Yourself

When you think of "youth crime," what images and information come to mind? What are the sources of those images and that information?

"Youth" and "deviance" frequently go hand in hand in the public mind, whether reading newspaper headlines about youth crime being out of control or expressing concerns about the music, movies, or video games youth are consuming (Tanner, 2015). More than any other age group, youth are perceived as having lifestyles built around deviance. They are seen as both "troubling" and "troubled"—and "troubling *because* they are troubled" (Tanner, 2001, p. 2). **Troubling youth**, such as young offenders, gang members, and street youth, are primarily seen as threats to society. **Troubled youth** are first and foremost viewed as threats to themselves (for example, through substance abuse); however, they have the potential to become threats to society, to become "troubling" if their problems are not solved early enough. However, at some level *all* youth are viewed as potential threats to both themselves and the larger society. It is not just *some* youth who are perceived as deviant; rather, youth culture, and indeed this period in the life cycle itself, is deemed to be deviant and in need of social control.

But precisely what time in life is captured by the term "youth"? **Youth** has been defined in several different ways. In some cases, it refers to a specific stage in life, referring to a transitional time in life between childhood and maturity; one is no longer a "child" but is not yet an "adult." However, how this stage is operationalized varies across cultures, over time, and even across contexts within a culture at a specific point in time; in other words, the concept of "youth" is socially constructed (Tyyskä, 2014). Some constructions define it based on age. For instance, the *Youth Criminal Justice Act* (YCJA) defines youth as those aged 12 to 17, and the United Nations defines youth as those aged 15 to 25. Others define youth based on social status rather than age; for them, youth refers to anyone who has not achieved full economic and social independence. In everyday conversation, the meaning of the term can be much more diverse, referring to adolescents or teenagers, university-age adults, and even individuals in their mid-twenties (Tyyskä, 2014). Yet others define youth not as a certain stage in life, but rather as a process: "From a sociological perspective, youth is a social process ... that describes how groups of young people and individuals experience being young, how this is defined through institutions and policies, and how it is related to social, economic, and political circumstances" (White, Wyn, & Albanese, 2011, p. 3). As you progress through the chapter, you should consider which definitions underlie the discussion of the various topics.

Deviant Youth: "Troubling" Youth

Youth Crime

Before continuing, take a moment to look at the *Ask Yourself* exercise. When we think of deviant youth, those who are criminals are likely to come to mind first. Indeed, when the search terms "youth and deviance" are used in academic databases or Internet search engines, most results are about youth crime. Calls for a "crackdown" on youth crime can be heard on the news, in politicians' comments to the press, and from victims of youth crime. The view that youth crime is out of control and worse than ever pervades public discourses, and is evident in media images (McCormick, 2016; Tanner, 2015). But to what extent is this perception of youth crime accurate? Are teenagers out of control? Is youth crime worse than ever?

A closer examination reveals significant differences between the *perceptions* of youth crime and *patterns* of youth crime (McCormick, 2016; Tanner, 2015). At least when we look at official statistics (which measure crimes reported to the police), the extent and nature of youth crime is far from approximating the frightening picture painted in the popular mind by media images. Official statistics have been gathered through the Uniform Crime Reporting Survey since 1962. This data reveals that Canada's crime rate increased steadily from 1962 to 1991, when it reached its peak (Statistics Canada, 2016a).

Since 1992, there has been a steady downward trend in adult (ages 18 and over) and youth (ages 12 to 17) crime rates, such that in 2013, the overall crime rate was at its lowest point since 1969 (Statistics Canada, 2016a). Similar trends are evident in other countries as well, and may reflect a variety of social factors: changes in policing practices; aging populations; legislative changes; evolving attitudes; trends in patterns of substance use; and more (Statistics Canada, 2016a). Not only have crime rates declined over time, but so has the severity of crime. The crime severity index is a measure that reflects both the volume and the severity of crime. Although there may be small increases or decreases from year to year, there has been an overall downward trend. Figure 6.1 illustrates the declining crime severity index for youth crime in particular.

The crimes most frequently committed by youth are theft of $5000 or under, mischief, and common assault (Statistics Canada, 2016b). Although youth crime is not of the magnitude suggested by public perceptions, it is still a serious issue. Youth are overrepresented in the criminal justice system. Those aged 12 to 17 are twice as likely to be accused of crimes compared to people ages 25 and over, and rates of property crime in particular are highest among youth. If we include young adults ages 18 to 24 (who are not governed by youth justice legislation but who are considered "youth" based on other definitions), the problem is magnified. Young adults ages 18 to 24 have the highest crime rate overall, and for every category of crime other than property crimes (Statistics Canada, 2016b). In closing, adolescents and young adults are overrepresented in the criminal justice system, but the rate and severity of their crimes have been on a steady decline for several decades.

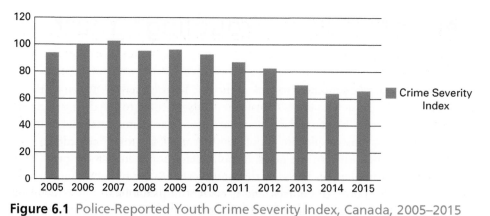

Figure 6.1 Police-Reported Youth Crime Severity Index, Canada, 2005–2015

Based on Statistics Canada (2016d). *Table 252-0052. Police-reported crime severity index, Canada, 2005–2015*. CANSIM. Accessed: January 28, 2017.

Where does the gap between the perceptions of youth crime as worse than ever and the declining patterns of youth crime come from? Many criminologists and other deviance scholars attribute the gap in part to **moral panics**. This concept was popularized by Cohen (1973) based on his analysis of the aftermath of a minor altercation between two groups of youths ("Mods" and "Rockers") at a British seaside resort in 1964. Although the incident itself was relatively minor, in the following days (and in fact for the next three years) the media exaggerated and distorted the magnitude of the events with headlines such as "Day of Terror by Scooter Groups" and "Seaside Resorts Prepare for Hooligans' Invasion." Public fear grew, and law enforcement and politicians faced pressure to crack down on the youth-inspired terror that was gripping the nation.

The concept of moral panic refers to exaggerated and sensationalized concerns of a social phenomenon. Goode and Ben-Yehuda (2009) list five elements of a moral panic: heightened concern, hostility toward the offending group, a certain level of consensus that there is a real threat, disproportionality (the attention given to the phenomenon is far greater than the level of objective threat that the phenomenon presents), and volatility (it erupts suddenly and then may just as suddenly disappear, although some may become institutionalized and therefore reappear time and again). This concept has since been applied to the analysis of diverse youth cultural phenomena (e.g., concerns over youth-oriented media) and has been used to explain the gap between the perceptions and patterns of youth crime.

Moral panics are constructed within the media, wherein youth crime is overrepresented, portrayed as a new problem for society, and linked to certain ethnic groups and classes (McCormick, 2016; Tanner, 2015). But as Pearson's (1983) analysis of British media illustrates, this portrait of youth crime has been repeatedly painted since the early twentieth century—public concerns about youth crime today are quite like public concerns about youth crime 100 years ago. Even a century ago, there were gaps between the perceptions and realities of youth crime, and moral panics about youth crime were conveyed in popular discourse, creating a distorted view of youth crime in the eyes of the public. Moral panics about youth crime are not limited to contemporary North American society; they have also been found in Austria, Germany, and other European societies as far back as the late nineteenth and early twentieth centuries (Wegs, 1999).

Even though the nature and extent of youth crime diverges considerably from public perceptions and media portrayals, concerns about young people who *are* involved in criminal activity have stimulated a significant body of research over the past several decades. Thus, research on the causes of youth crime abound. Many of the theories of deviance that lean toward the more objective end of the objective–subjective continuum (which were addressed in Chapter 2) are used to explain youth crime. Its existence (or its absence) has been variously explained as resulting from the following: learning deviant techniques and motives from peers (differential association theory); bonds with others that restrain most of us from crime (social bonds theory); the level of self-control developed early in life (self-control theory); structural inequalities in access to legitimate opportunities (Merton's strain theory) and illegitimate opportunities (differential opportunity theory); negative emotions that arise because of strain (Agnew's general strain theory); and the system of rewards, punishments, and role models we have been exposed to in life (social learning theory).

Historically, empirical research has also analyzed a variety factors to determine the extent to which they contribute to youth crime. This research has investigated the roles of intelligence (Liska & Reid, 1985); family structure and processes (Baumrind, 1991; Thornberry, Lizotte, Krohm, Farnworth, & Jang, 1991); school performance (Davies, 1994); and peer influences (Regioli & Hewitt, 1994). Factors related to school, families, and peers continue to be addressed in contemporary research. That research finds the single most effective predictor of criminal activity among youth is criminal activity among friends (Zeman & Bressan, 2008). However, school- and family-related factors also play important roles. Youth who have positive school experiences (e.g., feel safe and happy at school; feel like a part of the school; feel close to people at school) are significantly less likely to engage in criminal activity (Dufur et al., 2015). The same is true for youth who have positive experiences with parents (e.g., are satisfied with the relationship they have with their parents; feel close to their parents; see their parents as warm and loving). The parent–child relationship is especially important, having a greater influence than school experiences, and controlling for variables such as family structure (i.e., single-parent versus two-parent family), family income, characteristics of the neighbourhood, and even criminally-active peers (Dufur et al., 2015).

Strong parent–child relationships are associated with children who select higher quality peers as friends; have closer, more emotionally intimate and trusting relationships with those friends; and are less susceptible to negative peer influences. These relationships have been found in several different countries, including Colombia, where, despite high societal levels of drug use and violence, parenting variables improve child outcomes and mediate negative peer influences such as criminal behaviour and marijuana use (Brook et al., 1999). Although the parent–child relationship

Youth who feel close to their parents are much less likely to become involved in criminal activity.

plays an especially important role, the International Youth Survey (administered in more than 30 countries, including Canada) finds that a complex set of factors is associated with criminal behaviour among youth (Zeman & Bressan, 2008) (see Box 6.1).

Box 6.1

Factors Influencing Youth Crime

Property Crime
- single-parent or blended family
- absence of university aspirations
- truancy
- perception of school environment as unsafe
- personal experience as victim of theft
- out at night without adult supervision
- time spent alone rather than with family
- time spent with friends rather than with family
- peer acceptance of illegal acts

Violent Crime
- male
- absence of university aspirations
- truancy
- personal experience of discrimination on the basis of race, language, or religion
- personal experience as victim of theft
- personal experience as victim of threats
- perception of school as unsafe
- negative relationship with father or mother
- out at night without adult supervision
- time spent with friends rather than with family
- peer acceptance of illegal acts

Although the crime problem, and in particular the youth crime problem, is not at the level that public images suggest, crime is a social issue in need of control. In recent years, one form of youth criminal behaviour has come to predominate in the public mind: gang activity.

Exercise Your Mind

To further explore the linkages between theory and empirical research, identify which of the risk factors in Box 6.1 might fit within (a) Merton's strain theory; (b) Cloward and Ohlin's differential opportunity theory; (c) Sutherland's differential association theory; (d) social learning theory; (e) Hirschi's social bonds theory; (f) Agnew's general strain theory; and (g) Gottfredson and Hirschi's self-control theory.

Gang-Involved Youth

Gang-involved youth are a popular topic for newspaper articles, politicians' speeches, movies, and both fictional and nonfictional television. They are found throughout much of the world; however, the prevalence of gangs in the United States, combined with the emphasis placed on gang-involved youth in the American media, means that much of the research done on gangs is American. In fact, Canadian research on youth gangs continues to be comparatively sparse and is often decades old. A 2002 survey of police officers reported a total of almost 6000 gang-involved youth in Canada in more than 400 gangs (Public Safety Canada, 2016; Tanner, 2015; Totten, 2016). Young people are more likely to be involved with street gangs than gangs associated with organized crime, and they are likely to have been criminally active even before joining a gang (Public Safety Canada, 2016; Totten, 2016). Membership in gangs is fluid, and typically includes a range of ages (although most gang members tend to be under the age of 30) and diverse racial and ethnic backgrounds (Totten, 2016). However, there is a greater risk of gang involvement among youth who experience high levels of marginalization (e.g., street-involved youth; Indigenous youth) (Greenberg, Grekul, & Nelson, 2016; MacLaurin & Worthington, 2016; Tanner, 2015).

Because of the predominance of American research on gang-involved youth, it has dominated Canadian academic, public, and governmental policy discussions (Tanner, 2015). The American-centric nature of gang research is problematic when one considers Canadian–American differences in gun control legislation, drug laws, government policies, ethnic and cultural composition, and social supports (Grekul & LaBoucane-Benson, 2007).

Two broad streams of research on youth gangs can be identified. One of those streams focuses on causation or motivation: why gangs form, why youth join gangs, and why gangs engage in certain behaviours. The second stream of research focuses on various aspects of the social construction of the "gang problem," such as how and why moral panics about gangs emerge and even the problems involved in the very definition of "gang" itself.

The "How" and "Why" of Gangs

As with the theorizing about youth crime in general, the theorizing on gang-involved youth also brings us back to a number of the theories reviewed in Chapter 2. For instance, the underlying proposition of strain theories is that gangs will emerge in socially and economically disadvantaged communities. In such communities, where legitimate opportunities to achieve social status and economic success are limited, gangs form as an alternative way of achieving status, social acceptance, and economic success (e.g., Merton's strain theory).

The status and economic success to be gained via gang activity is not to be under-estimated, given the amount of money that can be made in the drug trade. However, the pursuit of economic success is not central to the activities of all youth gangs. Other theorists have asserted that different types of gangs have different types of activities as their foundation. Status frustration theory suggests that lower-class boys, if unable to live up to the middle-class measuring rod that pervades the education system, would join with other similar boys in forming gangs that engage in expressive, destructive, non-utilitarian behaviours (e.g., vandalism, violence) rather than econo-mically driven activities (Cohen, 1955).

Differential opportunity theory proposes that the nature of the illegitimate oppor-tunities present in the community determines the nature of gang behaviour; certain types of illegitimate opportunities result in the formation of gangs that may be eco-nomically enterprising, violent, or drug using and retreatist (Cloward & Ohlin, 1960). Although the pursuit of economic success is not a component of all youth gangs, the pursuit of status is—but the type of status that can be achieved through gang mem-bership depends on the gang in question.

Although positivist theories dominate the area, research on gangs does also come from more subjective theoretical orientations. For instance, drawing on the critical Marxist perspective of the Birmingham Centre for Contemporary Cultural Studies in England, Bourgois (1995) analyzed youth gangs as sources of identity and expres-sions of resistance among youth who are structurally marginalized. Pointing to the interactionist perspective, Venkatesh (2003) discusses the fact that individual mem-bers within a gang have different interests, motivations for gang membership, and understandings of what it means to be in a gang member.

Ethnographic research, emerging from the interactionist perspective, involves researchers embedding themselves in gangs for extended periods of time, interview-ing gang members, and observing their daily activities. For example, Jankowski's (1991) ethnographic study was one of the first pieces of research to explore the rela-tionships between gangs, other people, and other organizations within the commu-nity. Jankowski concluded that individuals join gangs for a variety of different reasons rather than for any one reason (such as blocked opportunities).

The various reasons for joining a gang are based on a rational calculation of what is in the best interests of the individual at the time. First, Jankowski (1991) suggests that one reason for gang membership is **material incentives**. Some people join gangs based on the belief that the gang will provide an environment that increases the chances of making money—more regular money and with less individual effort than if pursuing economic success individually. Jankowski found that material incentives also include financial security for gang members and their families during difficult times, as well as networking for future economic endeavours.

Recreation serves as another reason for gang membership. That is, gangs provide entertainment and a social life, and in some communities may serve as the primary social institution in the neighbourhood, promoting social events and supplying drugs and alcohol. The comments of one gang member illustrate the recreational aspect of gang membership: "'Man, it [the gang] was a great source of dope and women. Hell, they were the kings of the community so I wanted to get in on some of the action'" (Jankowski, 1991, p. 283). Gangs may serve as a **place of refuge and camouflage**, motivating some individuals to seek gang membership. Being just "one of the gang" provides a level of anonymity, removing a sense of personal responsibility for illegal activities—"'the gang is going to provide me with some cover'" (p. 283).

Other people are drawn to gangs for the **physical protection** they provide from known dangers in the neighbourhood. As gang member Cory points out, "'Now that I got some business things going I can concentrate on them and not worry so much. I don't always have to be looking over my shoulder'" (Jankowski, 1991, p. 284). For some people, joining a gang may serve as a **time to resist** living the kinds of lives their parents lived. In this vein, becoming a gang member is a statement of rejection to society, a rejection of the type of lives being offered. At the same time, the economic prospects of gang membership may be a way of avoiding just that type of life: "'Hey, I just might make some money from our deal-ings...If I don't [make it, at least] I told those fuckers in Beverly Hills what I think of the jobs they left for us'" (p. 284).

In some neighbourhoods, certain gangs have existed for generations, so that indi-viduals whose fathers, uncles, and grandfathers have been members of the gang at some point in their lives feel a **commitment to the community** and join the gang to continue a tradition. As Pepe states, "'A lot of people from the community have been in [the gang]. ... I felt it's kind of my duty to join 'cause everybody expects it'" (Jankowski, 1991, p. 285). Feeling a commitment to the community, along with the other possible motivations for gang membership, leads individuals to conclude that joining a gang is currently in their best interests.

Grekul and LaBoucane-Benson (2007) combine positivist (social bonds), criti-cal (conflict), and interactionist (labelling) theories in their analysis of Indigenous gangs in Canada. Interviews with former gang members, police officers, and correc-tions workers reveal that weak bonds of attachment, commitment to conventional society, involvement in conventional society, and beliefs that support conventional society play a significant role in gang membership. The legacy of colonization and residential schooling (which will be discussed further in Chapter 9) has had a lasting effect on Indigenous families, contributing to family instability and violence.

For example, Grekul and LaBoucane-Benson (2007) report that in the Edmonton area Indigenous children are six times more likely to be involved with child protection services, and it is these children who are prime targets for gang recruitment efforts in that region.

Although there have been increases in high school completion and post-secondary education, dropout rates continue to be considerably higher among Indigenous youth, with higher unemployment rates as a consequence. Ongoing discrimination continues to be a problem as well: "One of our respondents recalled being called a 'dumb little Indian who would never amount to anything' by one of his school teachers" (Grekul & LaBoucane-Benson, 2007, p. 33). The negative effects of being labelled have an impact; one respondent states, "'police called them a gang so they began to act that way and identify themselves that way'" (p. 42). These factors have an interactive effect, and gangs are able to step in and "fill the gap for disenfranchised and marginalized" (p. 2) Indigenous youth.

Several different variables, including personal, family, community, and educational factors, increase the likelihood of gang involvement (e.g., Public Safety Canada, n.d.; Tanner, 2015; Totten, 2016). In Box 6.2 you will find a summary of these factors, illustrating that gang involvement emerges in part from unhealthy personalities,

Box 6.2

Factors Influencing Gang Involvement

Family Indicators

- excessive parental controls
- lax parental controls
- low parental nurturance
- abuse/neglect
- low parental educational level
- criminality among other family members

Personal Indicators

- low self-control
- low motivation
- truancy
- failing grades
- low aspirations or goals in life
- substance abuse

Community Indicators

- community disorganization
- high crime rate
- high population turnover
- lack of cultural resources
- lack of recreational resources
- gang presence

School Indicators

- negative school environment
- violence in the school
- low expectations for students
- inadequate funding for school resources (e.g., library books, extracurricular activities)
- lax control over students

unhealthy relationships, unhealthy families, and unhealthy communities. Interviews with 125 Toronto youth (ages 16–24) who identify themselves as gang members found that a combination of push and pull factors are associated with gang affiliation. Unstable home environments drove many to hang out on the streets, while negative school experiences (e.g., bullying, histories of school discipline) propelled some to turn to similar others for support. Gang affiliation offered many benefits, including companionship and social support (which was typically lacking in their home lives), money, and respect. As one gang member states, "It was the image. It was the money. It was the power" (Tanner, 2015, p. 193).

The Construction of the "Gang Problem"

While the first stream of gang research explores the causes of or motivations for gang emergence, membership, and behaviour, the second stream concentrates on a different set of issues related to social construction. Within the latter stream, some researchers emphasize the social construction of "gangs" themselves. For instance, Sanday (cited in Venkatesh, 2003) asks why fraternities are not considered to be gangs. One of the more commonly used definitions of **"gang"** (albeit far from being agreed upon) is "any denotable...group [of adolescents or young adults] who (a) are generally perceived as a distinct aggregation by others in the neighbourhood, (b) recognize themselves as a denotable group (almost invariably with a group name), and (c) have been involved in a sufficient number of [illegal] incidents" (cited in Chatterjee, 2006). Fraternities are most certainly perceived as a distinct group, both by others and themselves, and Sanday points out that "theft, vandalism, sexual conquest (read: harassment), and the imbibing of alcohol (read: underage drinking)" (Venkatesh, 2003, p. 5) are common and are even explicitly included in some fraternity charters or manifestos.

Others who are embedded within the latter stream of research focus more on the social construction of the **"gang problem."** Discussions of media representations of gangs have been central to research from this perspective. The way youth gangs are represented in the media and other forms of public discourse is similar to the portrayal of youth crime more generally. Gangs are portrayed as a new and growing problem for society, one that is out of control (Tanner, 2015).

Just as with images of youth crime more generally, public images of gangs surpass their actual existence. Not only are stories about gangs found on television news and in newspapers, they can also be easily found in the fictional media—on television crime dramas, in movies, and in the glamourized images of gangs within some rap and hip hop music lyrics and videos (Delaney, 2005; Tanner, 2015). The involvement of certain ethnic and age groups is a significant component of public images of gangs.

Canadian media **racialize** the "gang problem." In other words, stories about gangs frequently include references to specific racial or ethnic groups. This is problematic on two fronts. First, a distorted picture of Canadian gangs is presented to the audience, when the reality is that gangs are ethnically diverse (Tanner, 2015). Second, race and ethnicity are only overtly linked in the media to gang activity when it is non-whites that are involved. "We read and hear of the 'Asian' gang problem, the problem of Jamaican Blacks in the east, and 'Aboriginal gangs.' We don't often hear of 'Caucasian' or 'White' gangs. Racial and ethnic stereotyping leads to processes such as racial profiling and creates misunderstanding, labelling, mistrust, and hostility between groups" (Grekul & LaBoucane-Benson, 2007, p. 25). The media's overrepresentation of gangs, its racialization of gangs, and its distortion of the age composition of gangs all contribute to a view of Canada's gangs that is quite different from the reality—showing that a "moral panic" has been created.

Certain groups may benefit from the creation of a moral panic about street gangs. Drawing on the critical theoretical perspectives addressed in Chapter 3, a number of researchers suggest that not only does the media benefit from the creation of moral panics, so do some politicians, interest groups, and law enforcement agencies (Cohen, 1973; Schissel, 2001; Tanner, 2015). By presenting sensationalistic and fear-provoking stories, the media draws an audience and thereby increases profit. Some politicians may similarly engage in fear mongering and then vow to toughen legislation and enforcement if elected. By contributing to moral panic and then promising to reduce the social problem, they can obtain more votes. Interest groups and community agencies who want legislation strengthened or who provide social programs may receive more funding by exaggerating the nature of the problem. Law enforcement agencies may also benefit in some communities by receiving more funding to hire more officers or create specialized gang units if they are able to convince municipal, provincial, and federal politicians that the "gang problem" is out of control. Some researchers suggest that even gangs themselves may benefit from this moral panic, which provides them with free publicity and may thereby increase their membership and power in the community. Youth who are currently not involved in gangs may form new gangs to protect themselves from the perceived threat (Tanner, 2015).

However, although the gang research done in this second stream suggests that the moral panic surrounding gang-involved youth surpasses actual patterns and that various groups benefit from this moral panic, it does not claim that gangs are a figment of the social imagination or that gangs are nothing to worry about. Indeed, the gangs that do exist must be socially controlled.

Controlling Youth Gangs and Youth Crime

"How do you deal with youth crime? 'Toughen up' the *Youth Criminal Justice Act*, send 'bad guys' (and girls) to jail for a very long time … and keep the problem away from our homes and families. Easy, simple, quick fix" (Grekul & LaBoucane-Benson, 2007). In fact, as Grekul and LaBoucane-Benson go on to point out, the effective control of gangs and of youth crime more generally is far from an easy, quick fix. Throughout North America, street gangs are socially controlled at multiple levels—formal and informal, retroactive and preventative. These social control efforts occur in families, communities (schools, community agencies, community organizations, businesses, and religious institutions), and the criminal justice system (government, courts, and law enforcement).

At a formal level of regulation, many schools have integrated gang awareness programs to teach children about the dangers of gangs and the consequences of gang membership. These programs are intended to prevent children from joining gangs. Community agencies, particularly those operating in gang-ridden neighbourhoods, frequently have both retroactive and preventative programs. Retroactive programs are designed to try to persuade existing gang members to leave that lifestyle. They may offer educational upgrading, job training, assistance in finding employment, free tattoo removal, and various types of counselling.

Preventative programs in communities may operate in conjunction with schools, teaching young children basic life skills (e.g., nutrition, grooming) and social skills (e.g., problem solving, anger management), or providing organized community activities. Many police departments in North America have specialized gang units who become familiar with and closely monitor known gang members, as well as deal with gang issues and events that arise. Governments provide gang-related legislation and social programs (e.g., job-training programs).

Informal social controls occur at the level of everyday social interaction, typically focusing on preventative efforts. This can include parenting efforts (e.g., child socialization; parenting style, talking to your children about gangs) and community involvement with neighbourhood children (e.g., becoming a soccer coach, helping the neighbourhood children organize a food drive).

The Comprehensive Gang Model outlines key strategies for prevention, intervention, and suppression (cited in Totten, 2016): mobilize community residents to take preventative and retroactive actions; take social interventions (e.g., tutoring, advocacy) directly to gang members where they are located; develop programs that provide economic, educational, and social opportunities; suppress gang activity by holding members accountable within the justice system; and facilitate organizational change by coordinating the social control efforts of different community organizations. The Community Solution to Gang Violence (CSGV) in Edmonton illustrates this model. Administered through Native Counselling Services of Alberta, this program combines prevention, intervention, and suppression, bringing together 40 community organizations, the Edmonton Police Service, and all levels of government (municipal, provincial, and federal).

Measures to control youth gangs are intertwined with the regulation of youth crime in general. Many of the formal and informal social controls that were discussed in the context of gangs are also used in relation to youth crime—it is presumed that the prevention of gang involvement is also the prevention of crime at a broader level. For instance, strong parent–child relationships, community involvement in children's lives, and effective classrooms will reduce not only the likelihood of gang involvement, but also the likelihood of all types of criminal activity.

Over the past century, there have been considerable changes in the way youth crime has been formally controlled or regulated. Public concerns about youth crime gained force during the late nineteenth century. This was a period of tremendous social and economic change in Canadian society. The process of industrialization was well underway, cities were growing, and an identifiable working class was present. Because of the long hours that working-class parents had to spend at work simply to ensure the survival of their family, their children were left unsupervised more than the children of middle-class parents. Social reformers during that era were concerned with the lack of supervision these children faced as well as the subsequent danger they presented to middle-class personhood and property (Leon, 1977; Sutherland, 1976).

Various small pieces of legislation encompassed the control of youth crime, neglected children, and abandoned children. Children under the age of 7 were presumed not to know the difference between right and wrong, and so could not be charged with criminal offences. If it was proven that a child between the ages of 7 and 14 knew the difference between right and wrong, the child could be subject to the same sentence as an adult; thus, it was possible for a 7-year-old child who had committed a crime to be sentenced to life in prison or even death. Youth over the age of 14 were considered equal to adults in criminal law.

In 1908, the Canadian juvenile justice system was created with the implementation of the *Juvenile Delinquents Act*. Its foundation was the principle of **parens patriae** ("parent of the country"), meaning that the state would act in the best interests of children under the age of 16 if it became clear that their own parents were unwilling or unable to—and both neglected and delinquent children were presumed to need such legislative attention. Although it controlled youth criminals, the *Juvenile Delinquents* Act was more a *child welfare* piece of legislation since it was believed that with the right assistance and correct teaching, young criminals could be set on the right path in life. Separate detention facilities and jail facilities were created for youth based on the belief that integrating juvenile delinquents with adult criminals would simply further juvenile delinquency (Reitsma-Street, 1989–1990).

The *Juvenile Delinquents Act* was amended several times over the ensuing decades, and in 1984 it was replaced by the *Young Offenders Act*. This new piece of legislation was based on *justice* principles rather than child welfare principles. It extended the legal rights of adult offenders (e.g., due process, the right to an attorney) to youth as well, who were not guaranteed such protections under the *Juvenile Delinquents Act*. Youth who committed crimes were no longer perceived as juvenile delinquents but as **young offenders**; an offending youth was now seen as a *criminal* rather than a child gone astray (West, 1984; West, 1991). After a number of amendments throughout the 1990s, the *Youth Criminal Justice Act* replaced the *Young Offenders Act* on April 1, 2003.

Under this most recent legislation, chronic or violent young offenders are treated more stringently, while first-time and non-violent young offenders are more likely to be treated via community and alternative measures. Because only a small proportion of young offenders are responsible for most of the serious crimes (and especially violent crimes) committed by youth, this means that the majority of young offenders are supervised in the community rather than in custody (Public Safety Canada, 2016). For instance, in 2016, 90 percent of young offenders who were in correctional services were being supervised in the community. Those in custody were primarily older teens, ages 16 to 17 (Correctional Services Program, 2016).

The *Youth Criminal Justice Act* is one component of the federal government's Youth Justice Renewal Initiative, a multifaceted initiative involving the criminal justice system, schools, community agencies, and more. Its underlying principles are prevention, meaningful consequences for youth crime, and intensified rehabilitation and reintegration.

However, Oudshoorn (2015) points out that the youth justice system continues to fall short of meaningful change. This is because it fails to sufficiently address youth trauma, which Oudshoorn argues plays a key role in youth crime. Trauma can be either individual or collective in nature. At the individual level, young people may experience poverty, abuse or neglect, discrimination, victimization by crime, or cyberbullying. Collectively, certain social groups may have been subjected to ongoing intergenerational trauma at a more macro level—such as that experienced by Indigenous groups because of colonization (Oudshoorn, 2015). This type of collective trauma contributes to the overrepresentation of Indigenous adults and youth in the criminal justice system, and in custodial (rather than community) settings (Correctional Services Program, 2016; Greenberg, Grekul, & Nelson, 2016). If one considers trauma to be a key source of youth crime, then the youth justice system must provide the resources necessary to heal that trauma (Oudshoorn, 2015). For Indigenous youth this includes cultural resources integrated into the youth justice system, but also broader measures of reconciliation in society at large (Truth and Reconciliation Commission of Canada, 2015).

The social control of youth crime has been modified in substantial ways over the past century, and more recently has included efforts to control gangs. Although legislation, criminal justice programs, and social programs are continually changing, the desire to control "troubling" youth is as old as civilization itself. However, youth who are perceived as threats to society because of their criminal activities are not the only ones considered deviant and in need of social control—"troubled" youth are a focus of concern as well.

Deviant Youth: "Troubled" Youth

Some youth are considered deviant and are made subject to measures of social control not because they are "troubling," and therefore currently a danger to society, but because they are "troubled." "Troubled" youth are first and foremost a danger to themselves; their behaviour threatens their own well-being, physical or mental health, and future. But "troubled" youth are also perceived as potentially "troubling"—if they are uncontrolled or if their problems are not effectively dealt with they may become not only a danger to themselves but a danger to society as well.

Youth who abuse drugs or alcohol, engage in premature sexual activity, become teenage parents, or engage in self-harm are just some of those youth who are considered "troubled." When considering "troubled" youth, one of the areas of greatest public concern today are youth who are victimized by bullying, and who may, as a result, be pushed toward other troublesome behaviours (see Box 6.3).

Substance Use among Youth

We live in a culture where substance use, in some form, is widely evident. Step outside the doorway of office buildings, shopping malls, and even hospitals and you will see groups of

Box 6.3

Being Bullied

In Chapter 2, you learned about Agnew's general strain theory, which proposes that experiencing strain can lead to negative emotions, which then increase the likelihood of a wide range of deviant behaviours; these behaviours can be self-directed (e.g., self-harm, suicide, substance abuse) or directed at others (e.g., criminal activity) (Agnew, 2001; Hay & Meldrum, 2010). Negative emotions are most likely to arise when strain is perceived as unjust, is severe, and the individual lacks control over the situation. Agnew (2001) proposes that bullying is a form of strain that fits those three criterial.

Bullying is an activity that can occur both online or offline. However, computer-mediated communication provides a level of anonymity that does not exist in offline bullying (Hinduja & Patchin, 2008). **Cyberbullying** refers to "the use of information and communication technologies...to support deliberate, repeated, and hostile behavior by an individual or group that is intended to harm others" (Li, 2010, p. 373). It can consist of numerous specific behaviours, ranging from excluding someone from an online group to harassing individuals with threats of harm to posting embarrassing information about someone. Although several instances of cyberbullying have been covered in the news media, the 2012 suicide of British Columbia teenager Amanda Todd captured the public mind, perhaps largely because prior to committing suicide she posted a heart-wrenching video on YouTube that described her experiences of being bullied—a video that was played repeatedly in the media following her death.

Estimates of cyberbullying vary, in part based on age. Among junior-high (or middle-school) students, 7 percent report being victimized by cyberbullying and 5 percent report engaging in cyberbullying (Rice et al., 2015). When considering junior- and senior-high students, numbers increase, where almost 20 percent report engaging in cyberbullying (Li, Holt, Bossler, & May, 2016). By the time youth reach university, 40 percent say they have been cyberbullied at some point in their lives (Reyns, Henson, & Fisher, 2012). Some youth are more likely than others to experience cyberbullying: visible minorities, girls, and sexual minorities are especially at risk. As with being victimized by cybercrime (which was discussed in Chapter 4), those who spend more time online are more likely to be cyberbullied, especially if they share a great deal of personal information on those sites (Rice et al., 2015).

Although the specific effects of being cyberbullied can vary based on the frequency, magnitude, and severity of the experience, as a whole victims of cyberbullying experience higher rates of depression and other mental health problems, as well as substance use (Calvete, Orue, & Gámez-Guadix, 2016; Gámez-Guadix, Orue, Smith, & Clavete, 2013; Smokowski, Evans, & Cotter, 2014). And as illustrated by the case of Amanda Todd and many other youth since, the impacts of cyberbullying can become as severe as suicide. Furthermore, the experience of being cyberbullied leads some youth to become perpetrators as well (Rice et al., 2015; Smokowski, Evans, & Cotter, 2014). Thus, resources have been developed in multiple arenas (e.g., schools, communities, media) as measures of social control.

people gathered, a haze of cigarette smoke hovering over their heads. Attend a wedding, retirement party, or dinner party and alcohol will likely be served. Some single people who are searching for Mr./Ms. Right (or Mr./Ms. Right Now) carry out those searches in bars—bars that likely have a happy hour (when drinks are less expensive) or even a ladies' night, where schoolgirl attire buys five drinks for five dollars. Across genres (hip hop, country, pop, rock), music lyrics not only include references to alcohol, but frequently specific brands of alcohol. Alcohol brands sponsor many festivals and concert tours, and in fact, a growing number of musical artists have their own brands of alcohol (e.g., Jay-Z, Pharrell Williams, Sammy Hagar, Hanson). Attend certain concerts, and although cameras may be confiscated, marijuana will not, and even those members of the audience who are not drug users will find themselves getting a secondhand high.

The related social controls we see around us are further evidence of substance use. Walk into your university's student resource centre and you will find pamphlets about alcohol abuse, smoking, and "club drugs." Prior to reading week (or spring break), abuse prevention campaigns might be displayed throughout your campus. If you tell someone you are going to a club, they may warn you about the dangers of "date rape" drugs. In school, you may have been exposed to educational programs about smoking, alcohol use, and drug use, often beginning in early elementary school. Rarely does a day go by when each of us does not see someone using such a substance (whether in person or in the media) or see some type of substance control efforts.

A large-scale survey of Ontario students in grades 7 to 12 finds that the three most commonly used substances are alcohol (46 percent in the past year), cannabis (21 percent), and e-cigarettes (12 percent) (Boak, Hamilton, Adlaf, & Mann, 2015). Substance use among youth peaked in the 1970s and then steadily declined until the early 1990s. Usage increased throughout the 1990s, but has subsequently declined once again (although the use of some specific substances, such as opioid pain relievers, is higher) (Adlaf & Paglia-Boak, 2007; Boak, Hamilton, Adlaf, & Mann, 2015).

Tobacco

The health risks associated with smoking and secondhand smoke exposure have been well established by medical research. When those risks were first publicized during the 1970s, smoking rates among youth began a steady decline that lasted until 1990. But beginning in 1990, youth smoking increased once again and continued to grow throughout the decade (Health Canada, 1999). Another shift has occurred since that time, such that smoking among youth has shown a significant downward trend (see Figure 6.2). Because most adult smokers indicate they started smoking prior to the age of 18 (Janz, 2012; Shields, 2005), declines in youth smoking are most likely indicative of further declines in adult smoking in the coming years.

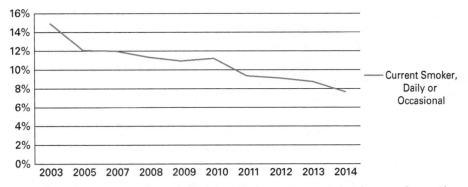

Figure 6.2 Proportion of Canadian Youth (Ages 12 to 19) Who Smoke Daily or Occasionally, 2003 to 2014

Based on Statistics Canada (2016e). *Table 105-0501. Health indicator profile, annual estimates, by age group and sex, Canada, provinces, territories, health regions (2013 boundaries) and peer groups.* CANSIM. Accessed: February 3, 2017.

Youth say that the primary motivation for smoking comes from friends or peer pressure (Health Canada, 2005). Research also shows that youth are less likely to smoke if their parents are non-smokers, and if they live in households with higher incomes and higher levels of parental education (Janz, 2012; Shields, 2005).

Youth smoking is socially controlled in a variety of ways. The federal *Tobacco Act* prohibits the sale of tobacco products and e-cigarettes to those under the age of 18, although provincial legislation can increase the minimum age requirement to 19. This kind of legislation has existed for many years, but enforcement has been lax for much of that time. In the 1970s, it was not uncommon for children as young as six or seven to be sent to the corner store to buy cigarettes for a parent or an older sibling. More recently, enforcement has become more stringent and penalties for selling cigarettes to minors have become more severe. For example, Alberta retailers can be fined up to $3000 for a first offence and up to $100,000 for a second offence (Government of Alberta, 2015).

And most retailers in Canada are complying. Health Canada conducts regular investigations of more than 5000 retail outlets in 30 cities across Canada. A research team of one youth and one adult go into a retail outlet (although not as an identifiable pair), and the youth requests a package of cigarettes. The youth lies about his or her age, if asked, but does not carry any identification. Using this methodology, research found that almost 85 percent of retailers complied with legislation, refusing to sell cigarettes to the youth, although there were some small variations based on the type of retail outlet (e.g., corporate-owned versus privately-owned convenience store) (Government of Canada, 2015).

Social control efforts specifically aimed at curtailing youth smoking are part of broader forms of regulation for smoking. We have come a long way from the days when cigarette commercials appeared on television, people smoked anywhere they wished (including university classrooms and hospitals), and doctors prescribed smoking as a weight-loss tool. Today, cigarette commercials are prohibited on television, and cigarette advertising is widely restricted.

In many communities, recent laws have banned smoking in many workplaces, shopping malls, hospitals, and restaurants. Other communities have taken this legislation a step further, prohibiting smoking in all public buildings, including bars. And, of course, instead of prescribing smoking as a weight-loss tool, contemporary doctors try to convince their patients to stop smoking and provide resources to help them quit (e.g., nicotine patches, access to support groups).

The tobacco industry itself has faced retroactive measures of social control arising, in part, from its past efforts to recruit youth smokers. Because most adult smokers began smoking while still in their teens, historically tobacco manufacturers focused much of their marketing efforts on youth. For several decades, tobacco companies denied these marketing efforts. In the 1990s, however, the seven major tobacco companies were sued by 46 states in the U.S. In 1998, five of the companies signed a Master Settlement Agreement that required, in part, placing online all the internal company documents they were forced to produce during the trial. This became the foundation for the Legacy Tobacco Documents Library (LTDL), recently renamed

Joel W. Rogers/Getty Images

The use of this animated character in cigarette advertising was highly criticized for its apparent attempts to attract the attention of youth.

Truth Tobacco Industry Documents; it is curated by the library at the University of California, San Francisco. The collection now includes more than 14 million documents, in a searchable database that is available to the public. Industry documents reveal efforts to improve cigarette marketing to youth. For instance, one company memo states, "It's a well-known fact that teenagers like sweet products," while another says, "The smoking patterns of teenagers is especially important to [our company]" (cited in Truth Tobacco Industry Documents, n.d).

However, research done in more than a dozen countries around the world has clearly demonstrated that images of smoking in movies have as large of an impact on youth smoking as—or an even a greater impact than—does tobacco advertising. There is a strong dose-response effect, in that (controlling for other variables associated with smoking initiation) the more images of smoking in movies that youth are exposed to, the more positive their attitudes are toward smoking and the greater the likelihood they will initiate smoking (World Health Organization, 2011). How common are images of smoking in movies? The *Thumbs Up, Thumbs Down* project regularly collects data on tobacco images in top-grossing films. Although tobacco images are more prevalent in adult-rated than youth-rated films, smoking in youth-rated (i.e., G/PG and PG-13) films is quite common, and is typically carried out by the movie's main characters. For example, in 2015, almost half of films rated PG-13 included images of tobacco, with an average of 19 tobacco incidents per film. Of the six major studios producing PG-13 films (Comcast Universal, Fox, Sony, Time Warner, Viacom, and Disney), Disney had the worst track record, with an average of 31 tobacco incidents per film. Movies rated for younger audiences (G/PG) were less likely than those rated PG-13 to include tobacco images, but those that did include such images had more of them—an average of 29 tobacco incidents per film (Polansky, Titus, Atayeva, & Glantz, 2016).

Because of the influences of tobacco images in movies on youth smoking initiation, the World Health Organization (2011) recommends several control measures. These include (but are not limited to) the following: R-ratings for all movies that include images of smoking (except by real historical figures who smoked); anti-tobacco messages prior to any film that includes tobacco images; movie producer certifications that they did not enter into any agreements with tobacco companies in exchange for including tobacco images; no public (i.e., government) subsidies for films that include smoking.

The health dangers of smoking are well known and have led to comprehensive anti-smoking efforts for people of all ages. However, smoking among youth is a public concern not only because of the health dangers, but also because of its association with other forms of substance use. Youth who smoke are more likely to use other drugs, particularly marijuana (Health Canada, 2005).

Drug Use

Cannabis is the most widely used drug among Canadian youth (Adlaf & Paglia-Boak, 2007). The *Ontario Student Drug Use and Health Survey (OSDUHS)* found that 21 percent of adolescents in grades 7 through 12 have used cannabis within the past year, a proportion second only to alcohol (at 46 percent) (Boak, Hamilton, Adlaf, & Mann, 2015). Similarly, the *Canadian Tobacco, Alcohol and Drugs Survey (CTADS)* finds that 22 percent 15- to 19-year-olds and 26 percent of those aged 20 to 24 have used cannabis within the past year (Health Canada, 2013).

Other illicit drugs have considerably lower rates of usage than cannabis. Among youth in grades 7 to 12, the most commonly used illicit drugs (excluding cannabis) are ecstasy (used by 5 percent of students in the previous year) and mushrooms/mescaline (used by 3 percent) (Boak, Hamilton, Adlaf, & Mann, 2015). Even among older youth (ages 20 to 24), illicit drug use (excluding cannabis) remains low, at only 6 percent in the previous year (Health Canada, 2013). Young people are more likely to abuse prescription (e.g., opioid pain relievers) or over-the-counter medication (e.g., cold medication) than they are illicit drugs (Boak, Hamilton, Adlaf, & Mann, 2015; Health Canada, 2013).

Although the regular use of psychoactive drugs is fairly uncommon among Canadian youth, those who do regularly use psychoactive drugs may do so problematically, increasing their risk of negative life consequences. Approximately 8 percent of young people aged 15 to 24 report harms from drug use—in physical health, friendships, home life, work or school opportunities, legal issues, learning, or housing (Health Canada, 2013). The more frequently youth use illicit drugs, the greater the likelihood of harms. For example, a study done in Quebec some years ago found that of those adolescents who have used an illegal substance more than five times, more than half have gone to school stoned or used an illegal substance in the morning or while participating in a competitive sport (Roberts et al., 2001).

The reasons for drug use vary among different groups of Canadian youth (Kerley, Copes, & Griffin, 2015; Norman & Ford, 2015; Phil, 2014). Some may use drugs for reasons similar to adult drug users—to relieve stress, as a form of escapism, or as a social activity. However, youth may also have distinctive motivations for drug use, such as to satisfy their curiosity, show their independence, become part of a peer group, or adapt to demands placed on them by parents or teachers. The relationship between an individual's drug use and drug use among peers is especially strong. Among youth who report having friends who use drugs, 80 percent also use drugs themselves; in comparison, only 7 percent of youth whose friends are drug free use drugs themselves (Hotton & Haans, 2004).

As with youth crime, the factors influencing youth drug use are multidimensional (Norman & Ford, 2015; Phil, 2014; Roberts et al., 2001). *Individual* factors that influence whether substance use becomes problematic include the following: genetic and environmental predispositions, degree of personal competence (e.g., extent to which the individual feels in control of his or her life and optimistic about the future), connection with violent behaviour, and gang involvement. *Community* factors include norms about substance use, prevalence of crime, price and availability of substances, economic conditions, and nature of peers. At the level of the *family*, parenting style, degree of parent–child emotional attachment, and family history in relation to substance use play significant roles. Finally, within the *school*, academic success, reading skills, problem-solving abilities, participation in extracurricular activities, and feelings of belonging influence the nature and extent of drug use.

Due to the multiple factors operating at different levels that influence youth drug use, effective programs are comprehensive, targeting factors at all levels and thus involving families, communities, schools, and youth themselves (Brotnow & Sinha, 2014; Roberts et al., 2001; Sinha & Brotnow, 2014). Programs must be age-appropriate and occur *prior to* the child's likely exposure to drugs. Effective programs integrate youth's own perceptions of drugs and drug use and realistically take their lifestyles into consideration. For example, the "Just Say No" campaign is seen by many adolescents as being unrealistic, not providing them with the tools they really need to deal with the situations they will encounter in their lives.

The problematic nature of drug use among regular users makes the reduction of drug use an important goal for these comprehensive programs. However, it is important to keep in mind that only a small percentage of youth use drugs and an even smaller percentage use them regularly. In contrast, the use of alcohol is far more prevalent among Canadian youth.

Alcohol Use

Alcohol use is a normative behaviour for youth in Canadian society. Just under half of youth in grades 7 to 12 have consumed alcohol within the previous year, although the majority have consumed alcohol at some point in their lives (Boak, Hamilton, Adlaf, & Mann, 2015). However, by grade 12 more than 70 percent of youth have had a drink in the previous year, and half within the past month (see Figure 6.3). In many cases, it is not just "a drink," but rather several drinks. Among youth in grade 12 who have consumed alcohol, approximately one-third have engaged in binge

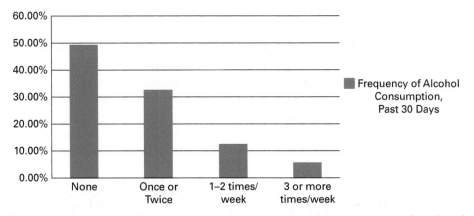

Figure 6.3 Frequency of Alcohol Consumption Within the Past 30 Days (Grade 12)

Based on Boak, A., Hamilton, H. A., Adlaf, E. M., & Mann, R. E. (2015). *Drug use among Ontario students, 1977–2015: Detailed OSDUHS findings*. (CAMH Research Documents Series No. 41). Toronto, ON: CAMH.

drinking and a similar proportion report having been "drunk" within the past month (Boak, Hamilton, Adlaf, & Mann, 2015).

The alcohol industry has been widely criticized for its role in facilitating or even promoting this phenomenon by targeting adolescents with the creation of flavoured alcoholic beverages (FABs) (low-alcohol beverages intended to taste like soda)—also known as "alcopops" or flavoured malt beverages. These beverages are very popular among youth. Almost two-thirds of adolescent drinkers (especially girls) report having consumed an FAB within the previous month, compared to less than one-third of drinkers in their late twenties (Mosher, 2012). The most popular FAB is Smirnoff Ice, consumed by almost 18 percent of youth ages 13 to 20 within the previous month (Fortunato et al., 2014). Mosher (2012) outlines the sophisticated youth-oriented marketing campaign surrounding Smirnoff Ice. Between 1970 and 1997 beer overtook distilled spirits (i.e., "hard" liquor), in large part because of its popularity in the youth market, where spirits were viewed as a beverage for older generations. Facing declining sales, the company that owns the Smirnoff brand (Diageo) developed a new marketing strategy, and even hired a former vice president of a tobacco company to steer its public relations. The first phase of Diageo's marketing strategy was to develop a drink that would taste like soda. Thus, Smirnoff Ice was introduced in 1999. It carried the brand capital of Smirnoff vodka, but was made with a flavourless malt liquor that enabled the fruit flavours of the beverage to shine through. Next, Diageo began advertising Smirnoff Ice in youth-oriented media venues: during television shows where 30 percent (or more) of the audience was under the legal drinking age (violating a voluntary guideline established by the alcohol industry); on Internet gaming sites; on youth-oriented websites; and subsequently on YouTube and Facebook. Finally, because people tend to leave FABs behind by the time they reach their late twenties, Diageo developed another new beverage that consumers could transition to—Smirnoff Twist, a flavoured vodka only slightly lower in alcohol content than regular vodka. As a result of these efforts to capture the youth market, Smirnoff has become the top alcohol brand in the world and Diageo has gone on to use a similar marketing strategy with some of its other brands (e.g., Jose Cuervo tequila, Captain Morgan rum).

Ask Yourself

How do you define "binge drinking"? What proportion of students at your university do you think engage in binge drinking?

Although drinking is common in youth of all ages, one particular aspect of problematic alcohol use has garnered public attention: binge drinking among university students.

Binge Drinking among University Students. Research on **binge drinking** (five drinks in one sitting for males and four drinks in one sitting for females) among university students has found it to be a rather unique pattern of behaviour, different from alcohol use in younger youth or even among youth the same age who are not university students. The unique nature and pattern of university binge drinking necessitates distinct social control measures.

In many people's minds, university life and alcohol go hand in hand. Students events—especially those that mark the beginning of a new academic year—are often sponsored by alcohol companies, such as Molson. University bookstores frequently stock not only textbooks and office supplies, but also beer mugs and shot glasses. Popular university rating guides often rate universities not only on academic factors but also on social factors, such as the best "party universities." Picture yourself at a university party such as a fraternity party. The images that come to mind likely contain large numbers of people present and loud music playing. Some of you might picture a few party attendees smoking marijuana or using other types of drugs, but in all likelihood it is images of alcohol that prevail—kegs of beer, drinking games, and large punch bowls of brightly coloured and highly potent beverages. You might imagine people at these parties consuming five, six, or even more drinks in one evening, perhaps even passing out.

Students say that the university environment is "conducive to binge drinking" (Hundersmarck, 2015, p. 44). When their post-secondary education begins, oftentimes so does their "apprenticeship in drinking" (p. 40). Even youth who did not drink in high school find themselves immersed in an environment where alcohol consumption—and even binge drinking—are normative. Students indicate that in the new social environment of the university, alcohol serves as a "social lubricant" (p. 46) and drinking to excess becomes a way to "fit in" (p. 46). However, they do see binge drinking as limited to the university environment, indicating that with graduation come new obligations and responsibilities that are no longer conducive to binge drinking. Most of our knowledge about university binge drinking comes from the United States, where research shows that between 35 and 40 percent of university students are binge drinkers (i.e., have engaged in binge drinking within the past few weeks), a proportion that has remained consistent for more than 20 years (Byrd, 2016; Johnston et al., 2016; Wechsler & Nelson, 2008). However, the prevalence of

Pressmaster/Shutterstock

Binge drinking and the university lifestyle go hand in hand in the popular imagination, and also in practice.

binge drinking varies across various subgroups of students. The "traditional" university student (aged 18 to 23 and living away from parents) is much more likely to binge drink. Binge drinking is also more common among members of on-campus groups, such as athletic teams, bands, fraternities, and sororities (Hundersmarck, 2015; Lewis et al., 2017; Wechsler et al., 2002).

Although the proportion of binge drinkers has remained consistent since the early 1990s, some changes in binge-drinking patterns have emerged. Alcohol use among university students has become more polarized: the proportion of abstainers (people who do not drink alcohol) has increased, yet so has the proportion of more frequent and higher-risk binge drinkers (Johntson et al., 2016). Another change in binge drinking is that it has increasingly moved off campus (Hundersmarck, 2015).

It has been suggested that more stringent university alcohol policies that emerged during the 1990s may have created a more supportive environment for abstainers, contributing to the increase in the proportion of non-drinkers. However, for heavier drinkers and for student subcultures in which drinking is more common, the more stringent policies may have facilitated resistance and rebellion. As these subcultures isolate themselves within their more accepting social networks and move their drinking activities to less-supervised off-campus areas, bingers' social contact with non-drinkers declines. Bingers are increasingly surrounded by heavier drinkers, subsequently raising the proportion of university students who are "frequent" binge drinkers (Keeling, 2002).

Individual binge drinking is correlated with the rate of binge drinking among peers, particularly close friends; that is, binge drinkers associate with other binge drinkers, and non–binge drinkers associate with other non–binge drinkers (Byrd, 2016). Patterns of binge drinking change during the academic year. There is a significant amount of binge drinking at the beginning of the year, but as class demands increase during the middle portion of the academic year and students become entrenched in their study routines, binge drinking declines. However, it increases once again following exams (Brower, 2002).

University binge drinking is not associated with problem drinking in later life, but there is no doubt that it does contribute to negative outcomes, such as accidents, sexual assault, unsafe sexual practices, and academic problems (Hundersmarck, 2015). Thus, a wide range of preventative and retroactive social control measures have been implemented on campuses throughout North America to curb the problematic consequences of binge drinking.

Most students in the Harvard College Alcohol Study report that they have been exposed to the following preventative controls: being informed of the university's alcohol rules and penalties for violating those rules, being targeted by educational campaigns about the dangers of consuming too much alcohol, and being informed of where they can seek help for alcohol problems (Wechsler et al., 2002). For students who have violated university alcohol policies or who have been otherwise identified as problem drinkers, a wide range of retroactive controls are used—written reprimands, fines, mandatory attendance at alcohol education programs, community service, and referral to alcohol treatment programs (Wechsler et al., 2002).

Preventative and retroactive social controls that target the individual and attempt to motivate them to refrain from problematic drinking are the most common social controls found at universities. In other words, the most prevalent university controls are efforts at stimulating self-control or self-regulation. However, the effectiveness of these efforts is questionable, as illustrated by the fact that, despite increasing control efforts, the prevalence of binge drinking has remained unchanged for over two decades. And although there are more abstainers than in the past, there are also more "frequent" binge drinkers.

Brower (2002) proposes that the shortcoming of many traditional social control efforts is that they mirror approaches for controlling alcohol abuse in society at large, which is based on the presumption that students who binge drink are "problem drinkers" who have problems with alcohol dependency. However, the fact that binge drinking usually stops following graduation suggests that it is a product of the university environment rather than being associated with alcoholism or other types of "problem drinking." Treating alcoholism (or other types of problem drinking) effectively typically means using individual treatments that are based on complete abstinence from alcohol. But if binge drinking is a product of the university environment, then control efforts must modify the role that alcohol plays in that environment.

Because university binge drinking tends to be treated as an individual problem, there is a **prevention paradox** in the university environment (Weitzman & Nelson, 2004). The growing efforts to help "problem" drinkers on campus have not reduced the extent of harm caused by alcohol consumption because, in fact, most of the harm comes from the larger number of students who engage in occasional binge drinking (e.g., on weekends) rather than the smaller number of students who may have problems with alcohol dependency (Scribner et al., 2011; Weitzman & Nelson, 2004).

A growing body of evidence from several countries suggests that the only effective means of control may be changes to regulatory environments, that is, changes in the university environment and the larger societal environment. At a societal level, a considerable body of research has found that the harmful consequences associated with binge drinking are significantly lower in communities that have higher alcohol taxes, a higher minimum drinking age, and stricter legislation or policies regarding alcohol accessibility and availability and driving while intoxicated (Goeij et al., 2016; Scribner et al., 2011; Wechsler & Nelson, 2008).

Thus, a *population prevention* approach has been found to be most effective in reducing harm (Goeij et al., 2016; Scribner et al., 2011; Wechsler & Nelson, 2008). This type of approach targets the university environment as a whole, rather than trying to change the behaviour of particular individuals. It includes regulating the prices of alcohol in university venues (e.g., policies governing drink specials, promotions, and alcohol advertising on campus), mandatory responsible beverage service (e.g., policies requiring employees at

Ask Yourself

What is your university doing to curb binge drinking? Your student resource centre may have information on the various aspects of your university's social control efforts— education programs, peer support, services for students with serious drinking problems, and university policies.

university venues to refuse further service to intoxicated people), limitations on the number of campus outlets that sell alcohol, and policies governing the overall accessibility and availability of alcohol (Scribner et al., 2011; Weitzman & Nelson, 2004).

However, it is also the case that taking extreme measures in which students are not consulted (e.g., "dry" campuses) is ineffective as well, because "students—like most of us—will react defensively and angrily to actions taken 'against' them" (Keeling, 2002, para. 29). What controls *do* students approve of? Wechsler and colleagues (2002) found that students approve of the following measures: making the rules clear, providing more alcohol-free recreational and cultural activities, offering more alcohol-free residences, prohibiting kegs on campus, and banning alcohol advertising on campus.

Binge drinking among university students, teenage alcohol use, drug use, and teen smoking are harmful to the individual consuming those substances but are also perceived as potentially dangerous to society. Youth who engage in these behaviours are therefore seen as both "troubled" and potentially "troubling." Young offenders, youth gang members, and young people who engage in substance use are just some of those youth who are considered deviant in our society and made subject to various measures of social control. However, other youth are also considered "troubled" or "troubling," such as street kids, runaways, and those who are prematurely sexually active. More recently, the concept of "at-risk youth" has emerged, which is able to encompass all of these groups of deviant youth—and even more.

TIME TO REVIEW

Learning Objective 4

- What are the characteristics of cyberbullying, and in what ways is it related to other troublesome behaviours?

- How have the patterns of youth tobacco use changed over time, and in what ways is youth smoking formally and informally controlled?

- What are the patterns of drug use among youth, and what problems do regular users of drugs experience?

- Why do youth use drugs, and what factors determine whether drug use becomes problematic?

- What are the patterns of alcohol use among adolescents, and why has the alcohol industry been criticized for these patterns?

- What proportion of university students engage in binge drinking, and how does this proportion vary over time and across different groups of students? What are the consequences of binge drinking?

- How is binge drinking among university students most commonly controlled, and why have these controls been criticized? What are the implications of the "prevention paradox" for effectively controlling the harm caused by alcohol use?

Youth "At Risk"

The concept of "**at-risk youth**" has come to permeate many sectors, including health, social services, education, policing, and even industry (Bessant, 2001; Ericson & Haggerty, 2001). This concept emerges from the broader notion of a **risk society**, which Beck (1992, 1999) suggests has emerged over the past several decades—a society in which knowledge experts warn us that risks are everywhere around us. It is the job of professionals to then identify those populations that are "at risk" of various negative outcomes and implement programming that will manage those risks. The precise nature of those risks and their potential negative consequences depend on the particular social group in question. For youth, the risks and consequences are seen as many: "It has become part of the contemporary common sense that leaving school 'early,' living in certain family arrangements and having a particular socio-economic or ethnic background put a young person 'at risk' of various other social ills like unemployment, crime, suicide, homelessness, substance abuse and pregnancy" (Bessant, 2001, p. 31).

Particular groups of youth are labelled "at risk" because of numerous personal, family, community, and educational factors, similar to those we addressed in looking at youth crime, gang involvement, and substance use. Those particular outcomes are just some of the possible consequences when risks remain unmanaged; thus, "at-risk youth" has become a label that replaces "troubling," "troubled," "delinquent," and "maladjusted." It is an encompassing category into which those youth who are threats to the social order or threats to themselves can be placed and then subsequently controlled through the **science of risk** (Bessant, 2001; Ericson & Haggerty, 2001). The science of risk, constructed by those experts and professionals who are presumed to have the necessary knowledge in that area, enables management of young criminals, gang members, substance abusers, street kids, teenagers who are prematurely sexually active, runaways, and even those youth whom the science of risk identifies as having a higher probability of any of those outcomes *in the future*.

Via the social typing process, "at-risk" youth are identified in schools, community agencies, or by the police, and they are then subjected to particular risk management strategies. For example, schools in "high-risk" neighbourhoods may have their own police officers to provide drug education, interact with students to create more favourable perceptions of the police, help resolve conflicts so that they do not escalate, and liaise with other individuals or agencies that can help individual youth whom the police have identified as facing more "risks" than others (Ericson & Haggerty, 2001). High-risk youth will find themselves on the receiving end of an array of risk management strategies. They may be entered into special educational programs in their school to increase their commitment to education and grades, they may be provided with necessary types of counselling or personal programs (e.g., anger management), or their families may be provided with needed resources or counselling.

In practice, professionals in the numerous sectors permeated by the science of risk frequently implement risk management strategies with *all* youth, rather than distinguishing between those who are and are not "at risk"; the implication is that all youth are "at risk" (Bessant, 2001; Ericson & Haggerty, 2001). Bessant (2001) suggests that although the label "at risk" has replaced older categories of troubled and troubling youth, "the youth-at-risk categories are different from the older categories in terms of their capacity to incorporate the entire population of young people" (p. 32). All youth are perceived as being potential threats to the social order, or threats to themselves and their own futures. The very nature of youth itself is seen as being deviant and in need of social control. "The wider culture constitutes youth as a symbolic threat. Disorderly youth are an expression of 'respectable fears'...about disorder and decline in general" (Ericson & Haggerty, 2001, p. 107).

Aren't All Youth Deviant?

One magazine writer speaks of her own experiences with parenthood: "It was about the fourth time my daughter Katie had made cookies on her own. She was 12, which is precariously close to 13, which in humans is not an age but a serious mental disorder" (Beck, 2001, p. 69). Although intended to be humorous, her statement reflects the perception that youth are problematic—not just *some* youth, but *all* youth. The popular image of the teenager is imbued with both "troubled" and "troubling" facets. Most of us have heard (or even participated in) conversations about the problems of adolescents. Themes in these conversations typically include phrases like the following: "They have no respect for authority anymore!" "When I was young, things were different!" These kinds of laments portray adolescents as a distinct and separate group, a group that is at the very least an annoyance and that may even pose a danger to themselves, to society, and to the future of civilization. As the title of Patricia Hersch's (1998) book suggests, they are considered "a tribe apart."

The problematic nature of adolescence began receiving widespread public attention not long after the "teenager" was labelled in the 1950s. At that time, articles about how to parent teenagers could be found in women's magazines such as *Ladies' Home Journal* and *Good Housekeeping*, and parenting manuals were written that focused specifically on teenagers. However, since the 1950s the problem of teenagers has been seen not only as a problem for the parents raising them, but also as a problem for society. That is, those problems that result in conflicts between parents and teenage children in individual families are perceived as indicative of problems between the adult and adolescent generations in the broader society.

A euphemism that many of us are familiar with—the **generation gap**—captures this perception. Why does a generation gap exist between adults and teenagers? According to this widespread perception, the generation gap is certainly not because of the adults—it is because of the teenagers, who are the problem that needs to be controlled. Adolescence itself has come to be defined as a time in the life cycle that is inherently deviant. We can see this perception reflected in the media; for instance, in an article titled "Your Teenager: An Owner's Manual (For the Bewildered Parent)," a popular Canadian women's magazine refers to adolescence as a time that is characterized by four "technical glitches" (*Canadian Living*, 2006, p. 162), implying that there is something inherently wrong with teenagers. Surveys reveal that more than 70 percent of adults describe youth as rude, wild, and irresponsible; they state that compared to youth 20 years ago, young people today are more selfish, materialistic, and reckless (Bostrom, 2001). Because perceptions of adolescents are based on these types of characteristics, considerable social control or regulation is seen as necessary.

We can see the formal regulation of adolescents in debates over the value of school uniforms in high schools, community curfews for those under the age of 18, special laws for teenagers (e.g., in Canada, the *Youth Criminal Justice Act*), special risk management programs in many junior high and high schools, and more. In these instances, the intent is to regulate, monitor, and control what is perceived as the inherently problematic nature of adolescence. We can see informal regulation in the changed approaches to parenting once adolescence arrives, the greater monitoring of teenagers in retail stores, the desire to sit as far away from a group of teenagers on the subway as possible, and the informal conversations we hear about "kids today." Such forms of formal and informal social control are intended to manage the deviant nature of adolescence and the subsequent "generation gap."

The Generation Gap: The Past

The perception of youth as a problem in need of control is nothing new, extending back thousands of years. For instance, Aristotle (384–322 BCE) described youth as having an absence of self-control (especially sexual self-control), being prone to angry emotional outbursts, spending too much time with friends, and thinking they know everything (*Rhetoric, Book II*). At the turn of the twentieth century, psychologist G. Stanley Hall (1904) spoke of the **sturm und drang** (storm and stress) of adolescence, suggesting that individual development mirrors the evolution of the human species. According to Hall, the process of growing up is a transition from "beast-like" to "human-like" where the period of adolescence mirrors the evolutionary stage of primitive man. The problems of adolescence could not be avoided, but with the appropriate controls to deal with that stage of psychological development and to minimize the damage adolescents might do, adolescents would eventually "grow out of it" as they reached the civilized stage of adulthood.

The "original" teenagers of the 1950s (Doherty, 1988, p. 45) were born during and immediately after World War II. They differed from previous generations in terms of their sheer number, economic prosperity, and generational cohesion in that they had an "awareness of themselves as teenagers" (Doherty, 1988, p. 45). Society accorded them a particular social status—"teenager"—and this group became part of a recognized youth culture. There was some dismay at the arrival of the teenager and its associated youth culture, which "cultural guardians … likened to *barbaric hordes descending upon a city under siege* [emphasis added]" (Doherty, 1988, p. 51).

Research in the mid-twentieth century frequently concluded that teenagers were a distinct and oppositional subculture and that the future of society was at risk. For example, research found that for teenage boys, being a star athlete was of ultimate importance, and for teenage girls, being popular was most important. These kinds of empirical results reinforced the perception that teenagers were as different from adults as possible and that all adolescents were "troubling," a threat to the social order (Tanner, 2001). Other researchers (e.g., Berger, 1963), who suggested otherwise, were largely ignored in popular discourse. They claimed that the generations are far more similar than they are different, that most parents and their teenage children get along fairly well, and that there are many issues on which they agree. Berger suggested that it is parents who bring the emphasis on sports to their sons' lives and the emphasis on popularity to their daughters' lives. Furthermore, interests in sports and peer acceptance are not limited just to the lives of teenagers but pertain to adult lives as well. Moving to the present day, we can still see the reality of Berger's claims.

The Generation Gap: The Present

Why do children get involved in organized sports? They play sports because their parents get them involved, and this occurs at increasingly younger ages. How many 4-year-olds insist that they want to join the community T-ball league? Parents enroll these young children in sports because they are quite adorable to watch. Where do children learn that sports are important? Again, they learn this from the adults in their lives—parents, teachers, coaches, and the media. Children's sporting leagues have had to institute regulations governing parental behaviour simply because of the preponderance of cursing at the officials, name calling of children on other teams, and even physical violence. For instance, in just one month, police were called to two minor hockey games in Edmonton; fearing for their safety at the hands of parents attending the game, the referees (who are teenagers themselves) had to lock themselves in their dressing room until police arrived. Five parents were suspended as a result, in addition to the five parents who were suspended earlier in the season (Huncar, 2017). In that same month, Burnaby RCMP were called to a peewee hockey game for the same reason (Larsen, 2017). One teenage referee describes his own similar experiences: " … at the end of the game, 10 parents were waiting at the gate we come off at to swear at us and tell us to go die …" (Judd, 2015).

The extreme behaviour of parents at children's sporting events demonstrates to children from an early age how important sports are. The importance of sports is also emphasized by the fact that some of the most highly paid people in North America are professional athletes, who make millions of dollars every single season. Dozens of television channels are devoted solely to sports, as are entire sections in the daily newspaper. If sports are important to teenagers, it is only because their parents and other adults put so much stress on them. Berger (1963) made this basic claim 40 years ago, but in contemporary society this pattern is even more evident than it was then.

Why is popularity important to teenagers? Again, it is because adults have made it so. Parents, teachers, and other adults encourage children to "make friends" and express concern if their children have too few friends. At a very young age, how many of us have heard adults say, "You must share your toys *or the other kids won't like you*," or "You have to be nice, *or the other kids won't want to play with you anymore*"? The importance of having the other kids like you and want to play with you is made clear before a child even enters grade 1.

Popularity is also important in the adult world, although we are unlikely to use the word "popularity" to describe it. The phrase "keeping up with the Joneses" refers to adults who want the same status of car, house, boat, or vacation as their neighbours or co-workers. This begs the question of whether these examples are really any different than teenagers who want the same kind of clothes or shoes as their peers. Many of us have felt obligated to go along with a group of co-workers for drinks or coffee after work, even when we would rather have gone straight home. As adults, when we move to a new city or some traumatic life change occurs (e.g., divorce), the advice we are given is to join clubs or community organizations so we can make new friends—as if finding more friends is the solution to our problems. And recent research being widely reported in the media points out the link between physical health and the extent of one's social network; these popular magazine articles are telling us we have to "make friends" because our lives really do depend on it!

Adults and youth are more similar than early research claimed. Most teenagers conform to the larger society, get good grades in school, go on to post-secondary education, and never get into trouble with the law, use drugs, or get pregnant (or get someone else pregnant). In fact, by taking a closer look at families, we see that parent–teen conflict is not as large a problem as popular images suggest. Disagreements are quite common, with 39 percent of teenagers saying they have disagreements with parents at least once per week (Bibby, 2009). However, conflicts are usually over everyday issues (e.g., household tasks) rather than large life-altering issues (Bibby, 2009; Weymouth, Buehler, Zhou, & Henson, 2016).

Even though conflicts do increase during adolescence (Weymouth, Buehler, Zhou, & Henson, 2016), 67 percent of teenagers say family life is "very important" to them (the highest proportion in the more than 30 years that sociologist Reginald Bibby has been conducting regular surveys of Canadian adolescents), 80 percent say they get a "high level" of enjoyment from interactions with their mothers, and 89 percent say that their mothers have a high level of influence in their lives (82 percent say the same about their fathers) (Bibby, 2009). In the end, the clear majority of teenagers turn out all right. In fact, Bibby finds that in many ways, today's Canadian adolescents are doing better than ever.

Thus, some scholars say that the concept of the "generation gap" is an exaggeration facilitated by stereotypes of teenagers, sensationalistic media portrayals that will attract an audience, and moral panics stimulated by interest groups who want to advance a political or economic agenda. Even research itself tends to focus on problems with teenagers rather than on the rather mundane everyday lives of most teenagers. Although Bibby's research finds that twenty-first-century teens are doing remarkably well compared to earlier social generations, concerns about adolescents are more prevalent than ever. For instance, Bibby says, "I've sometimes been appalled at the negative reaction of people involved in the drug field when I bring some good news about drug use being down—or the wincing of teachers when I suggest students are feeling more positive about school than they did in the past. I am treated like the bearer of bad news" (Bibby, 2009, pp. 67–68). Our cultural focus on problems leads us to lose sight of the fact that most families and most teenagers are doing just fine.

The Generation Gap: The Question of the Future

A considerable amount of research has claimed that the concept of the "generation gap" and the notion that adolescence is an inherently deviant time in the life cycle are exaggerations. However, some social analysts are now expressing the concern that, given contemporary social patterns and family trends in particular, the possibility of a significant generation gap may arise in the near future.

Some scholars suggest that beginning in the late 1990s contemporary family life became more characterized by a culture of busy-ness, where scattered work, education, and extracurricular schedules of family members often mean that they spend little time with each other. The lives of teenagers may be especially impacted by these changes, in that they are perceived as needing less direct supervision than younger children, making it easier for parents to leave them on their own amid complex family schedules. To some people, contemporary teenagers have become "a vague mass of kids growing up in a world that rushes past them until one of them steps out of the shadows and demands attention by doing something extraordinarily wonderful or troublesome, outrageous or awful. The rest of the time, especially for the average, everyday kid who goes along not making any waves, the grown-up world doesn't pay much attention" (Hersch, 1998, p. 11).

Two decades later, research reinforces Hersch's view. The American Time Use Survey finds that parents spend the most time with their younger children, and that time spent with children drops significantly as children become older (US Bureau of Labor Statistics, 2016). Of course, time spent with children can vary in quality. Some of that time is *accessible* time, where parents are available but are not interacting with children. This stands in contrast to *engaged* time, where parents and children are participating together in activities. Recent research finds that engaged time (especially with both parents) may, in fact, be more important for adolescents than for younger children, having a greater impact on academic (e.g., grades), emotional (e.g., mental health), and behavioural (e.g., criminal activity) outcomes (Milkie, Nomaguchi, & Denny, 2015).

It is in this adolescent aloneness that the potential for a new and significant generation gap emerges. In living, to some extent, separate lives, the possibility of similar values, similar interests, and an enjoyment of time spent together declines. Furthermore, considering the central roles that parenting factors (like the quality of parent–teen relationships) and community structures (that support and integrate youth) play in the emergence of youth crime, gang involvement, and substance use, adolescents' aloneness may set the stage for such "troubling" and "troubled" behaviours to emerge in the future.

The exaggerated generation gap of the past may become a reality in the future, although Bibby's research suggests that this may not be the case. But even if a growing generation gap does emerge, will it be because of the inherently deviant and problematic nature of adolescence itself? It may be that just as in the past, today's teenagers are simply living the lives that adults are creating for them. Youth who end up being "troubled" or "troubling" and those who are identified as being "at risk" then require social control. But even more significant is that the perceived "deviant" nature of adolescence and youth culture may be reinforced by the resulting realities of their lives.

TIME TO REVIEW

Learning Objective 5
- What leads certain youth to be considered "at risk," and how has the science of risk expanded in recent years?

Learning Objective 6
- What does the "generation gap" refer to, and what has traditionally been considered the cause of the generation gap?
- How are teenagers perceived and socially controlled in society?

- How were youth perceived in ancient Greece, at the turn of the twentieth century, and in the 1950s?
- What led some mid-twentieth-century researchers to conclude that teenagers formed a distinct and oppositional subculture?
- Why do some people claim that youth are *not* an oppositional subculture?
- Why might a new and significant generation gap emerge in the future?

CHAPTER SUMMARY

- Youth and deviance seem to go hand in hand in Canadian culture. Of concern are "troubling" youth, "troubled" youth, and "at-risk" youth; however, to some extent, all youth are perceived as deviant. (1)

- The "troubling" youth who receive the greatest attention are those involved in crime and those who are members of gangs. However, a gap exists between popular images of youth crime and gangs and their actual prevalence and nature. The media particularly contributes to a moral panic, from which various groups potentially benefit. (1)

■ Concerns over youth who *are* involved in crime and gangs have stimulated a wealth of research. Research has highlighted the role of family factors in explaining youth crime and a complex set of individual, family, educational, and community factors in explaining the emergence of and involvement with gangs. The social control of gangs is intertwined with the control of youth crime more generally, which has shown considerable variation over the past century. (2, 3)

■ "Troubled" youth who are of particular concern in contemporary society include those who use various substances. Although almost all youth have used alcohol by the time they graduate from high school, fewer youth regularly use tobacco, marijuana, or other drugs. Over the past decade, binge drinking on university campuses has drawn widespread attention, resulting in a wide range of social control efforts. (4)

■ The concept of "at-risk youth" is a recent formulation that integrates various types of "troubling" and "troubled" youth. The science of risk attempts to identify youth who are at greater risk of negative outcomes in their lives and then target risk management efforts at those youth. (5)

■ To some degree, *all* youth are perceived as being deviant and in need of social control. Adolescence is seen as an inherently deviant time in the life cycle, creating a "generation gap" between teenage and adult generations. Although the generation gap may be more of an exaggeration than a reality, some researchers suggest that current social patterns open the door for a real generation gap to emerge. (6)

> To learn more about the topics discussed in this chapter and to complete chapter quizzes, visit the Companion Website for *Deviance, Conformity, and Social Control in Canada.*

Chapter 7
Looking Deviant: Physical Appearance

Learning Objectives

After reading this chapter, you should be able to

1   Explain the role of "body projects" in people's lives and what the appearance of people's bodies tells us.

2   Describe the different kinds of information that are obtained about body modification when studied from various locations along the objective–subjective continuum.

3   Define the "ideal" body weight according to scientific standards and social standards, and describe how many people are "too fat" and "too thin" according to these standards.

4 Explain how people who are overweight are viewed and treated, and describe the range of social control measures targeted at "too fat."

5 Explain how people who are underweight are perceived and treated, and describe the range of social control measures targeted at "too thin."

6 Describe the various ways that people who have been labelled "too fat" or "too thin" resist the social typing process.

An old Chinese proverb claims that "talent counts thirty percent; appearance counts seventy" (Simply Reference, 2017). Half a world away and several centuries later that statement still rings true in many ways. We do live in a culture where physical appearance is important. Think of the myriad ways you maintain your own physical appearance. You have chosen a certain hairstyle and perhaps even hair colour. Every morning you might blow dry, straighten, curl, gel, or spray your hair to achieve a specific look. Perhaps you put on makeup. Then you choose certain clothes, depending on what your plans are for the day. Are you going to work, school, a job interview, a date, dinner with your grandparents, a club, or to write a final exam? For all but the last item on that list, you probably choose your clothes carefully. Maybe you have a tattoo, piercings, or some other type of body art. Perhaps you are dieting to lose weight, working out to become more sculpted, or taking supplements to increase muscle mass. As one of a select few, you may be gulping milkshakes to gain weight. You may even be contemplating cosmetic procedures to fix your nose, reduce wrinkles, suck the fat out of your love handles, or increase the size of your breasts. The time, effort, and money we spend on our physical appearance illustrate how important it is to us.

Our appearance is important to us in part because we wish to express ourselves and paint a picture of who we are. But our appearance is also important because we know people judge us by how we look. The way we look can affect whether we are hired for a job, what our grandparents think of us, who will and will not want to start a conversation with us, whether the person we are interested in will go on a date with us, and whether people stare at us as we walk down the street.

Physical appearance is the stimulus for the social typing we do every day and to which we are subject every day. But social typing based on physical appearance goes beyond our own individual likes and dislikes. Regardless of our own personal preferences for appearance, there are larger patterns of social typing that occur in our society. For instance, we all know that our chances of being hired are small if we appear at a job interview wearing sweatpants. Similarly, we know that someone with brown hair is far less likely to be stared at as they walk down the street than is a person with blue hair—and yet some people choose to dye their hair blue anyway, despite (or perhaps because of) that reaction.

Voluntary and Involuntary Physical Appearance

Some forms of physical appearance are voluntarily adopted—hairstyles, clothing, makeup, and body art. Precisely which forms of voluntary physical appearance are considered deviant depends on the sociohistorical context. Slicked-back hair, "dungarees" (jeans), and leather jackets were perceived so negatively in the 1950s that they were prohibited in many high schools. Men with long hair who wore beads were considered deviant in the 1960s and 1970s. Some store windows contained signs saying "No Hippies Allowed." Today, many schools have student dress codes that prohibit revealing clothing for female students and gang colours for students of all sexes—although there is considerable debate surrounding precisely what constitutes revealing or gang-affiliated clothing (CBC News, 2016b; Sagan, 2015).

Voluntary aspects of physical appearance that may be stigmatized also include those associated with certain lifestyle groups, such as dance music cultures (Jaimangal-Jones, Pritchard, & Morgan, 2015), drag cultures (Horowitz, 2013), punk rockers (Force, 2009), skinheads (Pollard, 2016), and cosplayers (people who dress up as characters from works of fiction, like comics) (Schiele & Venkatesh, 2016). In these cases, appearance is only one aspect of an overall lifestyle based on political, philosophical, or social foundations.

Other forms of physical appearance are involuntary in nature, such as height, the size of one's nose or shape of one's eyes, or visible disabilities. Although individuals have little or no choice regarding these aspects of their physical appearance, they may still be stigmatized in our society—stared at, laughed at, teased, or excluded from opportunities, activities, and relationships (Chaudoir, Earnshaw, & Andel, 2013). In Nazi Germany, people with visible disabilities were even targets of genocidal efforts (Mostert, 2002).

However, the boundary between voluntary and involuntary forms of physical appearance is somewhat blurred. Some forms of physical appearance combine voluntary and involuntary aspects. A good example of this is body weight. People choose how much to eat and how much physical activity to participate in (voluntary); however, psychological factors, social factors, and biological factors may influence those outcomes (involuntary). Furthermore, what is considered "voluntary" varies across cultures and over time, and may even vary across subgroups within a single culture. For instance, in Canada today, members of specific ethnocultural or religious groups may adhere to certain aesthetic standards, whether due to cultural tradition or religious requirements. For members of those groups, cultural socialization places boundaries around the choices they make regarding clothing or hairstyle. Sometimes people who are not members of those groups may adopt similar physical appearances—such as Justin Bieber sporting dreadlocks or music festival attendees donning Indigenous headdresses. This practice of turning culturally-significant aesthetic standards into fashion commodities has led to public debates over **cultural appropriation** (i.e., adopting elements of another culture without regard for their history or meaning) (Huffington Post Canada, 2016; O'Neil, 2016).

Shilling (1993) uses the term **body projects** to refer to the ways that each of us adapts, changes, or controls characteristics of our bodies and whether those characteristics are voluntary or involuntary. If you have poor eyesight, you may get glasses; if you do not like the look of glasses, you might get contact lenses. If you think you are too short, you may wear shoes with higher heels; if you think you are too tall, you may slouch as you walk. If you consider yourself too fat, you may start working out or go on a diet; if you consider yourself too thin, you may begin taking supplements to build muscle mass.

> ### Ask Yourself
> We all engage in various types of body projects. What types of body projects do you engage in and why? What makes your body projects similar to or different from those of people you see around you?

There are four different categories of body projects. First are **camouflaging** projects—"normative . . . techniques of body manipulation, learned in socialization processes" (Atkinson, 2003, p. 25). Examples include makeup, clothing, and hairstyle. Second are **extending** projects that attempt to overcome one's physical limitations, such as in the case of using contact lenses or a cane. Next are **adapting** projects, where "parts of the body are removed or repaired for a host of aesthetic . . . or medical . . . reasons" (p. 26). These include weight loss, muscle building, and laser hair removal. Finally, there are **redesigning** projects that "reconstruct the body in lasting ways" (p. 26), such as cosmetic surgery, tattoos, and body piercing. Various body projects may change the functioning of our bodies (e.g., contact lenses) or modify the appearance of our bodies (e.g., weight loss). This chapter emphasizes the latter, not only because physical appearance is important in our culture, but also because the appearance of people's bodies tells us something.

What is it that people's bodies tell us? The answer depends on one's location along the objective–subjective continuum. When looking at the issue from the more objective end of the continuum, bodies tell us about the characteristics of individuals involved in specific body projects, such as their age, sex, socioeconomic status, family structure and functioning, academic performance, personality, and psychopathology. Moving toward the more subjective end of the continuum, instead of learning about the characteristics of an individual person, we learn about the role that physical appearance plays in how people come to understand themselves, others, and the world around them.

From this more subjective vantage point, people's understandings form through social interactions with others, within a broader societal context. Thus, not only do people's bodies tell us about the way they attribute meaning to themselves and others, but also the structures and processes of the social fabric within which they live. Bodies are "text[s] upon which social reality is described" (Foucault, cited in Schildkrout, 2004, p. 319). For example, Lévi-Strauss explained the purpose of tattooing in the

Maori culture of New Zealand as "not only to imprint a drawing onto the flesh but also to stamp onto the mind all the traditions and philosophy of the group" (cited in Schildkrout, 2004, p. 321).

Among the endless variety of body projects that can affect physical appearance, two types are noteworthy. First, there are redesigning projects commonly known as body modification or body art—activities such as tattooing, piercing, branding, and scarification. These activities have become increasingly common over the past few decades, as well as increasingly accepted. They are an interesting illustration of how perceptions of what is deviant and normal change over time. Second, there are adapting projects related to body size or body weight. The social typing of body weight saturates all of us living in Canadian society today, permeating the fields of medicine, media, commercial industry, education, and even our daily interactions. Because the social typing of body size is so pervasive and affects so many lives, it is an interesting illustration of how the social construction of deviance and normality is an ongoing part of all our lives.

With all forms of physical appearance that may be socially typed as deviant, it is not necessarily appearance itself that generates a negative reaction but rather the meanings, stereotypes, and interpretations that are attached to that appearance. Physical appearance constitutes what Howard Becker (discussed in Chapter 3) called a **master status**, the primary label we attach to a person that subsequently defines who the person is. The auxiliary traits we attach to master statuses are what make them significant. Thus, people with disabilities were systematically killed by the Nazis not simply because of their appearance, but because they were perceived as a drain on society. Similarly, people who are obese are not stigmatized because of their appearance per se, but because that appearance is presumed to be indicative of laziness, a lack of self-control, and psychological problems. Some forms of body modification are socially typed as deviant in part because they are perceived as being associated with other risk-taking behaviours and with a broader opposition to the social order.

Body Modification

The history of tattooing, piercing, branding, and scarification is a long one, perhaps as long as the history of humanity itself. The remains of a 5000-year-old mummy discovered in the Alps had several visible tattoos, and archaeologists have found evidence of tattooing and piercing on bodies and represented on artifacts on every continent except Antarctica (DeMello, 2016). Whether forms of body modification have been stigmatized or considered acceptable has varied across cultures and over time. Body modification has been "variously used to mark outlaw status and nobility, insiders and outsiders, soldiers and slaves" (Schildkrout, 2004, p. 325).

In the early Christian and medieval eras, some Europeans had tattoos representing their religious affiliations and dedication, although that practice was abandoned over time (Atkinson, 2003; Schildkrout, 2004). European exploration and colonization brought such practices to broader public awareness, leading to the "first tattoo revolution" (DeMello, 2016, p. 25). As European explorers encountered new lands and new peoples and European governments colonized those lands, innumerable body modification practices were seen. In these various cultures, tattooing, branding, piercing, scarification, and implanting served as rites of passage, sacred symbols, signs of beauty, indicators of social position, and more. For example, "in Indigenous societies, tattoos were deeply embedded in social institutions, and while they were decorative, they also functioned to communicate rank, religious devotion or affiliation, marital status, important accomplishments, and other social markers to the world at large" (DeMello, 2016, p. 23). European sailors brought back their own body modifications akin to souvenirs from their travels.

However, European discourses that supported colonization emphasized the "civilized" nature of European societies in contrast to the "primitive" nature of other cultures. From this perspective, body modification was equated with savagery (Atkinson, 2003). Colonization also meant Christianization, and the Old Testament dictates that "Ye shall not make any cuttings in your flesh for the dead nor print any marks upon you" (Leviticus 19:28, cited in Cronin, 2001, p. 380). Although body modification was socially typed as deviant in Euro-dominant societies, the public's fascination with "primitive" cultures meant a growing interest in it. During the late eighteenth and early nineteenth centuries, people with extensive body modifications were featured in carnival side shows, partially nude and frequently dressed as savages (Atkinson, 2003; DeMello, 2016).

Over time, body modification left the carnival community. In Victorian England, some members of the privileged classes obtained tattoos as part of an ongoing fascination with other cultures or as mementos of their own leisure travels in the expanding leisure industry. In the early twentieth century, changes in technology made tattooing quicker, easier, and more affordable, and thus it entered society at large (although its availability to society's masses caused the privileged classes to leave the practice behind). By the 1950s, tattoos had become an established means of symbolizing masculinity and brotherhood in working-class communities, the military, and criminal groups (Sanders, 1989). The 1960s and 1970s brought in the "Tattoo Renaissance" (DeMello, 2016, p. 25). In the countercultural and anti-war movements of the 1960s, and then the New Age movements of the 1970s, youth used tattooing and other types of body modification as "collective representation" (Atkinson, 2003, p. 41) of their subcultures and political or social ideologies. This era brought body modification into middle-class communities, the backgrounds of most of the participants in these social movements.

In the twenty-first century, body modification has an even greater reach. It is pervasive within popular culture, from tattooed celebrities to television series (e.g., *Ink Master*). The commodification of body modification, particularly tattoos, is also evident when one sees the range of tattoo-related products targeted at children, "such as

Tattoo Barbie, *The Sesame Street Talent Show: Tattoo Tales, Around the World in Tweety Time: Tattoo Storybook*, and the Power Puff girls' *Ruff n' Stuff Tattoo Book*, that include tattooed figures, colour-in tattoo kits, and temporary tattoos" (Kosut, 2006). Now you can even obtain a tattoo or body piercing in a chain outlet at your local shopping mall, between your shampoo purchase and a new pair of shoes.

In this marketplace, body modification has become more prevalent. In 2003, 16 percent of adults ages 18 and over had at least one tattoo. By 2012 that proportion increased to 21 percent, although there was some variation by age (see Figure 7.1) (Harris Interactive, 2012). Not only does the prevalence of body modification vary by age, but also by other characteristics within age groups. For instance, although Harris Interactive (2012) found that 22 percent of young adults ages 18 to 24 overall have tattoos, more than 40 percent of university students (who are largely within that age group) have tattoos (Dickson, Dukes, Smith, & Strapko, 2015; Hill, Ogletree, & McCrary, 2016).

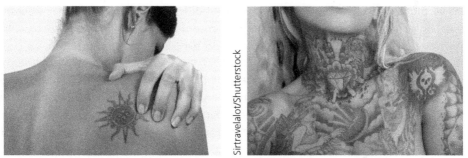

The practice of tattooing spans a wide range of people, from individuals who obtain one small tattoo to elite tattoo collectors who display artwork across their bodies.

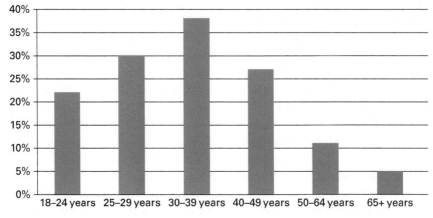

FIGURE 7.1 Proportion of the Adult Population with Tattoos, by Age

Based on Harris Interactive (2012). *One in five U.S. adults now has a tattoo.* Retrieved from www.prnewswire.com.

Although males were more likely than females to have tattoos for much of the twentieth century, the situation today is quite different. Females are now just as likely to have tattoos, and in some populations even more likely (Kluger, 2015). One study of 300 university students found that 51 percent of females had tattoos, compared to only 31 percent of males (Hill et al., 2016). Body piercings (excluding earlobes) are less common than tattoos, but also vary by gender. For example, 19 percent of female university students have facial piercings, compared to only 5 percent of males (Hill et al., 2016). The increasing prevalence of body modification has led to an upsurge in research on its participants. There is consensus that body modification conveys important information, but there are different points of view on precisely what that message is.

What Do Modified Bodies Tell Us?

Characteristics of Body Modifiers: Risk and Motivation

As we move from one end of the objective–subjective continuum to the other, we learn that bodies with tattoos, piercings, and other forms of body modification can potentially provide us with a great deal of information. Beginning at the far objective end, we hold the individual under the microscope—tattooed and pierced bodies tell us about the characteristics of that individual. From this viewpoint two central issues are emphasized: risk and motivation. Here, the presence of tattoos and piercings (above all, among youth) is associated with a broader range of risk, such that youth who have forms of body modification are perceived as being "at risk" more generally. For example, in an analysis of more than 4000 members of an online body modification site, Liu and Lester (2012) find extensive histories of physical, sexual, and mental abuse as well as emotional abandonment, particularly for females (and especially for those with body piercings).

Much of the risk-oriented research highlights psychological and behavioural risk, analyzing the association between body modification and other problematic characteristics such as risky sexual behaviour, substance use, violence, eating disorders, educational difficulties, criminal activity, and psychological problems (Dukes, 2016a; Kluger, 2015; Koch, Roberts, Armstrong, & Owen, 2010; Owen, Armstrong, Koch, & Roberts, 2013). For example, in a review of the existing literature on people with tattoos, Kluger (2015) finds several studies that highlight an association between tattoos and other risky behaviours. However, other research does not find this relationship. For instance, an analysis of middle-class adults with body modifications finds no association with mental health history, criminal activity, substance use, or risky sexual behaviours. In fact, this research found that the only statistically significant difference to emerge in comparing those with and without body modifications was that people with body modifications were more likely to engage in a range of *positive* behaviours, such as eating well, engaging in regular physical activity, donating money to charities, and doing volunteer work (Giles-Gorniak, Vandehay, & Stiles, 2016).

The extent to which body modification may be associated with other risky behaviours seems to vary based on several other factors, such as the number of body modifications an individual has and age. Risks appear to be higher for people who have more body modifications. Research suggests that the threshold number may be four; university students who have four or more tattoos are significantly more likely than their peers to engage in drug use, binge drinking, and risky sexual behaviours (Koch, Roberts, Armstrong & Owen, 2015). Risks are also greater for adolescents than for adults, and the younger the age at which an adolescent obtains body modification, the greater the risk (Dukes, 2016a; Kluger, 2015). This may be for a variety of different reasons (Dukes, 2016a). First, those forms of risk tend to decline as people mature into adulthood, in part because of the responsibilities they assume (e.g., full-time employment, parenthood). That means risky behaviours that were a part of adolescence may dissipate as the individual matures. Second, adolescents may be more likely to internalize stigmatizing labels; being stigmatized for body modification may lead some to adopt other deviant behaviours as part of a growing deviant identity and lifestyle. Third, just as certain adolescents are more likely than others to engage in criminal activity and substance abuse (see Chapter 6), the same may be true regarding body modification. Adolescents who obtain body modifications at a young age may be those who are already experiencing other difficulties at the individual, family, school, or community levels—difficulties that also increase the likelihood of substance use, criminal activity, risky sexual behaviours, and poor mental health.

From this more objectivist vantage point, tattooed and pierced bodies tell us about the psychology and the behaviours of individuals who have them, although there is debate about precisely what characteristics such individuals have. The proposed association between body modification and other risks is directly linked to social control efforts, especially for adolescents. Pediatric professionals are advised to consider tattoos or piercings in adolescents to be indicators of potential psychological and behavioural problems and to conduct assessments for other high-risk behaviours (e.g., Burger & Finkel, 2002; Carroll, Riffenburgh, Roberts, & Myhre, 2002).

Researchers with a more objectivist orientation also draw attention to the potential harms of body modification itself, although Mayers and Chiffriller (2008) found that only 19 percent of individuals in their sample who had piercings (and no individuals who had tattoos) experienced any medical complications. However, numerous health risks can be associated with tattooing and piercing, such as allergic reactions, sun sensitivity, surface-level skin infections, deeper bacterial infections, and life-threatening systemic infections (Dieckmann et al., 2016; Serup, Hutton, & Sepehri, 2015). Given the potential risks of harm inherent in body modification, the question then becomes one of motivation or causation. Why would an individual engage in a behaviour that carries these risks?

Research identifies several different motivations for obtaining body modifications (Hill et al., 2016; Kierstein & Kjelskau, 2015; Kluger, 2015). However, many of those motivations are reflections of *aesthetics* and *individuality*. In one study of university students with tattoos, three of the ten reasons given for getting a tattoo were related to aesthetics: "to look attractive," "because they look good," and "to be creative." Another four were related to individuality: "to express myself," "to be an individual," "to be unique," and "to feel independent" (Hill et al., 2016).

Although the pursuit of individuality is important to many people, it is especially so with youth, for whom identity formation is a significant developmental trajectory. Strivings for individuality are a key aspect of determining who they are, independent of their families. Exploration and experimentation enable them to, over time, achieve this goal. For some youth, body modification may be part of this experimentation. Yet the results of experimentation through body modification can be long lasting. Changing a tattoo is far more difficult than changing your clothing or hairstyle, the genre of music you listen to, or your hobbies—some of the other ways that young people may experiment and explore. Consequently, approximately one-third of adolescents with tattoos express regret (Dukes, 2016b). Because body modifications obtained as adults tend to be less exploratory and more personally meaningful, only half as a many adults say they regret their choices (Dukes, 2016a, 2016b).

Thus, from a more objectivist view, when we see modified bodies we learn something about those individuals. We may learn that they are experimenting as part of a specific developmental stage in the lifespan (adolescence), or may be engaging in a variety of high-risk behaviours (such as drug use), or could be experiencing psychological problems, or may come from marginalized backgrounds that contribute to a variety of negative outcomes. As we move toward the more subjective end of the objective–subjective continuum, the lens through which we view body modification shifts so that we are learning not just about individuals, but also broader social structures and processes.

The Self and Society: Understanding, Meaning, and Resistance

From a subjectivist view, body projects are part of people's understandings of themselves, others, and the world around them. According to interpretive approaches, these understandings are not purely individual in nature, but rather emerge through our social interactions. As we interact with those with whom we are close (significant others) and with society in general (the generalized other), we try to view the world through their eyes (role-playing) and to understand what they see when they look at us (the looking-glass self). Their points of view, and their views of us, influence how we understand ourselves and our places in the world. According to critical approaches, some people's viewpoints are more likely than others' to be legitimized and reflected in society's institutions, such as the education system and the economy. Thus, through our interactions with others (which occur within a larger structure of power), we come to attribute certain meanings to body modification and understandings of the role body modification will play in our own lives.

Some subjectivist scholars study body modification using a dramaturgical perspective. From this perspective, the decisions about whether to engage in body modification and the precise nature of any body art are all part of constructing our "front-stage" selves and "back-stage" selves (see Chapter 3). We decide on the image that we intentionally project to others and whether we want body art to be a part of that image. People with body art engage in impression management surrounding that art, deciding how large it will be, where it will be located, and to whom it will be displayed (Roberts et al., 2016). Will the tattoos, piercings, or brandings be visible to the public, co-workers, and parents on the front stage? Or will the modifications be visible only to intimate partners on the back stage? Will it be part of the costume on all front stages, or only on certain ones (e.g., at a concert, but not at work)?

Other subjectivist scholars study body modification using a narrative approach. From this perspective, body art tells the stories of our lives. For instance, tattoos can signify important life events (e.g., completing a marathon), represent one's religious or spiritual beliefs (e.g., a religious symbol), proclaim a personal mantra (e.g., a motivational quotation), identify social group membership (e.g., a sports team), or reflect a personal relationship (e.g., a child's name). As one person with body art states, tattoos "mark moments in my life, sort of a story of myself and my beliefs" (Orend & Gagné, 2009, p. 501). Whether you are looking at body modification in terms of performances on the front and back stages or as telling a story, the reactions of other people to one's body art are important. Various audiences interpret our front-stage performances or the stories told by our bodies. Their interpretations have implications for the choices we make, how we feel about ourselves, and the measures of social control we encounter. We can see this when we consider body art within the contexts of gender, work, and interpersonal relationships.

Stories of Gender. The stories that are told by people's body modifications give us insight into the social construction of gender in society today, as well as their own gender identities. Certain tattoo designs and locations of the body are more traditionally associated with femininity or masculinity. Thus, the type of tattoo a person has indicates, in part, their gender identity and the extent to which it emerges from the acceptance of or resistance to traditional constructions of masculinity and femininity. The act of getting a tattoo, in itself, can tell a story of gender as well (Leader, 2016; Yeun Thompson, 2015).

For instance, Atkinson (2002) has found that some women use tattoos in the construction of their gender identities, which emerge from and have an impact on structures of power in society. Some women use tattooing in the development of an established femininity, while others use it in the development of a resistant femininity. **Established femininity** embodies the dominant cultural constructions of what a female body should look like. Thus, some women interviewed by Atkinson used tattooing to enhance their femininity.

> ### Ask Yourself
> If you have tattoos, piercings, or other types of body modification, consider the following questions: What story does your body modification tell? What do your tattoos or piercings tell us about gender in Canadian society today? What do they tell us about norms governing the workplace? What do they tell us about your personal relationships? What do they tell us about your self-concept, that is, your understandings of yourself? If you do not have any body modifications, consider what stories you are telling by virtue of their absence.

Their thoughts about how men would perceive their bodies played a role in their initial decision to get a tattoo. One woman said, "I think it looks sexy, and so do all my male friends" (p. 224). They spoke of their tattoos as making them more attractive to their boyfriends or to men in clubs, and perceived too many tattoos or too-large tattoos as unattractive and unfeminine. Their choice of images reflected the desire to enhance their femininity—for example, small flowers, celestial motifs, and insects such as ladybugs—as did their chosen tattoo locations, such as sexualized parts of the female body like the back of the shoulder. Thus, just as with breast implants and extreme dieting, some women's use of tattooing reinforces traditional gender ideals where the female body is an object for men's desires (Bordo, cited in Atkinson, 2002). Atkinson's discussion of tattooing and established femininity emphasizes constructions of female physical attractiveness. However, established femininity can also refer to other traditional female roles, such as motherhood; this is illustrated in a growing trend of women getting tattoos of their children's names or portraits (Withey, 2012).

Resistant femininity opposes dominant gender ideals, and thereby serves as a form of resistance to existing structures of power in society. For some women, tattooing is part of this resistance. They get tattoos precisely because of the practice's historical association with male communities. These women select larger designs, images that are more traditionally masculine (e.g., daggers) and more visible locations to actively express the self and resistance to patriarchal power relations. One woman stated, "My temple [body] is worked with symbols that read—a strong and independent woman lives here . . . forever" (Atkinson, 2002, p. 228). For other women, their statement of resistance is private rather than public, a negotiation between established and resistant femininity. Their tattoos are a form of personal liberation from traditional discourses of gender, yet their concern about possible stigmatization leads them to get their tattoos in concealable locations.

Women's use of tattooing today is within the context of the practice's traditional association with working-class masculinity. Even though there has been a significant increase in the prevalence of tattooing among females, Roberts and colleagues (2016) point out that this cannot be equated with "mainstream acceptance" (p. 795). Research shows that females with tattoos remain stigmatized, being perceived as more promiscuous, less attractive, and heavier drinkers (Swami & Furnham, 2007). Hawkes, Senn, and Thorn (2004) presented Canadian undergraduate students with various written scenarios about a female university student. The scenarios varied in terms of the presence of a tattoo, its size, and its visibility. Researchers found that, overall, tattooed females were viewed more negatively than non-tattooed females. Females with large or highly visible tattoos were seen more negatively than those with small or nonvisible tattoos. In another study, researchers found that a woman's age (23 versus 48) and tattoo design (masculine versus feminine) also affect university students' evaluations of her body modification. Older women run a greater risk of being deviantized for having tattoos, especially if their tattoos have masculine designs, than younger women (Musambira, Raymond, & Hastings, 2016).

Popular discourse reflects this negative view of women with tattoos, wherein a large tattoo at the base of a woman's spine is labelled a "tramp stamp." More recently, young women have moved away from that type of tattoo, in part to avoid that stigmatization. Now large tattoos along the rib cage are gaining in popularity, but Rocky Rakovic (editor of *Inked* magazine) points out that this new form of tattoo is viewed in similar ways. Rather than being labelled a "tramp stamp," large tattoos on the rib cage are labelled "skank flank" (Kwong, 2012). Rakovic states that tattoo artists have a responsibility to make female clients aware of that label, saying, "You have to tell [young women] that" so that they can make more informed decisions about tattoo design and location (Kwong, 2012).

Thus, tattoos tell stories of negotiation, resistance, or conformity to social norms governing gender. Those stories are interpreted by others, so that tattoos may mean something quite different to observers (e.g., promiscuity) than to the individuals who have tattoos (e.g., strength). We can learn more about the stories told by modified bodies within another context, that of the workplace.

Stories of Work.   Body modification and work are intertwined in several ways. In some cases, body art may signify membership in a specific occupational group, such as members of the military and first responders (DeMello, 2016; Strike the Box, 2017). This is even the case for illicit occupational groups such as criminal gangs and organized criminals. For example, the *yakuza* in Japan (i.e., the Japanese mafia) commonly bear full-body tattoos (Westlake, 2012). In other cases, body art may reflect an individual's identity as a worker. For example, many well-known chefs have tattoos of food items (e.g., bacon), pieces of cooking equipment (e.g., kitchen knives), or culinary terminology (e.g., *mise en place*) (Fitzgerald & MacNaughton, 2016).

Just as social norms governing gender influence observers' responses to people's tattoos, workplace norms have a similar influence. Certain workplaces may accept body art, while others do not. Attitudes toward body modification may vary depending on whether the modified body is that of a physician or rock star, financial advisor or landscaper, warehouse employee or daycare worker. In some workplaces, tattoos may be an asset. For instance, people who work in correctional facilities or with at-risk youth say that their tattoos serve as conversation starters and facilitate positive social interactions (Timming, 2015). The extent to which body art may be accepted depends its location, the organization or industry type, the proximity of the worker to customers or clients, and the design of the tattoo (Timming, 2015). Roberts and colleagues (2016) argue that the location of the tattoo is crucial: "After all, people are not fired for having four tattoos instead of two, nor are they fired for having a 12-inch tattoo instead of a 3-inch tattoo; they are fired for having unconcealed tattoos on the front stage" (p. 801). And in the tattoo industry itself, tattoo artists refer to tattoos in specific locations (e.g., hands, neck) as "job-stoppers" (Kwong, 2012). Consequently, many individuals who have various forms of body modification report face discrimination in hiring, or are required to cover tattoos and remove piercings while at work (Ellis, 2015).

Stigmatization is a result of the ways that observers interpret certain forms of body modification. As part of the second component in the social typing process (*evaluation*), certain auxiliary traits may be associated with having body art. For instance, one study found that people consider physicians with facial piercings to be less competent and less trustworthy (Newman, Wright, Wrenn, & Bernard, 2005). Thus, although body art is central to understandings of self, the expectations associated with one's professional role may place constraints on the nature and extent of self-expression. In the case of physicians, their desire for self-expression must be balanced with their obligation to make patients feel comfortable, to put them at ease, and to reduce their anxiety.

Some people respond to stigmatization through concealment, that is, by selecting locations and forms of body modification that are easy to hide at job interviews or in the workplace. Other people respond by embracing their body modifications, despite the ramifications. Although they realize they may face problems with employment, they consider it more important to make their authentic selves visible to observers (Roberts, 2015, 2016). Still others respond collectively by actively trying to change workplace norms. For example, the group "Tattoo Acceptance in the Workplace" (which can be found on Facebook) seeks to change workplace policies.

The stories told by body modification within the context of work are stories of people's understandings of themselves as workers and of their workplaces. Employers, co-workers, and clients or customers then interpret these stories in ways that lead to acceptance in some instances, but more often deviantization and social control. In addition to body modification telling stories of work and of gender, it also tells stories about interpersonal relationships.

Stories of Interpersonal Relationships. People's close interpersonal relationships are interwoven with their body modifications. Interactions with family members and peers may influence decisions about body art. Within families, interactions with parents may influence the individual's decisions about whether to obtain body art, its design, and its location. If people perceive their parents as disapproving of body art, they may select a design their parents are less likely to disapprove of (e.g., a small tattoo of a flower) or a location that can be easily hidden from their parents (e.g., a nipple or genital piercing). However, having body art that they know their parents disapprove of or having to continually hide it from their parents can have an impact on people's perceptions of self (Atkinson, 2003).

Peers play somewhat different roles. Individuals are more likely to actively seek the opinions of their peers when deciding whether to engage in body modification. Once the decision to obtain some form of body art has been made, individuals intentionally seek out more interactions with peers who also have body art. Interviews reveal that these interactions make individuals feel better about their decisions and provide a validation of self (Atkinson, 2003).

Body art designs may integrate close interpersonal relationships as well. In one study of undergraduate students, more than 20 percent of those with tattoos indicated that their first tattoo represented a bond or connection with certain people in their lives, a reminder of people who were no longer in their lives, or a memorial to a deceased loved one (Dickson, Dukes, Smith, & Strapko, 2015). Memorial tattoos have a long history, associated with the traditional practices of many cultures, including some Inuit and Polynesian cultures (Davidson, 2016; DeMello, 2016). Today some people even take the involuntary tattoos of the past and turn them into voluntary tattoos in the present. For example, prisoners at Auschwitz during the Second World War involuntarily had their prisoner numbers tattooed on their forearms. Some of their descendants now voluntarily tattoo that number on their own bodies, as a memorial to their ancestors and recognition of the significance of that event in world history (DeMello, 2016).

From a subjectivist view, body art does not just tell us something about the individual, but also larger social structures and processes. We learn about norms governing gender and the ways that people may accept or resist those norms through their choices in body modification. We learn about the structure of workplaces and how the auxiliary traits associated with body modification may constrain workplace opportunities. We learn about the nature of parent–child relationships, peer groups, and social bonds. More broadly, we learn that people's physical bodies are interwoven with their understandings of themselves, others, and the society they live in.

TIME TO REVIEW

Learning Objective 1

- What are the differences between voluntary and involuntary physical appearance?
- What are the different types of body projects?

Learning Objective 2

- In what ways does one's location along the objective–subjective continuum determine one's perception of what people's bodies can tell us?
- How have body modification practices changed over time?

- Based on the more objective end of the continuum, what risks are associated with body modification and what motivations are involved in modification practices?
- Based on the more subjective end of the continuum, how can the dramaturgical perspective and narrative approaches be applied to an understanding of body modification?
- What stories of gender, work, and relationships are told by people's body modifications?

Ask Yourself

Try to picture the ideal body. Notice the details. What does the ideal body look like? Is it a female body? If so, who does that body type most closely approximate—a model like Gigi Hadid, an actress like Jennifer Lawrence, a "plus-size" model like Ashley Graham, a member of the Canadian National Women's hockey team (like Marie-Philip Poulin), or the average woman you see on the street? If it is a male body, who does that body most closely approximate—a hockey player like Connor McDavid, actor Channing Tatum, a male figure skater like Patrick Channing, or the average man you see on the street?

"Too Fat," "Too Thin," and "Ideal"

Early-twentieth-century socialite Wallis Simpson claimed that "you can never be too rich or too thin" (Klauer, 2005). In the twenty-first century, does that phrase still hold true? Is thinner better? Is it possible to be too thin? In any culture at any specific time in history, only a certain range of body sizes are perceived as normal, conforming, or ideal. A body outside of that ideal is considered unacceptable, deviant, and requiring modification—overweight or underweight or, using more popular terminology, "too fat" or "too thin."

Take a moment to look at the *Ask Yourself* exercise. Once you have done so, consider the image that first emerged in your mind. If the ideal body you initially pictured was a female body, you should not be surprised. Body size and weight are more likely to be used as an evaluative criterion for women than for men (Kłonkowska & Maj, 2015). But even though men tend to have more freedom in what is considered an acceptable body, at some point they are also subject to the judgments of others based on their weight or the size of their bodies.

What is the ideal body according to our current cultural standards? To some extent, the answer to that question depends on whose criteria we are using—the criteria used by physicians in their evaluations of health, or the criteria used by average people in their judgments of people's physical appearance.

The Ideal Body According to Science

In the field of medicine, acceptable and deviant body weights are determined based on "risks" for negative health consequences. Relative risk can be measured in many ways, such as waist-to-hip ratio and simple height–weight tables. However, the most common measurement tool used by physicians and scientists today is the **body mass index (BMI)**. Although BMI is not an indicator of health risks for certain individuals with high levels of muscle mass (e.g., bodybuilders, people of specific ethnic backgrounds), it is considered a valid measure of risk at a population level (World Health Organization, 2016). BMI is determined through a comparison of height and weight according to the following formula:

[weight in pounds ÷ (height in inches × height in inches)] × 703

The standards of the World Health Organization (2016) categorize a BMI between 18.5 and 24.9 as in the "normal" range, because it is associated with the lowest health risks. A BMI between 25.0 and 29.9 is considered **overweight** because of increased risks of high cholesterol, type 2 diabetes, heart disease, high blood pressure, arthritis, and more. A BMI of 30.0 and higher is categorized as **obese**, with considerable risks for these illnesses. A BMI of 18.4 and lower is considered **underweight** because of greater risks of heart problems, lowered immunity, anemia, depression, and death.

According to these standards, being overweight is a significant problem throughout much of the world. Globally, 39 percent of adults are overweight or obese, and most of the world's population lives in countries where more people die of complications from being overweight than of complications from being underweight (World Health Organization, 2016). In Canada, 62 percent of men and 46 percent of women are overweight or obese (Statistics Canada, 2016b). Even among youth, obesity is a serious problem. In Canada, almost one in four youth ages 12 to 17 (i.e., 23%) are overweight or obese (Statistics Canada, 2016b). Throughout much of the world, children are developing diseases related to being overweight (e.g., type 2 diabetes, high cholesterol, cardiovascular disease), diseases that used to be limited to adults (World Health Organization, 2016).

Far fewer people worldwide are underweight than overweight, and they tend to be concentrated in developing nations where being underweight is often associated with malnutrition and stunted growth. In Canada, the proportion of people who are underweight declines from childhood to adulthood. While 7 percent of 18- to 19-year-olds are underweight, only 1 percent of adults ages 55 to 64 are (Statistics Canada, 2016b).

In the developed world, extreme thinness may signal the presence of anorexia for some people. **Anorexia nervosa** is one of several different eating disorders, all of which are mental disorders. Anorexia is characterized by a combination of physical and psychological symptoms that are dependent on the progression of the illness, including (but not limited to) the following: extreme weight loss to the point of emaciation, which is achieved through severe calorie restriction and/or obsessive exercise; distorted body image, where the individual denies any problem and continues to see herself as overweight; loss of female menstruation; growth of fine white hair over the body (in the body's attempt to keep warm); yellowing of skin; anemia; heart problems; brain damage; and multi-organ failure. Anorexia nervosa has the highest mortality rate of any mental illness; 10 percent of people with anorexia die within 10 years of onset (Centre for Addiction and Mental Health, n.d.). Between 1 and 3 percent of females (and fewer males) experience anorexia. It is more common among female adolescents and young adults, where the prevalence may be as high as 5 percent (Centre for Addiction and Mental Health, n.d).

Among males, **muscle dysmorphia** is more common than anorexia and is sometimes called "bigorexia." This refers to a preoccupation with being unmuscular and results in an obsession with weightlifting accompanied by anxiety or mood disorders, extreme body dissatisfaction, distorted eating attitudes, and anabolic steroid use. There is less research on the prevalence of muscle dysmorphia than anorexia, in part because of disagreement about the diagnostic criteria. Nevertheless, in some male populations it may be quite prevalent. For instance, one study of males who were participating in resistance training found that 12 percent met the criteria for muscle dysmorphia (Nieuwoudt et al., 2016).

The negative health and social consequences of anorexia, muscle dysmorphia, being overweight, or being obese have stimulated an abundance of research on how people come to have these experiences. Genetic, psychological, family, and larger socio-cultural factors have all been areas of focus for those researchers who take a more objective approach to these conditions by searching for causes (Centre for Addiction and Mental Health, n.d.; Chen, Jaenicke, & Volpe, 2016; Fiese & Bost, 2016; Hruby et al., 2016; World Health Organization, 2016). For example, while some people may have genetic predispositions for obesity, stress can contribute to poor food choices or a lack of physical activity, and the characteristics of certain neighbourhoods (e.g., high crime rates, poverty, a lack of access to stores with nutritious, low-cost food) place constraints on the availability of nutritious, low-cost food and opportunities for physical activity.

The research on causation and prevalence that emerges from scientific definitions of the ideal body is positioned on the more objective end of the objective–subjective continuum. Deviance specialists working from the more subjective end shift their attention elsewhere—to social definitions of the ideal body, the social control of body weight, and the implications of those social messages. While scientific definitions are based on medical implications, social definitions have a very different foundation. Social judgments of body weight more typically emerge from tacit definitions of the ideal body rather than scientific definitions; that is, when we react to our own weight or the weight of people we see, health risks are rarely the stimulus for our responses.

The Ideal Body According to Social Standards

As we judge the physical appearance of others or as our own physical appearance is judged, medical standards such as BMI or the diagnostic criteria for eating disorders rarely come into the picture. Instead, social standards determine the nature of the social typing process. These standards vary across cultures and over time, but at any given cultural moment we can identify what standards constitute the ideal body (see Figures 7.2 and 7.3).

Looking at our current cultural standards, a small range of bodies is considered "ideal." Note that the ideal body for both men and women leans toward the "thin" side of the continuum; our current cultural standards define more "thinness" than "fatness" as being acceptable. You will also note that the ideal range is thinner for females than for males. The ideal female body is "curvaceously thin," that is, thin with

FIGURE 7.2 The "Ideal" Female Body: Current Cultural Standards

FIGURE 7.3 The "Ideal" Male Body: Current Cultural Standards

large breasts. The ideal male body is "v-shaped," that is muscular, with broad shoulders, narrow waist, and low body fat (Flynn, Park, Morin, & Stana, 2015, p. 174).

A body outside of this ideal range is judged as in need of fixing—popular discourse labels it as either "too thin" or "too fat." At the extreme ends of the continuum are "anorexic" and "obese"; however, the popular usage of these terms is based on appearance alone, and does not necessarily correspond to the medical criteria for those conditions. In fact, there is a considerable discrepancy between what people consider to be a "normal" body weight and what they consider to be an "attractive" body weight. In one study, participants ages 4 through 26 were shown a series of photos that varied in terms of the body sizes represented. They were asked to rate the photos in terms of body normality and body attractiveness. In all age groups, the bodies rated high in attractiveness were considerably thinner than those rated high in normality (Brown & Slaughter, 2011).

The ideals of physical attractiveness stem, in large part, from media portrayals. Tylka and Calogero (2011) describe these media-perpetuated ideals as "fictions," "fashions," and "functions" (p. 448). They are *fictions* in that only a select few can realistically achieve them. In fact, bodies can be easily altered in digitized media, such that even the models and celebrities captured in professional images (or even in selfies on social media platforms) do not have the bodies pictured. These media-perpetuated ideals are *fashions* in that they become the standards for attractiveness in society. Although body ideals may also be communicated and reinforced through interpersonal interactions with strangers, co-workers, friends, and family members, people identify the media as the primary source of the thin ideal (Couch et al., 2016). They are *functions* in that they "dictate gender-specific functions of women's and men's bodies" (Tylka & Calogero, 2011, p. 448). Women's thin (yet busty) bodies are prescribed functions associated with sexuality and passivity, while men's "ripped" (Couch et al., 2016, p. 63) bodies are primed for physical action and dominance.

Contemporary ideals of female and male bodies emerge from significant changes in media representations during the latter half of the twentieth century that have continued to today. Female media bodies have become taller and thinner, and male media bodies leaner and more muscular (Calogero & Thompson, 2010). From the 1950s onward, *Playboy* centrefolds became increasingly thinner (Owen & Laurel-Seller, 2000), such that by the end of the twentieth century they were at their thinnest point ever. At that time, almost all centrefolds were underweight according to health standards, and approximately 30 percent met the weight criteria for anorexia (Spitzer, Henderson, & Zivian, 1999). In the twenty-first century, the trend continues in the modelling industry. A 2007 survey of British fashion models found that half considered anorexia to be a problem in the modelling industry, and 70 percent claimed that over the previous five years, the trend had been for models to be increasingly thinner (British Fashion Council, 2007). More recently, *Victoria's Secret* model Erin Heatherton was outspoken about her decision to leave the company because of the unrealistic weight criteria for its models. Despite starving herself and working out twice a day, she still was unable to meet the evolving standards (Elan, 2016). Current and former female models report that the standard in the modelling industry today is a height of 5 feet 11 inches, with a clothing size of 0 to 2 (Elan, 2016).

Outside of the modelling industry, women on television have become increasingly thinner as well. By the late twentieth century, the gap between the body size of women in the media and that of the average woman in society was considerable. In an analysis of the 10 most popular television shows during the 1999–2000 season, only a small percentage of female characters were overweight or obese, and a large proportion were underweight (Greenberg, Eastin, Hofschire, Lachlan, & Brownell, 2003). In the twenty-first century, this pattern remains evident. Actress Julianne Moore has said, "'All actresses are hungry all the time'" (Anderson, 2015), and Jennifer Lawrence indicates that "'In Hollywood I'm obese . . . I'm considered a fat actress'" (*Daily Mail*, 2012). The "real" people who appear on reality television also conform to the thin ideal. An analysis of several reality television shows on MTV found that two-thirds of the women conformed to the thin ideal (Flynn et al., 2015).

Media representations of male bodies also changed significantly in the latter half of the twentieth century, resulting in the V-shaped ideal that continues today. In various forms of media, images of men became larger and more muscular during the latter half of the twentieth century (Wroblewska, 1997). An analysis of male images in *GQ*, *Rolling Stone*, and *Sports Illustrated* between 1967 and 1997 illustrates the emergence of the muscular ideal (Law & Labre, 2002). The proportion of "very muscular" images increased over that period from 9 to 35 percent, while the proportion of "not muscular" images declined from 42 to 16 percent. As with female media bodies, this trend has also continued into the twenty-first century. Actor Channing Tatum has talked about the intense exercise and restricted eating plan that was necessary to transform his body for the movie *Foxcatcher* and the *Magic Mike* franchise, in some cases leading him to lose 15 pounds in a single day—"'I was not feeling very well after that'" (Ernst, 2015). This trend is also evident with "real" men's bodies on reality television shows, with three-quarters conforming to the thin, V-shaped ideal (Flynn et al., 2015).

By scientific standards, bodies are classified as overweight, underweight, or normal, based on health risks. By social standards, bodies may be considered too fat, too thin, or ideal. The nature of social standards means that even those who may have normal or underweight bodies according to science, may be labelled "too fat." To be considered "too thin" according to social standards, people must be extremely thin. Whether by scientific or social standards, those bodies that are deemed deficient are subject to negative evaluations and subsequent measures of social control.

"Too Fat": Commercialization, Societal Reaction, and Social Control

Perceptions of People Who Are Overweight

Although more than half of Canadian and American adults are either overweight or obese, people who are overweight face considerable stigmatization. They are stereotyped as emotionally and socially handicapped, lazy, sad, sloppy, and as having poor hygiene

(Taylor, 2011; Vartanian, Trewartha, & Vanman, 2016). Even health professionals who specialize in treating obesity stereotype obese individuals as lazy, unattractive, ugly, and bad (Puhl & Heuer, 2009). These stereotypes are accompanied by negative emotions, with people of varying ages saying they feel contempt and disgust when looking at images of obese people (Vartanian, Trewartha, & Vanman, 2016; Wirtz, van der Pligt, & Doosje, 2016).

Among the general population, 46 percent of adults say they would rather die one year earlier than be obese, and 30 percent would prefer divorce over obesity (Schwartz et al., 2006). The stigma we attach to people who are overweight is overwhelmingly clear when looking at the perceptions of children. Latner & Stunkard (2003) presented children in grades 5 and 6 with photographs of various types of disabled children (on crutches, in a wheelchair, with an amputated hand, and with a facial disfigurement) and overweight children. The overweight children were rated as the least desirable as friends. Anti-fat bias is pervasive in children as young as grade 3 (Bissell & Hays, 2011).

The popular perceptions of people who are overweight constitute the evaluation component of the social typing process. Of course, this leads to our discussion of the third component of the process: prescription. Various social control measures, both informal and formal, are directed at people who are deemed to be "too fat."

Controlling "Too Fat"

Negative perceptions of people who are overweight are accompanied by particular behaviours or forms of social control. Children and adolescents who are "too fat" most frequently experience direct and intentional teasing or name calling by classmates. They are verbally teased, physically bullied, and face social exclusion by peers (Puhl & Latner, 2007; Warschburger, 2005); obese children are twice as likely to be victimized in these ways than non-obese children (Hayden-Wade et al., 2005). A study of children in elementary school finds that they are aware overweight classmates are likely to be teased and bullied. More than 100 children viewed line drawings of an overweight child and a normal-weight child. They then read a story in which a child was called "stupid" by a peer. Two-thirds of the children indicated that it was likely the overweight child who was being victimized in the story. Furthermore, they stated that the overweight child was more likely to be teased and less likely to be popular (Nabors, Meriano, & Olsen, 2016). In adulthood, teasing and name calling may become less frequent, replaced by subtler messages from peers and strangers such as staring and whispering.

Behaviours extend beyond the casual comments of peers, family members, and even strangers. Research has consistently found that people who are overweight face discrimination in the institutions of society—education, health care, and employment (Glock, Beverborg, & Müller, 2016; Puhl & Brownell, 2001; Puhl & Heuer, 2009). In lab settings, several studies have asked participants to pretend to be employers making hiring decisions. They were provided with hypothetical resumés and photographs of job applicants. The results of these studies conclude that people who are overweight are significantly less likely to be hired for jobs, even given equivalent qualifications as normal-weight applicants. In the political realm, simply reading disparaging media comments about a politician's weight discredits that politician in observers' eyes, leading them to consider that candidate as less competent (Bresnahan, Zhuang, Zhu, & Nelson, 2016).

Many social control measures are directed specifically at trying to "fix" people who are "too fat." Some measures aim to reduce the health risks associated with the scientifically defined categories of overweight and obese, while others are based on reinforcing the overly thin social standards that define the ideal body. All of these control efforts ultimately are related to self-regulation; in the end, we are supposed to monitor and control our own body weight. However, the media, commercial industry, medicine, government, and community programs all make efforts to "fix fatness."

Media.   As you learned in Chapter 4, media permeates our lives. According to Couch and colleagues (2016), because the thin ideal is so pervasive, "various media messages considered together form a Gestalt which then acts as a form of social control" (p. 62). In other words, the thin ideal found within media is a type of social control itself. Not only does the media contain images of the ideal body, it also tells us how to control our bodies. Websites, online magazines, and a plethora of books share secrets for how to lose weight, get in shape, or attain the body of a certain celebrity. Morality is frequently linked to body weight, fitness, and food choices. The "right" body, fitness level, and eating habits are represented as indicators of strong morality, while the "wrong" physical characteristics are indicative of a lack of morality in the individual. For example, ads for a certain type of low-fat breakfast bar have a photograph of a woman with a giant pastry around her waist or cinnamon buns protruding from her hips. The tag line reads, "Respect yourself in the morning," suggesting that only by eating this low-fat breakfast bar can women respect themselves—and conversely, eating pastries means they are undeserving of respect.

Exercise Your Mind

Do an online search for "lose weight" or "get in shape." How many results are obtained from that search? Then look at a handful of those websites. What images of female and male bodies do you see? Then look at the headlines and associated written text. To what extent do they focus on weight loss or fitness in terms of health? To what extent do they focus on weight loss or fitness in terms of physical appearance?

Media portrayals of the "curvaceous thin" ideal for women and "V-shaped" ideal for men are forms of social control in themselves.

Media are also a tool used by other agents of social control. For example, a public health campaign by the organization Children's Healthcare of Atlanta featured billboards, online videos, and local television commercials to educate parents on the emotional and physical harms that can accompany being overweight. However, the campaign itself was immediately criticized for contributing to the stigmatization of children who are overweight, such as by featuring an image of an overweight, unhappy girl accompanied by the text, "Warning: It's hard to be a little girl if you're not" (Youngblut, 2012).

An additional aspect of the media's control of body size lies in its integration of advertisements and commercials for weight-loss and fitness products. The commercialization of weight loss exists not only in the media, but also outside of the media.

Commercialization. Commercial industry provides a massive range of products for controlling body size—books, videos, packaged foods, weight-loss programs, gym memberships, fitness equipment, pills, powders, patches, and more. It is estimated that by 2019, the global weight loss and weight management market will be worth $206.4 billion. It is in the best interests of commercial industry to attract as many consumers as possible; thus, the more of us who can be convinced that our bodies are lacking in some way, the more money the diet and fitness industry makes.

The role of commercial industry in regulating "too fat" extends to children as well. In 2012, Disney World created its "Habit Heroes" attraction, intended to educate children about healthy habits in a fun way. Shortly after opening the attraction, Disney closed it in the face of intense criticism. Part of the attraction involved children fighting overweight villains, such as "Snacker," "Glutton," and "Lead-Bottom." Critics argued that these portrayals would not improve health habits in children, but rather stigmatize overweight children even more (Anderssen, 2012). Freedhoff (2012) asked, "What kid doesn't want to be made to feel like a personal failure while on a Disney family vacation?"

Medicalization. Despite the profit-driven motives of the diet and fitness industries, which may distort facts through their efforts to convince people they are overweight, there is no doubt that being overweight is a health risk. The World Health Organization and many national governments emphasize these health risks. Heart disease is the number-one cause of death in adults in North America, and being overweight is one of the central risk factors for heart disease. Consequently, the medical community is heavily involved in the social control of people who are "too fat" by telling patients to change their diets or increase physical activity. In most cases, these forms of medicalization are based on the goal of reducing the health risks associated with being overweight.

However, the medical control of people who are "too fat" sometimes steps outside the realm of health and into the realm of physical appearance—in the past, for example, doctors told women who wanted to lose weight to take up smoking! From the 1950s through the 1970s, amphetamines were prescribed for weight loss. Beginning in the 1980s, other medications purported to decrease appetite, increase metabolism, or change the body's absorption of fat were developed. Since that time, several of these medications have been taken off the market because of health complications (and deaths), but are continually replaced by new drugs. Even the normal side effects can include nausea, vomiting, headaches, and uncontrollable bowel movements. The complications from weight-loss surgery are even more frightening. Even the normal consequences of weight-loss surgery sound unappealing, where eating more than a few tablespoons of food can lead to vomiting, explosive diarrhea, and fainting. Liposuction, which is surgery that uses a vacuum-like instrument to suck fat cells out of specific parts of the body, has nothing to do with health and is based solely on physical appearance. In fact, medical criteria for the procedure say that liposuction should not be done on someone who is medically overweight.

Governments.   The health risks associated with being overweight have a significant impact on the health of the world's population. By negatively impacting the health of large numbers of people, nations experience economic drains from consequences like health care costs, absenteeism from work because of illness, lower levels of productivity at work, and lost tax revenue. Globally, the economic costs of obesity have been estimated at $2 trillion per year (Associated Press, 2014). As a result, several governments have recently initiated considerable efforts to reduce the proportion of overweight people in their countries.

In 2011, Denmark became the first country to implement a "fat tax," that is, an additional tax levied on foods containing high levels of saturated fat. One year later the tax was repealed. Insufficient time had passed to determine whether the tax was effective in changing people's eating behaviours, but sufficient time had passed for opponents to draw attention to the negative economic consequences. They argued that lower-income households were unduly affected by the tax, that retailers had increased prices beyond the fat tax, and that the Danish economy was losing money because of increased cross-border shopping into Germany and Sweden. Despite Denmark's repeal of the fat tax, other countries are moving in a similar direction. France has implemented a tax on products containing palm oil, and Hungary a tax on foods that are high in fat, salt, and sugar. In Canada, the Ontario Medical Association lobbies for the taxation and labelling of unhealthy foods (Ha, 2012).

In Canada, a collective framework (involving federal, provincial, and territorial governments) has been developed for increasing the proportion of the population who have healthy weights, with a special emphasis on curbing childhood obesity (Public Health Agency of Canada, 2010, 2011a, 2011b). Strategies target individuals (e.g., health services and intervention), communities (e.g., workplaces and schools), and the broader social environment (e.g., tax credits for children's sports activities, food labelling policies, urban planning). You may be familiar with programs such as *ParticipACTION* (to increase physical activity) or *5 to 10 a Day* (to increase consumption of fruits and vegetables). But federal, provincial, and territorial governments are not the only bodies developing effective programs and policies for weight loss: so are individual communities.

Communities. Individual communities have developed a wide range of measures to reduce the proportion of people who are overweight. For instance, the Honour Your Health Challenge (HYHC) is available in several Indigenous communities across British Columbia. It includes nutrition education, tobacco awareness, and culturally based physical activities such as snowshoeing, traditional dance-off competitions, and games (Aboriginal Sport BC, 2012).

Efforts to reduce the proportion of overweight children have also been integrated into many school programs throughout Canada. For example, at Evangeline Middle School in New Minas, Nova Scotia, all children are required to play intramural sports; however, this school program goes one step further by having intramural games played during regular classroom hours rather than at lunchtime or after school. The gymnasium remains open every evening, every weekend, and throughout the summer for those students and parents who want to use the facilities (Evangeline Middle School, 2017).

Informal interactions, community programs, government programs and policies, members of the medical community, commercial industry, and the media all interact to create a complex web of social control for body size and shape. Some of these control measures emerge from concerns over the health consequences of being overweight. However, the regulation of body size extends beyond health to concerns over physical appearance for those who are perceived as "too fat" (by others or by themselves), regardless of whether they are overweight.

Consequences of Social Control

We are surrounded by a multitude of measures to control bodies that are deemed "too fat." For females, social control emphasizes extreme thinness while for males, it stresses a combination of thinness and muscularity. While some measures of social control can lead to healthier choices in diet and exercise, the pervasiveness of such measures also contribute to a "fear of fatness" (Couch et al., 2016, p. 63) and body dissatisfaction. Even the youngest of children are affected. A study of 144 children found that almost two-thirds of girls who had healthy weights were unhappy with their bodies; in fact, twice as many girls who had healthy weights experienced body dissatisfaction compared to girls who were overweight (Tremblay, Lovsin, Zecevic, & Larivière, 2011).

The pressure placed on youth by the media is particularly intense and influences body image and dieting practices (Bell & Dittmar, 2011; Dye, 2016). In contemporary society, social media is especially significant. Physical appearance is central on social media, such as through profile pictures, selfies, and other shared images (deVries, Peter, de Graaf, & Nikken, 2016). Research with both adolescents and adults finds that those who spend more time on social media have higher levels of body dissatisfaction (deVries et al., 2016; Stronge, Greaves, Milojev, & Sibley, 2015). However, some people are influenced by media portrayals more than others. For example, although social media use is associated with body dissatisfaction overall, this is especially the case for women in their late 30s and 40s. Women in this age group may be "stuck between societal pressure and an unattainable youthful ideal" (Stronge et al., 2015, p. 209).

Historically, research suggested that females experienced greater body dissatisfaction than males. Recent research finds that men and women are equally likely to be unhappy with their bodies, particularly in response to media messages (Dye, 2016; Stronge et al., 2015). In interviews with adult men, Hervic and Fasting (2016) find that many men do report being concerned about their bodies' appearance. However, the men appeared uncomfortable in voicing these concerns, which suggests body dissatisfaction continues to be viewed as a feminine trait.

Social control measures may trigger the adoption of a "fat" identity in individuals. Even people who may have been overweight since early childhood do not come to see themselves as "fat" until external cues give them that indication (Degher & Hughes, 2003). External cues may be of an active type (e.g., comments from others) or a passive type (e.g., seeing one's own reflection in a store window). These external cues lead to the personal recognition that one does not have a "normal" body but a "fat" body. A deviant definition of the self is subsequently internalized and a "fat" identity emerges. Being subjected to the social typing process by others thus leads people to socially type themselves, changing an individual's understanding of self. Fat identities are not limited to people who are overweight according to scientific standards. Current social standards contribute to people who are at healthy weights developing fat identities as well.

The social controls placed on body size, especially the controls exerted by the media, peers, and family members, have considerable influence on the way people feel about themselves, their self-esteem, and their self-regulation practices (like dieting or using anabolic steroids). However, as public control measures for body size have expanded at a rapid pace, the proportion of both adults and children who are overweight or obese has grown rather than declined.

Resisting a Label of "Too Fat"

The fact that being overweight has become so stigmatized in society and that the social definition of what constitutes "too fat" has reached absurd standards has done more than simply raise a few eyebrows. Many individuals and various organizations are taking active steps to curb this social typing process. Several "fat acceptance" groups have formed in Canada, the United States, and Western Europe (e.g., the National Association to Advance Fat Acceptance). They provide information on current obesity research, facts about weight-loss drugs and surgeries and the dangers of them, and litigation updates. They also facilitate advocacy by, for example, providing instructions on writing effective complaint letters and leading activism efforts. Other organizations have created beauty magazines, websites, and clothing lines for people who are overweight.

Although the media is one of the primary social control agents for "too fat" and the central reproducer of overly thin body images, at times it also resists that social typing process. For instance, social media includes comments and images that highlight #fatpride. Fitness websites may include articles about the dangers of fad diets. Some celebrities are critical of the thin ideal, and respond to online trolls who criticize their weight (Anderson, 2015). However, these instances constitute the minority in contemporary media and are contradicted by the preponderance of thin images.

Fat acceptance organizations, websites, and celebrities are all participants in resisting the social typing process. The areas of emphasis for these resistance activities are twofold: first, to promote sound nutrition and physical fitness in pursuit of good health; and second, to remove the social stigma from people who are overweight, thus broadening the standards of physical attractiveness in our culture. Views of health and physical appearance are the two foundations (albeit sometimes contradictory ones) in the stigmatization and social control of "too fat," just as they are key elements in the resistance to these processes. Health and physical appearance are also foundations to discussions of the other deviant body size in our society— "too thin."

"Too Thin": Commercialization, Societal Reaction, and Social Control

Perceptions of People Who Are Underweight

The ideal body size in a society is one that is perceived as normal or conforming. In many Western industrialized societies today, widespread cultural perceptions support an extremely thin ideal. Consequently, considerable thinness is necessary before a "too thin" label is attached and the social typing process is triggered. This is especially true when considering social definitions rather than scientific ones.

Based on scientific definitions, between 1 and 7 percent of adults in Canada are underweight (Statistics Canada, 2016b). Social definitions put those numbers even lower, considering the value placed on underweight females as images of beauty. In a classic analysis, McLorg and Taub (1987) found that even among people belonging to an eating disorders support group, family members and friends did not perceive them as "too thin" or "anorexic" until they had reached the point of being emaciated. Prior to that point, family members and friends encouraged them in their pursuit of weight loss and congratulated them on their successes.

However, at some point a "too thin" label does emerge. Interviews reveal that people who are too thin are viewed as "nauseating," "emaciated," and "look[ing] like junkies," and observers report feeling "repulsed" by them (Couch et al., 2016, p. 64). Views of people with anorexia combine positive and negative aspects as well. After reading a story about a young woman with anorexia, female research participants stated that they perceived her as self-centred and wanting attention from others

(Mond, Robertson-Smith, & Vetere, 2006). They also were not sure they would want to hire her for a job. Yet their attitudes were more positive than negative, and one-third thought that it would not be too bad to have that woman's problem.

Controlling "Too Thin"

Medicalization, Education, and Formal Intervention. "Too thin" is socially controlled at various formal levels. The medical community, frequently in conjunction with social agencies and programs, makes people who are at the most extreme end of thinness (anorexic) subject to social control efforts. When an individual is in immediate danger of sudden death, the medical community pursues intervention. The difficulty in preventing and treating anorexia and other eating disorders has resulted in a range of approaches that are employed at different points in the progression of this condition (Levine & Maine, 2005; National Eating Disorder Information Centre, 2014).

Physicians, psychiatrists, psychologists, and nurses carry out some of the formal social control measures described in Box 7.1, while social agencies and programs carry out others. For example, at Eastwood Collegiate Institute in Kitchener, Ontario, guest speakers are brought into the school to talk to girls about eating disorders and body image. Eating disorder associations frequently sponsor group meetings and peer support for people who have eating disorders like anorexia. People who work with adolescents in a variety of arenas—schoolteachers, coaches, school counsellors, and youth care workers—are educated about the signs of anorexia and other eating disorders.

Even governments and the fashion industry are becoming involved in the control of extreme thinness by banning underweight models from various types of work. In 2006, runway model Luisel Ramos died of complications from anorexia during a runway show; six months later, her sister Eliana (also a model) died for the same reason (Beckford, 2007). Since that time, the fashion industry in some countries (e.g., France, Italy, Spain, Israel) have banned underweight models. The legislation in some countries prohibits the hiring of models with a certain BMI (e.g., below 18.0), while in other countries, models must provide a medical certificate that indicates their health "is compatible with the practise of the profession" (*BBC News*, 2015). Employers who violate these laws can face fines or even jail time. For instance, in France violators can receive fines of up to $75 000 and six months in jail (*BBC News*, 2015).

Media. The social control of "too thin" is evident in the media as well, although to nowhere near the extent of the social control of "too fat." For example, celebrity-following websites often comment on the health of shrinking celebrities such as Khloé Kardashian, Rachel Zoe, Miley Cyrus, and Angelina Jolie. Kim Kardashian's and Beyoncé's ample bottoms, initially the subject of media jokes, are now described as a "sexy" alternative to the waif-like look of many other female celebrities.

Box 7.1

Preventing and Treating Anorexia

1. Prevention

You know the old saying: "An ounce of prevention is worth a pound of cure." Many different social organizations emphasize the value of preventing eating disorders (Berman & White, 2013; Canadian Mental Health Association, 2016; National Eating Disorder Information Centre, 2014).

Primary prevention involves efforts to prevent eating disorders from occurring in the first place. It entails school and community programs that raise awareness of eating disorders and their associated dangers as well as the unrealistic body ideals portrayed in popular culture (Berman & White, 2013; National Eating Disorder Information Centre, 2014). However, primary prevention must also go much further than this. At a societal level, the culture's obsession with thinness must be dismantled, the gendered norms that constrain both men and women must be changed, and institutions (e.g., schools) must adopt processes that facilitate the development of self-esteem and efficacy in a wide range of areas (Centre for Addiction and Mental Health, n.d.).

Secondary prevention involves identifying those young men and women who may be in the very early stages of an eating disorder. This kind of prevention entails educating parents, teachers, and coaches about the warning signs of eating disorders and effective means of intervention (e.g., National Eating Disorders Association, 2014).

2. Treatment

An extensive range of treatments are available for eating disorders, though which treatments are most effective depends entirely on the individual. People with eating disorders may choose from diverse forms of therapy and counselling—psychotherapy, group therapy, family counselling, and cognitive behavioural therapy (Canadian Mental Health Association, 2016; Centre for Addiction and Mental Health, n.d.; Levine & Maine, 2005). For therapy to be effective, it must deal not only with the eating disorder itself but also with the psychological, familial, and cultural factors that contributed to the eating disorder in the first place (Levine & Maine, 2005). There are medications that can be prescribed to some individuals with eating disorders, such as anti-anxiety drugs or anti-depressants, although their effectiveness is debated. Support groups are useful tools. The nature of support groups is quite varied, with some following a program pattern like Alcoholics Anonymous (e.g., Anorexics and Bulimics Anonymous). When severe health dangers are imminent, hospitalization or residential programs may be necessary so that medical monitoring and health supports are available around the clock.

Just as celebrities who are considered overweight are subjected to fat-shaming on social media and in the comments sections of websites, those who are viewed as too thin are subjected to thin-shaming (e.g., "eat a cheeseburger"; "looks like a 9-year-old girl").

Interpersonal Interactions.   When individuals are finally socially typed as "too thin," everyday interactions exert measures of control. Interviews with people who are very thin (but do not have eating disorders) find that they feel treated as an Other because of their body size—not only by friends and family members, but by complete strangers as well (Beggan & DeAngelis, 2015). They find themselves on the receiving end of three types of comments. First are those related to *attractiveness* (or lack thereof). People refer to them negatively as "bird legs" or "concentration camp victim," and positively as "supermodel thin" (p. 378). Second are comments related to levels of *concern*. Some observers express true concern, asking them if they have anorexia, while others merely have curiosity, such as asking them how much they weigh. Third are comments indicative of *resentment*, such as "I hate you," or "You wouldn't know what my struggle [with controlling my weight] is like" (p. 378). Even when comments from others express admiration or envy, the individuals interviewed said that being singled out made them feel uncomfortable. Despite their discomfort at being treated as an Other, they were generally satisfied with their bodies as they were.

A classic study by McLorg & Taub (1987) explores how social interactions change for people with anorexia as their disorder progress. Friends and family members closely watch their eating habits, and blame those habits for falling grades and the loss of friendships. People with more moderate degrees of "too thin" may have food pushed on them as family members and friends try to get them to eat more. Once others identify them as "anorexic," on the other hand, people may not offer them anything to eat or drink, even at social gatherings. Friends and family members withdraw from interactions with them, making them feel increasingly isolated and stigmatized. Even so, many people who have anorexia nevertheless feel that the stigma attached to their emaciated appearances and strange eating patterns is preferable to the stigma of being overweight. It is through these everyday social interactions, however, that people with anorexia eventually develop an "anorexic" identity. McLorg and Taub (1987) apply labelling theory (discussed in Chapter 3) to this process. Labelling friends or family members as "anorexic" leads to the distinct types of treatment described above. People labelled in this way are isolated from "normal" relationships in their lives, and even say that others come to expect them to act anorexic. An "anorexic" identity forms and a lifestyle becomes entrenched—processes that are the hallmarks of the transition from primary to secondary deviance.

Resisting a Label of "Too Thin"

Although "too thin" is considered deviant and made subject to measures of social control, people who have been so labelled resist the social typing process in several ways. The idea that you can never be too rich or too thin, for example, illustrates resistance to the idea that thinness is deviant and in need of social control. The extent to which weight-loss products and messages permeate our media and commercial industry reinforces this notion. Celebrities who are criticized for being too thin respond through the media, sometimes to emphasize that fact that they are naturally thin (and not anorexic). At other times, they *condemn the condemners*, a technique of neutralization (see Chapter 2). For instance, when followers on social media accused Victoria's Secret model Bridget Malcolm of have anorexia, she responded by pointing her finger back at them—"questioning why 'some followers feel the need to shame strangers on the Internet about their bodies'" (Blair, 2015).

Beggan and DeAngelis (2015) find that people who are thin (but who do not have eating disorders) use different strategies to cope with the comments they receive from others. Some of these strategies are problem-focused, used to avoid being the target of negative (or positive) comments. For example, they avoid wearing shorts so that others will not see their thin legs. They avoid going to the bathroom immediately after eating, so people will not think they have an eating disorder. They do not complain about feeling cold at work, because they know that someone will attribute it to being too thin. Other strategies are emotion-focused, used to re-frame negative comments in less disturbing ways. For instance, they say that negative comments are an indication of low self-esteem in the people making the comments.

Although most of us would agree that the extreme thinness of anorexia needs both preventative and retroactive measures of control, resistance to the social typing and social control of anorexia is also evident in some arenas, including the Internet.

In the twenty-first century, popular discourse has come to include "Ana." Innumerable websites are devoted to "Ana," which refers to anorexia. These websites do not provide help with and support for ending anorexia; rather, they help maintain anorexia (Haas, Irr, Jennings, & Wagner, 2011). They include photographs of models and actresses as motivation for continuing the pursuit of weight loss. There are tips for losing weight faster, charts listing the calorie count of different foods and the calories burned by different activities, and advice for maintaining motivation. Additional advice tells people how to dress so that others will not detect their extreme weight loss and how to fool others into thinking they are eating normally. Avoiding a deviant label is important because detection results in social control measures, which interfere with weight loss. There are even tips on how to resist active control efforts, such as how to avoid weight gain while hospitalized for treatment. Chatrooms and discussion groups provide an arena for support in resisting the deviantization of anorexia. "Ana" websites themselves have now been identified as dangerous, and Internet providers remove pro-anorexia sites once

Ask Yourself

How is the appearance of your body affected or socially controlled by other people in your life, groups you belong to, and cultural norms? What influence does the appearance of your body have on other people, groups you belong to, and the larger society?

they are discovered. Because of these social control measures, many Ana websites are located on the Dark Net (see Chapter 4). But even on mainstream social media platforms, there are debates over whether "thinspiration" posts are intended to improve health or promote eating disorders.

Look in the mirror. Is your body "too fat," "too thin," or "just right"? Answering that question rests on the foundation of our cultural standards of the ideal body. The bodies we see in the media and elsewhere around us, as well as people's responses to those bodies, tell us what "too fat," "too thin," and "just right" mean. The medical community, commercial industry, social agencies and organizations, and individual people we encounter in our lives let us know the status of our own bodies and exert means of control if our bodies need to be "fixed" in some way. In the end, we are expected to self-regulate our bodies—realize when we are "too fat" and take steps to lose weight, or notice when we are "too thin" and take steps to gain weight.

Body weight is only one of many aspects of physical appearance that can potentially be socially typed as deviant and made subject to measures of social control. Additional aspects include tattoos, piercings, and other forms of body modification. The appearance of our bodies is an expression of other characteristics we may have (e.g., personality traits), our selves and identities, our culture's (or subculture's) norms and ideologies, and structures of power in society. Our bodies say a great deal—what does your body say?

TIME TO REVIEW

Learning Objective 3

- How is the ideal body defined according to scientific standards and social standards? How prevalent are "deviant" bodies according to each of these standards?

- What are the causes of overweight/obesity and anorexia?

- In what way are ideal male and female bodies reflected in the media and how has that changed over time?

Learning Objective 4

- How are overweight people perceived and how are they socially controlled by the media, commercial industry, medicine, government, and communities?

Learning Objective 5

- How are people who are "too thin" perceived and how are they socially controlled at formal and informal levels?

Learning Objective 6

- How are the labels of "too fat" and "too thin" each resisted?

CHAPTER SUMMARY

- Physical appearance is extremely important. All of us engage in body projects that change our bodies' functioning or appearance. Social scientists propose that the appearance of people's bodies can convey many important messages. (1)

- A growing proportion of people alter their appearance through body modification. Body modification may tell us about the characteristics of individuals, the processes involved in coming to understand the self, and the discourses and structures of power in the larger society. (2)

- Other body projects are based on body weight and size. Body size and weight are a nexus for social typing that occurs everywhere around us daily. The "ideal" body weight can be defined scientifically based on health risks or socially on the basis of social standards. (3)

- People who are considered "too fat" are perceived negatively in our society and subjected to a wide range of informal and formal social controls. Informal social interactions, discriminatory practices, the media, commercial products, medical services, government programs, and community services all target "too fat." (4)

- A label of "too thin" is usually not attached to people until they reach an extreme level of thinness. Once that label is attached, social control efforts are initiated through formal prevention and intervention measures, the media, and personal interactions. (5)

- Labels of "too fat" and "too thin" are resisted in numerous ways. The former is resisted through fat acceptance organizations and some elements of the media. The latter is resisted through the pervasive thin ideal in the media, individuals' strategies to cope with thin-shaming, and pro-anorexia websites. (6)

> **To learn more about the topics discussed in this chapter and to complete chapter quizzes, visit the Companion Website for *Deviance, Conformity, and Social Control in Canada*.**

Chapter 8
Mental Disorders

Paradox/Fotolia

Learning Objectives

After reading this chapter, you should be able to

1 Describe the prevalence of mental disorders in Canada and worldwide, as well as patterns of mental disorders across various social groups.

2 Describe the costs of mental illness for individuals, their families, and the larger society.

3 Explain how mental disorders are subject to social control through (1) the stigmatization of mental illness and (2) the medicalization of mental disorder.

4 Describe the efforts to reduce the stigmatization of mental illness and to improve the resources that are available to people with mental disorders.

5　Explain why the diagnostic handbook used by mental health professionals is criticized.

6　Describe Rosenhan's classic study on mental illness and explain the consequences of his research.

What images come to mind when you think of mental disorder? Caplan (1995) suggests that "usually, images of difference and alienation" first come to mind, "suggesting that 'they' are not as competent, human, or safe to be around as the rest of 'us'" (p. 11). The concept of mental disorder consists of two different dimensions. First, it entails the experience of the disorder itself—its specific symptoms. Second, mental disorder also has a social dimension. Human beings attribute meaning to their symptoms, and that meaning arises from their interactions with other people. Thus, the ways that others perceive and treat people with mental disorders play a central role in their experiences of illness.

Research on mental disorder reflects both of these dimensions as well and emerges from various points along the objective–subjective continuum. It includes research on the prevalence and patterns of mental disorder, the costs of inadequately treated mental illness, stigmatization, and medicalization. Contemporary sociological research on mental disorder tends to lean toward the more subjective end of the continuum, focusing on stigmatization, experiences of self, and the social construction of mental illness, with a strong interactionist theoretical foundation.

Mental disorder, by definition, is a psychological, biological, or behavioural dysfunction that interferes with daily life—"alterations in thinking, mood or behaviour ... associated with significant distress and impaired functioning" (Public Health Agency of Canada, 2015). The "bad day" (or "bad week") that all of us have at times is not sufficient to be considered mental illness; the distorted thoughts, moods, and behaviours must be of a magnitude and duration substantial enough to interfere with daily functioning. The *Diagnostic and Statistical Manual of Mental Disorders* (DSM) and the *International*

Exercise Your Mind

You can find a copy of the *DSM-V* in the DSM Library at www.psychiatryonline.org. Browse through the diagnostic categories to see what types of thoughts, moods, or behaviours are defined as constituting mental illness. Select three different diagnostic categories—a psychotic disorder, a mood disorder, and an anxiety disorder—and look at their descriptions and lists of symptoms. How do these three different disorders encapsulate the "distress" and "impaired functioning" that definitions of mental illness focus on? In what ways would everyday life differ for people who are and are not experiencing these symptoms? In what ways would everyday life be similar?

Classification of Diseases (ICD) are diagnostic handbooks that clearly outline precisely what types of thoughts, moods, and behaviours constitute a mental disorder and under what circumstances. In common conversation, the term "mental illness" is frequently used interchangeably with "mental disorder."

Who Has Mental Disorders?

Mental disorders can strike anyone and affect the majority of Canadians either directly (through experiencing a mental disorder themselves) or indirectly (by having a friend, family member, or co-worker with a mental disorder). Approximately 20 percent of adult Canadians have a mental illness and 80 percent of Canadians know someone with a mental illness (Health Canada, 2002; Mental Health Commission of Canada, 2015; World Health Organization, 2013). Half of Canadians will experience a mental disorder by the age of 40, and between 65 and 70 percent by the age of 90 (Mental Health Commission of Canada, 2013a). In any given year, there are more Canadians who experience a mental disorder than heart disease and type 2 diabetes combined (Mental Health Commission of Canada, 2013a). Some mental disorders are more prevalent than others (see Figure 8.1) (Mental Health Commission of Canada, 2013a).

Although mental illness can strike anyone, some social groups are more susceptible than others. For instance, while anxiety and mood disorders affect 12 percent of Canadian adults overall in any given year, those disorders affect fewer immigrants (7 percent) and Northern residents (10 percent), but more individuals who identify as LGBTQ (29 percent) (Mental Health Commission of Canada, 2015). Mental illness has a complex etiology that includes genetic, biological, and psychological factors.

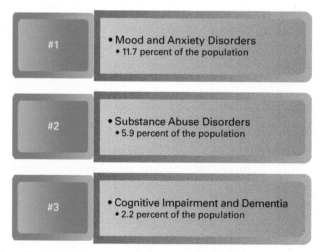

Figure 8.1 The Three Most Common Mental Disorders

Based on Mental Health Commission of Canada. (2013a). *Making the case for investing in mental health in Canada*. Ottawa, ON, and Calgary, AB: Author.

However, seeing the variations in mental disorder across social groups draws our attention to the social factors that contribute to mental illness as well. According to the World Health Organization (2013), mental illness emerges from "not only individual attributes such as the ability to manage one's thoughts, emotions, behaviours and interactions with others, but also social, cultural, economic, political and environmental factors such as national policies, social protection, living standards, working conditions, and community social supports" (p. 7).

Just as with other types of illness, the single greatest predictor of mental illness is socioeconomic status. Although socioeconomic status interacts with other variables (e.g., gender, ethnicity), across social groups people of low socioeconomic status have higher rates of most types of mental illness, especially mood and anxiety disorders (World Health Organization, 2013). A longstanding question about the relationship between socioeconomic status and mental illness concerns the direction of causation. The **social causation hypothesis** suggests that more life stresses and fewer resources characterize the lives of the lower class, contributing to the emergence of mental illness.

This was, in fact, mentioned in Robert Merton's strain theory (discussed in Chapter 2). Although his theory and its later applications largely focus on crime, he did suggest that mental illness can emerge in response to the gap between institutionalized goals and the legitimate means for attaining those goals. The mode of adaptation that he labelled **retreatism**, wherein people give up on pursuing the goals as well as the legitimate means of attaining those goals, can include voluntary behaviours such as alcohol and drug use, but also involuntary outcomes such as mental illness. In contrast, the **social selection hypothesis** proposes the reverse—that people with mental disorders can fall into lower economic strata because of difficulties in daily functioning (Eaton, 2001).

Although some debate continues among mental health experts, recent research finds that the direction of causation depends on the specific mental disorder in question. Individuals with schizophrenia, conduct disorders, and attention deficit disorder are more likely to fall into the lower socioeconomic strata and are less likely to be able to rise out of the lower strata, supporting the social selection hypothesis. Conversely, social causation appears to underlie the more common mood and anxiety disorders. The life stresses associated with economic difficulties contribute to the emergence of these disorders (World Health Organization, 2013). Economic difficulties can be tied not only to overall social class (e.g., lower class versus middle class), but also changes in financial status due to local, regional, national, or global economic patterns. Research done in Canada, Hong Kong, Spain, and Greece has found a significant increase in mood and anxiety disorders following the 2008 global economic recession (Economou et al., 2016; Gili, Roca, Basu, McKee, & Stuckler, 2013; Lee et al., 2010; Wang et al., 2010). For instance, prior to the economic recession, approximately 3 percent of the Greek population had major depression. By 2009 that proportion had more than doubled, and it continued to increase such that by 2013 that proportion had risen to more than 12 percent (Economou et al., 2016).

Although socioeconomic status is the single greatest predictor of mental illness, there is also a strong correlation with age. Mental illness is most common in young adults. While 20 percent of the adult population overall experiences a mental disorder in any given year, among those ages 20 to 29, that proportion increases to 28 percent (Mental Health Commission of Canada, 2013b). Furthermore, most adults who have been diagnosed with mental disorders state that their symptoms began during childhood (Mental Health Commission of Canada, 2016b). However, mental health difficulties can exist even for those youth who have not been diagnosed with a mental disorder. One study of more than 10 000 junior- and senior-high school students in Ontario found that approximately one-third report symptoms of anxiety or depression, such as chronically feeling nervous, hopeless, or worthless (Boak, Hamilton, Adlaf, Henderson, & Mann, 2016).

Biological factors play a role in the correlation between age and mental illness, as do psychological and social factors such as the struggles involved in identity formation during this time, the dramatic nature of the transitions that occur with high school graduation, and the stresses associated with developing an "adult" role (e.g., deciding what type of education and career to pursue, becoming financially independent, and participating in the mate-selection process). Among the students in the study by Boak and colleagues (2016), the closer they were to high school graduation, the larger the proportion who reported symptoms of psychological distress. These researchers also found a correlational relationship between social media and psychological distress, in that the more time adolescents spend on social media platforms, the more likely they are to experience symptoms of anxiety and depression.

Some groups of youth are at greater risk of mental illness or psychological distress than others, such as those that live in families of low socioeconomic status, those that are forced to flee their countries of origin as refugees, and those that are marginalized because of LGBTQ identities or expression (Mental Health Commission of Canada, 2016b; Mullaney, 2016). For Indigenous youth living in some communities in Canada, the legacy of colonization (which you will learn more about in Chapter 9) has created an especially dire situation in this regard. In 2016, states of emergency were declared in several Indigenous communities because of a rash of youth suicides (CBC News, 2016c; Markewich, 2016). In Attawapiskat (in northern Ontario), there were 11 youth suicides in one day alone (CBC News, 2016c). The risk varies considerably across different Indigenous communities, in that 90 percent of Indigenous youth suicides occur in only 10 percent of communities (McCue, 2016). These are communities that face complex challenges that can affect the psychological well-being of youth. For instance, the state of emergency declared in Attawapiskat because of youth suicide was the fifth state of emergency declared in that community within a decade (Canadian Press, 2016). Previous states of emergency

Ask Yourself

Considering what you have learned about media in the course thus far, why do you think a relationship exists between social media use and psychological distress? What might be the nature of that relationship? Do you think social media use contributes to psychological distress, or rather that youth in psychological distress are more likely to turn to social media? What is it about the social media environment that may contribute to psychological distress?

were declared because of contaminated drinking water (2006), homes contaminated by sewage (2009), a housing shortage that resulted in people living in tents without heat or water (2011), and a massive sewer backup (2013). However, Lalonde (cited in McCue, 2016) argues that overall, the Indigenous communities that experience high rates of youth suicide are those that are the least "culturally healthy"—where cultural continuity has been the most disrupted. As you will see at a later point in the chapter, because the level and nature of risk varies across different social groups, the types of resources required to reduce that risk vary as well.

Certain types of mental illnesses are more prevalent in particular social groups. For example, mood and anxiety disorders are more common in women while antisocial and conduct disorders are more prevalent in men; post-traumatic stress disorder (PTSD) is more common in refugee populations and certain occupational groups (e.g., emergency responders) (Health Canada, 2002; Mental Health Commission of Canada, 2016b). However, mental disorders can affect anyone, as illustrated by the fact that half of Canadians will experience a mental disorder by the time they reach the age of 40 (Mental Health Commission of Canada, 2013a). Thus, the resulting costs of mental illness are substantial.

The Costs of Mental Illness

Mental disorders have a considerable impact on individual people's lives as well as the larger society. Research that emerges from the more objective end of the objective–subjective continuum shows us that having a mental disorder can contribute to a wide range of negative life outcomes. For example, having a mental disorder is associated with higher rates of teen pregnancy and a greater risk of marital instability, all of which contribute to difficulties for the children being raised in those environments (Barrett, Katsiyannis, Zhang, & Kingree, 2015; Perry, 2014). Mental illness (and particularly severe mental illness) is also associated with lower levels of educational attainment, lower employment rates, and lower incomes (Mental Health Commission of Canada, 2013c). In addition, individuals with mental illnesses, along with their families, must bear direct and indirect financial costs (e.g., the costs of health care or the costs associated with unemployment) (Mental Health Commission of Canada, 2013a).

Some mental illnesses are correlated with other physical ailments; for example, depression is related to a higher risk of heart disease. Furthermore, people with mental disorders are less likely to comply with medical instructions for other physical ailments, such as high blood pressure, diabetes, or cancer, resulting in poorer health overall and a greater likelihood of complications (Coventry, Dickens, & Todd, 2014). Finally, the emotional burden of living with a mental disorder creates a challenge to many aspects of daily living and influences the quality of life overall.

Beyond the level of individuals and their families, insufficiently treated mental disorders also have a considerable impact on society. National economies experience costs from mental illness because of premature deaths from suicide, absenteeism from work, lower levels of productivity while at work, family members' absence from work to provide care, treatment costs, and more (Mental Health Commission of Canada, 2013a). Conservative estimates are that the economic costs of mental illness in Canada total $50 billion every year, and are projected to rise to almost $90 billion by 2023. One-third of short- and long-term workplace disability claims are due to mental illness, with insurance costs of $15 billion to $33 billion per year (Stonebridge & Sutherland, 2016).

The magnitude of these various impacts means that effective treatment of mental illness would benefit the individuals who have mental illnesses, their families, and society as a whole. The Mental Health Commission of Canada (2013a) reports that by reducing the incidence of mental illness by a mere 10 percent, within 10 years the Canadian economy would save $1.7 billion every year, and after 30 years those savings would be almost $5 billion per year; reducing remission rates by 10 percent would increase savings even further. However, many people with mental disorders do not receive treatment. In high-income countries (such as Canada), 35 to 50 percent of people with severe mental disorders receive no treatment. In low- to middle-income countries, 76 to 85 percent receive no treatment (World Health Organization, 2013). This can be for a variety of reasons including lack of services (e.g., long waiting times), perceptions of treatment as inadequate, discomfort with the level of self-disclosure that accompanies diagnosis and treatment, perceptions of stigmatization, or neglect within their own families and communities (Mosher, 2002; Sareen, Cox, Afifi, Yu, Stein, 2005; World Health Organization, 2013). In Canada, research has found that 60 percent of adults with mental disorders who avoid treatment do so because of a fear of being stigmatized (Mental Health Commission of Canada, 2016c).

Coming from a more subjectivist perspective, Wolff (2007) suggests that cost-of-illness estimates should be viewed with some level of caution. First, Wolff points out that these estimates "are not just a product of biochemistry; biochemistry interacts with economics and social norms" (p. 73). For example, if pharmaceutical companies established lower drug costs, then the costs of mental disorder would be lower as well. Second, Wolff points out that these estimates fail to take into account the many ways that individuals with mental disorders contribute to society outside of the labour force as parents, neighbours, and volunteers. That is, cost-of-illness estimates themselves are, in part, reflective of the negative attitudes that surround mental illness. Overall, she argues that cost-of-illness estimates only take on social meaning when we look at "the ways in which we collectively view and treat people with mental illness" (p. 75).

Controlling Mental Disorder: Stigmatization and Medicalization

The reactions of other people are an integral part of the experience of having a mental disorder. As we have already seen, one of the main reasons that people with mental disorders do not seek assistance from health professionals is because of the presumed reactions of other people, as well as the general stigma that is associated with mental illness in our society. The *stigmatization of mental illness* constitutes one of the major dimensions of social control, and this will be the first aspect of social control that we will explore. The second major dimension of control, which we will explore later in the chapter, is embodied by the *medicalization of mental disorder*.

The Stigmatization of Mental Illness

From the perspective of one individual with a mental disorder, having a mental illness is "sort of like having 'crazy bitch' stamped across my forehead and everybody treats you differently" (cited in Bassett, Lampe, & Lloyd, 1999). More than a half century ago researchers began identifying the prejudice and discrimination that people with mental disorders face (Scheff, 1966). Decades later, stigmatization continues in many ways.

We have only to look at the media to see the way mental illness continues to be stigmatized. When people with mental disorders are addressed in the media, they are framed in terms of negative stereotypes (Parrott & Parrott, 2015). Both fictional and nonfictional media frame people with mental disorders as unpredictable, violent, dangerous, and criminal (Aragonès, López-Muntaner, Ceruelo, & Basora, 2014; Goodwin & Tajjudin, 2016; McGinty, Webster, Jarlenski, & Barry, 2014; Parrott & Parrott, 2015). For instance, Parrott and Parrott (2015) analyzed 65 episodes of the popular American television crime dramas *NCIS* and *Criminal Minds*; at the time of the study, these two shows had weekly audiences of more than 30 million viewers in the U.S. alone. Compared to characters without mental disorders, those with disorders were more often portrayed as involved in crime, violent, unemployed, and having poor hygiene. Similarly, an analysis of almost 700 newspaper articles finds that mental illness is framed negatively—as dangerous, incoherent, and eccentric (Aragonès et al., 2014). In addition to television programs and news stories, negative portrayals of people with mental disorders are pervasive in Hollywood movies, children's novels, video games, and graphic novels (Fekete, 2012; Goodwin & Tajjudin, 2016; Wahl, 2003).

This type of media imagery has a notable impact on people's own perceptions of mental illness. Aguiniga, Madden, and Zellman (2016) found that one-quarter of the undergraduate students they surveyed said the media is their primary source of information about mental illness. Those students are more likely to believe that media portrayals of people with mental disorders are realistic, and they are more likely to have negative attitudes toward people with mental disorders. The impact of media portrayals on viewers' perceptions of mental illness has been demonstrated in experimental settings as well. McGinty, Webster, and Barry (2013) had research participants read a news story that associated mass shootings with severe mental illness. After reading this story, research participants were more likely to associate mental illness with dangerousness and express a desire for greater social distance from people with mental illnesses. Similarly, Green and Brock (2000) found that research participants who read a fictional short story ("Murder at the Mall") that associated mental illness with violence had more negative attitudes about mental illness (and malls) as a result.

Given the biased portrayals of mental illness in the media and their impact, it is not surprising that public attitudes toward mental illness are negative as well (Mental Health Commission of Canada, 2015). In addition to being associated with violence and unpredictability, DeLenardo and Terrion (2014) find that people with mental disorders are sometimes perceived as making excuses to avoid life's responsibilities, as having a "weak character" (p. 48), or as being "weak-minded" (p. 50). Family members, co-workers, or peers may not understand why someone struggling with recovery can't just "suck it up" (p. 50). For example, one young male varsity football player states, "I would try to help them out but at a certain point you have to get better... man up, we have a game on Saturday" (p. 49). The stigmatization of mental illness is so pervasive that 40 percent of parents say if their child had a mental disorder, they would not admit it to anyone—not even a doctor (Pietrus, 2013).

These negative attitudes are not limited to the general public, but are also found among health care practitioners, mental health professionals, and other human service providers. In fact, members of these groups may subscribe to even more stereotypes than the general public because they typically see clients when symptoms are at their worst (Covarrubias & Han, 2011; Stuart, Arboleda-Flórez, & Santorius, 2012). Anti-stigma professional development sessions in hospitals and community health settings tend to be poorly attended, so negative attitudes are maintained (Pietrus, 2013). Covarrubias and Han (2011) found that among students pursuing a master's degree in social work, more positive attitudes toward people with mental disorders are not associated with their formal education and training, but rather with their personal experiences; those students who have close friends or family members with serious mental disorders subscribe to fewer stereotypes.

At a personal level, stigmatization has a negative impact on the quality of life of people with mental disorders. Even if an individual has not personally experienced instances of direct stigmatization or discrimination, awareness of the negative attitudes that pervade society can lower self-esteem and increase feelings of demoralization, contributing to **self-stigma** (Kroska & Harkness, 2006). For example, the terminology used by military veterans with mental disorders who were taking part in a work-therapy program reflects their own stigmatizing attitudes: they referred to the program facility as the "VA Nut House," and their periodic health evaluations as "crazy checks" to determine if they were still "nuts" (Feinstein, 2015, p. 15). Some individuals may experience higher levels of self-stigma than others. High levels of self-stigma create consequences similar to those described by labelling theories (see Chapter 3); individuals who internalize the label (i.e., see themselves as "mentally ill") and its evaluative components (e.g., uncontrollable) become less likely to conform to treatment regimens or even to seek treatment (Kroska & Harkness, 2006). Whether through stigmatization by others or self-stigmatization, the effectiveness of treatments is hindered and recovery impeded.

These negative perceptions impact the lives of people with mental disorders in many ways, ranging from affecting their personal relationships to discrimination in employment, health care, and housing (Hipes, Lucas, Phelan, & White, 2016;

Despite the fact that mental illness is a leading cause of disability in the world, and hundreds of billions of dollars are lost each year as a result, mental health policies and programs are not perceived as priorities.

- Almost 40 percent of countries have no mental health policy.
- Approximately 30 percent of countries have no mental health plan.
- Globally, governments spend an average of less than US$2 per person per day on mental health care.

- The gap in mental health care resources between lower-income and higher-income countries is growing.
- 50 percent of the world's population lives in countries that have less than 1 psychiatrist per 200,000 people.
- Among higher-income countries, Canada lags behind others in mental health care spending.

Pietrus, 2013). The stigmatization of mental illness affects program and policy development as well; societies that are characterized by negative attitudes toward mental disorder also tend not to rate mental illness as a policy or programming priority. Unfortunately, this is characteristic of most countries in the world, including Canada (Mental Health Commission of Canada, 2016a; World Health Organization, 2011) (see Box 8.1).

TIME TO REVIEW

Learning Objective 1

- What is "mental illness" and how many people have mental disorders?
- How do the prevalence and patterns of mental illness vary on the basis of socioeconomic status, age, and other social factors? What are the explanations for these variations?

Learning Objective 2

- What costs are associated with mental illness for individuals, their families, and society?

- How many people with mental disorders seek professional help and what prevents some people from doing so?

Learning Objective 3

- How is mental illness portrayed in the media and what perceptions of mental illness are found in the general population and among health practitioners?
- How does the stigmatization of mental disorders influence quality of life, discrimination, and mental health policies and programming?

The Medicalization of Mental Disorder

The medicalization of deviance has been addressed in previous chapters. For example, in the chapter on physical appearance (Chapter 7) we saw how medical science defines what deviant body sizes are, explains why those body sizes are deviant, and then provides social control measures to ameliorate those problems (e.g., prescriptions for diet pills, references to a nutritionist, or information about physical fitness). Similarly, mental disorders are also medicalized. Psychiatrists determine which thoughts or behaviours constitute mental illness and then incorporate that into the *DSM* or *ICD*. They explain that these particular thoughts and behaviours are deviant because they cause significant distress and impairments in daily functioning. Finally, they provide measures of social control—that is, treatments for mental disorders to improve quality of life and level of functioning. However, a historical analysis reveals that medical treatment to improve functioning has not always been the focus of social control measures.

The History of the Social Control of Mental Illness

Through much of Western history, the thoughts and behaviours that we now define as mental illness were instead seen as the result of demonic possession, and the "treatment" was physical torture to drive out the demons. During the Middle Ages and early Renaissance, refusing to conform to society's norms (even by those people who would now be considered to have mental disorders) was considered a sign of allegiance with the devil. As a result, people were labelled "witch" or "heretic," put on trial, convicted, and put to death (e.g., by burning at the stake).

During the Middle Ages, people with mental illnesses were some of those convicted of witchcraft and burned at the stake.

As religious explanations were replaced by scientific explanations, authorities no longer saw these non-normative behaviours as signs of possession or allegiance with the devil. Instead, families and communities assumed responsibility. As the size of communities grew, prisons were built to house not only criminals but also the poor and people with mental illnesses (Foerschner, 2010; Grob, 1994). In the eighteenth century, "madhouses" were created specifically for those with mental illnesses. The purpose of these madhouses was not treatment or rehabilitation, but simply warehousing the disordered so that society's "normal" citizens could feel safe and secure (Foerschner, 2010; Rothman, 1971). In the late nineteenth century, madhouses were replaced by "asylums" as some doctors proposed that, with appropriate treatment, people with mental illnesses could be trained to conform to society's norms. This is the era when the medicalization of mental illness came to predominate in Western cultures (Foerschner, 2010; Grob, 1994). These "asylums," later to be known as "mental hospitals" or "psychiatric institutions," continued to grow well into the 1950s.

The treatments for people with mental illnesses provided in psychiatric institutions included practices that many people now see as almost barbaric—lobotomies and fever therapies, for example (Foerschner, 2010; McGovern, 1985). The failure of these types of therapies to "cure" mental illness combined with social concerns about their harshness eventually led many of them to be abandoned. Broader concerns about the effectiveness of hospitalization itself began to take hold in the late 1950s as well. People began to wonder how removing individuals from their homes, from the support of their families, and from the semblance of normality that existed within their communities and instead placing them in institutions where they were dehumanized and isolated could possibly help in recovery from mental illness. These questions, along with new drug therapies that effectively controlled many forms of mental disorder, eventually led to **deinstitutionalization**—the social control of people with mental illnesses in community-based programs rather than in institutions.

Treating Mental Illness Today

The medicalization of mental disorders in contemporary society involves an extensive range of treatment options—psychotherapy, cognitive-behavioural therapy, medication, occupational therapy, and social supports. Treatment options today have become quite effective in improving functioning and the quality of life for individuals with mental disorders. The combination of medical support (e.g., medications) and psychosocial support (e.g., therapy, community resources) is particularly effective for even the most severe mental illnesses (World Health Organization, 2002). For example, without any treatment 55 percent of people whose schizophrenia goes into remission will have a relapse within one year. Among those who receive psychopharmaceutical treatment alone, 20 to 25 percent will relapse within one year. Of those who receive both psychopharmaceutical treatment and psychosocial supports for the family, only 2 to 23 percent will relapse within one year (World Health Organization, 2002).

The Legacy of Deinstitutionalization. When the deinstitutionalization movement began in the early 1960s, it was perceived as an evolution in treatment that would bring nothing but benefits—to the individuals who would receive treatment in their own homes and communities, to society in terms of the higher rate of recovery, and to the government and taxpayers in terms of cost savings. Indeed, many of these benefits have been realized to some extent. Treatment in the community is generally more effective in the long term than treatment in institutions, and it is considerably less expensive (World Health Organization, 2011, 2013). There is also no doubt that many people consider it to be more respectful, more humane, and less emotionally disturbing. However, deinstitutionalization has had its drawbacks as well (Mental Health Commission of Canada, 2013d). The *Ask Yourself* exercise begins to explore some of these drawbacks.

> ### Ask Yourself
>
> In order for people with mental illnesses to be successfully treated in the community rather than in institutions, what kinds of resources are necessary? That is, what might people with mental illnesses need if they are to successfully recover in their own homes and neighbourhoods?

In the *Ask Yourself* exercise, perhaps you mentioned close families or friendship networks that can help provide necessary support or care. Deinstitutionalization did, in fact, emerge during an era when the image of the "ideal" family was everywhere. Popular television series such as *Leave It to Beaver, Father Knows Best,* and *Ozzie and Harriet* portrayed family life in a way that few people in reality ever experienced (Coontz, 1992). This type of popular imagery helped create the assumption that families were always caring, supportive, united, and happily willing to work together to overcome any difficulties. This was one of the key underlying assumptions of deinstitutionalization; that is, shifting the care of people with mental illnesses into the community was perceived as non-problematic because it was assumed that they would have loving families to help them (Accordino, Porter, & Morse, 2001).

Of course, many of us do not have that type of network of family relationships. Some of us are closer to our families than others are; some of us are able to depend on our families more than others are; some of us may have close marital relationships that are a source of support while others do not; furthermore, the experience of any type of serious illness contributes to the dissolution of many marriages. With all of these variations in family form and quality of family relationships, the assumption that there exists a social support network within the family for people with mental illnesses is a precarious one. Those people who have close support networks may do very well with community-based treatment, but those who are lacking such networks may not.

In your response to the last *Ask Yourself* question, you may have said that an accepting community that is free from stigmatization is necessary for successful community-based treatment. The prejudice and negative attitudes that pervade public perceptions of people with mental disorders have been addressed earlier in this chapter; stigmatization is a central obstacle to successful recovery and integration into the community (Pietrus, 2013).

Perhaps you listed adequately funded community resources as necessary for successful non-institutional treatment for people with mental disorders. In fact, this is one of the biggest problems worldwide that has plagued the deinstitutionalization movement (Mental Health Commission of Canada, 2016a; World Health Organization, 2011). Although the intent was quite different, the reduction in hospital-based service was accompanied by insufficient increases in community-based resources. This was because of the stigmatization of mental illness (that make related programs and policies difficult for politicians to "sell" to voters), a lack of adequate health care funding overall, and the prioritizing of other areas of government spending. The nature of available resources is also dependent on community size. Individuals living in large urban centres have more community mental health resources available to them than do those living in rural areas.

You may have mentioned that in order for people to have a successful recovery in their own homes, they actually need their own homes—that is, somewhere to live. Simply having a place to live can be a considerable challenge for some people with mental disorders, especially when we consider insufficient community resources and the stigmatization that inhibits integration within communities. As a result of discrimination or the symptoms of their disorders, some are unable to find employment or housing and may become dependent on family or friendship support networks. If those networks are lacking, possible outcomes can include homelessness. More than half of people who are homeless or vulnerably-housed have been diagnosed with a mental disorder, and approximately two-thirds have had a traumatic brain injury at some point in their lives (Research Alliance for Canadian Homelessness, Housing, and Health, 2010). There are more than 500 000 Canadians with mental illnesses who have inadequate housing, and 100 000 of those are homeless. At the same time, there are fewer than 30 000 housing units for people with severe mental illnesses (Mental Health Commission of Canada, 2013d).

Fmalot/Fotolia

The deinstitutionalization movement has benefited many people, but others have fallen through the cracks of the mental health care system.

Homelessness adds one more dimension to the social typing process that individuals must experience: not only do they face the consequences of being socially typed as mentally ill, they also must face the consequences of being socially typed as homeless. Homeless people with mental disorders who also have substance abuse problems face the additional predicament that some community resources are designed to deal with either substance abuse or mental illness, but not both. Recently, a growing number of communities have piloted new projects based on the principle of "housing first"—placing individuals in safe and comfortable housing to begin with, and then building specific treatment programs to address mental illness and addiction. One of the first of these programs, a five-year $110 million project known as "At Home," housed almost 1000 people with mental illnesses in several cities across Canada and provided them with mental health support (McIlroy, 2012).

The costs of community-based treatment are usually described as being lower than the costs of hospital-based treatment. However, when a significant number of people fall through the cracks of the community mental health system, other costs accompany deinstitutionalization. The costs associated with reducing homelessness are compounded by the social and economic losses emerging from higher suicide rates among individuals with untreated mental illnesses, more accidents, and a greater number of untreated physical illnesses (Mental Health Commission of Canada, 2013a). For some individuals with serious mental disorders, factors such as homelessness, substance abuse, and a lack of social supports can contribute to criminal activity.

The media perpetuates stereotypes of people with mental disorders being violent and dangerous. In fact only 3 percent of violent crimes are committed by people with mental disorders. Furthermore, people with mental illnesses are far more likely to be victims of crime than perpetrators. Nevertheless, they are overrepresented in the criminal justice system. Furthermore, the number of provincial and federal inmates who require mental health care far exceeds the available resources (MacPhail & Verdun-Jones, 2013).

As with homelessness, criminality adds a second dimension to the social typing process for some individuals with mental disorders. They face the consequences of not only being socially typed as mentally ill, but also being socially typed as criminals. Problems with mental health programming emerge in some communities, in that community resources that help people with mental illnesses may not help those with criminal records, and resources that help former criminals may not be equipped to deal with the mentally ill. Consequently, "the streets and prisons [have become] the asylums of the 21st century" (Bailey & Bronskill, 2007).

More than a half century ago, Penrose (1939) proposed that a *hydraulic* relationship exists between the mental health care system and the criminal justice system: when one contracts the other expands. Wolff (2007) argues that this is precisely what occurred when deinstitutionalization was not accompanied by sufficient community resources—the mental health care system contracted and the prison population expanded. Conversely, expanding the extent and nature of resources within the mental health care system should reduce the prison population.

The Deviance Dance: Resisting Stigmatization, Inadequate Care, and Psychiatry Itself

Mental disorders are socially typed as deviant at many different levels. Perceived as "dangerous" and "unpredictable" by the general public (a view perpetuated by the media), people with mental illnesses face stigmatization in everyday interactions and discrimination in employment, housing, and medical care. Stigmatization and discrimination constitute one of the ways they are subjected to measures of social control. They also face social regulation through processes of medicalization. Once diagnosed with particular mental disorders, individuals have a wide range of treatments available to them. The nature of these treatments has changed and expanded over time, making possible the deinstitutionalization movement that began in the 1960s. The move toward community-based treatment has benefited many and is the preferred form of treatment among people with mental disorders. However, it has also had a number of unintended negative consequences for people who happen to fall through the cracks of the community mental health system. Such consequences include a lower quality of life, and for some individuals, substance abuse, homelessness, or criminality. Individuals and groups in society are, therefore, engaging in resistance against both stigmatization and inadequate treatment, trying to change the nature of the social typing process.

The policies and programs addressing treatment and support available to people with mental disorders arise from the **disease paradigm** of mental illness, which emphasizes ameliorating symptoms that distress and impair individuals' functioning. Other policies and programs emerge out of the **discrimination paradigm** of mental illness, which emphasizes the role that stigmatization plays in the daily experiences of people with mental illnesses. These programs and policies constitute part of the "deviance dance"—that is, people resisting and fighting back against the inadequate treatment of mental illness and the social rejection or discrimination faced by individuals with mental disorders.

Resisting Stigmatization

People with mental illnesses may use a number of stigma management techniques to deal with their spoiled identities (see Figure 8.2). Some may **try to pass** by hiding their disorders. Some may **divide their social worlds**, carefully managing who is and is not permitted to know about their illnesses. However, others more actively resist the imposition of stereotypes about mental illness. Two such techniques are **deflecting** and **challenging** (Thoits, 2011, 2016; Thoits & Link, 2016).

Efforts at deflecting block the stigmatizing external force. Through a variety of means, individuals are able to distance themselves from the label of "mentally ill."

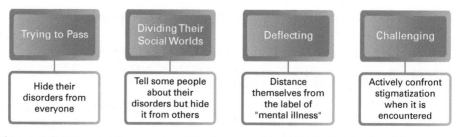

Figure 8.2 Stigma Management Techniques Used by Individuals with Mental Disorders

Based on Thoits, P. A. (2016). "I'm not mentally ill": Identity deflection as a form of stigma resistance. *Journal of Health and Social Behavior*, 57 (2), 135-151; Thoits, P. A. (2011). "Resisting the stigma of mental illness." *Social Psychology Quarterly*, 74 (1), 6–28.

Individuals may draw upon the public, mass-mediated images of people with mental illnesses as dangerous and unpredictable, emphasizing how they personally bear no resemblance to those images. They may emphasize that their disorder is only one small part of their lives, so that their identities are not based solely on the disorder. For instance, they may identify themselves as someone who *has* a mental disorder rather than someone who *is* mentally ill. Some individuals resist the label altogether, arguing that they do not have a "mental illness," but rather are just tired or overworked.

In contrast to deflecting, efforts at challenging more actively fight back against the external stigmatizing force. Sometimes this involves directly confronting people who stigmatize them or who express a stigmatization of mental illness more generally. At other times, challenging is less about confrontation, and more about educating others when those situations arise. Challenging can also take on a more personal form, where individuals overcompensate for stigmatization, trying to show themselves as being extra competent compared to the average person (Thoits, 2011).

Under what conditions will people with mental disorders actively resist stigmatization rather than try to pass or divide their social worlds? Thoits (2011, 2016) finds that several factors are associated with active resistance: past experience with stigma resistance (such as in response to racial or gender discrimination); past familiarity with mental illness in a friend or family member; greater coping resources, such as high self-esteem and a strong support network; holding and identifying with multiple roles in daily life; and less severe, more time-limited mental illnesses. Different stigma management strategies have varied effects. People who engage in deflection tend to have higher levels of well-being, although that positive effect wanes to some extent with more serious mental illnesses (Thoits, 2016). Those who engage in challenging tend to have a better quality of life, fewer symptoms, higher levels of self-esteem, and a stronger sense of empowerment, even among those with more serious disorders (Thoits & Link, 2016).

At the government level, many nations have instituted legislation and policies prohibiting discrimination against people with mental disorders in housing, employment, health care, and more. Some policies target persons with mental illnesses specifically. In other cases, people with mental illnesses are included under broader human rights legislation. For example, the Canadian *Charter of Rights and Freedoms* guarantees equality and prohibits discrimination on (among other things) the basis of mental and physical disability. At an international level, the *Universal Declaration of Human Rights* has a similar declaration. Provincial human rights codes also integrate similar policies.

The health care community is also involved in trying to reduce negative attitudes toward mental illness. For example, Alberta's "My Mental Health" campaign was created to eliminate misconceptions about mental illness to reduce stigmatization and increase people's attention to their own mental health (including their willingness to seek out services). The World Psychiatric Association coordinates an international program ("Open the Doors") to reduce the stigma of schizophrenia in many countries, including China, Egypt, Greece, and India. The World Health Organization (WHO) devoted 2001's World Health Day to mental health, emphasizing issues of prejudice and discrimination. Reducing the stigma associated with mental illness is one of the dimensions of their Mental Health Global Action Programme (mhGAP), whereby they coordinate advocacy efforts in member states to educate the public about mental illness and protect or promote patient rights (World Health Organization, 2013).

Self-help or advocacy groups for people with mental illnesses can be found in many countries as well. One of their mandates is acting to reduce the stigmatization of mental disorders through education, communication, and media information. For example, the Canadian Mental Health Association sponsors an annual Mental Health Week that is intended to dispel myths and reduce stereotypes. These types of groups also provide information about legislation, updates of mental health–related court cases, and materials to assist persons with mental illnesses in employment, housing, parenting, and more.

Just as some of the stigma management techniques used by individuals have more positive effects than others, certain types of stigma management programs are more effective than others. In a review of the literature, Pietrus (2013) finds that broad-based public education campaigns tend to have little impact. More effective are programs that are developed for very specific target audiences, such as new Canadians, health care practitioners, employers, and youth. For example, the organization Jack.org consists of "programs designed for young people by young people." Youth can establish local Jack.org chapters on their own high school or university campuses, drawing upon the organization's toolkits, TEDx talks, and funding opportunities (Jack.org, 2017).

Not only do a variety of organizations and groups act to reduce the stigma associated with mental illness, they are also involved in the resistance to inadequate care for individuals with mental illnesses.

Resisting Inadequate and Insufficient Care

In addition to providing public awareness to reduce stigmatization, advocacy groups are also involved in lobbying governments for better funding and improved services for people with mental disorders, as well as providing information to mental health consumers about the nature and appropriateness of the resources that are available to them. Support groups for specific mental disorders provide detailed information about new medications that are available, the effectiveness of specific types of treatments, and research about potential negative side effects of different medications and treatments.

The health care community, of course, is continually engaged in research on new and improved treatments for different disorders. They also monitor the professional behaviours of their members and negatively sanction those who do not provide appropriate care to patients. On an international level, groups like the World Health Organization integrate their anti-stigmatization efforts with efforts to increase government funding for mental health and improve the training of mental health professionals. Their Mental Health Global Action Programme's mission is to "support Member States to enhance their capacity to reduce risk, stigma, and burden of mental disorders and to promote the mental health of the population" (2002, p. 11). To this end, their approach includes four core strategies (see Figure 8.3).

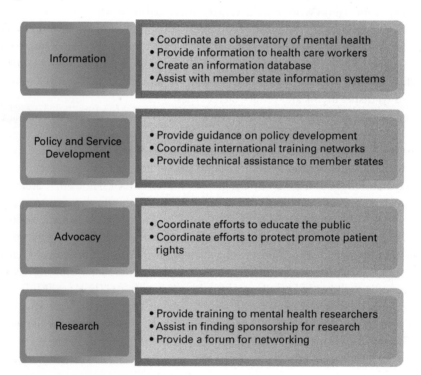

| Information | • Coordinate an observatory of mental health
• Provide information to health care workers
• Create an information database
• Assist with member state information systems |

| Policy and Service Development | • Provide guidance on policy development
• Coordinate international training networks
• Provide technical assistance to member states |

| Advocacy | • Coordinate efforts to educate the public
• Coordinate efforts to protect promote patient rights |

| Research | • Provide training to mental health researchers
• Assist in finding sponsorship for research
• Provide a forum for networking |

Figure 8.3 Strategies of the World Health Organization's Mental Health Global Action Programme

Based on World Health Organization (2002). *Mental Health Global Action Programme*. Geneva, Switzerland.

Within Canada, one of the WHO's member states, the Standing Senate Committee on Social Affairs, Science, and Technology subsequently analyzed the status of mental health services, releasing its final report (*Out of the Shadows at Last*, also known as the "Kirby Report") in 2006. One of its recommendations was that a Mental Health Commission of Canada (MHCC) be created (and funded) by the federal government to move forward on the fact that Canada was the only G8 nation to lack a national mental health policy. The foci of the MHCC are (1) an anti-stigma campaign, (2) a program to reduce homelessness, (3) a knowledge exchange centre, and (4) a mental health strategy. Extensive consultation with researchers, service providers, individuals affected by mental illness, and the general public serves as the foundation for the MHCC's work. A series of open consultations was held across Canada to inform the creation of a national mental health strategy, based on a foundation of eight goals. Arising from those consultations, Canada's Mental Health Strategy was developed and shared with the public in 2012. The strategy is composed of six strategic directions (see Box 8.2) (Mental Health Commission of Canada, 2012).

Since its implementation, the strategy has served as the foundation for a number of different mental health policies, programs, and initiatives. However, a recent analysis reveals that one area where considerable work remains to be done is in the development of targeted services for specific social groups (Mental Health Commission of Canada, 2015). As you learned earlier in the chapter, the level and nature of risk for developing particular mental health problems varies across social groups. Consequently,

Box 8.2

Canada's Mental Health Strategy

The Mental Health Strategy for Canada is the country's first. Released by the Mental Health Commission of Canada in 2012, it has six strategic directions:

- Promote mental health across the lifespan in homes, schools, and workplaces, and prevent mental illness and suicide wherever possible.

- Foster recovery and well-being for people of all ages living with mental health problems and illnesses, and uphold their rights.

- Provide access to the right combination of services, treatments, and supports when and where people need them.

- Reduce disparities in risk factors and access to mental health services, and strengthen the response to the needs of diverse communities and Northerners.

- Work with First Nations, Inuit, and Métis to address their mental health needs, acknowledging their distinct circumstances, rights, and cultures.

- Mobilize leadership, improve knowledge, and foster collaboration at all levels.

Source: Mental Health Commission of Canada. (2012). *Changing Directions, Changing Lives: The Mental Health Strategy for Canada: Executive Summary.* Calgary, AB: Author.

the resources needed to reduce that risk vary as well. For example, supportive parenting helps youth who are transgender deal with the stigmatization they frequently encounter at school and, as a result, these youth have significantly lower levels of mood and anxiety disorders (Travers et al., 2012). Thus, targeted resources that enable parents to be more supportive in the face of marginalization and stigmatization are important for improving the mental health of this particular group of youth (Gender Creative Kids Canada, n.d.).

Similarly, mental health programming must be developed that addresses the specific needs of immigrant, refugee, ethnocultural, and racialized groups (Mental Health Commission of Canada, 2016b). The distinct circumstances of Indigenous peoples in Canada create a need for particular types of programs, policies, and initiatives as well. Earlier in the chapter, you learned that in 2016 alone, several Indigenous communities declared states of emergency because of a rash of suicides among youth (CBC News, 2016c; Markewich, 2016; McCue, 2016). Although the majority of suicides among Indigenous youth occur in only a small proportion of communities, the risk of suicide in those particular communities is extremely high. Lalonde (cited in McCue, 2016) argues that these are the communities that are the least "culturally healthy." Consequently, reducing the level of risk among youth in these communities requires programs and initiatives that enable them to re-establish a sense of cultural continuity: "What we have found is when communities have a sense of their collective past and have the tools and resources to navigate toward their future, those are the places that support youth health and well-being better than others" (McCue, 2016). For example, there are several Aboriginal Support and Crisis Intervention Response Teams (ASCIRTs) in British Columbia, consisting of Indigenous volunteers and support workers. Individual communities determine what their immediate needs are, and the ASCIRT creates a foundation for those needs to be addressed. In Nanaimo, the Snuneymuxw First Nation established a number of cultural programs for youth (along with other initiatives) and, as a result, has been suicide-free for more than five years (McCue, 2016).

Individuals and groups who are involved in reducing the stigmatization of mental illness and ameliorating the problems of insufficient and inadequate care are trying to change aspects of the social typing process. Groups involved in the former efforts are working toward removing the label of "crazy," the evaluation of persons with mental illnesses as "dangerous" and "unpredictable," and reducing the social rejection and discrimination that result. Groups involved in the latter efforts are trying to improve the ways that persons with mental disorders are treated in the mental health system—ensuring that enough of a priority is placed on mental health, that there are sufficient resources available, and that those resources are developed to address the distinct needs of particular social groups.

However, resistance to stigmatization and to inadequate treatment is not the only way the "deviance dance" is evident in the realm of mental illness. Some people resist the medicalization of mental disorders overall, and even question the very notion of mental illness.

Resisting Medicalization

Resistance to the medicalization of mental disorders can occur at a number of levels, from criticisms of the diagnostic manuals used by mental health professionals to criticisms of the daily practices of mental health professionals to questions about whether "mental illness" even exists.

Criticizing the *DSM*

Although both the *DSM* and the *ICD* have faced criticisms, the *DSM* has been the focus of particular attention. Much of the criticism has been based on the inclusion of particular disorders in the *DSM*. For example, homosexuality was included in the *DSM* from 1952 until its removal in 1973—it was first classified as a "sociopathic personality disorder" and then as a form of "non-psychotic sexual deviance." Factors contributing to its removal from the *DSM* included research demonstrating that homosexuality was not pathological and was not related to pathological outcomes, as well as the activism of gay and lesbian rights groups (see Chapter 5).

More recently, controversy has emerged over the diagnostic category of attention deficit hyperactivity disorder (ADHD). Most experts agree that this is a disorder that affects people's lives by interfering with their abilities to concentrate on tasks, follow instructions, and sit still in situations that require it. However, critics argue that in North America, far too many children are being diagnosed.

One concern is that normal childhood restlessness and inattention is being diagnosed as a mental disorder. Another concern is that behavioural or attention problems that are actually being caused by social forces (e.g., family conflicts) are being diagnosed as mental disorders, while the true cause of the problems remain untreated (Shute, 2000). Furthermore, some social analysts suggest that the inability to focus or pay attention is a logical outcome for children growing up in a society in which the adults pride themselves on multitasking, and where being "stressed out" is seen by many as a sign of importance and value. All of these concerns reached a climax in 2000, when a class action lawsuit was launched against the American Psychiatric Association and the pharmaceutical company that manufactured the first drug for ADHD (Ritalin) for constructing a nonexistent mental illness. The lawsuit was later dismissed (Shute, 2000; Peck, 2001).

While some critics of the medicalization of mental disorder focus their disapproval on the inclusion of specific categories of disorder within the *DSM*, other critics express concerns over the *DSM* itself and the power it holds. Critics of the *DSM* point not only to methodological shortcomings in its creation, but also to the role played by power (and economics) in determining what is and is not included in the list of mental disorders, and the influence of the pharmaceutical industry. Critics include Allen J. Frances, a prominent psychiatrist and Chair of the task force that led the revision of the *DSM-IV* (Frances, 2013).

Despite its shortcomings, there is considerable agreement that the *DSM* and *ICD* do capture many diagnostically useful sets of symptoms that *are* distressful to the people that experience them and that *do* impair effective daily functioning. However, even those social analysts and health professionals who acknowledge the validity of the handbooks recognize that problematic patterns in its usage and in other practices of mental health professionals can occur. Research finds that variables other than medical ones may influence the diagnoses and treatments for mental disorders.

Being Sane in Insane Places: Criticizing Mental Health Professionals

Rosenhan (1973) was one of the early mental health professionals who documented the influence of social factors and other biases on psychiatric diagnoses. His influential study stirred tremendous controversy in the mental health community, but also motivated considerable changes in the mental health system. Rosenhan began with the question, "If sanity and insanity exist, how shall we know them?" That is, his fundamental question was whether the salient characteristics leading to diagnosis lie within the individual or in the environment. The medical view is that people present themselves with symptoms, which are then recognized by professionals as constituting a diagnosis, leading to treatment. As a parallel, people who present themselves with certain other characteristics may also be told by professionals that those are not symptoms of any mental disorder.

Rosenhan had eight research associates (including students, homemakers, and a psychiatrist) attempt to have themselves admitted to psychiatric hospitals. These "pseudo-patients" presented themselves to mental health admissions people at 12 different hospitals, claiming that they had been hearing voices for the past few weeks that were saying "empty," "hollow," and "thud." Rosenhan's underlying assumption was that if their sanity was not detected, it would indicate that the salient characteristics involved in psychiatric diagnosis reside more in the environment than within the individual. All of these research associates were admitted to hospitals with diagnoses of schizophrenia.

Once they were admitted, they were to begin acting normally, report that the voices had stopped, and try to get discharged. In interactions with the mental health professionals, they were to be truthful about the characteristics of their lives (with the exception that those in mental health professions would allege another occupation to avoid special treatment)—their relationships with family members, their life histories, their frustrations and joys in life. As patients, they were completely cooperative with staff, doing everything they were told to do (although they did surreptitiously flush their medication down the toilets). In the end, the pseudo-patients spent between 7 and 52 days hospitalized prior to being discharged, with the average stay being 19 days. The psychiatrists at the hospitals never detected the pseudo-patients' sanity; they were discharged with diagnoses of "schizophrenia in remission," suggesting that their mental illness was still there but simply dormant for the present moment.

The lack of detection was not because they were acting abnormally. They received daily visitors, who were to look for any inadvertent behavioural consequences resulting from hospitalization, but the visitors detected no abnormal behaviours. Furthermore, in many cases *other patients* detected the sanity of the pseudo-patients, saying things like "You're not crazy" or "You must be a journalist or professor checking up on the hospital." Inside the hospitals, the mentally ill label that they had received affected the nature of all of their interactions with staff.

Normal behaviours were overlooked or misinterpreted through the lens of the diagnosis of mental illness. For example, although the pseudo-patients initially tried to hide their note-taking (for fear of being detected), it quickly became apparent that note-taking was seen as a *sign* of their mental disorder. As boredom set in and mealtime became a highlight of the day, waiting in the hallway for the cafeteria doors to be opened was described as indicative of the "oral-acquisitive nature" of schizophrenia. In a session with a psychiatrist, one male pseudo-patient spoke of how, as a little boy, he was closer to his mother but as he progressed through adolescence he became closer to his father and more distant from his mother; psychiatric notes described this as "considerable ambivalence in relationships." When he described his marriage as generally positive with just occasional arguments, the case notes identified those occasional conflicts as "angry outbursts."

Of course, one factor that might contribute to misdiagnosis is the desire of mental health professionals to err on the side of caution. It may be safer to mistakenly label a healthy person as ill than to mistakenly label an ill person as healthy and not provide them with the treatment they need. Rosenhan suggested that this desire to err on the side of caution can explain misdiagnosis at the initial time of admission but is less able to account for continued misdiagnosis after a lengthy period of observation and analysis.

So, why *did* the misdiagnosis continue all the way until the time of discharge? One reason could be the lack of interaction between the mental health professionals and the patients. Nursing attendants, nurses, and even the psychiatrists actively avoided contact with the pseudo-patients. When the pseudo-patients intercepted staff members to ask them simple questions, the psychiatrists averted their eyes and walked away 71 percent of the time, as did 88 percent of the nurses and nursing attendants. Another reason, one emphasized by Rosenhan, is the power that a diagnosis of mental illness carries. He concluded that the initial "schizophrenic" label given upon admission to the hospitals provided staff with a **schema**, or mental framework, that affected their interpretations of the pseudo-patients' behaviours—*all* behaviours then came to be interpreted as indicative of pathology. In contrast, those very same behaviours exhibited by someone who had not been diagnosed as mentally ill would not be perceived as indicative of pathology. What was Rosenhan's conclusion? The salient characteristics in the diagnosis of mental illness lie more within the social context, or the environment, than within the individual.

As you can imagine, the results of this research project caused quite a stir in the psychiatric community. An outcry from psychiatric hospitals throughout the United States occurred. Critics claimed that something like that could certainly never happen at their hospitals, suggesting that the hospitals used in Rosenhan's study must have been poorly run. Rosenhan therefore created a follow-up study to look into this possibility.

This time Rosenhan selected a well-known and very well-respected teaching hospital. He told administrators that within the next three months, at least one pseudo-patient would attempt to be admitted as a psychiatric patient. Hospital staff, including the psychiatrists, were asked to rate each person admitted during that time as to the likelihood that this was one of the pseudo-patients. During that period of time, a total of 191 psychiatric patients were admitted to this hospital. Of these patients, the hospital staff identified 41 as having a high likelihood of being pseudo-patients. At least one psychiatrist identified as many as 23 patients, and both a psychiatrist and at least one additional staff member identified 19 patients as being likely pseudo-patients. How many pseudo-patients had Rosenhan actually sent in? None. Rosenhan concluded that even mental health professionals have difficulties distinguishing the sane from the insane.

Rosenhan's research seemed to present a resounding critique of the efficacy of mental health professions. First, by illustrating that people without mental disorders could be kept in hospitals and not have their "sanity" detected, it raised significant concerns about those patients who had been committed to psychiatric hospitals involuntarily. It was possible that some of these patients being kept against their wills did not have any mental disorder. These types of concerns stimulated governments throughout the Western world to create or intensify legislation governing involuntary psychiatric admissions. In Canada, all provinces have mental health legislation that outlines the conditions under which individuals can and cannot be admitted for psychiatric care against their wills and sets procedural safeguards in place for reviewing such cases at regular periods following admission. Within the government, many provinces have a Mental Health/Psychiatric Patient Advocate Office whose role is to advise involuntarily committed patients and their families of their rights in such situations.

Second, Rosenhan's research described the dehumanizing treatment that patients in psychiatric hospitals frequently faced, such as being ignored by staff when asking a question, being prescribed large numbers of pills (altogether, the eight pseudo-patients in the first study were given a total of 2100 pills during their hospital stays), and being mistreated in many other ways. For example, in one instance a nurse unbuttoned her shirt to adjust her bra right in front of a group of male patients. It was not a teasing or sexual demonstration, but rather reflected her view that it was no big deal because these were "mental patients" rather than "real" men. These observations reinforced Goffman's (1961) argument that psychiatric hospitals were *total institutions*, similar to prisons and concentration camps, wherein "inmates" had no choice but to accept restriction and dehumanization; their identities were dismantled and new "inmate" identities created, identities that would be carried into the community following release from the institution. Although Goffman's sociological work of more than a decade earlier had pointed to some of the negative implications of treatment within an institutional setting, Rosenhan's empirical documentation of dehumanization raised greater awareness, contributing to changes in the practices in psychiatric hospitals and the growth of mental health advocacy groups.

Third, Rosenhan's research had, and continues to have, broader theoretical implications. Rosenhan's first study illustrates important aspects of labelling theories, which emphasize the influence that labels have on the way people are subsequently treated. In particular, it reflects the assumption that labels have negative consequences by closing the doors of acceptance within the "normal" world. However, even though Rosenhan's research is reflective of the negative consequences of labels, stigmatization can have potentially positive consequences as well (see Chapter 3). Several decades later, debates over whether stigmatization on the basis of mental health has positive or negative effects continue. One perspective points to the harmful effects that stigmatization has on the self-concept, which has implications for treatment outcomes and the magnitude of symptoms.

Opponents in this deviance dance bring attention to the fact that stigmatization can improve self-concept, in that being labelled is the key factor in opportunities for effective treatment, which improves well-being. It may be that receiving a formal label of mental illness enables the individual to be assigned a **sick role**. Parsons (1951) claimed that although illness was dysfunctional for society in general, under certain conditions people with illnesses could be assigned a role that would accord them certain rights; but along with those rights came certain responsibilities. A person who has been assigned a sick role is given a temporary reprieve from some of life's responsibilities and is not blamed for the condition, but rather is given sympathy. However, that person must clearly be trying to get well, must seek professional help, and must adhere to the physician's treatment plan. Consequently, having received a formal label can be considered indicative of seeking professional help and attempting to get well.

Perry (2011) found that being labelled as mentally ill has a positive impact on people with more severe, rather than less severe, mental disorders. For these individuals, being formally labelled results in larger, more functional support networks for the individual. Why might labelling have a more positive impact on people with more severe mental illnesses? More severe psychiatric symptoms may be more overt, resulting in others placing less blame on them for their behaviours; milder symptoms may be more subtle to outside observers, such that others may wonder why the individual cannot simply "snap out of it." In fact, De Maio (2010) suggests that not everyone who is ill will be assigned a sick role. The process is dependent, in part, on the severity of the illness.

Finally, Rosenhan's research pointed to the unintentional influence of social factors on diagnostic processes. Considering the awareness stimulated by Rosenhan's research, one might think that, since that time, the influence of social factors in diagnosis has declined. Is this the case?

The Role of Social Factors in Diagnosis and Treatment

Given the way that social factors permeate every aspect of our daily lives and the subsequent influence they have over our thoughts, feelings, and behaviours, it should not be too surprising that social factors continue to have the potential to influence diagnosis and treatment. Research reveals that there are diagnostic biases based on clients' gender, race, or ethnicity (Eriksen & Kress, 2008; Hicks, 2004; Neighbors, Trierweiler, Ford, & Muroff, 2003). For instance, one study found that even when clinicians were using the same diagnostic instrument, black clients were more likely to be diagnosed with schizophrenia while white clients were more likely to be diagnosed with bipolar disorder (Neighbors et al., 2003). Furthermore, black individuals are less likely to be diagnosed with mental disorders and more likely to be criminalized for their actions (Foulks, 2004). Similarly, women and men who present similar symptoms may also face differential diagnosis, and women are more likely to be prescribed psychiatric medications (Eriksen & Kress, 2008). More broadly, Nakash and Saguy (2015) find that there is more misdiagnosis of clients from marginalized social groups, especially if the clinician is not a member of that marginalized group.

> ### Ask Yourself
> Why do you think social factors influence the diagnosis and treatment of mental disorders?

When you thought about your answer to the *Ask Yourself* exercise, you may have referred to something like stereotypes—assumptions about what people of different social groups are like or should be like. Because of biased attitudes that continue to pervade society, members of different races or ethnic groups are often perceived in different ways. So are men and women. Indeed, researchers working in the various critical theories that were explored in Chapter 3 (e.g., feminist theories) explain these research results in precisely those terms (Eriksen & Kress, 2008).

Thus far, we have looked at resistance to the medicalization of mental disorder in three different ways. One form of resistance emphasizes the ways that some normal social behaviours have been deviantized within the DSM. A second form of resistance launches broader critiques against the DSM, showing us the political dimension of the document. The third form of resistance focuses on some of the inaccuracies and biases that occur in the daily practices of mental health professionals, revealing the power of the labelling process and the influence of social factors on diagnosis and treatment.

There is one last form of resistance to the medicalization of mental illness that moves to a much broader, more abstract level, criticizing the concept of "mental illness" itself as being a false label that denies free will (Szasz, 1994). Thomas Szasz (a psychiatrist himself) acknowledges that there are physical diseases of the brain, but argues that virtually none of the disorders listed in the DSM have been proven to be physical diseases of the brain. Instead, people use the diagnostic categories of the DSM to involuntarily treat people who do not want treatment and to enable others to avoid responsibility for criminal acts. Szasz's arguments have stimulated controversy since the 1950s and continue to stimulate controversy today.

However, most people agree that mental disorders *do* exist, and that some people with mental disorders do not have everything they need to successfully recover or achieve a high quality of functioning in daily life. The continued stigmatization of mental illness is one of the central obstacles to recovery and high functioning, and even influences the extent and quality of policies and programs available. Governments, the medical community, and self-help/advocacy groups continue to work toward improving the lives of people with mental disorders—reducing the stigma and increasing the available resources. At another level, people are bringing to the forefront the political nature of the process by which diagnostic categories are created and the social factors that can influence or bias diagnosis and treatment.

TIME TO REVIEW

Learning Objective 3

- How has the social control of mental illness changed throughout Western history?
- What are the necessary prerequisites for deinstitutionalization to be successful, and why has reinsitutionalization emerged?
- What role does mental illness play in homelessness and in crime?

Learning Objective 4

- What types of policies and programs emerge from the *discrimination* and *disease paradigms*?

Learning Objective 5

- What criticisms have been directed at the *DSM*?

Learning Objective 6

- What happened in Rosenhan's two studies and what were his conclusions?
- What were the implications of Rosenhan's research?
- What influence do social factors (such as ethnicity and gender) have on the diagnosis and treatment of mental disorders and why?
- What are Thomas Szasz's criticisms of the medicalization of mental illness?

CHAPTER SUMMARY

- *Mental illness* refers to thoughts, moods, and behaviours that cause significant distress or impaired functioning for individuals. The nature of these impairments is further delineated in the diagnostic categories listed in the *Diagnostic and Statistical Manual of Mental Disorders* (DSM) and the *International Classification of Diseases* (ICD). (1)

- Although 20 percent of people experience mental illness in any given year, the lifetime incidence of mental illness is much higher. The level and nature of risk varies across social groups. People in low socioeconomic status groups show higher rates of mental illness, as do adolescents and young adults. The level of risk in a small proportion of Indigenous communities is extremely high. (1)

■ Considerable costs are associated with mental illness for the individuals experiencing the illness, their families, and society as a whole. (2)

■ The stigmatization of people with mental disorders is evident in media representations, attitudes of the general public, and even attitudes of health professionals. Stigmatization hinders recovery of people with mental disorders, contributes to discrimination in many areas, and results in mental health programs and policies not being seen as priorities. (3)

■ Although mental illness has been treated in various ways throughout history, in the late nineteenth century it became *medicalized*. Over the last several decades, the *deinstitutionalization* movement has helped millions of individuals with mental disorders; however, there have also been unintended negative consequences. (3)

■ Mental health policies and programs are embedded within two different paradigms: the *disease paradigm* and the *discrimination paradigm*. The first paradigm emphasizes the role of symptoms of the disorders themselves in people's experience of mental illness. The second paradigm emphasizes the role of stigmatization and prejudice in people's experience of mental illness. (4)

■ The medicalization of mental disorder is being resisted and changed in a number of different ways. Critics express concerns about the diagnostic handbook, the *DSM*, for (1) the inclusion of some normal behaviours as "disorders," such as homosexuality and ADHD, and (2) the political nature of the process by which disorders are included in the *DSM* and the subsequent power the handbook has. (5)

■ Other people have raised questions about mental health professionals themselves. Rosenhan's classic study concluded that the salient characteristics in diagnosis lie more within the social context than in the individual. Decades later, researchers continue to find that social factors have an impact on psychiatric diagnosis and treatment. Thomas Szasz (1994) takes his criticisms of psychiatry the furthest, suggesting that mental illness is a "myth." (6)

To learn more about the topics discussed in this chapter and to complete chapter quizzes, visit the Companion Website for *Deviance, Conformity, and Social Control in Canada.*

Chapter 9

What Do You Believe? Religion, Science, and Deviance

Marekuliasz/Shutterstock

Learning Objectives

After reading this chapter, you should be able to

1　Identify the two types of relationships that exist between belief systems and deviance.

2　Describe the traditional typology that helps determine which religions are "deviant," and explain why sects and cults are considered "deviant."

3　Describe the different levels of social control that are directed at "deviant" religions and the ways that deviant labels are resisted.

4　Explain how religion served as a social typer of deviance in the cases of the witch persecutions, residential schooling, and the child-savers movement.

5 Describe the origins, causes, and control of scientific misconduct.

6 Explain why a science's location on the deviant science–real science continuum may change over time.

7 Describe why science is a powerful social typer of deviance and how that power has manifested itself through history.

Scientist J. B. S. Haldane (1927) suggested that "the wise man regulates his conduct by the theories of both religion and science. But he regards these theories not as stringent statements of ultimate fact but as art forms." This quotation indicates that both religious and scientific belief systems are vital parts of our daily lives. It also suggests that these belief systems can serve social control functions, and if we are wise we will act on the basis of religion and science. In the quote, Haldane also points to the subjectivity of religious and scientific belief systems. Although these belief systems proclaim truths, they emerge through processes of social construction or creation, just as art does.

Anything that you personally think is true represents one of your **beliefs**, regardless of whether it is actually true or not. Some of your beliefs might be unique to you, while in other cases a group of people might accept the same truths that you do. Frequently, single beliefs are combined with other interrelated beliefs into organized sets of **belief systems** (Oxford Dictionaries, 2017). Religious doctrines (e.g., Christian, Islamic), the knowledge contained in particular disciplines of science (e.g., astronomy, zoology), and the ideologies of specific political parties (e.g., Liberals, New Democrats) are all belief systems that are shared among large groups of people.

There are two different types of relationships between belief systems and deviance. First, we can look at belief systems *as* deviance, when acts of deviance occur within groups of people who adhere to particular belief systems or when an entire belief system itself is socially typed as deviant. Second, we can explore belief systems as social typers of deviance, wherein the truths proclaimed by belief systems dictate to us who should be considered deviant and what the consequences should or will be. Both religion and science have these two types of relationships with deviance.

Religion

Sociological analyses of religion explore the social embeddedness of religious belief systems—the processes by which religious belief systems emerge, the role that religion plays in people's lives, and the relationships between religion and other social structures or processes.

Look at the first *Ask Yourself* question. It leads you to make the transition from thinking about religion as a belief system to thinking about religion as a social organization that holds a particular place in the community and in the larger society. If you are like the majority of Canadians, you have a religious affiliation but you do not necessarily attend a church, temple, mosque, or synagogue on a regular basis. In fact, weekly or monthly attendance at organized religious services declined from 48 to 28 percent between 1986 and 2008 (Eagle, 2011). If you do regularly attend a place of worship, you will be aware that it holds a particular role in the community in terms of the way it is viewed by other members of the community and the activities it may engage in within the community. Your religious belief system may be disparaged by others, that is, considered to be "deviant." Conversely, your religious belief system may provide you with a moral code that defines certain others as being "deviant."

Religion as Deviance: "Deviant" Religions

When considering religion and deviance, many of you may initially think of abuses carried out by representatives of different religions, such as instances of child sexual abuse by religious leaders and allegations that churches put other priorities before the safety of children (Kirchgaesser, 2017). In addition to deviant acts carried out by religious institutions or representatives of those institutions, talking about **religion as deviance** also brings to mind those religious groups that are thought of as deviant in their entirety.

Which religions are considered deviant and which are considered normal? Traditionally, religious belief systems were categorized using various typologies based on characteristics of the particular group in question. A religious group's location in the typology determined whether it was considered deviant. More recently, these traditional typologies have been questioned and even abandoned by some researchers, resulting in quite a different view of "deviant religions."

Deviant Religions According to Traditional Typologies

Different scholars have proposed various typologies of religious groups, but a review of these frameworks reveals that four categories of religious groups are common (Bromley & Melton, 2012; McGuire, 2002; Stark & Bainbridge, 1996). Deviance is determined by which category a religious group is assigned to.

Ecclesia refers to state religions: a specific religious belief system is adopted at a governmental level and becomes a nation's "official" religion. Islam is an ecclesia in Iran, as is the Anglican denomination of Christianity in England and the Lutheran denomination of Christianity in Sweden. The extent to which other religions are practised in these countries depends on the nation in question. Some nations identify an ecclesia and yet declare freedom of religion for their citizens (e.g., England); in other cases, non-ecclesiastic religions are banned (e.g., Europe during the Middle Ages).

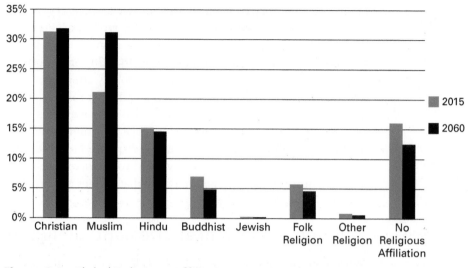

Figure 9.1 Global Religious Affiliations, 2015 and 2060

Data from Pew Research Center (2017). *The changing global religious landscape*. Washington, DC: Author.

Churches are not "official" religions of an entire society, but they are large and powerful religious groups. The religious groups commonly perceived as being the world's major religions—Islam, Judaism, Hinduism, Buddhism, Sikhism, and Christianity—are categorized as *churches*. They are well established in society, highly bureaucratized (having complex hierarchies of leadership and administration, as well as formalized rituals and practices), and have millions of members around the world. The largest religious groups in the world are Christianity, Islam, and Hinduism. By 2060, it is projected that Christianity and Islam will continue to grow, while some other churches will decline (see Figure 9.1). Churches are further subdivided into **denominations**, such that there are different types of Christianity (e.g., Catholicism), Islam (e.g., Sunni), and Judaism (e.g., Orthodox). The same can be said of all of the other churches of the world. In Canada, the predominant religious denomination is Roman Catholicism, practised by 39 percent of Canadians who have a religious affiliation (Statistics Canada, 2013).

Sects are smaller religious groups that have usually broken away from larger churches at some point in their history. They are less established in society than churches, have fewer members, more rigid doctrine formed in reaction to the doctrine of the larger church, and require higher levels of commitment from their members (e.g., clothing, behaviour, and food). The Amish and the Hutterites are examples of sects that are offshoots of the larger Christian church, while the Taliban is a sect that has broken away from mainstream Islam.

Cults are usually smaller than sects, frequently having only a handful of members. Their doctrine is even more reactionary and oppositional, and intense levels of commitment are required of members. A single, charismatic leader serves as a source

The Hutterites are a Christian-based sect living primarily on the western prairies of North America whose beliefs include communal goods and pacifism.

of inspiration, convincing followers that the secret to salvation can be found in that group. Examples are the Branch Davidians, Heaven's Gate, and The Family of Love.

This framework has traditionally been used as the foundation for decisions about whether a particular religious group is deviant. Ecclesia, which declare an entire nation's citizens as members (at least on a theoretical level), are not considered deviant in those societies. Of course, there may be some groups in those societies that do attempt to deviantize that religion as part of the "deviance dance." For instance, there are some groups in England who are critical of the Anglican church as an ecclesia. Churches, with millions of members worldwide and their high level of integration in many societies, are also perceived as normal or conventional religions, although members of one church may attempt to deviantize members of another church. For example, the "deviance dance" between the Christian church and the Islamic church was responsible, in part, for the Crusades—a series of battles lasting from the eleventh century to the sixteenth century.

Sects and cults—which have fewer members, are more isolated from mainstream society, and have doctrine that is more reactionary or oppositional—are the religious groups that are traditionally seen as deviant and in need of social control. In other words, those religious groups that are characterized by high levels of tension with the broader society are perceived as deviant, while those that are characterized by low levels of tension are seen as normal (Stark & Bainbridge, 1996).

The "Deviant" World of Sects and Cults

Although both sects and cults are viewed as deviant, thereby existing in a state of tension with wider society, the deviance of cults is of a greater magnitude than that of sects. Cults are based on novel beliefs, while sects tend to have more traditional belief systems as their foundation, creating some differences in the level of tension that exists with society and the level of social control exerted on the religious groups (Stark & Bainbridge, 1996).

Sects. According to some scholars, sects are "churches of the disinherited" (Niebuhr, cited in Schwadel, 2014, p. 100). That is, people of lower social status and members of marginalized groups are drawn to the doctrine of sects, which frequently emphasizes that rewards come not in life, but rather in the after-life. Because of this belief, sects are less aligned with the secular world than churches are (Niebuhr, 1929; Schwadel, 2014). Higher levels of commitment are required of members of sects, and their beliefs and life habits are strictly controlled. Members who fail to think or act in accordance with the belief system are punished, and in some sects the most extreme punishment is excommunication from the group (McGuire, 2002; Stark & Bainbridge, 1996).

Although the levels of commitment required of members and the levels of control exerted over members' lives are higher in sects than in churches, there is considerable diversity among sects in these characteristics—that is, some sects have more rigid requirements than others. Similarly, the degree of tension between sects and the wider society also varies. Such tension is fundamental to the social control of sects within society. The level of tension experienced by a particular sect is determined by three factors: (1) the magnitude of the differences between the sect and society; (2) the level of antagonism that the sect feels for society; and (3) the extent to which the sect separates itself from the larger world (Stark & Bainbridge, 1996). For example, although Seventh-day Adventists and Jehovah's Witnesses have similar origins, over time Seventh-day Adventists have integrated with the larger society (such as through building schools, universities, and hospitals) to a greater extent. Because of these different trajectories, today Jehovah's Witnesses experience higher levels of tension with their surrounding societies than do Seventh-day Adventists. As a result, Seventh-day Adventists are considered a **denominational sect**, suggesting they are verging on being seen as a conventional Christian denomination. In contrast, Jehovah's Witnesses are considered an **established sect** because of the tension that continues to exist with the societies in which they reside (Lawson, 1995).

However, it is important to point out that the level of tension that exists between a sect and the larger society is not solely due to characteristics of sects. It is also a product of characteristics of the wider society, such as public attitudes toward the sects and how authorities interact with them. Tension between a sect and society is bidirectional in that a sect may have certain levels of antagonism toward society, but society may have certain levels of antagonism toward a particular sect. Furthermore, existing hostilities in society toward specific religious groups may cause a sect's belief system to become more polarized. When a deviantized group becomes more extreme as a response to hostilities or social control efforts from outsiders, it is referred to as **deviancy amplification** (Becker, 1963).

Although the tensions between different sects and the sociocultural environment vary, some degree of tension must exist for a religious group to be considered a sect rather than a church. Tension is also characteristic of the types of religious groups known as cults. When looking at cults, the tensions with the wider society are typically of an even greater magnitude, especially in the realm of public attitudes. Simply mentioning the word "cult" fuels a flood of images in most people's minds.

Cults.   Your thoughts about cults likely draw heavily on the media, particularly news stories about specific cults. When cults are covered in the media, it is usually because of some sensationalistic incident, such as the mass suicides of the Order of the Solar Temple in 1994, or the storming of the Branch Davidians' compound in Waco, Texas, by the American government in 1993. These are the kinds of cults typically represented in the media—doomsday suicide cults and cults that engage in various criminal activities.

The ways that cults are portrayed in the news media has changed over time (McCloud, 2007). In the 1950s, new religious groups were framed as exotic and largely harmless, although some were viewed as potentially politically subversive. When a variety of new religious groups emerged alongside the countercultural youth movements of the 1960s and 1970s, their portrayals evolved. News stories drew attention to the "cult menace" (McCloud, 2007, p. 219), highlighting the dangers of brainwashing and physical harm—dangers realized in the Manson Family murders in 1969 and the mass suicides of the People's Temple Agricultural Project ("Jonestown") in 1978. The "cult menace" frame continues to dominate news coverage of cults into the present day. Doherty (2014) highlights the factors that contribute to distorted news coverage of alternative religious groups. First, the sources used often have one-sided views of the group (e.g., disgruntled former members). Second, the news industry faces constraints in both time and money, which impedes comprehensive investigations of the events. Third, journalists themselves frequently have limited knowledge about the group and fall prey to sensationalistic stereotypes. Finally, because the news industry depends on sensationalism to attract more readers or viewers, there is a tendency to over-report stories in the beginning but then ignore later developments.

Through its framing of cults, the media constructs them as "folk devils," which can contribute to moral panics (Laycock, 2013, p. 73). However, it is important to note that popular images of cults are not always unfounded. Some groups are very real threats to people's well-being, such as through acts of mass violence or mass suicide, sexual abuse, economic exploitation, or other criminal activities (Beit-Hallahmi, 2003; Bereska, 2017). Behaviours that violate cultural norms do occur in some cults,

Eiji Hori/AP Photo/The Canadian Press

In 1995, 12 people were killed and thousands injured when members of Aum Shinrikyô, a Japanese cult with Christian and Buddhist foundations, released sarin nerve gas in the Tokyo subway. Incidents like this one strongly influence public perceptions about cults.

such as The Family of Love (see Box 9.1) (Bainbridge, 2002; Gardner, 2016; Kent, 1994; Lewis & Melton, 1994). In these cases, media coverage can provide important information on controversial or criminal activities (Manca, 2017).

Although there is some foundation to the popular images of cults, such as mass suicide, violence, mind control, child abuse, and sexual deviance, these qualities are characteristic of only a small proportion of the thousands of groups in the world that are considered "cults." Cults, like sects, are characterized by diversity in beliefs and practices, as well as the level of overt tension that exists with society. However, popular images of cults and the resulting public attitudes contribute to more overriding tensions for cults. For both cults and sects, these tensions are played out in the "deviance dance"—the various means of social control of these deviant religions and the corresponding resistance to those means of control.

The Family of Love

The Family of Love, formerly known as the Children of God (and now calling itself "The Family International") is a group that has been a target of attention for cult watchers for more than 40 years. Its founder, David "Moses" Berg, brought together a group of young hippies in the 1960s based on his revelation from God that he would be the prophet who would play a key role in the second coming of Jesus Christ. Members fully devoted themselves to the group by abandoning all ties with their families, giving up personal possessions, and evangelizing. Actors River Phoenix, Joaquin Phoenix, and Rose McGowan were all raised, as children, within this group. Although the Children of God were initially located in several communes across the United States, a revelation that the nation would be destroyed for its impurity led Berg to disperse members throughout the world. There, they continued their attempts to recruit new converts.

Controversy surrounded many of Berg's teachings, such as his concept of flirty fishing. Because Jesus was called a "fisher of men," Berg claimed that the women in the group should also be "fishers of men," seducing and offering sexual favours to men to convert them. Sexual sharing was another component of Berg's doctrine—sex was to be freely shared among group members, except between two men. Whether sex was freely shared between adults and children is debated. Analyses of the group's newsletters, as well as testimony from former members, point to pedophilia. Although criminal investigations in many countries have not been able to prove these allegations in court, some civil suits have been successful.

In 1987, Berg declared an official prohibition on adult–child sex and decreed that offenders would be excommunicated. Flirty fishing has also been eliminated because of the danger of sexually transmitted diseases. However, some researchers suggest that these practices were only removed from official documentation to prevent further investigation by authorities, and that the practices continued after that time (e.g., Kent, 1994). Although Berg died in 1994, The Family is alive and well, claiming more than 12 000 members worldwide. They present musical performances at youth shelters and women's shelters free of charge, and bring humanitarian efforts after natural disasters and in developing countries.

Cults, Sects, and the "Deviance Dance"

Controlling "Deviant" Religions. The international community has repeatedly declared the importance of religious freedom. The United Nations *Universal Declaration of Human Rights*, created in 1948 and signed by more than 100 countries around the world, states that freedom of thought, conscience, and religious belief and practice are fundamental human rights. However, this right is not unbridled. Threats to public health, public order, and infringement on the rights of others constitute valid reasons

Learning Objective 1

■ What are beliefs and belief systems?

■ What are the two ways that deviance can be explored within the context of belief systems?

Learning Objective 2

■ What typology has traditionally been used to categorize religious

groups, and which groups are socially typed as deviant?

■ What factors influence the level of tension between sects and the larger society?

■ How are cults framed in the news media?

■ What factors contribute to the framing of cults, and are these frames accurate?

for governments to violate religious freedom, according to human rights documents themselves. These caveats to freedom of religion serve as the basis for the various measures of social control that target sects and cults. Measures of social control emerge from the anti-cult movement, counter-cult movement, media, and governments.

During the twentieth century, a number of social organizations emerged in response to the perceived problems caused by "deviant" religions. Acting as moral entrepreneurs, they apply measures in their efforts to control "deviant" religions. In particular, during the late 1960s and early 1970s, the **anti-cult movement** materialized (Bromley & Shupe, 1993; Jenkins, 2000; Shupe & Bromley, 1995). Initially, it consisted of parents whose hippie children had joined new religious groups that were part of the broader countercultural movement. Concerned because their children had severed ties with their families, and fearful that their children would be brainwashed into deviant behaviours, parents coalesced into support groups. These support groups later became information networks to make other parents aware of the dangers of these new religious groups. Over time, numerous mental health, legal, and political professionals, along with academic researchers, became involved in anti-cult groups.

The anti-cult movement targets only certain religious groups—those considered to be "destructive." When the word "cult" is used in this movement, it refers specifically to those religious groups that have dangerous or destructive characteristics (see Box 9.2) (Langone, 2015; Ontario Consultants on Religious Tolerance, 2004; reFOCUS, 1998–2012).

Although the anti-cult movement is a relatively recent construction, the **counter-cult movement** is noticeably older, going back more than a century (Cowan, 2003). Unlike the anti-cult movement, this movement does not base its philosophy on internationally recognized legitimate limits to religious freedom discussed earlier. In fact, members of the counter-cult movement are overwhelmingly opposed to religious

Box 9.2

Characteristics of Destructive Cults

Although there is some disagreement over precisely what the characteristics of "dangerous" cults are, there are some common warning signs pointed out by various organizations:

- The leader places the group above the law, telling members they are not bound by the same laws as outsiders.

- The leader does not have to follow the same rules as the other members.

- The leader exerts control beyond the realm of religious doctrine, extending control to members' personal lives, education, jobs, or finances.

- "Mind control" techniques are used on members to facilitate indoctrination.

- The group follows a formal or informal policy of deceiving outsiders when recruiting, fundraising, or answering to authorities.

- The group is based on an apocalyptic vision in which the group will play a key role. For example, the group may stockpile weapons to prepare for battle with the outside world.

freedom itself. These groups primarily consist of conservative Christians drawn from fundamentalist denominations. They are not concerned about the possibility of brainwashing or abuse in cults, but instead express a theological concern about groups using the "wrong" interpretation of the Bible. Any religious group that does not follow fundamentalist, evangelical Christian doctrine is labelled a cult. Thus, not only are the groups that are commonly categorized as sects or cults targets of the counter-cult movement's control efforts, so are mainstream Christian religions (e.g., Catholicism) and all Eastern religions (e.g., Hinduism, Islam, Buddhism). Franklin Graham (son of the well-known evangelist Billy Graham) referred to Islam as a "wicked and evil" religion, Jerry Vines (former president of the Southern Baptist Convention) called Islam's prophet Muhammad "a demon-possessed pedophile" (Goodstein, 2003), and Pat Robertson (Southern Baptist minister, television host of *The 700 Club*, and one-time presidential candidate) blamed poverty in nations like India and Bangladesh on the "demonic cults" of Islam, Buddhism, and Hinduism (Vuijst, 1995).

Counter-cult groups engage in measures to eliminate "deviant" religions in a larger attempt to recruit converts to their own religious groups, including lobbying governments and law enforcement officials to enforce the law harshly against target religions. However, due to some of the negative perceptions that fundamentalist Christian religious groups themselves face in society, their lobbying efforts are not as successful as those of the secular anti-cult movement. Consequently, the counter-cult movement tends to operate on a less formal level inside religious communities.

The anti-cult and counter-cult movements make use of various forms of media, such as online environments, to convey their messages. But the media's own representations of cults are also powerful measures of social control, in that they influence public attitudes (Green & Brock, 2000). This is not the case with just news coverage of real events, but also fictional (or quasi-fictional) portrayals of cults in entertainment media. The "cult narrative" frames cults in five specific ways (Neal, 2008, p. 93). First, cult members are shown wearing *distinctive clothing*; for example, they might wear grey uniforms rather than the normative clothing of other characters on the show. Second, storylines often locate cults in *isolated areas*, such as farms. Third, cult members are shown living in *communes*, unlike most people in society. Fourth, the groups' belief systems are portrayed as *delusional*, such as based on extraterrestrial influence. Finally, the group's peculiarities in belief and practice are made *highly visible*, such as through group chanting in a public park. Taken together, these frames construct symbolic boundaries between acceptable beliefs or practices and the cultic Other. Whether highlighting a purely fictionalized group (such as the Heaven's Helpers Youth Cult in *Family Guy*), a quasi-fictional group (such as the Church of Scienetics in *LA Complex*), or a real religious group (such as Scientology in *South Park*), the cult narrative is a form of social control that reinforces, reproduces, and maintains the Othering of certain religious beliefs and practices.

At the most formal level of social control, governments have the power to create legislation, policies, and programs that will curb the destructive nature of "deviant" religions. When governments do enact legislation or alternative forms of policy, they often do so under the rubric of threats to public health, public order, and the rights of others (US Department of State, 2015). Determining at what point governmental measures of control can be enacted without violating the right to religious freedom is an especially grey area in those nations that declare an official separation of church and state.

Thus, in many Western nations, efforts are directed at those religious groups commonly recognized as sects and cults. For example, the Canadian Security Intelligence Service (CSIS) monitors doomsday and apocalyptic cults, those cults whose members may commit mass suicide or inflict mass harm. In the United States, the FBI does the same thing. The actions of some nations, however, are not without controversy. In the late 1990s, the government of France formed the Interministerial Mission in the Fight Against Sects/Cults (MILS) to monitor and control the 173 groups identified as sects or cults in a 1996 government report—groups like the Church of Scientology, Jehovah's Witnesses, Latter-day Saints (Mormons), and doomsday cults (Palmer, 2011). After certain groups were forced to disband and members of other groups were arrested for violating pieces of the new legislation, the European Court of Human Rights overturned many convictions on appeal.

Concerns about violations of religious freedom at the hands of government are of considerable interest to the international community. The United States Department of State releases an annual report that documents violations of religious freedom in specific countries and the measures being taken to improve religious freedom in other countries (US Department of State, 2015).

Resisting a Deviant Label. Anti-cult groups, counter-cult groups, media, and governments all act as social control agents in minimizing the perceived dangers of "deviant" religions. However, their efforts are counteracted to some extent by acts of resistance. The right to religious freedom is an international concept that serves as a nexus for many of these measures of resistance, but the social typing of "deviant" religions is resisted in numerous other ways as well.

In some cases, religious groups may engage in resistance within the legal system. Some groups (e.g., the Family of Love) defend themselves in court when accused of wrongdoings, such as child sexual abuse. Other groups initiate legal action themselves. For example, the Church of Scientology is well known for its litigious responses to criticism, having threatened or launched legal proceedings against filmmakers, journalists, and researchers (Beit-Hallahmi, 2003; *The Walrus*, 2015).

Other forms of resistance take place using the media, a "contested arena" where the religious fringe and religious mainstream are debated (McCloud, 2007, p. 225). Deviantized religious groups use the media for impression management. For instance, during the Waco standoff between the Branch Davidians and federal authorities in 1993, Seventh-day Adventists used the media to make it clear to the public that the Branch Davidians were a "cult" that distorted Seventh-day Adventist teachings and were in no way representative of the larger group (Lawson, 1995). More recently, Muslim individuals and groups use the media—such as the Muslims Are Not Terrorists Facebook page—to educate the public on the fact that violent acts by extremists are not reflective of Islamic doctrine. Impression management can emerge from other media sources as well. For example, the Church of Scientology is well known for its recruitment of celebrities as members, and increasingly for using those celebrities as the public faces of Scientology (Bereska, 2017; Kent, 2017). The media is also an arena where religious groups' ideologies are communicated—not only overtly on their websites, but also creatively within literature, artwork, or music (Evans, 2017; Raine, 2017; Shaw & Raine, 2017).

One of the most significant forms of resistance to the social typing of "deviant" religious groups comes not from the groups themselves but from academia. The traditional distinction among ecclesia, churches, sects, and cults was used for most of the twentieth century. The distinctions among these different types of religious groups were not questioned, although debates would sometimes emerge about how a specific religion should be categorized. However, as time passed, questions about these distinctions were raised and criticisms grew. Ecclesia were easily recognized in that official state religions are identified in legislation. By contrast, with continued discussion it became evident that the boundaries between churches, sects, and cults may not be as definitive as they seem.

What Are "Deviant" Religions? The Traditional Distinction Reconsidered. As you have read through this chapter thus far, you might have already begun to feel somewhat confused about which religions are actually deviant. We began with academic definitions of cults and sects, but as the chapter progressed we saw that different kinds of religious groups were labelled in this way at various times. The anti-cult movement prefaces the term "cult" with the descriptor "destructive," identifying as cults only those groups that have certain characteristics, such as mind control.

The counter-cult movement uses the term "cult" to refer to the theology of certain religious groups, those that do not adhere to fundamentalist Christian doctrine. We also saw that when media use the word "cult," they usually do so in the context of a distorted image of cults—those religious groups involved in destructive events captured in the news. Finally, we saw that in an international context, any religious groups that a particular government does not approve of are categorized as cults.

The boundaries between churches, sects, and cults become blurred even further when we incorporate a historical perspective. All of the world's major religions, now categorized as churches, began as cults—small groups of highly committed members who followed a single charismatic leader and whose doctrine was oppositional to a society's conventional belief system at the time (Hadden & Bromley, 1995; Jenkins, 2000). As these religious groups became more established, attracted larger numbers of members, and became integrated in a society's power structure, they progressed to being churches.

Even when we temporarily set aside the debates over which groups are cults or sects, the notion of *religion as deviance* crosses all boundaries. Every religious belief system in the world has been considered deviant at some time, in some place. There is no group of religious believers that has not at some moment in history been persecuted or perceived as evil, dangerous, or a threat to the social order. This is evident in looking at the former Soviet Union, where *all* religion was at one time prohibited, but is also apparent when looking at historical events such as the Crusades, the Israel/Palestine conflicts, and the bloodshed between Protestants and Catholics in Europe over hundreds of years.

For all of these reasons, many contemporary academics have abandoned the traditional terminology of ecclesia, churches, denominations, cults, and sects and instead use more encompassing terms, such as "ideological groups." Some scholars

TIME TO REVIEW

Learning Objective 3

- What forms of social control are directed at religious groups?

- In what ways do the anti-cult movement and the counter-cult movement differ in terms of who their members are, which religious groups they target, and their ideologies?

- What is religious freedom and what are its exceptions?

- In what ways have "deviant" religious groups themselves acted in resistance to social typing?

- What limitations are there in the traditional typology that distinguishes between churches, sects, and cults?

distinguish the world's major religions from more recent religious groups by using the term **new religious movements** (Bromley & Melton, 2012). Although some scholars find the traditional typology valid and, for various reasons, continue to use it, a historical and global perspective shows us that *any* religion can be socially typed as "deviant" and made subject to measures of social control.

Religion as a Social Typer of Deviance

While various religions have been socially typed as deviant at different times and in different places, religious belief systems also play a role in the social typing *of* deviance; that is, their proclamations of truth incorporate moral truths as well, dictums of what is right and wrong. At the individual level, the religious belief systems we adhere to present us with guidelines for our own behaviour, dictate how we should evaluate the behaviours of others, and influence the way we interact with people.

Beyond the individual level, religious belief systems also serve as social typers of deviance at the societal level. This is of particular interest when the boundaries between religious and political belief systems become blurred; that is, when a particular religious belief system becomes institutionalized by the government and serves as the foundation for the construction of governmental policy and law. Those people and behaviours considered deviant according to religious beliefs thereby become the people and behaviours considered deviant at the political level.

Religion and Politics in History

The Witch Persecutions.   From the fourteenth through the seventeenth centuries, the Christian church was essentially the core of government in Europe. It either served as the main governing body itself or acted in a key advisory capacity for governing bodies in most of Europe. Thus, its belief system was the foundation for law and governance. It was in this capacity that the "witch craze" occurred (Anderson & Gordon, 1978; Barstow, 1994; Quaife, 1987).

It is estimated that, during this time, between 40 000 and 100 000 "witches" were persecuted, sometimes by being burned at the stake. One of the best-known victims was Joan of Arc, who was convicted of witchcraft and burned at the stake in 1431. Witches were declared to be in league with Satan and responsible for plagues, floods, stillborn babies, infertility, crop failures, and any other unfortunate events in families or communities.

Those accused of witchcraft included a wide range of people, the list growing longer as the witch craze snowballed—followers of the pre-Christian religions, women who were financially independent or who outlived their husbands, midwives who used herbs and other natural techniques to ease the pain of childbirth, village "wise women" who used herbs in healing illness and injury, and peasants. The majority of people prosecuted as witches were women; however, there were considerable regional variations (e.g., in Iceland, 90 percent of the accused were male) (Briggs, 1996). At the peak of the witch craze (1550–1650), just about anyone could be accused of witchcraft.

Its belief system established as "law," the Christian church was central to the persecution of witches from the fourteenth to the seventeenth centuries.

Bettmann/Getty Images

Once arrested, torture was used to elicit confessions. The torture was so horrendous (e.g., having one's toenails pulled out or being stretched on the rack) that many people did confess. The content of their confessions was virtually guaranteed, given that a handbook (the *Malleus Maleficarum*) had been written in 1486 about how to question and torture witches. The nature of the questions asked typically led to specific types of responses, and torture would progress until that point. Upon being found guilty, the witch was put to death via hanging, decapitation, burning at the stake, or other means. With the invention of the printing press, church documents about the "witch problem" flooded the educated classes. Various witch-hunting manuals, church sermons, and pamphlets made people aware of the extent of the problem, frequently exaggerating the magnitude of persecution to gain more support and strike more fear into the populace.

The witch craze was not a uniform phenomenon. Witch trials occurred more often in some countries than in others, ranging from 26000 deaths in Germany to four deaths in Ireland (Briggs, 1996). Ben-Yehuda (1980) explains that following the Protestant Reformation, persecutions flourished in the regions of Europe where the Catholic church had weakened (e.g., Germany), while they were rare in those countries where Catholicism continued to hold its traditional power (e.g., Italy); however, both the Catholic and Protestant churches participated in the persecutions, each using the trials to demonstrate their religious dominance.

In some regions, the church was directly responsible for the arrest and trial of witches, while in other regions it was local authorities that searched for and tried them. In these latter instances, even though the church was not directly involved, church doctrine provided the theological foundation for persecution. In some regions, local authorities steered the witch trials, while in other regions it was national authorities. Capital punishment was virtually guaranteed in the former, while in the latter it was possible to hold onto one's life by turning in fellow witches to the authorities. Witch persecutions frequently followed peasant rebellions against the political elite or preceded them in an attempt to distract peasants from rebellion. As Quaife (1987, p. 208) concludes, the witch hunts were the result "of either the godly zeal of the political and religious elite and their peasant allies or the furious rage of her discomforted and ill-fortuned neighbours."

The persecution of witches is not relegated to the past (Horowitz, 2014). The United Nations has released several reports (e.g., Cimpric, 2010) that document an increase in violence linked to accusations of witchcraft in the twenty-first century. Thousands of people who are accused of witchcraft are imprisoned or killed every year. For example, most of the homeless children living in the Democratic Republic of Congo have been abandoned by their parents because members of the community consider the children to be witches. Women in Papua New Guinea have been accused of sorcery and stoned to death by mobs. In Saudi Arabia, the religious police formed an Anti-Witchcraft Unit in 2009; hundreds of people have been arrested, many imprisoned, and some sentenced to death for casting spells. In several countries, people with albinism (a physical condition characterized by a lack of pigmentation in the hair and skin) are at particular risk of being accused of witchcraft—so much so, in 2015 the United Nations launched a special campaign and website to educate people about albinism.

Residential Schooling. Following the colonization of North America, European colonizing governments began to establish a long list of laws and policies designed to assimilate Indigenous peoples. An integral part of this process was eradicating Indigenous spiritual beliefs and practices and replacing them with Christian beliefs and practices (Fournier & Crey, 1998; Miller, 1996; Milloy, 1999). Every aspect of Indigenous culture was perceived as deviant and in need of elimination.

Efforts on this front began when, upon settlement, Christian missionaries were among the first Europeans sent to North America. At a later point, laws prohibiting various Indigenous spiritual practices were enacted, and spiritual leaders faced up to

30 years in prison for violating some of these laws. In 1879, the Canadian government adopted a **residential schooling** policy that it hoped would guarantee assimilation. Indigenous children were removed from their homes and families and taken to residential boarding schools where they would be given an education—not only in reading, writing, and arithmetic, but also in Christianity and learning to act "white." Taking children from their homes would remove the cultural influence of their communities and facilitate assimilation. Residential schools were a part of government policy and were funded by the government but were operated by Christian churches. Residential schooling occurred for more than a century, beginning in 1879; the last residential school closed in 1996. Approximately 150 000 children went through these schools.

Parental consent was not necessary, because legislation made all Indigenous people wards of the state. Communities that refused to have their children taken were threatened with the loss of government resources and even arrest. In many of the schools, children received formal teaching for only half of the day. For the remainder of the day, they engaged in physical labour on school grounds or nearby farms. Even more important than education in reading, writing, and math was education in Euro-Canadian beliefs and practices.

Behaviours related to traditional Indigenous spirituality and culture were prohibited, and children were punished if caught engaging in these behaviours. What was perceived as being normal punishment in that environment, however, is now considered physical abuse. Furthermore, thousands of children were sexually abused in some of these schools. Of the 150 000 children who went to residential schools, 91 000 have reported being physically or sexually abused. The psychological abuse the children experienced is too great to even be estimated. Many children went years without being able to see their parents; some never saw their parents alive again. On a daily basis, many children were told that their parents, having not found God, would burn in hell for eternity—as would they if they did not do as they were told.

In the 1990s, government and religious authorities acknowledged the intergenerational trauma caused by the residential schooling initiative, recognizing the high rates of substance abuse, suicide, and family violence as well as the loss of traditional cultures. In 2008 Prime Minister Stephen Harper offered a formal apology on behalf of the government, stating that "there is no place in Canada for the attitudes that inspired the Indian residential schools system to ever again prevail" (CBC News, 2008).

The government and churches not only issued formal apologies for residential schooling but also offered restitution. Former residential school students received $10 000 plus $3000 for each year spent in a residential school. In addition, the federal government invested $10 million in an existing commemoration initiative, provided $125 million to the Aboriginal Healing Foundation, and established the Truth and Reconciliation Commission (TRC) to further analyze the legacy of residential schools. As part of its mandate, the TRC held a series of dialogue forums across Canada over a period of four years, where survivors of residential schools were able to share their stories and have them formally documented. The last TRC event was held in

Edmonton in 2014, and the TRC subsequently released a final report and a list of recommendations for reconciliation in areas such as child welfare, education, language, and justice (Truth and Reconciliation Commission, 2015).

Victorian Child-Savers.   At the same time as residential schooling was being implemented in Canada, the Victorian **child-savers movement** was at its apex, another example of religious belief systems influencing political belief systems. During the late nineteenth and early twentieth centuries, this movement played an essential role in child welfare reforms, compulsory education legislation, prohibition, and many other government policies in Canada, the United States, and Britain (Jordon, 1998; Platt, 1977; Valverde, 1991). An aspect of Protestant theology known as the **Social Gospel** informed the child-savers movement, whereby Christian principles were applied in real-world settings to solve social problems (providing humanitarian aid to the less fortunate in society was seen as one way of achieving salvation).

Ask Yourself
Are blurred boundaries between religious and political belief systems relegated only to the past? Where do you see these boundaries being blurred in Canada and the rest of the world today?

The child-savers were especially interested in social problems that involved children. Children were corrupted by growing up in immoral homes, leading to drunkenness, poverty, and vice. The child-savers believed it was the state's responsibility to provide a moral environment for children whose parents were unwilling or unable to do so. Child abuse and neglect were deviantized, and over time the efforts of the child-savers led to legislation dictating that children whose parents were abusive or neglectful should be removed from their homes. They were placed in foster homes with morally upstanding families who could teach the children the path to good citizenship and salvation.

That path was, however, based on middle-class, Protestant norms. Interpretations of doctrine at the time suggested that material success could be considered a sign of strong morality. Thus, the fact that people of the middle class had material success meant that whatever beliefs and norms they adhered to were the "moral" ones, ordained by God. Members of the lower classes were automatically considered immoral—after all, if they were moral they would have material success and would not be lower class! Consequently, simply being of a lower socioeconomic class was automatically considered deviant, so virtually all of the efforts of the child-savers were directed at lower-class families.

Ask Yourself
In your own life, what roles are played by the truths proclaimed by the religious belief system you adhere to and scientific belief systems? Which of these belief systems plays a larger role in your life?

A historical perspective provides excellent examples of blurred boundaries between religious and political belief systems. With the witch craze, residential schooling, and the Victorian child-savers, those behaviours, beliefs, and people that were considered deviant within specific religious belief systems came to be socially typed as deviant in political belief systems as well. As components of religious beliefs were incorporated into the political realm, social control shifted to legislation and other forms of government policy.

Learning Objective 4

- What role does religion play as a social typer of deviance at the individual level?

- How did religion act as a social typer of deviance during the witch craze?

- What was the nature of religious social typing involved with residential schooling?

- Which groups were socially typed as deviant in the child-savers movement and why?

Science

Science can be broadly defined as "knowledge or a system of knowledge covering general truths of the operation of general laws especially as obtained and tested through scientific method" (Merriam-Webster, 2017c). Belief systems in the sciences are twofold. First, there are claims about the nature of reality, the way the world works. Second, there are ethical and moral claims embedded in the scientific belief system. For example, in gene editing research, claims are being made about both the biological or genetic foundations of gene editing and the implicit morality of gene editing.

Some beliefs are characteristic of science as a whole (e.g., that the truths about nature can be discovered), but other beliefs are specific to each of the disciplines or subdisciplines of science. For instance, biology and sociology each have their own distinct truths based on the specific objects of study.

In the first half of this chapter, we saw that religion is subjected to social control and yet also steers processes of social control—it is socially typed but also socially types others. The same is true for scientific belief systems. Science serves a social control function, dictating to us what is deviant and providing a means for controlling that deviance. It is also made subject to social control itself to prevent and resolve deviance.

Science as Deviance: Scientific Misconduct and Pseudo-Sciences

In the pursuit of the goal to "find, describe, and analyze . . . the truth" (Ben-Yehuda, 1990), scientists can be thought of as deviant in two ways. First, individual scientists may be socially typed as deviant when they engage in scientific misconduct. Second, an entire discipline may be deviantized for not being an authentic science, but rather a pseudo-science.

By permission. From Merriam-Webster's Collegiate® Dictionary, 11th Edition © 2017 by Merriam-Webster, Inc. (www.Merriam-Webster.com).

Scientific Misconduct

In any occupation or profession, some individuals engage in deviant acts. Some elite members of the business world embezzle funds or participate in insider trading, some retail employees steal products from stores, and some police officers use excessive force. Similarly, some scientists engage in acts of scientific misconduct.

Scientific misconduct is used as an umbrella term to refer to scientific practices deemed unacceptable or inappropriate because they intentionally manipulate research outcomes. For instance, data fabrication, data falsification, and plagiarism are intentional acts of deception. In contrast, questionable research practices (QRP) refer to acts that may not intentionally manipulate research outcomes, but do contravene accepted research practices. Examples can include ethical violations, poor data management, sloppy data collection, and even errors (Kingori & Gerrets, 2016). Concerns about the nature and extent of scientific misconduct intensified in the 1970s, partially due to the 1974 Patchwork Mouse incident. This incident involved a researcher who claimed to have grafted skin from a black mouse onto a white mouse but had actually drawn patches on the white mouse using a black marker (Bleicher, 2003; Judson, 2004). Concerns with how to prevent, detect, and punish scientific misconduct have grown since that time.

The social sciences and other disciplines outside of the hard sciences are not immune to such instances of fraud. Several of the twin studies and adoption studies from the 1970s and 1980s that claimed genetic traits were responsible for various psychological and behavioural characteristics have been accused of scientific misconduct (Joseph & Baldwin, 2000). Cases of fabrication, falsification, and ethical violations have been found in the social sciences, health services (e.g., nursing), and human services (e.g., counselling) (Gibelman & Gelman, 2005). A well-known case of scientific misconduct in the social and behavioural sciences is that of social psychologist Dr. Diederik Stapel. A prolific researcher, he was an "academic star in the Netherlands and abroad" (Bhattacharjee, 2013). If you have taken a course in social psychology, you may have learned about some of Stapel's research about the social influences on attitudes. For example, he reported that messy environments increase racist attitudes, and eating meat contributes to selfishness. As it turns out, Stapel built his career on data fabrication and falsification. Some junior researchers reported their suspicions, and as a result, Stapel was fired from his position. "Overnight, Stapel went from being a respected professor to perhaps the biggest con man in academic science" (Bhattacharjee, 2013).

Although scientific misconduct occurs in all disciplines, it is primarily associated with the hard sciences, especially biomedical research (Gibelman & Gelman, 2005)—not because misconduct is necessarily more common in these fields, but because it is more likely to be looked for and detected. Ben-Yehuda (1986, p. 18) suggests that deviance is far more likely to be detected in research on hot issues and in breakthrough research because of the interest that is generated—in the twenty-first century, these terms often characterize biomedical research. Furthermore, it is this type of research that receives the most funding from external agencies (Gibelman & Gelman, 2005), and accountability of funds is another factor that stimulates greater interest in potential research misconduct. The economic costs of misconduct in biomedical fields can be considerable. For instance, the alleged misconduct of only one scientist at Duke University was associated with $200 million in federal research grants funded by taxpayer dollars (McCook & Retraction Watch, 2016).

The Extent of the Problem. The prevalence of scientific misconduct is difficult to determine, and depends on the specific acts under consideration. In the largest meta-analysis of survey data to date, Fanelli (2009) found that 2 percent of scientists admitted to having falsified or fabricated data, and 14 percent were aware of those acts being committed by their colleagues. When considering other practices, the proportions increase. One-third report engaging in a variety of acts outside of falsification and fabrication, including "changing the design, methodology or results of a study under pressure from a funding source" and dropping data based on a "gut feeling." Almost three-quarters of scientists were aware of their colleagues engaging in these types of acts as well.

In addition to anonymous surveys of scientists, another way that the extent of scientific misconduct is estimated is by the retraction of articles in scientific journals (Hesselman, Graf, Schmidt, & Reinhart, 2017). A retraction occurs when a scientific journal publishes an announcement indicating that a previously published article should be disregarded by readers. Although retraction notices may or may not explicitly point to scientific misconduct, they are generally considered indicators of misconduct (Fanelli, Costas, & Larievière, 2015; Hesselman et al., 2017). For example, when Diederik Stapel's misconduct was discovered, more than 50 of his publications were retracted (Bhattacharjee, 2013). The number of retracted articles has been increasing over time, although there is some debate over whether that is indicative of growing misconduct, greater vigilance, or changing journal policies (Fanelli, 2014).

Explanations for Scientific Misconduct. There are two contrasting explanations for scientific misconduct—**bad apple/person theory** and **iceberg theory** (Ben-Yehuda, 1986). For many years, deviant acts committed by scientists were explained based on individual factors—the *bad apple/bad person theory* of scientific deviance. Just as a few "bad" people commit crimes because of psychological disturbances, personality factors, or free choice, a few "bad" scientists commit deviant acts in their work for similar reasons. This theory suggests that we need to find those few bad apples and throw them out so they do not spoil the whole barrel. For example, because only a small proportion of researchers account for most journal retractions (Hesselman et al., 2017), one could argue that the structure of science itself is sound and "the system of oversight currently in place has the power to self-correct when a transgression occurs" (*The Lancet*, 2006, p. 1).

In contrast, the *iceberg theory* of scientific deviance claims that it is far more common than we might think, and that those scientists whose misconduct is detected are just the tip of the iceberg. Most known cases of misconduct are discovered by accident rather than as a function of institutional processes or safeguards (Judson, cited in McCarthy, 2004). In the instances of scientific deviance that Barrett and Jay (2005) have been called upon to investigate, most of the scientists had been engaging in misconduct for five to ten years prior to being caught. For instance, Diederik Stapel had been falsifying and fabricating data for most of his career before he was finally caught (Bhattacharjee, 2013). Unless research is controversial or about a particularly hot issue, it is unlikely to stimulate questions and efforts at replication, because replicating someone else's research does not add much to the prestige of scientists. Because the chances of being caught are remote, there is little motivation to refrain from deviant acts (Kornfield & Titus, 2016).

Proponents of the iceberg theory argue that "focusing on a single 'bad apple' obscures complicity, institutional environments, and research contexts that produce or endorse fabrications—a 'bad barrel'" (de Vries et al., cited in Kingori & Gerrets, 2016, p. 151). In other words, the structure within which scientists work encourages deviance at a macro level. Many scholars have highlighted the pressure to publish as a key element of the scientific environment. The number of publications that a scientist has can determine hiring, increases in salary, promotion, likelihood of receiving research grants, and the degree of status within the scientific community. It is argued that these pressures increase the chance that scientists will use deviant means to produce these publications. However, Fanelli and colleagues (2015) call that claim into question, pointing out that the most prolific researchers are more rigorous in their scientific standards and less likely to engage in misconduct. However, there are other characteristics of the scientific environment that are associated with misconduct. An analysis of retracted journal articles finds that retractions are more likely when authors work in contexts where they receive financial rewards for publications, where mutual criticism among colleagues is stifled, and in countries characterized by lax research integrity policies and weak enforcement structures (Fanelli et al., 2015).

At a micro level, the reasons for scientific misconduct vary, depending on the specific roles held by individuals (Kornfield & Titus, 2016). For senior researchers, the low risk of getting caught may play an important role. In contrast, junior researchers or trainees may engage in misconduct because of inadequate mentorship or a fear of failure. Support staff (e.g., lab technicians) may engage in misconduct to deal with unrealistic workloads or to increase their incomes (if they are paid based on the number of tasks they complete). For example, research with field workers (i.e., people collecting data in the field) on medical research projects in sub-Saharan Africa found that misconduct arose from two sources: moral challenges and declining morale (Kingori & Gerrets, 2016). First, in some cases data fabrication or falsification was a way to deal with *moral challenges* encountered in the field. For instance, on one occasion a field worker found that a child who was part of the research project had died. The mother asked if her other child could take his place, so that he could receive the free medical care associated with the project. The worker agreed, and continued to report data as though the original child was still alive. In other cases, field workers filled out survey data themselves to avoid interfering with community activities (such as a funeral) or embarrassing a respondent (such as by asking them sensitive questions). Second, in some instances scientific misconduct was a response to *declining morale*. Data fabrication became a tool for resistance against unpaid overtime, draconian supervisors, or unrealistic interview targets.

The scholars who consider the detected cases of scientific misconduct to be just the tip of the iceberg have applied various specific theories that we addressed in Chapter 2 to explain this form of deviance. Ben-Yehuda (1986) proposes that *techniques of neutralization* (Sykes & Matza, 1957) play an important role in scientific deviance. Techniques like *denial of injury* or *denial of responsibility* help scientists justify their actions, convincing themselves or others that what they are doing is not wrong or that they are not responsible for the misconduct. For example, Diederik Stapel shifted the responsibility for his misconduct to changes in academia. He argued that academia has become a big business that creates pressure to obtain research grants, and that legitimately practised science is too "messy" to be able to rise to those pressures (Bhattacharjee, 2013).

Bechtel & Pearson (1985) discuss the usefulness of Robert Merton's *strain theory*. They point out that scientific deviance can be considered an example of the mode of adaptation called *innovation*; that is, the gap between legitimized goals and access to the legitimate means of attaining those goals leads some people to pursue those goals in "innovative" ways. Just as some people who want expensive cars will sell drugs to earn the money to purchase them, some scientists who want career success will engage in misconduct rather than obtain it legitimately.

Gottfredson and Hirschi's (1990) *self-control theory* has not been used to study scientific deviance specifically, but it has been applied to occupational deviance more generally. Research has found that self-control plays a role in occupational deviance, particularly when low self-control is combined with an environment in which co-workers are engaging in deviance (Donner & Jennings, 2014). If co-workers appear to be rewarded for their deviance, such as by receiving promotions or large research grants for their productivity in publishing, the pull toward deviance may be even greater.

Misconduct and the Corporatization of Science.   The prevalence and reasons for scientific misconduct are influenced by ties with corporate industry. A growing proportion of scientific research is funded by commercial industry, especially in biomedical fields. These scientist–industry partnerships can result in scientific misconduct that is steered by the funding source or done by the funded scientists without the funder's knowledge. Corporate funding and the nature of the research results frequently go hand in hand (Born, 2004; Caulfield, 2004).

Exercise Your Mind

Go back to the various theories discussed in Chapters 2 (positivist theories) and 3 (interpretive and critical theories). Select one positivist, one interpretive, and one critical theory that you think best explains scientific misconduct. What makes each of those theories preferable to the others in those chapters?

Martinson (cited in Dyer, 2005) found that 15 percent of 3200 medical researchers surveyed had "changed the design or results of a study under pressure from a funding source" (p. 1465). And resulting publications from industry-sponsored research are far more likely to report positive findings than those sponsored by public (i.e., government) funds (Krimsky, cited in Thompson, Baird, & Downie, 2005). This pattern is most evident in therapeutic/drug research sponsored by pharmaceutical companies. For example, "an analysis of 70 studies of specific cardiac drugs showed that 96 percent of authors with ties to the pharmaceutical company produced favorable results, while only 37 percent of independently funded studies *of the same drugs* showed favorable results" (Stelfox, Chua, O'Rourke, & Detsky, cited in Born, 2004, para. 12).

In many cases, the contracts between pharmaceutical companies and researchers stipulate that the company retains the right to determine which research results do and do not get published (Born, 2004). Even in those instances where the company does not retain the right to publish, the company may delay the publication of negative results (Thompson et al. 2005), which enables the company to "quickly fund a new study that produces a favorable response and then publish only the positive results" (Born, 1994, para. 14). In addition, most clinical drug research is now done by commercial centres hired by the pharmaceutical companies, compared to 15 years ago when it was done in university research departments, a phenomenon that has been labelled **post-academic science** (Ziman, cited in Montgomery & Oliver, 2009). This creates a structure within which researchers face considerable pressure to obtain the results that will make their funding sources happy, a structure that is conducive to scientific misconduct.

Pinto (2015) claims that the corporatization of science "has encouraged the *production of ignorance* [emphasis added]" (p. 294). First, when science serves commercial interests, research areas are governed by those interests; this leaves other important areas unstudied, creating gaps in scientific knowledge. Second, commercialization can also contribute to the "deliberate manufacture of ignorance" (p. 295) by providing the public with false information about the nature of scientific knowledge on important policy issues. Historically, the tobacco industry engaged in public disinformation campaigns stating that cigarette smoking did not have negative health effects, even though their own scientists were well aware of those effects. That industry even went a step further by creating scientific societies and journals that falsely gave the impression of unbiased science. Thus, "the tobacco industry is not just *corrupting* science, but *creating* it" (Proctor, 2011, p. 458). More recently, internal industry documents have revealed similar distorted science and public disinformation campaigns on the part of the sugar industry (denying the health effects of excessive sugar consumption), and the oil industry (denying the effects of fossil fuels on global warming) (Kearns, Schmidt, & Glantz, 2016; McKibben, 2015; Surowiecki, 2016).

Controlling Scientific Misconduct. Scientific misconduct can be controlled in a number of ways. Workplace gossip is a type of informal regulation. Interviews with scientists in India, the United Kingdom, and the United States reveal that gossip is a common response to colleagues suspected of scientific misconduct or other questionable research practices. Rather than explicitly alleging misconduct, workplace gossip labels their work as careless or sloppy, and advises that there are certain colleagues that graduate students or junior researchers should not align themselves with (Vaidyanathan, Khalsa, & Ecklund, 2016).

Misconduct is controlled in formal ways as well. Scientists who have engaged in misconduct can face temporary or permanent disbarment from public research funding and from serving on public research bodies, have their published articles retracted by journal editors, and lose their positions. In some cases, they may even face criminal prosecution. For example, in 2015 Dr. Dong-Pyou Han of Iowa State University was sentenced to 57 months in prison and given a $7.2 million fine for fabricating and falsifying data about an HIV vaccine (Reardon, 2015). However, criminal prosecution is very rare and, in this case, occurred only because it drew the attention of Senator Charles Grassley, who placed pressure on the district attorney's office (Reardon, 2015).

Some scientists argue that preventative social control is even more important than retroactive control. Just as effective efforts to curb binge drinking on university campuses must target the whole environment rather than just those students who are problem drinkers (see Chapter 6), reducing scientific misconduct also requires a population prevention approach (Nylenna & Simonsen, 2006). This approach includes the following: regular informational and educational seminars at research institutions; focusing on misconduct at its broadest level, rather than only on fabrication, falsification, and plagiarism; mentoring of young researchers to transmit guidelines; investigation mechanisms at the national level; and a restructuring of the academic reward system to remove the climate of "publish or perish" (Kornfield & Titus, 2016; Nylenna & Simonsen, 2006; Titus, 2014).

Population prevention is a relatively recent approach to controlling scientific misconduct. Montgomery and Oliver's (2009) analysis of the "institutional logics" (p. 139) that govern social control measures directed at scientific misconduct reveals three distinct time periods. Prior to 1975, the institutional logic emphasized science as self-governing, based on the assumption that science was inherently about objectivity and the search for truth. Sociologist Robert Merton (1973) described this as the *normative structure of science*, and listed four norms of science: **communism** (scientists freely give up rights to the knowledge that they create so that this knowledge can be shared by all); **skepticism** (all ideas must be subjected to rigorous scrutiny); **disinterestedness** (scientific work is done in the name of truth rather than for any personal gain or vested interests); and **universalism** (knowledge is free from any biases based on characteristics such as race, gender, or religion). Although Merton himself recognized that not all scientists would necessarily adhere to these norms, the institutional logic of the time suggested that normative pressures within the scientific community would be sufficient to prevent misconduct.

However, with the growing awareness of specific cases of misconduct (such as the Patchwork Mouse incident discussed earlier), it became increasingly clear that the normative structure of science was not sufficient to prevent acts of misconduct. Consequently, from 1975 to 1990 the institutional logic became one of coercive measures to both punish and prevent misconduct. This heralded an era when institutional research boards emerged, and research institutions that received public research funding were required to implement procedures for investigating allegations of misconduct.

Since 1990, the growth of private research funding (through scientist–industry partnerships) has removed some of the power behind the coercive social control mechanisms of the previous time period. It has also subjected scientists to new and different pressures that can increase the likelihood of misconduct.

As a result, the institutional logic has once again shifted from a focus on preventing and punishing misconduct to an emphasis on "promoting research integrity" (Montgomery & Oliver, 2009, p. 146). This entails a cooperative, multifaceted effort among governmental organizations, universities, professional academic societies, credentialing associations, and academic journal editors (Kornfield & Titus, 2016; Titus, 2014). It is within this discourse, and its resulting network of stakeholders, that the population prevention approach has emerged.

The history of scientific misconduct is almost as long as the history of science itself (Judson, 2004). But with the proliferation of science over the last century, we have also seen the escalation of scientific misconduct. From the Piltdown Man of 1912 (a hoax where bone fragments were passed off as an early human ancestor) to some of the industry-sponsored research of today, the list of instances of scientific misconduct continues to grow, as does the debate over how to best control it.

Science and Pseudo-Science

As we have seen thus far, deviance can occur in science when scientists engage in misconduct. Deviance can also occur in science when a whole discipline of science is perceived as deviant in its entirety and is rejected as a legitimate science (Ben-Yehuda, 1990). An entire science may be socially typed as deviant when its belief system or technologies are significantly called into question. If subject to enough doubt, the belief system or technologies may be determined not to be a science at all; instead, they may be labelled a "non-science." Particular combinations of belief systems and technologies can be thought of as falling along a continuum (Figure 9.2).

At one end of the continuum lie those belief systems, such as astrology, magnetic therapy, and Bible codes (i.e., pseudo-sciences) that have not been supported by empirical research using scientific methods. At the other end of the continuum are those belief systems that have been consistently supported by the most research evidence, such as evolution and quantum mechanics. Falling at various points between these two extreme ends of the continuum is the bulk of other belief systems and technologies (Shermer, 2001).

TIME TO REVIEW

Learning Objective 5

■ What are some forms of scientific misconduct?

■ How is misconduct explained by the bad apple/person theory and the iceberg theory?

■ In what ways may the relationship between commercial industry and science promote scientific misconduct?

■ How have the institutional logics of social control changed over time?

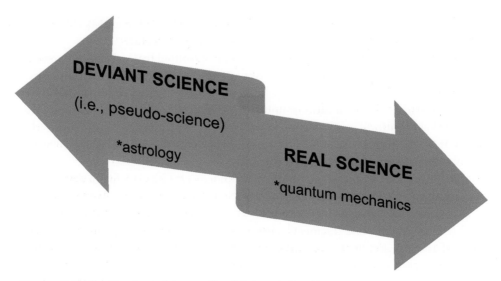

Figure 9.2 The Deviant Science–Real Science Continuum

Based on Shermer, M. (2001). *The Borderlands of Science: Where Sense Meets Nonsense*. New York: Oxford University Press.

The media plays an important role in reproducing pseudo-scientific beliefs. The stranger the scientific claim, the more likely it is to be reported in the media—unusual scientific claims are sensationalistic and can reliably attract an audience. The media ties into commercialization as well. Belief systems that are frequently labelled as deviant science are often linked to companies selling a marketable product or service related to those claims. Astrological charts, magnetic insoles for your shoes, and homeopathic remedies are just some of the services and products available.

Determining what is a pseudo-science may initially appear to be quite straightforward. However, that is not necessarily the case. A science perceived as deviant at one time may become an accepted science at a later date. This is what happened with radio astronomy in the early twentieth century (Ben-Yehuda, 1986, 1990). Radio astronomy essentially claims that scientists can identify events that are occurring in the solar system by measuring the radio waves the events emit. Those of you who are familiar with this field may ask how radio astronomy can be a deviant science when its claims are entirely accepted in the scientific community. Though this may be true today, it was not always the case. The scientists who argued for the validity of radio astronomy initially faced considerable censure. They had tremendous difficulty finding a research journal willing to publish their article, and for a number of years they were stigmatized in the scientific community. Eventually, other astronomers conducted research and concluded that their claims were, in fact, valid; thus radio astronomy entered the realm of mainstream science.

Debates over what constitutes pseudo-science and real science continue to this day. Thyer and Pignotti (2016) argue that there are several industry-approved continuing education programs for social workers that are based on pseudo-science, such as meridian-tapping, holding therapy, energy healing, and chakra wisdom. Other scholars call into question various elements of clinical psychology, including memory recovery techniques, dissociative identity disorder, antidepressant medications, and even clinical judgment itself (Lilienfield, Lynn, & Lohr, 2015).

Because of instances where the claims made by a deviant science eventually came to be adopted by the scientific community, proponents of deviant sciences today claim that the same might eventually become true of their belief systems. They argue that the methods for investigation in mainstream science have not evolved sufficiently to properly evaluate the claims being made (Shermer, 2001). Ben-Yehuda (1986, 1990) points out that one of the reasons that a science may first be considered deviant and later become accepted is the conservative character of the scientific community.

Although scientists pursue innovation via their research efforts, the tendency to resist change can sometimes prevail. Senior scientists who have become well established are usually the members of the scientific community who determine whether new ideas are viewed as valid or not. The cynical view they have developed as part of the scientific worldview (presuming that a claim is *not* true until it is proven beyond a doubt) contributes to this conservative dimension. The conservative aspect of science then increases the likelihood that any claim outside of the mainstream will, at least initially, be looked upon with suspicion.

Just as is the case with religion, science can also be socially typed as deviant and made subject to social control. Sometimes this occurs when scientists engage in specific actions that are considered deviant within the scientific community, such as data fabrication or ethical violations. At other times, the claims about reality or the ethical and moral assumptions of a discipline are called into question themselves. When this happens, the entire science is labelled deviant and made subject to control. However, science also steers the social typing process.

TIME TO REVIEW

Learning Objective 6

■ What is a deviant science?

■ What does the deviant science–real science continuum represent?

■ How have perceptions of radio astronomy changed over time?

■ Why are new scientific claims often regarded as deviant?

Science as a Social Typer of Deviance

In his book *Power/Knowledge*, Michel Foucault (1980) proposed that a relationship exists among knowledge claims, the positions of power from which those claims emerge, and the resulting influence they have. Thus, when claims to truth come from locations of institutionalized power, those claims also become institutionalized—people believe the claims being made simply because those claims are coming from "experts." This is the position that science holds in our culture today, such that the social typing done by scientists tends to be effective.

Scientific Social Typing in History: Social Darwinism, Eugenics, and the Nazis

Earlier in the chapter, we explored European colonization of North America and the role that religious belief systems played in the government initiative for residential schooling, a policy that caused long-term damage to Indigenous individuals, families, and cultures. European colonization did not occur just in North America, though; it also took place in Africa, Asia, Australia, Central America, and South America. Religious beliefs were central to the push toward colonization, serving as the primary rationalization for several centuries. However, by the end of the nineteenth century, scientific theory also provided a rationale for the last several centuries of European colonization and a justification for government policies regarding Indigenous peoples for years to come.

Social Darwinism applied the Darwinian concept of *evolution* to history and society, although some scholars point out that certain aspects of this approach actually pre-date Charles Darwin's work. It is associated with various sociologists of the late nineteenth and early twentieth centuries, but there is debate over which sociologists actually adhered to this view (Weiler, 2007). The theory proposed that just as biological species evolve over time, so do human societies, from "primitive" to "civilized." In the nineteenth century, European societies were seen by social Darwinists as the most highly evolved. Thus, the colonization of more "primitive" societies was justified as benefiting Indigenous peoples; in other words, European colonizers were seen as helping these cultures to evolve at a more rapid rate than they were doing on their own. Government policies based on the principle of assimilation also justified moving the evolution of Indigenous cultures forward.

Social Darwinism was soon popularized as the science of **eugenics** (Burdett, n.d.). Similar principles were applied, but to various individuals and groups within particular societies. Recent biological developments were used to support the argument that some social groups were more evolved than, and therefore biologically superior to, other groups. Although eugenics is most often associated with Nazi Germany, governments in Britain, the United States, Australia, and Canada also pursued eugenic ideals (Asbury, 2015; Dyck, 2012; Gibson, 2015; Kühl, 2013). According to a 1922 sociology textbook that spoke in favour of eugenics, the goals of eugenics were to ensure that "a larger proportion of superior persons will have children than at present . . . the most inferior persons will have no children . . . [and] other inferior persons will have fewer children than now" (Popenoe & Johnson, 1922).

Eugenics was based on "discourses of degeneracy and social reform" (Gibson, 2015, p. 320). Over time, those viewed as degenerate came to include non-whites, Eastern and Southern Europeans, "mental defectives," criminals, the poor, and the morally suspect (Asbury, 2015; Gibson, 2015; Wong, 2016). Precisely which groups were the focus of attention varied across nations, in that race was emphasized in some countries, while social class, immigration status, or disability were focused on in other countries (Kühl, 2013). Eugenics-inspired social reform took many forms. In many universities, biology and sociology students studied from eugenics textbooks just like the one quoted above. In churches, ministers presented sermons on eugenic ideals. At community fairs, families competed for awards from local eugenics societies (Seldon & Montagu, 1999). Eugenics societies influenced restrictions on immigration policies, legislation enforcing racial segregation and prohibiting interracial marriages, and involuntary sterilization (Dyck, 2012; Gibson, 2015; Wong, 2016).

In Canada, the eugenics movement is best exemplified by the province of Alberta, which had "the largest and longest-standing sterilization policy in Canada, and the only one in Canada or the United States to remove the need for informed consent" (Dyck, 2012, p. 21). This disturbing aspect of Canadian history reached widespread public attention in Canada in the 1990s, when Leilani Muir launched a lawsuit against the Alberta government for wrongful sterilization. In 1928, the Alberta government set up a eugenics board and instituted the *Sexual Sterilization Act*. The board would evaluate "mental defectives" when they reached puberty, and after an interview of only a few minutes would determine if they should be sterilized. When Muir was a pre-teen, her alcoholic and abusive mother dropped Muir off at the Provincial Training School in Red Deer. Shortly thereafter, she was classified as a "mental defective" and, without her knowledge or permission, was sterilized. After leaving the training school and embarking upon a normal life, she sought medical advice to determine why she had been unable to become pregnant. In the words of Buchanan (1997), "The doctor described her insides as 'being as if she'd been through a slaughterhouse.' Then, when she tried to adopt, she was refused because of the stigma of being a former inmate of Red Deer" (p. 46). Muir won her lawsuit and was awarded an undisclosed amount of money for the pain and suffering she had endured (Dyck, 2012). Shortly thereafter, the Alberta government introduced legislation to prohibit others from being able to sue the government.

The eugenics board attached the label "mental defective" to an extremely wide range of people—for example, those with low IQs, those who had "immoral" lifestyles (the board presumed that only a "mental defective" would live an immoral lifestyle), immigrants unable to speak English, Indigenous women, those who were considered burdens because of their poverty, and poverty-stricken women who dared to have children (Dyck, 2012; Gibson, 2015; Wong, 2016). In a significant proportion of cases, the "mental defectives" who were sterilized were people who had simply violated social norms (Grekul, 2002). For example, one young woman had been gang raped by local boys and as a result was labelled "sexually immoral" and entered into the juvenile justice system herself. Her father, unable to live with what had happened, placed her in the Provincial Training School, where she was sterilized (Buchanan, 1997).

The *Sexual Sterilization Act* was not repealed until 1978, thus lasting far longer than in other countries that used sterilization in pursuit of eugenic ideals. Even following World War II, at a time when "Nazis were being hung for their eugenic programs, 'lessons from this dark period of human history appeared to have little or no impact on the operation of the Alberta Eugenics Board'" (Wahlstein, cited in Buchanan, 1997, p. 46).

Of course, the Nazis in Germany went much further in their application of eugenics. Their eugenics program emerged from the disarray Germany experienced following its defeat in World War II. The program progressed through three phases (Asbury, 2015). In 1933, the *Law for the Prevention of Offspring with Hereditary Diseases* was enacted, along with its associated sterilization programs. Two years later, the Nuremberg Laws were established, which regulated various aspects of citizenship and marriage (e.g., removing citizenship from Jewish people living in Germany). Finally, beginning in 1939 there was the large-scale euthanizing of people who were disabled, diseased, and "feeble-minded," and the mass extermination of "degenerate races" in concentration camps. By the end of World War II, more than six million members of "degenerate races" had been exterminated in concentration camps, 400 000 "genetically defective" Germans were sterilized, and 75 000 "Aryans" whose medical care was too costly were euthanized (Conway, cited in Asbury, 2015). The Nazi government established a large science program as well, and significant strides were made in the area of genetics (such as through torturous experimentation on twins) in service to the Nazis' political strivings for racial purity.

Today, some scientists continue to make claims about evolutionary differences among the races, such as in terms of intelligence (e.g., Philippe Rushton, founder of the Charles Darwin Research Institute). Their scientific claims are heavily criticized

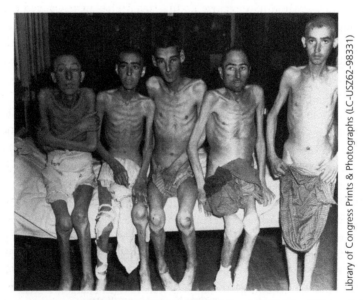

Library of Congress Prints & Photographs (LC-USZ62-98331)

The eugenics movement reached its historical apex in Nazi Germany, with millions of people killed in concentration camps. However, eugenic ideals were also being pursued to lesser degrees in Canada, Britain, Australia, and the United States.

(e.g., Brace, 1996; Lieberman, 2001; MacEachern, 2006) as racist and based on faulty science, but are widely used by white supremacist groups to support their ideals. Thus, although history provides us with rather dramatic illustrations of the power of science, the role that science plays in the social typing of deviance is not limited to the past.

Scientific Social Typing Today: Medicalization

In contemporary society, the role of science in determining and controlling deviance is even more pervasive than it was historically. Throughout the textbook, you have seen evidence of science's influence in medicalizing certain behaviours or characteristics, such as smoking, body modification, obesity, anorexia, and mental disorders. There is no doubt that medicine is of tremendous importance to people's health throughout the world. Being overweight or underweight *does* increase health risks. Advances in psycho-pharmaceuticals *have* cured many people of mental disorders such as depression and have enabled many people with ongoing mental disorders to lead high-quality, high-functioning lives. Smoking *is* dangerous to smokers and people around them. However, the primacy given to medical science in determining deviance has led to numerous questions and concerns, not the least of which is whether *social* characteristics are being medicalized.

This concern is illustrated by the practice of giving liposuction to patients solely for the purpose of physical appearance, by the categorization of social groups (e.g., immigrants, people who did not follow social norms) as "mental defectives" under the science of eugenics, and by the individualization of social problems in the over-diagnosis of ADHD in North America.

The medicalization of deviance and normality has now reached the level of the human genome and has resulted in debates over genetic technologies such as gene editing, pre-implantation genetic selection, and prenatal genetic selection (MacKellar & Bechtel, 2014). Some scholars refer to genetic testing and technologies as the **new eugenics**, whereby certain social groups are targeted with reproductive controls. For example, Asbury (2015) is critical of prenatal genetic counselling. Its purpose is to give parents-to-be information and resources when tests reveal their unborn child has a genetic condition; with this information, parents can decide whether or not to continue with the pregnancy. However, Asbury argues that because genetic counsellors often consider family income when determining parents' preparedness to raise a child with a disability, family income influences counsellors' advice. Thus, women in marginalized groups are more likely to be encouraged to end their pregnancies while those in higher status groups receive information on the resources that are available to them to aid in their childrearing.

More broadly, critics of genetic science draw attention to the dangers of labelling certain biological characteristics as superior or inferior, desirable or undesirable—as illustrated by the Nazi's World War II–era genetic program to create the perfect Aryan race (MacKellar & Bechtel, 2014). On what basis will decisions be made about which genes are desirable or undesirable? To what extent will these decisions be influenced by political ideologies or corporate interests? Will brown eyes be prioritized over blue eyes, or white skin over brown skin? Will genes associated with mathematical abilities be considered desirable while those associated with artistic abilities are dismissed as undesirable (or vice versa)? Will people with certain genetic conditions simply no longer be born, even if that condition brings with it some type of benefit (such as high intelligence), along with a type of disability (such as the inability to walk)?

International coalitions of governments have sought to address some of the ethical concerns raised by developments in genetic science. For example, member states of the United Nations have adopted the *Universal Declaration on the Human Genome and Human Rights* (UNESCO, 1997), which prohibits human cloning and provides guidelines for genetic science (such as the right to genetic equality, the use of research for peaceful purposes, and respect for uniqueness of individuals). Coalitions of scientists are also involved in developing safety protocols and ethical guidelines to address concerns, such as at the International Summit on Human Gene Editing (Crowe, 2015).

Like religious belief systems, scientific belief systems also have extensive relationships with the concept of deviance. Certain practices that occur in science can be considered deviant, and entire bodies of science can be considered deviant. However, science also serves as a powerful social typer of deviance—perhaps the most powerful social typer in society today. That power does not go unquestioned, and controls are being exerted on the social typing that occurs in science. Both religious and scientific belief systems are governing forces in the lives of billions of people in the world. The truths that they proclaim are a foundation for our own behaviours as well as our judgments of others. But as the quote at the beginning of this chapter suggests, both types of belief systems are socially constructed. The subjective dimension of religion and science means that neither belief system should operate unbridled or without question.

TIME TO REVIEW

Learning Objective 7

- What is social Darwinism and how is it related to the social typing of deviance?

- What is eugenics and what were the goals of the eugenics movement?

- In what countries were eugenic ideals pursued and how?

- What are some contemporary examples of how science socially types deviance?

CHAPTER SUMMARY

- Religion and science both compose belief systems. Belief systems may act *as* deviance, or they may be socially typed as deviant themselves and subjected to social control. (1)

- Traditionally, the typology distinguishing between ecclesia, churches, sects, and cults has been used to determine which religions are deviant. Within this typology, religious belief systems classified as sects or cults are more likely to be considered deviant. (2)

- Deviant religions face a wide range of social controls. The anti-cult movement and counter-cult movement are active in reducing the threat they consider cults present. The media exerts control in conjunction with these movements, as well as in their own representations of deviant religions. Governments also exert control over religions they define as deviant. (3)

- The internationally recognized right to freedom of religion is the foundation for religions to resist a deviant label. Individual religious groups use litigation in response to critique, and make use of the media to demonstrate that they are not deviant. Today, some scholars even call into question the traditional distinctions between churches, sects, and cults. (3)

- At a societal level, religion serves as a social typer of deviance when the boundaries between religious and political belief systems become blurred. Historically, this occurred with the witch persecutions, residential schooling, and the child-savers movement. (4)

- Various forms of scientific misconduct are possible, including data fabrication, data falsification, and plagiarism. Bad apple/person theories propose that individuals' characteristics are the cause of misconduct. Iceberg theory claims the structure of the scientific community sets the stage for misconduct. The increasing corporatization of science promotes misconduct. The nature of controlling misconduct changes over time, as the institutional logics change. (5)

- Deviant sciences are those where the claims being made about the nature of reality are questioned. What is considered to be a deviant science, or a pseudo-science, changes over time, as happened with radio astronomy; this occurs because of the inherently conservative nature of science (6).

- Science has served as a social typer of deviance in its application of social Darwinism, during the eugenics movement, and in Nazi Germany. The medicalization of deviance today, along with the "new eugenics" of genetic science, also illustrates science's power as a social typer. (7)

To learn more about the topics discussed in this chapter and to complete chapter quizzes, visit the Companion Website for *Deviance, Conformity, and Social Control in Canada*.

Chapter 10
The "Deviance Dance" Continues

Marekuliasz/Shutterstock

Learning Objectives

After reading this chapter, you should be able to

1 Describe how more objective and more subjective approaches to studying deviance have been reflected in the chapters in this text.

2 Describe how the notion of the social typing process has been reflected in the topics explored in this text.

3 Explain how the importance of power has been addressed in the chapters in this text.

4 Explain how the concept of the "deviance dance" has been integrated into the topics explored in this text.

5 Cite examples of human rights legislation, and explain how these documents can determine when it is and is not appropriate to attach a deviant label to people, behaviours, or characteristics.

Let's return to some of
the questions raised in
Chapter 1: Who are the
conformists in our
society and in our
world? Is life easier for
them? Are their
thoughts, behaviours,
and identities limited
by their conformity?
Who are the deviants?
Are they really the devi-
ants of our world, or
do they represent some
type of problem that
we need to control?
What is it that differen-
tiates a "deviant" from
a "conformist"? How
can we distinguish
between them? Given
what you have learned
during the course and
the ideas that the
course material has
stimulated, spend some
time thinking about
how you would answer
these questions now.

This text began with two quotations about deviance and conformity. Actress Gemma Arterton (Wiseman, 2016) stated, "It's easier
to conform and shut up." This suggests that our lives will run more
smoothly if we conform; however, it also makes the claim that we
may have to silence a part of ourselves to do so. Television producer David Lee (n.d.) pointed out that "you have to be deviant if
you're going to do anything new." The first quotation suggests that
conforming will make our lives run more smoothly; at the same
time, it points out that **conformity** is restricting. The second quotation suggests that we can achieve innovation and change only if
we're willing to risk being thought of as engaging in **deviance**. Now
that you have reached the last chapter, this is a good time to reflect
upon these concepts. In this chapter, we will look back at some of
the main ideas that were introduced in the first chapter and explore
how those ideas have been reflected in the various substantive topics
that have been addressed. As you read through this chapter, you will
be asked to do a lot of thinking on your own. This is the time when
you can reflect on the topics you have learned about and the ideas
you had during this course.

The Objective–Subjective Continuum

Various researchers approach the study of deviance differently.
Although the differences among researchers have traditionally been
characterized as a dichotomy or dualism, most deviance specialists
today combine some aspects of both objective and subjective
approaches. Thus, we can think of deviance research as falling along a
continuum, wherein virtually all scholars fit somewhere between the
two extreme ends. Some deviance specialists lean to the more objective
side of the continuum, while others lean to the more subjective side.

Scholars who lean to the more **objective** side of the continuum focus their analytical spotlight on the deviant act itself. For these scholars, the deviant act exists *a
priori* to the analysis and can be recognized by specific characteristics such as a negative societal reaction, harm, statistical rarity, or a violation of norms. With an overarching **positivist** interest in explaining the variation in human behaviour, they focus
on causation—what makes people act in deviant ways (Ashley & Orenstein, 2001).
Due to their focus on explaining the deviant act, they find that certain types of theories are more useful to them than to the scholars who lean toward the more subjective
side of the research continuum. These were the theories addressed in Chapter 2:
functionalist theories, social learning theories, and social control theories.

Deviance specialists who lean to the more **subjective** side of the continuum focus their analytical spotlight on the social processes by which certain people, actions, or characteristics come to be perceived as deviant and treated accordingly. They suggest that we cannot recognize deviance in any objective sense but instead must be taught that certain people, actions, and characteristics are deviant (Becker, 1963); that is, notions of deviance and normality are socially constructed. Power is perceived as central to determining what is deviant. Due to their emphasis on explaining the social processes that underlie deviant labels, certain types of theories are more useful to them than to scholars who lean toward the more objective side of the research continuum. These were the theories addressed in Chapter 3: interpretive theories and critical theories (Ashley & Orenstein, 2001).

Combining the results of both the more objective and more subjective research provides us with the most comprehensive understanding of deviance, wherein we learn something about the deviant act (why, when, and how it occurs) and the processes by which that act has come to be perceived and treated as deviant. Throughout this text you have seen many examples of research inquiry. In the chapter on media and deviance (Chapter 4), we saw that contemporary research on media is both objective (analyzing the effects of media consumption on attitudes and behaviours) and subjective (exploring how the media socially constructs events, issues, and identities, and how those constructions may be affected by changing structures of media ownership).

In the chapter on sexuality (Chapter 5), a historical context surrounded part of our exploration. In looking at the changing sexual cultures in North America before, during, and after industrialization (D'Emilio & Freedman, 1997; Valverde, 1991), we saw the various norms (i.e., a more objectivist interest) that shaped people's sexual behaviours. For example, we saw that prior to industrialization, reproduction within marriage was the guiding principle for sexuality. In contemporary society, we explored cultural norms that if violated are considered deviant (e.g., age of the sexual partner).

From a more subjectivist point of view, a historical context also enabled us to look at the culturally specific processes by which certain people, acts, or characteristics come to be labelled as deviant. Our discussion of the tremendous diversity in sexual cultures around the world and throughout history illustrated that what is considered sexually deviant stems not from the acts themselves, but from the evaluations of specific acts and identities based on the dominant moral codes in society at the time.

In the chapter on youth (Chapter 6), the objective and subjective dimensions were reflected in the various topics of youth-related deviance that were addressed— crime, gangs, substance use, and the nature of adolescence itself. An abundance of more objectivist research has been conducted on the factors that contribute to youth crime (e.g., Dufur et al., 2015), gang emergence and involvement (e.g., Greenberg, Grekul, & Nelson, 2016; MacLaurin & Worthington, 2016), smoking, alcohol use, and drug use (e.g., Kerley, Copes, & Griffin, 2015; Polansky, Titus, Atayeva, & Glantz, 2016). We explored some of the theoretical and empirical research that explains these "deviant" behaviours. Differential association theory, social control theories, and social learning theories have been applied to understandings of many of these acts, and empirical research reveals the complex web of factors that contributes to them as well. For instance, youth who have positive school experiences and high-quality relationships with parents are less likely to be involved in crime (Dufur et al., 2015). Because these behaviours emerge from the interaction of personal, family, school, and community factors, the programs and policies designed to reduce the frequency of these behaviours must address such multilevel factors.

Shifting our focus to the more subjectivist interest in the social processes that underlie the deviantization of youth, we also explored how the gap between the perceptions and actual prevalence of youth crime or the "gang problem" contributes to certain ways of trying to control these problems (McCormick, 2016; Tanner, 2015). In looking at the way in which youth itself, as a stage in the life cycle, is considered deviant, we saw that adolescents live the lives that we as adults create for them. The exaggerated generation gap of the past may become a reality in the future; however, it is not because of the deviant nature of adolescence, but rather because of the structure of society as created by adults. Even so, the misperceptions that all youth are both troubling and troubled influences the ways that youth are treated in society (Bibby, 2009).

Body size was one of the areas of emphasis for the chapter on physical appearance (Chapter 7), which addressed body images such as "too fat," "too thin," and "ideal." Certain body sizes are indeed associated with significantly higher risks of health problems (World Health Organization, 2016), and scholars with more objectivist interests have therefore analyzed various biological, psychological, and social factors in their attempts to determine why people become obese or anorexic and what treatments will help them (Fiese & Bost, 2016; Hruby et al., 2016). However, scholars with more subjectivist interests reveal that popular social perceptions of "too fat," "too thin," and "ideal" have little to do with health risks and much to do with current cultural standards of attractiveness—standards that critics say have reached alarmingly unrealistic proportions (Flynn, Park, Morin, & Stana, 2015).

Body modification was another area of emphasis in the chapter. More objectivist-based research has explored the motivations for obtaining tattoos or piercings and risk factors with which body modification is associated. From a more subjectivist point of view, scholars have explored what body modification tells us about social interaction (e.g., impression management) and the larger society (e.g., stories of gender).

Like obesity and anorexia, discussed in Chapter 7, mental disorders are medicalized forms of deviance. In the chapter on mental disorders (Chapter 8), the more objective approach to deviance was reflected in the material on prevalence, causes, and treatments of mental illness. We saw that mental illness affects most Canadians either directly (through their own experiences of mental illness) or indirectly (by having a friend, family member, or co-worker with a mental illness) (Mental Health Commission of Canada, 2015). The social and economic costs of mental disorders are tremendous, not only in Canada but throughout the world (Mental Health Commission of Canada, 2013a; Stonebridge & Sutherland, 2016). Therefore, a wide range of therapeutic techniques—counselling, medication, and family supports—are used to treat the combined biological and social aspects of mental disorders.

The more subjective approach to deviance is reflected in the research that emphasizes the political and social aspects of diagnosis and treatment. Although there is considerable overlap between North American and international diagnostic tools, scholars point out that there is a political aspect to determining what constitutes psychological deviance (Caplan, 1995). For example, homosexuality is no longer categorized as a mental disorder, but other behaviours (e.g., gender identity disorder) now are. Some critics suggest that *social* problems are being medicalized and treated as illnesses. For example, the high rate of ADHD diagnoses in North America may have more to do with the multitasking that characterizes modern life than with a psychological disorder in particular children (Shute, 2000).

The objective and subjective dimensions of deviance research are reflected in the chapter on religious and scientific belief systems as well (Chapter 9). More objective research on religion is reflected in the search to understand sects and cults, such as who might be more inclined to join those types of religious groups (Schwadel, 2014). Specialists in the study of cults have investigated specific groups (e.g., "The Family of Love"), testified in court as expert witnesses, and created guidelines for people to use in determining whether a specific religious group may be dangerous (Langone, 2015). Scholars with more subjective interests in deviance have questioned the traditional distinction between churches and sects, demonstrated that political factors frequently determine which groups are treated as deviant within a specific society, and analyzed the ways that certain religious groups are framed in the media (Bromley & Melton, 2012; McCloud, 2007; Neal, 2008). They have also pointed out the power that

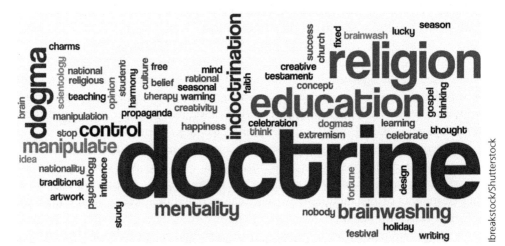

Deviance scholars with an objective approach to research analyze the characteristics of sects and cults, while those with a subjective approach study how we come to view some religious beliefs as more acceptable than others.

religion has frequently had as a social typer of deviance—that it dictates to us who or what should be considered deviant—and the potential dangers of the boundaries between religion and politics becoming blurred (Cimpric, 2010).

Like religion, science now has great influence over what society considers deviant. Chapter 9, therefore, also addresses science as a social typer of deviance as well as deviance in science. Researchers with more objective interests have studied "deviant" acts that occur in science, broadly referred to as **scientific misconduct** (e.g., Kingori & Gerrets, 2016). Many of them have concluded that these acts are more common than might be suspected. Some explanations of "deviant" scientific acts focus on individual factors (the **bad apple/person theory**), but others emphasize that the characteristics of the scientific community itself set the stage for "deviant" acts (**iceberg theory**) (Ben-Yehuda, 1986; Fanelli, Costas, & Larivière, 2015). In the latter approach, several specific theories have been applied, such as differential association theory, Merton's strain theory, and social control theories. The subjective dimension of deviance is explored in the analysis of science as a powerful social typer of deviance, telling us who or what should be considered deviant. When scientists make claims to truth, many of us automatically believe them and would likely never dare question them. Although in many cases the efforts of scientists benefit us all (e.g., regarding the health dangers of obesity and smoking), we must also remember the central role that science played in the eugenics movement and the ethical concerns surrounding genetic science today.

Exercise Your Mind

What are some other examples of research from this text that reflect more objectivist and more subjectivist interests?

Social Typing, Social Control, and Powerful Groups

The notion of deviance emerges out of the **social typing process** (Rubington & Weinberg, 2008). The first component of social typing is **description**, wherein a label is attached to a person, behaviour, or characteristic. The second component is **evaluation**, in which a judgment is attached to the person, behaviour, or characteristic because of the initial label. The last component is **prescription**, where the person is treated in specific ways only because of the label and the judgment that have been attached. This last component of the social typing process refers to measures of social control or regulation.

Deviance can be met with **informal social control** (through everyday social interactions) or with **formal social control** (at the hands of an institution or organization) (Rubington & Weinberg, 2002). The regulation of deviance may be through **preventative social control** (preventing a deviant act in the first place, such as through socialization) or **retroactive social control** (following a deviant act) (Edwards, 1988). **Self-control** is another form of regulation, wherein we all monitor our own behaviours to prevent and fix our own deviance (Edwards, 1988; Foucault, 1995).

The social typing of deviance is most effective when done by someone who has some institutionalized power in society (Rubington & Weinberg, 2002). Five different groups in society are especially powerful in that they can influence our decisions about who or what is "deviant" and to exert potent measures of social control: the media, commercial enterprise, government, religion, and science. At times, these powerful groups act as **moral entrepreneurs** themselves by trying to influence or change society's dominant moral code in relation to a specific issue. At other times, these powerful groups serve as tools used by other groups of moral entrepreneurs in their efforts.

The central role that the media plays in the daily lives of billions of people makes it the locus of claims-making in the struggles over moral codes and deviance. Commercial enterprise is another powerful group involved in the social typing process. Its efforts are intertwined with the media in two different ways. First, although there is a small nonprofit element in Canadian broadcasting, the media are predominantly a form of commercial enterprise—that is, an industry that is driven by the profit motive. Second, commercial enterprise uses the media as a tool for selling its products via advertising, commercials, and product placement in television shows, movies, or video games.

Another group using the media is, of course, politicians and government, who have ultimate power vested in them. In their hands lies the power to create or revoke legislation, to construct social policies that will be implemented through various means, and to influence the enforcement of society's dominant moral codes. Politicians may act as moral entrepreneurs or may be lobbied by interest groups acting as moral entrepreneurs. The work of politicians also exists in a bidirectional relationship with the media, where the media follow the work of politicians, and politicians use media to influence the public mind.

Exercise Your Mind

Social typers frequently rationalize the labelling of certain people, actions, or characteristics as deviant based on statistical rarity, social harm, negative societal reaction, or normative violation. As you read through the review of how social typing was addressed in the substantive topics in this text, consider the rationales that were used for the social typing of deviance in each of the various instances.

There are two other groups of moral entrepreneurs, however: religion and science. Religious institutions have played a vital role in the creation of dominant moral codes throughout history, maybe more so in the past than today. Finally, the power of scientists in the social typing process is perhaps granted more legitimacy today than any other group. Science is seen by many people as a purely objective discipline, such that its claims to truth are frequently considered unaffected by political, religious, or commercial interests.

Chapter 5, on sexuality, revealed that in any given culture at any time in history, certain sexual behaviours are socially typed as deviant and made subject to social control measures. Over the past several hundred years, what has been socially typed as deviant sexuality has varied based on the cultural norms of the time (D'Emilio & Freedman, 1997). When sexuality was perceived as solely for procreation, any non-procreative sexual acts (e.g., heterosexual coitus involving contraceptive use, homosexuality, masturbation) were socially typed as deviant. This is considerably different from society today, wherein personal fulfillment is perceived as the purpose of sexuality.

Although there is more freedom in sexual norms today than in the past, certain sexual acts are still socially typed as deviant (e.g., sex with a minor, having sex "too frequently," or being "kinky") (Goode, 1997). The way that sexuality is socially controlled has changed as well. During the sixteenth and seventeenth centuries, sexual deviance was primarily a religious and familial concern; for example, sexual deviance could result in excommunication from the church, and fathers would enforce "shotgun" weddings following premarital pregnancy. Today, religion has lost its hold over sexuality and has been succeeded by a diversity of social control measures. We have legislation that governs certain aspects of sexuality (e.g., degree of consent and age), medicalization (e.g., encouraging "safer" sex and the designation of "sexual disorders" as mental disorders), social organizations that try to encourage abstinence and contraceptive use in adolescents, and the pervasiveness of sexuality in all forms of the media.

In Chapter 6 on youth, we saw that certain behaviours and characteristics of youth are socially typed as deviant and made subject to social control. Youth crime is defined and controlled by government and the criminal justice system. Youth gangs are considered a widespread social concern, which is reflected in media reports of youth street gangs, specialized law enforcement units to monitor gang members, as well as various educational programs that discourage gang membership (Tanner, 2015; Totten, 2016).

The science of "risk management" attempts to intervene with youth who are seen as "at risk" of gang membership, criminal involvement, homelessness, substance abuse, teen pregnancy, and more. Law enforcement, social workers, psychologists, educators, health professionals, government, and social organizations all participate in such "risk management" (Bessant, 2001). Youth substance use is socially typed as deviant, seen as both a medical and a social problem. Public service campaigns via the media, education and intervention programs within various social organizations, and medical treatment are all means by which substance use is controlled (Brotnow & Sinha, 2014). Binge drinking in university is controlled through diverse programs that include peer education and support, university policies, and in some cases even "dry" campuses (Goeij et al., 2016). At the same time, it is not just youth behaviours that are subjected to measures of social control, but also institutions that influence those behaviours, including tobacco companies and the movie industry (Truth Tobacco Industry Documents, n.d.; World Health Organization, 2011).

Chapter 7 addressed how certain types of voluntary and involuntary physical appearances are socially typed as deviant. Those who choose certain hairstyles, makeup, and clothing (e.g., "goths") may find it difficult to find employment because of employers' attitudes and biases. Body modification that may be considered acceptable in some groups may be considered unacceptable in others (e.g., in physicians). People who stray beyond the "ideal" body size are socially typed as "too fat" or "too thin," although there is much more leeway for thinness before a deviant label is attached.

Body size is regulated in the realms of medicine for health reasons, but is controlled in other arenas as well. The media is a powerful social typing and social control agent for people who are both "too fat" and "too thin" (although extreme thinness is required before people are deviantized) (Couch et al., 2016; Dye, 2016). Commercial industry permeates social control over "too fat." Books, magazines, videos, pills, potions, and patches all promise to help us lose weight and look great. In the realm of everyday interaction, people who are considered "too fat" or "too thin" are controlled through stigmatization (e.g., name calling), prejudicial attitudes, and discrimination (Beggan & DeAngelis, 2015; Nabors, Meriano, & Olsen, 2016; Vartanian, Trewartha, & Vanman, 2016). Government programs target people who are overweight or out of shape, trying to encourage people to adopt healthier lifestyles (e.g., Public Health Agency of Canada, 2011b). Even some schools are attempting to reduce the proportion of children who are overweight by instituting daily fitness activities (Evangeline Middle School, 2017).

Chapter 8 discussed the social typing of psychological deviance as mental illness, which occurs at both formal and informal levels. Mental illness today is highly medicalized. The fields of psychiatry and psychology are intimately involved in social typing, determining what the "descriptions" are (e.g., "depression"), what the evaluation is (i.e., "ill"), and what the treatments should be (e.g., therapy, medication, hospitalization).

Exercise Your Mind

An important aspect of social typing is who benefits from the social typing process—the social typers themselves, particular groups in society, society as a whole, or sometimes even the people who have been socially typed. Select one specific issue from each of the substantive topics covered in the text—sexuality, youth, physical appearance, mental illness, religion, or science—and ask yourself who has benefited from the social typing in that instance.

In the past, mental illness was perceived quite differently. For example, for several centuries people who are now seen as "mentally ill" were instead perceived as being possessed by the devil or guilty of witchcraft. Control measures included religious rituals to exorcise the devil (in the case of possession) or, in the case of witchcraft, executions carried out by religious or governmental authorities. Over the last several decades, the **deinstitutionalization** movement has characterized most Western nations, with a shift from hospital-based treatments to community-based ones. Dein-stitutionalization has worked very well for those people who have strong support networks and who live in communities with sufficient resources. However, for people lacking support networks and community resources, deinstitutionalization has meant a lack of medical treatment. As a result, people with mental illnesses who do not receive medical treatment are at greater risk of being socially controlled as homeless persons or criminals (MacPhail & Verdun-Jones, 2013; Research Alliance for Cana-dian Homelessness, Housing, and Health, 2010).

In Chapter 9 on religious and scientific belief systems, we saw that many differ-ent religious groups are socially typed as deviant by governments, scientific "experts," or other religious groups. For example, the government of France lists almost 200 religious groups as "sects" in need of social control (Palmer, 2011).

The **anti-cult movement** socially types certain religious groups as deviant, empha-sizing those groups thought to use mind control techniques and authoritarian leader-ship. Organizations that are part of this movement provide information on cult awareness, support groups for parents of cult members, and in some cases deprogram-ming services for former cult members (Barker, 2001). The **counter-cult movement** consists of certain fundamentalist Christian groups that identify all nonfundamentalist Christians and all non-Christian religions as deviant. They spread their messages via the Internet, at church meetings, and through publications that teach members how to con-vince adherents of specific cults to leave those groups (Cowan, 2003).

One of the ways that social typing, social control, and power made themselves evi-dent in relation to science is in the concept of deviant sciences or pseudo-sciences (Shermer, 2001). The scientific community itself determines which belief systems, such as astrology, are not "real" sciences. Although the scientific community is the most qual-ified entity to evaluate scientific claims being made by others, some scholars suggest that its inherent conservatism often leads it to automatically rejecting anything that is new or too different from the status quo (Ben-Yehuda, 1990). This is particularly apparent in those instances where claims that were initially rejected as deviant later come to be accepted. The astronomy community socially typed the first radio astronomers as devi-ant; consequently, they had difficulty getting their work published and became outcasts in the astronomy community. At a later point, however, that same scientific community determined that radio astronomy was a "real" science after all (Ben-Yehuda, 1990).

Exercise Your Mind

What are some additional examples of the social typing process found in this text? Select a few examples and try to do the following: apply the three steps of the social typing process (i.e., description, evaluation, prescription); identify a variety of associated measures of social control (i.e., preventative; retroactive; formal; informal; control of others; control of self). In what ways has the structure of power in society influenced these processes?

The "Deviance Dance"

Another theme throughout this text is the notion of the **deviance dance**. This refers to the idea that with any specific person, action, or characteristic that has been socially typed as deviant, there will be differing points of view, debate, and resistance. The dance surrounding deviance is sometimes uniform (like a country line dance), with virtually everyone agreeing on the issue and what should be done with it; everyone moves in the same direction in pursuit of the same goal. At other times, the dance is more waltz-like, where various groups work toward the same goal but everyone is not taking the same steps to reach that goal. At yet other times, the dance is more like a mosh pit, with groups pushing, shoving, and slamming into each other to reach their own particular goals.

Every substantive topic we have looked at involves the deviance dance. In Chapter 4 on media, we see resistance to the media framing of ethnic minorities through hashtag activism (e.g., #whitewashedOUT), and debates over whether sharing videos of police brutality toward unarmed black men raises awareness or desensitizes viewers (*CBC News*, 2016d; Hess, 2016). In Chapter 5 on sexuality, we see debates over various aspects of sexuality, such as how often is "too often," whether exotic dancers are victims of violence in a patriarchal society versus legitimate workers, the purported harms caused by pornography, and social policies governing prostitution. We even see resistance to the legalization of same-sex marriage in the United States in the form of anti-LGBTQ refusal of service laws (Powers, 2016).

In Chapter 6 on youth, we also see differing opinions, several debates, and acts of resistance. For example, critics say that virtually every adolescent ends up being perceived as "at risk" within the knowledge and practices of "risk management" (Bessant, 2001; Ericson & Haggerty, 2001). That is, adolescence itself has become defined as a time of inherent risk. The deviance dance is also apparent in the debates that occur between politicians or interest groups that proclaim youth crime to be out of control and in need of tougher legislation, and those groups that point out that the public image of youth crime is tremendously overblown.

The topic of body size embodies differing views and resistance as well (Chapter 7). Although the cultural ideal of thinness continues to be perpetuated in the media and public opinion, various organizations are trying to change cultural ideals to accommodate a wider range of body sizes and are lobbying the media to integrate more realistic representations of the female body. Anorexia is an extremely dangerous disorder that frequently requires immediate medical intervention. However, media images promote anorexic ideals, and "Ana" websites even provide tips to people with anorexia to enable them to continue their pursuit of weight loss. Like the behaviours of these lobbyists and even the "Ana" websites, body modification may also be a form of resistance to social typing. For example, women may get tattoos to reject traditional discourses of gender in society (Atkinson, 2002).

In the chapter on mental disorders (Chapter 8), the deviance dance is evident in several ways, such as the stigma management strategies of **deflecting** and **challenging** that some people with mental disorders use. The deviance dance is particularly apparent in debates

At times, the struggle over deviance is characterized by intense debate and conflict.

surrounding specific diagnostic categories contained in the American Psychiatric Association's *Diagnostic and Statistical Manual of Mental Disorders* (e.g., Frances, 2013). For example, in contemporary society, debates over the extent to which ADHD is being diagnosed in North America are common. However, some groups have even gone a step further, suing the American Psychiatric Association for "manufacturing" a mental illness (Shute, 2000; Peck, 2001). Some scholars resist the medicalization of mental disorders even more profoundly, by arguing that the concept of mental illness itself is a "myth" (Szasz, 1994).

The deviance dance is perhaps at its most obvious in situations involving religion (see Chapter 9)—those in which certain groups have been socially typed as being sects or cults, and then the ways that they actively resist those labels. Religious groups defend themselves in court cases, pursue litigation themselves, recruit celebrities to improve the group's image, and communicate their ideologies through various forms of media (such as websites, art, and music) (Beit-Hallahmi, 2003; Kent, 2017; Shaw & Raine, 2017).

Difference, debate, and resistance are even evident in the world of science. There are ongoing debates over which belief systems are real science or pseudo-science (Lilienfield, Lynn, & Lohr, 2015). For many decades, the tobacco industry used its own science (characterized by misconduct and other questionable research practices) to defend itself and influence social policy (Proctor, 2011); today, the sugar industry and oil industry are doing the same (Kearns, Schmidt, & Glantz, 2016; Surowiecki, 2016). Historically, although the eugenics movement had considerable influence in Canada, the United States, Britain, and Germany, there were also scientists and social organizations in each of those nations who were critical of eugenic ideals. In contemporary society, while some groups of scientists proclaim the benefits that genetic testing and manipulation will bring to the world, others disagree, and some claim that modern genetics is nothing more than eugenics in twenty-first-century clothing (Asbury, 2015; MacKellar & Bechtel, 2014).

Exercise Your Mind

What are some other examples of varying opinions, debates, and acts of resistance that you have seen in this text?

The Search for Standards

Throughout this text, we have seen that, to some extent, "deviance" is in the eye of the beholder. That is, there is far more to the concept of deviance than the inherent nature of the person, act, or characteristic. The cross-cultural and historical examples that we have looked at show us that power is fundamental to determining what or who will be considered deviant in society. Actions considered criminal in certain cultures at specific historical moments are viewed as acceptable actions in other cultures and at other historical times. For example, homosexual acts were considered criminal throughout North America a century ago, but today they are not considered criminal in Canada, although they are criminalized in some other regions of the world.

Conversely, during most of the nineteenth century, child abuse and spousal abuse were seen as legally, socially, and morally acceptable, but today they are considered crimes in much of the world. The sexual relationships between boys and adult men in Sambian society would constitute pedophilia according to Canadian standards. Adultery, while merely frowned upon in North America, is considered criminal in other nations. A half century ago, youth (but not adults) could run afoul of the criminal justice system for misbehaviours like truancy, sexual promiscuity, and incorrigibility; today, the list of criminal offences is identical for youth and adults.

Historically, acts that were carried out by societal authorities with wide support from the rest of the community would be considered deviant by contemporary standards. The witch persecutions that swept much of Europe for centuries are now looked upon with disdain as an instance of religious and political authorities preying on the superstitious populace to further their own goals of power. Residential schooling is perceived as a regrettable event in Canadian history, even by those societal institutions that participated in it—that is, the federal government and several church bodies. Formal apologies have been issued, some reparations made, and various programs and policies developed in pursuit of reconciliation (Truth and Reconciliation Commission, 2015).

Social Darwinism and the subsequent eugenics movement, popular in Canada, the United States, Britain, and other nations during the late nineteenth and early twentieth centuries, targeted numerous social groups for forced sterilization. The eugenics movement itself is now looked upon as a deviant use of science and politics. The apex that the eugenics movement reached in the Holocaust is widely perceived as one of the most horrific events in human history; however, it is important to remember that for several years during the 1930s, the rest of the world (including Canada) looked upon the success of Nazi eugenics with admiration.

After exploring cross-cultural and historical variations, as well as the debate and differing points of view that exist within a single society at any given time, some people may understandably begin to think that there are no transcendent standards by which people, behaviours, or characteristics can be evaluated—and that no group has the right to impose its subjective standards of behaviour on any other group. Because deviance is in the eye of the beholder, "anything goes." Of course, if that belief were fully realized, anarchy would reign in society. So how can balance be achieved? How can we determine whether it is appropriate to socially type specific groups of people as deviant and subject them to measures of social control?

To some extent, subjectivity will always be involved in the social typing of deviance. Regardless of what norms, policies, programs, or legislation exist, there will always be some people (no matter how many or how few) who will be in opposition. However, one place to begin a search for possible universal standards is with documents that emphasize the notion of human rights.

The Universal Declaration of Human Rights, adopted by the member states of the United Nations on December 10, 1948, is the foundational document for other modern human rights policies, programs, and legislation throughout the world (including the Canadian *Charter of Rights and Freedoms*). A larger sample of human rights documents can be found in Box 10.1.

Box 10.1

A Sample of Human Rights Documents

- The Magna Carta (see the British Library website for scanned pages of the original Magna Carta and an English translation)
- Declaration of the Rights of Man and of the Citizen (from the French Revolution)
- Universal Declaration of Human Rights
- Canadian *Charter of Rights and Freedoms*
- Convention on the Rights of the Child
- International Covenant on Civil and Political Rights
- International Covenant on Economic, Social, and Cultural Rights
- European Convention on Human Rights
- Universal Declaration of Sexual Rights

- Universal Declaration on the Human Genome and Human Rights
- Declaration on the Elimination of All Forms of Intolerance and of Discrimination Based on Religion or Belief
- Declaration on the Rights of Disabled Persons
- Principles for the Protection of Persons with Mental Illness and for the Improvement of Mental Health Care
- Convention Concerning Indigenous and Tribal Peoples in Independent Countries

All of these documents can be found in their entirety on the Internet using any search engine.

Several themes run through the range of human rights documents that can be found in countries around the world. One of these is the right to **human dignity**, which is the right to be treated with respect. Numerous issues that have been addressed in this text can be considered in relation to this human right. The way that certain social groups were targeted by the eugenics movement can certainly be considered a violation of human dignity, as can the Nazis' racial hygiene program. European colonization and residential schooling also involved infringements on the dignity of Indigenous peoples. The notion of human dignity underlies other international documents as well, such as the *Declaration of Sexual Rights* (World Association for Sexual Health, 2014), and UNESCO's *Universal Declaration on the Human Genome and Human Rights* (UNESCO, 1997). The former document emphasizes that consensual adult sexual activities should not be deviantized and that freedom to sexual expression must prevail. The latter document suggests that certain genetic traits should not be considered superior or inferior to other traits; that is, individuals with specific genetic traits should not be deviantized.

Another theme in human rights documents is the prohibition of differential treatment on the basis of group membership (i.e., **discrimination**). The characteristics that are commonly listed in relation to this right are race, sex, ethnicity, colour, nation of origin, religion, political membership, and language; however, other categories (e.g., sexual orientation) are included in some human rights documents as well. The Canadian *Charter of Rights and Freedoms* and various pieces of provincial human

The United Nations is one international body that develops universal human rights standards.

rights legislation address the notion of discrimination in Canadian society. The World Health Organization's constitution declares that the right to physical, mental, and social health applies to all social groups, such as those just listed (World Health Organization, 2004). The *Universal Declaration on the Human Genome and Human Rights* prohibits discrimination based on genetic characteristics (UNESCO, 1997).

Historically, the right to freedom from discrimination was infringed upon in the eugenics movement and during European colonization. In contemporary society, people with visible body modifications often face discrimination in employment (Ellis, 2015). Members of certain religious groups are discriminated against in several countries, such as the groups identified by the government of France as sects or cults (e.g., Jehovah's Witnesses, Scientology) (US Department of State, 2015).

Security of person and property are also prevalent in human rights documents. Violent crimes (e.g., assault) and property crimes (e.g., theft) violate security of the person and property. The World Health Organization's constitution declares that the universal right to physical, mental, and social health is necessary for peace and security, not specifically for individuals but in societies and throughout the world (World Health Organization, 2004); thus, the failure to provide the necessary means for achieving health for any group is seen as unacceptable. The involuntary sterilization of "mental defectives," the torture and death involved in the Holocaust, the abuse suffered by tens of thousands of Indigenous children in residential schools, and the witch persecutions (wherein witches were not only executed but also had their property seized to pay for their persecution) can all be seen as infringements on the right to security of the person and of property. When the Canadian government defined Japanese-Canadians as "enemy aliens" during World War II, it placed thousands of Japanese-Canadian citizens in internment camps and subsequently seized their property and auctioned it to the highest bidder. Security of person and security of property were again violated by the Canadian government.

Human dignity, freedom from discrimination, and security of person and property are three of the core themes that are integrated into various types of human rights policies and legislation. Given the influence of subjectivity and power that has been involved in the social typing of deviance across cultures and throughout history, human rights policies represent some basic standards that we may be able to apply in determining whether it is appropriate to label anyone or anything as deviant. However, a level of subjectivity also exists in determining whether human rights have been violated in any specific instance. Human rights documents themselves state that there are circumstances where someone's human rights may legitimately be violated; typically, this is when there are threats to public order, public health, or other people's human rights. For example, although freedom of religion is a basic human right, many governments monitor, regulate, and even ban specific religious groups that are perceived as a threat to social order (US Department of State, 2015).

Although freedom of expression is a universal human right, Canada, the United States, and numerous other countries have hate crime or human rights legislation that prohibits spreading hatred or advocating the genocide of identifiable social groups. For

Ask Yourself

Now that you have completed all the chapters in this text, what people or behaviours do you consider to be "deviant"? In what ways have your views changed or remained the same compared to when you first began reading the text?

instance, some leaders and members of white supremacist groups have been charged with spreading hatred, even though charging them with that offence is a violation of their right to freedom of expression. International human rights documents condone this as a legitimate violation of that freedom based on threats to the public order and violations of other people's human rights.

Exercise Your Mind

Considering human dignity, freedom from discrimination, and security of person and property, think about which instances of social typing and social control that you have learned about in this course may be legitimate or illegitimate.

If you are interested in learning more about human rights, see the information contained in Box 10.2.

TIME TO REVIEW

Learning Objective 1

- How have more objective research interests been reflected in the chapters of this text?
- How have more subjective research interests been reflected in the chapters of this text?

Learning Objective 2

- What are some examples of how social typing and social control are evident with each of the substantive topics explored in this text?

Learning Objective 3

- In what ways are structures and processes of power apparent in the topics we have looked at?

Learning Objective 4

- In what ways is the "deviance dance" apparent in the topics we have looked at?

Learning Objective 5

- What themes are found in human rights documents, and what are some examples of those themes?

CHAPTER SUMMARY

■ Certain ideas that were introduced in Chapter 1 represent themes that have been carried through the various chapters in the text. One of these themes is the blending of *objective* and *subjective* approaches to the study of deviance.

■ In various chapters, the *positivist* interest in causation that characterizes more objective approaches was explored, such as in explanations of youth crime and substance use. (1)

■ The *interpretive* and *critical* interests in the social processes by which deviance is assigned, which characterize more subjective approaches, was addressed throughout the chapters as well. For example, we looked at how popular perceptions of "too fat," "too thin," and "ideal" have little to do with health risks and much to do with current cultural standards of attractiveness. (1)

■ A second theme throughout this text is the notion of the *social typing process*. Power plays a critical role in determining who or what will be considered deviant and what social control measures are directed at them. Governments, the media, religious institutions, scientists, and commercial industry are all intimately involved in the social typing and social control of various aspects of deviance. (2, 3)

■ The *deviance dance* can be seen throughout this text as well. Regardless of the specific issue in question, various individuals and groups have differing points of view on whether something or someone is deviant, how deviant they are, and what the most effective means of social control will be. (4)

■ Given the role of subjectivity in understanding deviance, does that mean "anything goes"? Does it mean that we cannot legitimately socially type anyone or anything as deviant? The concept of *human rights* is one place where we can begin looking at whether any standards can be applied. Numerous international human rights documents exist, and they give some indication of criteria that may be used to determine who should and should not be deviantized. (5)

To learn more about the topics discussed in this chapter and to complete chapter quizzes, visit the Companion Website for *Deviance, Conformity, and Social Control in Canada*.

Glossary

absolute others Individuals who are presented (through the media) as inherently evil.

adapting Body projects that involve removing or repairing aspects of one's body.

affirmative postmodernism A form of postmodern theory that deconstructs master narratives, overarching theories, or knowledge and focuses analysis on the local and specific.

androcentric bias A bias toward the experiences of males, whereby female experiences are ignored; a critique of functionalist theories.

anomie (1) In Durkheim's functionalist theory, a state of normlessness. (2) In Merton's functionalist theory, a state where society's institutionalized goals are emphasized more than the legitimate means of attaining those goals.

anorexia nervosa A mental disorder characterized by being significantly below the ideal body weight according to scientific standards, in conjunction with several additional physical and psychological characteristics.

anti-cult movement Individuals that educate people about dangerous or destructive cults and attempt to control their activities by lobbying governments and other organizations.

appealing to higher loyalties A technique of neutralization that rationalizes one's deviant behaviour as serving a higher purpose.

atavists In early criminological theories, the view that criminals were evolutionary throwbacks whose biology prevented them from conforming to society's rules.

at-risk youth Youth who have been identified as having a greater likelihood of negative outcomes.

attachment In social bonds theory, the bond characterized by one's emotional attachment to others.

back-stage self In the dramaturgical approach, individuals' identities and behaviours when they are no longer in front of any audience, but rather are alone or with those who are closest to them.

bad apple/person theory A theory that claims acts of scientific misconduct are rare.

behavioural coping strategies In Agnew's general strain theory, a possible response to strain where people attempt to eliminate the strain itself.

belief Any proposition that an individual considers to be true, regardless of whether it is true or not.

belief systems Organized sets of interrelated beliefs.

berdaches A derogatory term used by European explorers to refer to biological males who assumed female roles in some Indigenous cultures.

binge drinking The consumption of five or more drinks (for males) or four or more drinks (for females) in one drinking session.

body mass index (BMI) A calculation of height and weight that determines an individual's level of risk for a variety of health problems.

body projects The ways that people adapt, change, or control characteristics of their bodies.

bourgeoisie In Marxist conflict theory, the owners of the means of economic production.

camouflaging Body projects that reflect normative processes learned through socialization.

career contingencies In the theory of the deviant career, significant turning points that influence the directions that people take at various points in the deviant career.

challenging A stigma management technique in which individuals actively fight back against an external stigmatizing force, such as through confronting or educating others.

child pornography Any representation of someone under the age of 18 engaged in explicit sexual activity or any representation of someone under the age of 18, "the dominant characteristic of which is the depiction, for a sexual purpose, of a sexual organ or the anal region."

child-savers movement During the Victorian era, middle-class church groups who thought it was the state's responsibility to provide a moral environment for children whose parents were unwilling or unable to do so.

churches Religious groups, usually large and powerful, that are well established in society and highly bureaucratized.

cisgender People whose gender identity or expression corresponds to their birth sex.

cognitive coping strategies In Agnew's general strain theory, a possible response to strain that transforms the way people think about the strain.

commitment In social bonds theory, the bond characterized by one's vested interest in the conforming world.

commitment to the community A motivation for gang membership that involves continuing a family or neighbourhood tradition.

communism The assumption that scientists freely give up rights to the knowledge that they create so that this knowledge can be shared by all; part of the normative structure of science.

concentration The trend toward a small number of corporations owning the majority of the market share.

condemnation of the condemners A technique of neutralization that shifts the focus from the deviant's own behaviour to the deviant behaviour of others, especially people from the social groups that have pointed to this person's deviance.

conflict frame A frame used in the news media that emphasizes conflicts between nations, institutions, groups, or individuals.

conflict gangs In differential opportunity theory, gangs who engage in violent conflict with other gangs in pursuit of status and power.

conflict theories Critical theories that claim social rules emerge out of conflict and are made by the powerful to serve their own interests, that the powerful are less likely to break social rules, and that the powerless are more likely to break the social rules.

conflict view (of law) The view that laws are created by the powerful to serve their own interests.

conformity (1) A person, behaviour, or characteristic that is considered normal and acceptable; the opposite of *deviance*. In this case, the specific definition of conformity is dependent on the specific definition of deviance being used. (2) In Merton's strain theory, the mode of adaptation that involves acceptance of both the institutionalized goals and the legitimate means of attaining those goals.

conglomeration The trend toward companies merging, or some companies purchasing other companies to form large multinational conglomerates.

consensual view (of law) The view that suggests society's laws emerge out of consensus.

consent One of the criteria used to judge deviant and normal sexual activity, based on some level of agreement between the two sexual partners.

contextual constructionism A form of social constructionism that emphasizes the processes by which certain social phenomena come to be perceived and reacted to in particular ways in a given society at a specific time in history; also known as *soft constructionism*.

convergence The trend toward media companies owning multiple forms of media; for example, a single corporation owning not only several television stations, but also the cable companies that deliver the service.

counter-cult movement Fundamentalist Christian groups that express concerns about other religious groups they consider to be based on "wrong" theologies.

courtesy stigma A form of stigma where people are stigmatized not because of their own actions, but rather the actions of someone with whom they associate; also known as *stigma by association*.

criminal gangs In differential opportunity theory, gangs whose activities are economic in nature.

criminalized The social typing process within the context of the criminal justice system.

criminologists Scholars who exclusively study criminalized forms of deviance.

critical theories Theories that focus on the power relations that underlie the creation of social rules and that have an interest in emancipation and social justice.

cults Small religious groups characterized by a highly oppositional and reactionary doctrine, extremely high levels of commitment required of members, and a single, charismatic leader.

cultural appropriation Adopting elements of another culture without regard for their history or meaning.

cyberbullying Bullying behaviours that use information and communication technologies.

cyberdeviance Deviant acts that are committed using computer technology.

cyberespionage Forms of hacking that use computer viruses and malware to attack societal infrastructure; also known as *cyberterrorism*.

cyberterrorism Forms of hacking that use computer viruses and malware to attack societal infrastructure; also known as *cyberespionage*.

dancers Female exotic dancers who have considerable training in dance and who enjoy the artistic and creative expression of the industry.

date rape drugs Odourless, tasteless drugs that, when mixed with alcohol, cause intense drowsiness and memory impairment.

deflecting A stigma management technique in which individuals block an external stigmatizing force by distancing themselves from the labels they have been given.

deinstitutionalization The social control of people with mental illnesses in community-based programs rather than in institutions.

denial of injury A technique of neutralization that argues one's behaviour does not hurt anybody.

denial of responsibility A technique of neutralization that acknowledges one's behaviour but shifts the larger blame to someone or something else.

denial of the victim A technique of neutralization that argues the victim of one's behaviour was deserving of that behaviour.

denominational sect A religious sect that has become increasingly integrated into the larger society, such that it is on the verge of being considered a denomination of a larger church.

denominations Religious subgroups of larger churches.

description The first component of the social typing process, whereby a label is attached to a particular person, behaviour, or characteristic.

deviance A person, behaviour, or characteristic that is socially typed as deviant and subjected to measures of social control.

deviance dance The interactions, negotiations, and debates among groups with different perceptions of whether a behaviour or characteristic is deviant and needs to be socially controlled and, if so, how.

deviancy amplification The process by which a deviantized group becomes more extreme as a response to hostilities or social control efforts from outsiders.

deviant career An interpretive theory of deviance that claims deviance emerges, progresses through stages, and changes over time, similar to the developmental stages of a career.

deviantize To subject a person, behaviour, or characteristic to the complete social typing process.

differential association The process by which individuals learn deviant or conforming techniques and motives.

digital piracy The illegal downloading of music, software, or video.

discourse A body of knowledge, or all that is "known" about a particular phenomenon.

discrimination Differential treatment on the basis of group membership; a violation of human rights.

discrimination paradigm A view of mental illness that emphasizes the role that stigmatization plays in the daily experiences of people with mental illnesses and seeks to reduce those experiences.

disease paradigm A view of mental illness that emphasizes the symptoms of the disorder that distress and impair individuals' functioning and seeks to ameliorate those symptoms.

disintegrative shaming The process by which deviantized persons are rejected by the community.

disinterestedness The assumption that scientific work is done in the name of truth rather than for any personal gain or vested interests; part of the normative structure of science.

divide their social worlds A stigma management technique that involves carefully managing who is and is not permitted to know about one's stigmatized behaviour or characteristic.

dominant moral codes The "lists" of right/wrong, appropriate/inappropriate, moral/immoral that predominate in a particular society at a given time in history and that are enforced in multiple ways.

dramatization of evil In Tannenbaum's labelling theory, the judgment that it is no longer a particular behaviour that is deviant, but rather it is the person her- or himself who is deviant.

dramaturgy The interpretive school of thought that suggests social life is similar to performing in the theatre, wherein individuals have *front-stage selves* and *back-stage selves*.

ecclesia State religions that are sanctioned by the government and adopted as a nation's official religion.

economic consequences frame A frame used in the news media that highlights material costs and benefits for countries, regions, groups, or individuals.

emotional coping strategies In Agnew's general strain theory, a possible response to strain where people engage in measures to reduce the negative emotions caused by strain.

established femininity A form of femininity that embodies the dominant cultural constructions of what a female body should look like.

established sect A religious sect that retains a high level of tension with the larger society.

ethnographic research Research in which the researcher embeds her or himself with the groups being studied for an extended period of time.

eugenics Practices to increase sexual reproduction among individuals believed to be genetically superior while decreasing (or eliminating) sexual reproduction among those believed to be genetically inferior.

evaluation The second step of the social typing process, whereby a person, behaviour, or characteristic has judgments attached based on the label applied during the description component.

exhibitionists People who enjoy having sex in places where others might see them (i.e., public places).

extending Body projects that attempt to overcome physical limitations.

false consciousness In conflict theories, the false sense of freedom held by powerless groups.

folkways Norms that govern informal everyday behaviours.

formal regulation Forms of social control that emerge from organizations or institutions; also known as *formal social control*.

formal social control Forms of social control that emerge from organizations or institutions; also known as *formal regulation*.

framing The overall way that an issue is depicted in the media, which influences what we notice about reality.

front-stage self In the dramaturgical approach, the social roles people play when in front of a variety of audiences.

functional definition (of pornography) Forms of media or popular culture used by an individual for the purposes of sexual arousal.

functionalist theories Positivist theories that explain the causes of behaviour in terms of the various structures that fulfill important functions for society.

gang A debated term that frequently refers to "any denotable ... group [of adolescents or young adults] who (a) are generally perceived as a distinct aggregation by others in the neighbourhood, (b) recognize themselves as a denotable group (almost invariably with a group name), and (c) have been involved in a sufficient number of [illegal] incidents" (Sanday cited in Chatterjee, 2006).

gang problem The socially constructed representations of gangs that are communicated through the media.

gender-variant People whose gender identity or expression does not correspond to their birth sex; also known as *transgender*.

generalized other In symbolic interactionist theory, our perception of the viewpoints of generic "people" in society.

generation gap The perception that conflicts are inherent between the adult and youth generations.

genre definition (of pornography) Media or popular cultural products created for the purposes of arousing the consumer.

globalization Processes that create "tight global economic, political, cultural, and environmental interconnections and flows that make most current borders and boundaries irrelevant" (Steger, 2013, p. 9).

hackers People who access computer systems without authorization and sometimes use that access for malicious purposes.

harm An objective view that defines deviance as people, behaviours, or characteristics that cause harm.

hashtag activism A form of social activism that uses social media.

hegemony In conflict theories, the dominant way of seeing and understanding the world, as determined by the ideology of powerful groups and then taught to citizens as common sense.

high-consensus deviance Forms of deviance about which there are high levels of agreement in society.

human dignity The right to be treated with respect; a fundamental human right.

human interest frame A frame used in the news media that focuses on human life stories and emotions.

human trafficking Illegal trade in human beings for the purposes of sexual exploitation, forced labour, or slavery.

iceberg theory A theory that claims the acts of scientific misconduct that are detected are only a small proportion of all of the instances of misconduct that are actually occurring.

identity management Techniques used by individuals to manage their stigmatization; also known as *impression management*.

ideology In conflict theories, the worldview held by society's powerful groups.

impression management Techniques used by individuals to manage their stigmatization; also known as *identity management*.

informal regulation Forms of social control that emerge from everyday social interaction; also known as *informal social control*.

informal social control Forms of social control that emerge from everyday social interaction; also known as *informal regulation*.

innovation In Merton's strain theory, the mode of adaptation that involves accepting society's institutionalized goals but rejecting the legitimate means of attaining those goals.

institutionalized goals In Merton's strain theory, the goals that are culturally exalted, including wealth, status/power, and prestige.

interactionist view (of law) The view of law that suggests that society's powerful define the law at the behest of interest groups, who appeal to those with power to rectify a perceived social ill.

instrumental Marxism A form of Marxism that proposes social rules are created to serve the interests of the powerful, becoming tools to control the proletariat.

interpretive theories Theories that draw attention to people's intersubjective understandings of the world around them, other people, and themselves.

involvement In social bonds theory, the bond characterized by the time one spends involved in conventional activities.

labelling definitions (of pornography) Sexually explicit materials deemed obscene according to community standards.

labelling theories Interpretive theories that describe the process by which individuals are labelled as deviant, which then has implications for how others treat them and their own subsequent behaviours and identities.

latent functions In functionalist theories, those functions that are unintentionally served by society's structures.

learning theories Positivist theories that explain the causes of behaviour in terms of the learning processes that people are subjected to.

legitimate means In Merton's strain theory, socially acceptable ways of attaining the institutionalized goals in society.

les femmes du pays Country wives, or Indigenous women who formed intimate relationships with male European fur traders and settlers.

looking-glass self According to symbolic interactionist theory, the process by which our assumptions about what other people think of us influences what we think about ourselves and how we look or act.

low-consensus deviance Forms of deviance about which there are low levels of agreement in society.

manifest functions In functionalist theories, those functions that are intended to be fulfilled by society's structures.

master status A core characteristic by which others identify a person.

material incentives A motivation for gang membership involving the desire to make more, or more consistent, money.

McDonaldization of society The routinization of activities in contemporary capitalism, characterized by efficiency, predictability, control, and calculability.

mechanical solidarity In Durkheim's functionalist theory, preindustrial societies in which people were bonded together by their similarity to one another.

media Any form of communication that targets a mass audience in print or electronic format.

medicalized The social typing process within the context of medical or psychiatric science.

mental disorder "Alterations in thinking, mood or behaviour … associated with significant distress and impaired functioning" (Public Health Agency of Canada, 2015).

middle-class measuring rod In status frustration theory, the middle-class norms that permeate the school system and against which all students are compared.

moral entrepreneurs Individuals or groups who manufacture public morality by bringing a social problem to public awareness and then attempting to affect change in society's dominant moral codes.

moral panic An exaggerated and sensationalized concern over a particular phenomenon, characterized by heightened concern, hostility toward the offending group, a certain level of consensus that there is a real threat, disproportionality, and volatility.

moral regulation In Durkheim's functionalist theory, the extent to which norms are enforced in society.

mores Norms that are considered to be the foundation of morality in society.

motives In differential association theory, the rationales for deviance or conformity.

muscle dysmorphia A psychological disorder that involves a preoccupation with being too thin or small and results in an obsession with weightlifting accompanied by anxiety or mood disorders, extreme body dissatisfaction, distorted eating attitudes, and anabolic steroid use.

mutual conversion The way in which lower-class boys join with similar others in response to status frustration.

nature of the sexual act One of the criteria for determining deviant and normal sexuality, which identifies certain sexual activities as being acceptable or unacceptable.

nature of the sexual partner One of the criteria for determining deviant and normal sexuality, which identifies certain sexual partners as being acceptable or unacceptable.

negative affect In Agnew's general strain theory, the negative emotions that mediate the relationship between strain and deviance.

negative societal reaction An objective view that defines deviance as people, behaviours, and characteristics that society's "masses" respond to with negative feelings.

new eugenics According to some scientists, genetic testing and technologies that target certain social groups with reproductive controls.

new religious movements A term used by some scholars in place of the terms *sect* or *cult*.

nonconformists Female exotic dancers who come from privileged, educated backgrounds and who have the freedom to enter and leave the industry as they wish.

normative violation An objective view that defines deviance as people, behaviours, and characteristics that violate society's norms.

obese A person that has a body mass index (BMI) between 25.0 and 29.9.

objective The view of deviance as being defined on the basis of a single, common, clearly identifiable characteristic; also known as *objectivist*.

organic solidarity In Durkheim's functionalist theory, industrial societies in which people are bonded together by their interdependence.

overweight (1) According to scientific standards, a person that has a body mass index (BMI) 30.0 and higher. (2) According to social standards, a body that is larger than current cultural ideals.

Panopticon A prison design that enabled guards to observe prisoners at all times and yet did not allow prisoners to definitively know whether they were being watched or not.

parens patriae Parent of the country, or the child welfare approach to youth crime that was embodied in the *Juvenile Delinquents Act*.

physical protection A motivation for gang membership involving increased safety from the known dangers of the neighbourhood.

place of refuge and camouflage A motivation for gang membership involving a level of anonymity, removing a sense of personal responsibility for illegal activities.

pornography Forms of media or popular culture that include explicit sex.

positivist (theories of deviance) Theories that attempt to explain the causes of behaviour.

post-academic science A term that refers to the predominance of scientific research occurring in commercial centres rather than university environments.

praxis The Marxist view that social scientists have a responsibility to use their work in pursuit of practical, emancipatory goals.

prescription The third component of the social typing process, whereby measures of social control are directed at a person, behaviour, or characteristic because of the previously attached label and judgment.

preventative social control Forms of social control intended to prevent a deviant behaviour or characteristic from emerging in the first place.

prevention paradox The growing efforts to help "problem" drinkers on university campuses have not reduced the extent of harm caused by alcohol consumption, because most of the harms are caused by low- to moderate-risk drinkers.

primary deviance In Lemert's labelling theory, the occasional rule breaking everyone engages in, which is seldom noticed and rarely caught.

primary prevention (of anorexia) Efforts to prevent eating disorders from occurring in the first place.

proletariat In Marxist conflict theory, the employees of the owners of the means of production.

racialize The process by which representations of social phenomena become associated with specific racial or ethnic groups.

radical constructionism A form of social constructionism that claims the world is characterized by endless relativism; also known as *strict constructionism*.

reaction formation In status frustration theory, the oppositional standards that are developed by lower-class boys in the school system.

rebellion In Merton's strain theory, the mode of adaptation that involves replacing society's institutionalized goals and

legitimate means with new sets of goals and means.

recreation A motivation for gang membership involving opportunities for entertainment and socializing.

redesigning Body projects that involve fundamental, lasting reconstructions of bodies.

reintegrative shaming Individuals are temporarily stigmatized for their deviant acts, but then accepted back into the community.

religion as deviance Deviant acts that occur within accepted religions, or religious belief systems that are socially typed as deviant.

residential schooling A policy of the Canadian government that removed Indigenous children from their communities and placed them in boarding schools run by various Christian churches.

resistant femininity A form of femininity that opposes dominant ideals of what the female body should look like.

retreatism In Merton's strain theory, the mode of adaptation that involves rejecting both society's institutionalized goals and the legitimate means of attaining those goals.

retreatist gangs In differential opportunity theory, gangs whose activities revolve around substance use.

retroactive social control Forms of social control intended to punish, fix, or cure deviance that has already occurred.

risk society A society in which knowledge experts warn us that risks which must be identified and managed are everywhere around us.

ritualism In Merton's strain theory, the mode of adaptation that involves rejecting society's institutionalized goals but continuing to accept the legitimate means of attaining those goals.

role taking In symbolic interactionist theory, the process by which we vicariously place ourselves in the roles of others in order to see the world from their points of view, which then influences our own attitudes and actions.

schema A cognitive, or mental, framework that helps us organize and interpret information.

science "Knowledge or a system of knowledge covering general truths of the operation of general laws especially as obtained and tested through scientific method" (Merriam-Webster, 2017c).

science of risk The processes by which a variety of professionals are trained to identify populations that are "at risk" of various negative outcomes and implement programming that will manage those risks.

scientific misconduct An umbrella term used to refer to fabrication or falsification of data, breaches of ethics, plagiarism, and any other scientific practices deemed unacceptable or inappropriate.

secondary deviance A lifestyle and identity based on chronic rule breaking.

secondary prevention (of anorexia) Identifying those young men and women who may be in the very early stages of an eating disorder to provide early intervention.

sects Smaller religious groups that have usually broken away from larger churches and that have more rigid doctrine and higher levels of commitment required of members.

security of person and property A fundamental human right that protects individuals' physical well-being and entitles them to control over their own property.

self-control (1) Forms of social control that one directs at oneself; also known as self-regulation. (2) In self-control theory (also known as the general theory of crime), the factor that prevents most people from engaging in deviance.

self-regulation Forms of social control that one directs at oneself; also known as self-control.

self-stigma The process of stigmatizing oneself for a particular behaviour or characteristic.

sex hygiene movement During the Victorian era, moral entrepreneurs who equated social purity with sexual purity and who sought to solve problems such as prostitution, divorce, and illegitimacy; also known as the social purity movement.

sexting Sending nude or partially nude photos of oneself using forms of electronic communication.

sick role The role that ill individuals may be assigned, under certain conditions, in which they are given a temporary reprieve from some of life's responsibilities and are not blamed for their conditions.

significant others In symbolic interactionist theory, people who are personally important to us.

simulmedia The use of multiple forms of media simultaneously.

skeptical postmodernism A form of postmodern theory that postulates knowledge is not possible and only chaos and meaninglessness exist.

skepticism The assumption that all ideas must be subjected to rigorous scrutiny; part of the normative structure of science.

social causation hypothesis The proposal that more life stresses and fewer resources characterize the lives of the lower class, contributing to the emergence of mental disorders.

social constructionism The perspective proposing that social characteristics are creations or artifacts of a particular society at a specific time in history, just as objects are artifacts of that society.

social control theories Positivist theories that explain the causes of conforming behaviour rather than the causes of deviant behaviour.

social Darwinism The application of the Darwinian concept of evolution to history and societies.

Social Gospel A theology that informed the work of the child-savers movement during the Victorian era, whereby Christian principles were applied in real-world settings to solve social problems.

social integration In Durkheim's functionalist theory, the level of cohesion or social bonds in society.

social purity movement During the Victorian era, moral entrepreneurs who equated social purity with sexual purity and who sought to solve problems such as prostitution, divorce, and illegitimacy; also known as the *sex hygiene movement*.

social selection hypothesis The proposal that people with mental disorders fall into lower economic strata because of their difficulties in daily functioning.

social typing The process by which some people come to be perceived as deviant and others as normal.

soft constructionism A form of social constructionism that emphasizes the processes by which certain social phenomena come to be perceived and reacted to in particular ways in a given society at a specific time in history; also known as *contextual constructionism*.

spoiled identity In the dramaturgical approach, the stigmatization faced when an individual assumes a deviant role on the front stage.

status frustration In status frustration theory, the strain experienced by lower-class boys who are unable to live up to the middle-class standards of the school system.

stigma by association A form of stigma where people are stigmatized not because of their own actions, but rather the actions of someone with whom they associate; also known as *courtesy stigma*.

stigmatization The process of exclusion that follows a deviant master status.

stigmatized others Individuals who are presented (through the media) as threats to the way of life of decent people.

strain The structural gap that exists between institutionalized goals and the legitimate means of achieving those goals for people located in some parts of the social structure.

strict constructionism A form of social constructionism that claims the world is characterized by endless relativism; also known as *radical constructionism*.

structural Marxism A form of Marxism that proposes social rules are created to protect the capitalist economic system and may then be applied to members of the proletariat or bourgeoisie.

sturm und drang Storm and stress, perceived by G. Stanley Hall as being inherent during adolescence.

subjective The view of deviance where deviance is defined as those people, behaviours, and characteristics that society's dominant moral codes deem to be unacceptable and in need of control; also known as *subjectivist*.

survivors Female exotic dancers who have extensive histories of childhood abuse and who feel forced into the industry because of few available alternatives.

symbolic interactionism The theoretical perspective that describes society as composed of social interaction, which occurs via communication through symbols; the foundation for all interpretive theories.

tagging In Tannenbaum's labelling theory, the deviant label that we initially attach to an individual's behaviour.

tautological A circular argument, in which the latter part of the argument merely restates the former part of the argument; a critique of functionalist theories.

techniques In differential association theory, the skills that are required for deviance or conformity.

techniques of neutralization Self-rationalizations for deviant behaviour.

teleological An argument that proposes the existence of a phenomenon lies in the functions that it serves; a critique of functionalist theories.

tertiary deviance Following a person's transition to secondary deviance, his or her efforts to resist a deviant label and instead redefine normal in a way that includes the deviantized behaviour or characteristic.

time to resist A motivation for gang membership that involves a statement of rejection to society, a rejection of the type of lives being offered.

transgender People whose gender identity or expression does not correspond to their birth sex; also known as *gender-variant*.

troubled youth Youth who are considered to be primarily a threat to themselves, such as through substance use.

troubling youth Youth who are considered to be primarily a threat to others or to society, such as through criminal activity.

trying to pass A stigma management technique that involves hiding the behaviour or characteristic that is stigmatized.

underweight (1) According to scientific standards, a person that has a body mass index (BMI) of 18.4 or lower. (2) According to social standards, a body that is thinner than current cultural ideals.

universalism The assumption that scientific knowledge is free from any biases based on characteristics such as race, gender, or religion; part of the normative structure of science.

workers Female exotic dancers primarily from working-class backgrounds who become exotic dancers because of the money they can earn.

young offenders Individuals under the age of 18 who commit criminal acts.

youth A transitional time in life between childhood and maturity.

References

Aboriginal Sport BC (2012). Honour Your Health Challenge. Retrieved from www.aboriginalsportbc.ca.

Accordino, M. P., Porter, D. F., & Morse, T. (2001). Deinstitutionalization of persons with severe mental illness: Context and consequences. *Journal of Rehabilitation Medicine, 67* (2), 16–21.

Adlaf, E. M., & Paglia-Boak, A. (2007). *Drug use among Ontario students, 1977–2007.* CAMH Research Document Series No. 21. Toronto, ON: Canadian Association for Mental Health.

Adler, P. A., & Adler, P. (2006). The deviance society. *Deviant Behavior: An Interdisciplinary Journal, 27* (2), 129–148.

Adler, P. A., & Adler, P. (2016). *Constructions of deviance: Social power, context, and interaction* (8th ed.). Belmont, CA: Wadsworth.

Agnew, R. (1992). A foundation for a general strain theory of crime and delinquency. *Criminology, 30,* 47–87.

Agnew, R. (2001). Building on the foundation of general strain theory: Specifying the types of strain most likely to lead to crime and delinquency. *Journal of Research in Crime and Delinquency, 38* (4), 319–361.

Agnew, R. A. (2006). *Pressured into crime: An overview of general strain theory.* Los Angeles, CA: Roxbury.

Aguiniga, D. M., Madden, E. E., & Zellman K. T. (2016). An exploratory analysis of students' perceptions of mental health in the media. *Social Work in Mental Health, 14* (4), 428–444.

Ahmed, S., & Matthes, J. (2016). Media representation of Muslims and Islam from 2000–2015: A meta-analysis. *The International Communication Gazette, 0* (0), 1–26.

Akers, R. L. (1977). *Deviant behavior: A social learning approach.* Belmont, CA: Wadsworth.

Akers, R. L. (1991). Self-control as a general theory of crime. *Journal of Quantitative Criminology, 7,* 201–211.

Akers, R. L. (1998). *Social learning and social structure: A general theory of crime and deviance.* Boston, MA: Northeastern University Press.

Akers, R. L. (2000). *Criminological theories: Introduction, evaluation, and application* (3rd ed.). Los Angeles, CA: Roxbury.

Akers, R. L. (2006). *Social learning and social structure: A general theory of crime and deviance.* Boston, MA: Northeastern University Press.

Alberta Education (2016). *Guidelines for best practices: Creating learning environments that respect diverse sexual orientations, gender identities and gender expressions.* Retrieved from www.education.alberta.ca/.

Allen, M. (2015). Police-reported hate crime in Canada, 2014. *Juristat, 35* (1). Statistics Canada Catalogue No. 85-002-X. Ottawa, ON: Statistics Canada.

American Academy of Pediatrics (2016). Virtual violence. *Pediatrics, 138* (2), 1–48.

Anderson, A., & Gordon, R. (1978). Witchcraft and the status of women: The case of England. *British Journal of Sociology, 29,* 171–184.

Anderson, C. H. (2015). Refreshingly honest celebrity confessions. *Shape Magazine.* Retrieved from www.shape.com.

Anderssen, E. (2012, March 2). Disney closes exhibit over criticism for stigmatizing overweight kids. *Globe and Mail.* Retrieved from www.theglobeandmail.com.

Angus-Reid (2012, November 29). Most Americans and Canadians are ready to legalize marijuana. Retrieved from www.angus-reid.com.

Aragonès, E., López-Muntaner, J., Ceruelo, S., & Basora, J. (2014). Reinforcing stigmatization: Coverage of mental illness in Spanish newspapers. *Journal of Health Communication, 19*, 1248–1258.

Arkins, B. (1994). Sexuality in fifth-century Athens. *Classics Ireland, 1*, 1–8.

Armstrong, L. (2016). "Who's the slut, who's the whore?" *Feminist Criminology, 11* (3), 285–303.

Aronson, E., Wilson, T. D., Fehr, B., & Akert, R. M. (2017). *Social psychology* (6th Canadian ed.). Toronto, ON: Pearson Education.

Asbury, B. D. (2015). "Backdoor to eugenics"? The risks of prenatal diagnosis for poor, black women. *Duke Journal of Gender Law and Policy, 23* (1), 1–24.

Aseltine, R. (1995). A reconsideration of parental and peer influences on adolescent deviance. *Journal of Health and Social Behavior, 3* (6), 103–121.

Ashley, D., & Orenstein, D. M. (2001). *Sociological theory: Classical statements* (5th ed.). Boston, MA: Allyn & Bacon.

Associated Press (2014, November 20). Obesity's global costs hit $2 trillion a year, report suggests. *CBC News.* Retrieved from www.cbc.ca/news.

Associated Press (2016, December 14). Yahoo discloses 'shocking' hack affecting 1 billion accounts. Retrieved from www.cbc.ca/news.

Atkinson, M. (2002). Pretty in ink: Conformity, resistance, and negotiation in women's tattooing. *Sex Roles, 47* (5/6), 219–235.

Atkinson, M. (2003). *Tattooed: The sociogenesis of a body art.* Toronto, ON: University of Toronto Press.

Attwood, F. (2011). The paradigm shift: Pornography research, sexualization and extreme images. *Sociology Compass, 5* (1), 13–22.

Bagdikian, B. H. (2004). *The new media monopoly.* Boston, MA: Beacon Press.

Bailey, S., & Bronskill, J. (2007, January 30). Prison warehouses, 'open-air asylums' are home to the mentally ill. *Edmonton Journal.* Retrieved from www.canada.com.

Bainbridge, W. S. (2002). *The endtime family: Children of God.* New York, NY: State University of New York Press.

Balestrery, J. E. (2012). Intersecting discourses on race and sexuality: Compounded colonization among LGBTTQ American Indians/Alaska natives. *Journal of Homosexuality, 59*, 633–655.

Ball, R. A. (2012). Changing images of deviance: Nineteenth-century Canadian anti-prostitution movements. *Deviant Behavior, 33* (1), 26–39.

Bandura, A. (1986). *Social foundations of thought and action: A social cognitive theory.* Englewood Cliffs, NJ: Prentice Hall.

Bandura, A., Ross, D., & Ross, S. A. (1961). Transmission of aggression through imitation of aggressive models. *Journal of Abnormal and Social Psychology, 63*, 575–582.

Bandura, A., Ross, D., & Ross, S. A. (1963). Imitation of film-mediated aggressive models. *Journal of Abnormal and Social Psychology, 66*, 3–11.

Barker, E. (2001). Watching for violence: A comparative analysis of five types of cult-watching groups. Paper presented at the annual meeting of the Centre for Studies in New Religion.

Barman, J. (1997/1998). Taming Aboriginal sexuality: Gender, power, and race in British Columbia, 1850–1900. *BC Studies, 115/116*, 237–266.

Barrett, D., Katsiyannis, A., Zhang, D., & Kingree, J. (2015). Predictors of teen childbearing among delinquent and non-delinquent females. *Journal of Child and Family Studies, 24* (4), 970–978.

Barrett, J., & Jay, P. (2005). Clinical research fraud: A victimless crime? *Applied Clinical Trials, 14* (2), 44–46.

Barsley, M. (1967). *The other hand: An investigation into the sinister history of left-handedness.* New York, NY: Hawthorn Books.

Barstow, A. L. (1994). *Witchcraze.* San Francisco, CA: Pandora.

Bartlett, J. (2015). The dark net: Inside the digital underworld. Brooklyn, NY: Melville House Publishing.

Barton, B. (2015). How like perceives like: Gay people on "Gaydar." *Journal of Homosexuality, 62* (12), 1615–1637.

Bassett, H., Lampe, J., & Lloyd, C. (1999). Parenting: Experiences and feelings of parents with a mental illness. *Journal of Mental Health, 8* (6), 597–604.

Baumrind, D. (1991). Parenting styles and adolescent development. In R. Lerner, A. Peterson, & J. Brooks-Gunn (Eds.), *Encyclopedia of adolescence.* New York, NY: Garland Publishing.

BBC News (2016, December 12). Russian hackers threaten Germany 2017 election. Retrieved from www.bbc.com.

BBC News (2015, December 18). France passes bill banning 'excessively thin' models. Retrieved from www.bbc.com.

Beaver, W., & Paul, S. (2011). Internet pornography: Variables related to use among traditional-aged college students. *Sociological Viewpoints, Fall,* 25–38.

Bechtel, K., & Pearson, W. (1985). Deviant scientists and scientific deviance. *Deviant Behavior: An Interdisciplinary Journal, 6* (3), 237–252.

Beck, M. (2001, November). Embracing your inner brat. *O Magazine,* 69.

Beck, U. (1992). *Risk society: Towards a new modernity.* London, UK: Sage.

Beck, U. (1999). *World risk.* Cambridge, UK: Polity Press.

Becker, H. (1963). *Outsiders: Studies in the sociology of deviance.* New York, NY: Free Press.

Beckford, M. (2007, February 15). Sister of tragic 'size zero' model found dead. *The Telegraph.* Retrieved from www.telegraph.co.uk.

Beggan, J. K., & DeAngelis, M. (2015). "Oh my God, I hate you": The felt experience of being othered for being thin. *Symbolic Interaction, 38* (3), 371–392.

Beit-Hallahmi, B. (2003). Scientology: Religion or racket? *Marburg Journal of Religion, 8* (1), 1–56.

Bell, B. T., & Dittmar, H. (2011). Does media matter? The role of identification in adolescent girls' media consumption and the impact of different thin-ideal media on body image. *Sex Roles, 65,* 478–490.

Ben-Yehuda, N. (1980). The European witch craze of the 14th to 17th centuries: A sociologist's perspective. *American Journal of Sociology, 86* (1), 1–31.

Ben-Yehuda, N. (1986). Deviance in science. *British Journal of Criminology, 26* (1), 1–27.

Ben-Yehuda, N. (1990). *The politics and morality of deviance: Moral panics, drug abuse, deviant science, and reversed stigmatization.* Albany, NY: State University of New York Press.

Bender-Baird, K. (2016). Peeing under surveillance: Bathrooms, gender policing, and hate violence. *Gender, Place, and Culture, 23* (7), 983–988.

Bennett. T. H., Holloway, K. R., Brookman, F., Parry, O., & Gorden, C. (2014). Explaining drug misuse among students from a widening access university: The role of techniques of neutralization. *Drugs: Education, Prevention and Policy, 21* (3), 189–196.

Beres, M. A. (2007). 'Spontaneous' sexual consent: An analysis of sexual consent literature. *Feminism & Psychology, 17* (1), 93–108.

Bereska, T. M. (2014). Conformity. In C. Forsyth and H. Copes (Eds.), *Encyclopedia of social deviance.* Thousand Oaks, CA: SAGE Publications.

Bereska, T. M. (2017). Must see television. In S. A. Kent and S. Raine (Eds.), *Scientology in popular culture: Influences and struggles for legitimacy.* Santa Barbara, CA: Praeger.

Berger, B. (1963). Adolescence and beyond. *Social Problems, 10,* 294–408.

Bergstrom, K., Fisher, S., & Jenson, J. (2016). Disavowing 'that guy': Identity construction and massively multiplayer online game players. *The International Journal of Research into New Media Technologies, 22* (3), 233–249.

Berman, N., & White, A. (2013). Refusing the stereotype: Decoding negative gender imagery through a school-based digital media literacy program. *Youth Studies Australia, 32* (4), 38–47.

Bessant, J. (2001). From sociology of deviance to sociology of risk: Youth homelessness and the problem of empiricism. *Journal of Criminal Justice, 29,* 31–43.

Bhattacharjee, Y. (2013). The mind of a con man. *New York Times.* Retrieved from www.nytimes.com.

Bibby, R. W. (2009). *The emerging millennials: How Canada's newest generation is responding to change and choice.* Lethbridge, AB: Project Canada Books.

Bissell, K., & Hays, H. (2011). Understanding anti-fat bias in children: The role of media and appearance anxiety in third to sixth graders' implicit and explicit attitudes toward obesity. *Mass Communication and Society, 14* (1), 113–140.

Blair, O. (2015). Victoria's Secret model Bridget Malcolm criticises 'skinny shamers' for calling her anorexic. *Independent.* Retrieved from www .independent.co.uk.

Bleicher, P. (2003). Is change afoot? 21 CFR 11 in transition. *Applied Clinical Trials, 12* (6) 34–36.

Bloch, E. (2001). Sex between men and boys in classical Greece: Was it education for citizenship or child abuse? *Journal of Men's Studies, 9* (2).

Blumer, H. (1986). *Symbolic interactionism: Perspective and method.* Berkeley, CA: University of California Press.

Born, L. (2004). Fast-tracking the plague: Drugging America to death. *International Socialist Review, 33.* Retrieved from www.isreview.org.

Bostrom, M. (2001). *The 21st century teen: Perception and teen reality.* Washington, DC: Frameworks Institute.

Boak, A., Hamilton, H. A., Adlaf, E. M., Henderson, J. L., & Mann, R. E. (2016). *The mental health and well-being of Ontario students, 1991–2015: Detailed OSDUHS findings.* CAMH Research Document, Series No. 43. Toronto, ON: CAMH.

Boak, A., Hamilton, H. A., Adlaf, E. M., & Mann, R. E. (2015). *Drug use among Ontario students, 1977–2015: Detailed OSDUHS findings.* CAMH Research Documents Series No. 41. Toronto, ON: CAMH.

Bouffard, J. A., & Petkovsek, M. A. (2014). Testing Hirschi's integration of social control and rational choice: Are bonds considered in offender decisions? *Journal of Crime and Justice, 37* (3), 285–308.

Bourgois, P. (1995). *In search of respect: Selling crack in El Barrio.* Cambridge, UK: Cambridge University Press.

Brace, C. L. (1996). Racialism and racist agendas. *American Anthropologist, 98* (1), 176–177.

Braithwaite, J. (2000). Shame and criminal justice. *Canadian Journal of Criminology, 42* (3), 281–298.

Bresnahan, M., Zhuang, J., Zhu, Y., & Nelson, J. (2016). Obesity stigma and negative perceptions of political leadership competence. *American Behavioral Scientist, 60* (11), 1362–1377.

Brezhnev, L. I. (2006). The Quotations Page. Quoted in V. Rich (1977), *Nature, 270*, 470–471. Retrieved from www.quotationspage.com.

Briggs, R. (1996). *Witches and neighbors: The social and cultural context of European witchcraft.* New York, NY: Viking Penguin.

British Fashion Council. (2007). *The report of the model health inquiry.* Retrieved from www.modelhealthinquiry.com.

Bromley, D. G., & Melton, J. G. (2012). Reconceptualizing types of religious organization: Dominant, sectarian, alternative, and emergent tradition groups. *Nova Religio, 15* (3), 4–28.

Bromley, D. G., & Shupe, A. D. (1993). Organized opposition to new religious movements. In D. G. Bromley & J. K. Hadden (Eds.), *The handbook of cults and sects* (pp. 177–198). Greenwich, CT: JAI Press.

Brook, J. S., Brook, D. W., De La Rosa, M., Whiteman, M., & Montoya, I. D. (1999). The role of parents in protecting Colombian adolescents from delinquency and marijuana use. *Archives of Pediatrics & Adolescent Medicine, 153* (5).

Brotnow, L., & Sinha, R. (2014). A developmental approach to prevention and intervention. In M. Leyton and S. Stewart (Eds.), *Substance abuse in Canada: Childhood and adolescent pathways to substance use disorders* (pp. 68–81). Ottawa, ON: Canadian Centre on Substance Abuse.

Brower, A. M. (2002). Are college students alcoholics? *Journal of American College Health, 50* (5), 253–255.

Brown, F. L., & Slaughter, V. (2011). Normal body, beautiful body: Discrepant perceptions reveal a pervasive "thin ideal" from childhood to adulthood. *Body Image, 8*, 119–125.

Buchanan, E. (1997). A school for sterilization. *World Press Review*, June, 46.

Bucher, J., Manasse, M., & Milton, J. (2015). Soliciting strain: Examining both sides of street prostitution through general strain theory. *Journal of Crime and Justice, 38* (4), 435–453.

Burdett, C. (n.d.). Post Darwin: Social Darwinism, degeneration, eugenics. *British Library*. Retrieved from www.bl.uk.

Burger, T. D., & Finkel, D. (2002). Relationships between body modifications and very high-risk behavior in a college population. *College Student Journal, 36* (2), 203–213.

Burgess, R., & Akers, R. (1966). A differential association reinforcement theory of criminal behavior. *Social Problems, 25*, 128–147.

Buzzell, T. (2005). Holiday revelry and legal control of fireworks: A study of neutralization in two normative contexts. *Western Criminology, 6* (1), 30–42.

Byrd, K. M. (2016). Binge drinking in and out of college: An examination of social control and differential association on binge drinking behaviors between college students and their non-college peers. *Sociological Spectrum, 36* (4), 191–207.

Calogero, R. M., & Thompson, J. K. (2010). Gender and body image. In J. C. Chrisler and D. R. McCreary (Eds.), *Handbook of gender research in psychology* (pp. 153–184). New York, NY: Springer.

Calvete, E., Orue, I., & Gámez-Guadix, M. (2016). Cyberbullying victimization and depression in adolescents: The mediating role of body image and cognitive schemas in a one-year prospective study. *European Journal on Criminal Policy and Research, 22*, (2), 271–284.

Canadian Living (2006, August). Your teenager: An owner's manual (for the bewildered parent), pp. 159–162.

Canadian Mental Health Association (2016). Eating disorders. Retrieved from www.cmha.ca.

Canadian Press (2012, July 19). RCMP arrest Alberta man who U.S. says is a suspect in international cyber crime. Retrieved from www.canada.com.

Canadian Press (2016, April 11). Timeline: States of emergency Attawapiskat has declared in recent years. Retrieved from www.cbc.ca/news.

Caplan, P. J. (1995). *They say you're crazy: How the world's most powerful psychiatrists decide who's normal.* Reading, MA: Perseus Books.

Caputo, T., & Linden, R. (2016). Early theories of criminology. In R. Linden (Ed.), *Criminology: A Canadian perspective* (8th ed.). Toronto, ON: Nelson Education.

Carroll, S. T., Riffenburgh, R. H., Roberts, T. A., & Myhre, E. B. (2002). Tattoos and body piercings as indicators of adolescent risk-taking behaviors. *Pediatrics, 109* (6), 1021–1027.

Carter, M. J., & Fuller, C. (2016). Symbols, meaning, and action: The past, present, and future of symbolic interactionism. *Current Sociology, 64* (6), 931–961.

Caulfield, T. (2004). The commercialisation of medical and scientific reporting. *PLoS Medicine, 1* (3), 178–179.

CBC News (2007). Same-sex rights: Canada timeline. *CBC News Indepth.* Retrieved from www.cbc.ca/news.

CBC News (2008, June 11). Prime Minister Stephen Harper's statement of apology. Retrieved from www.cbc.ca/news.

CBC News (2012, January 31). Homosexuality an "illness." *CBC Digital Archives.* Retrieved from www.cbc.ca/news.

CBC News (2013, September 10). Charter of Quebec values would ban religious symbols for public workers. Retrieved from www.cbc.ca/news.

CBC News (2016a, February 28). Man imprisoned for being gay to get posthumous pardon from Trudeau. Retrieved from www.cbc.ca/news.

CBC News (2016b, March 22). School bans trendy teen clothing line, say it's gang wear. Retrieved from www.cbc.ca/news.

CBC News (2016c, April 11). Attawapiskat suicide emergency: Health Canada, province send in crisis teams. Retrieved from www.cbc.ca/news.

CBC News (2016d, July 9). 'There is no filter': Video of shootings could force public to confront issues of race and policing. Retrieved from www.cbc.ca/news.

Centre for Addiction and Mental Health (n.d.). *Eating disorders: Overview.* Retrieved from www.camh.ca.

Chambliss, W. J., & Seidman, R. (1982). *Law, order and power* (2nd ed.). Reading, MA: Addison-Wesley.

Chamlin, M. B., & Sanders, B. A. (2013). A time series analysis of integrative and coercive social control. *Journal of Crime and Justice, 36* (1), 53–66.

Chappell, A. T., & Piquero, A. R. (2004). Applying social learning theory to police misconduct. *Deviant Behavior, 25* (2), 89–108.

Chatterjee, J. (2006). *A research report on youth gangs: Problems, perspectives, and priorities.* Ottawa, ON: Research and Evaluation Branch, RCMP. Toronto, ON: HarperCollins.

Chaudoir, S. R., Earnshaw, V. A., & Andel, S. (2013). "Discredited" versus "discreditable": Understanding how shared and unique stigma mechanisms affect psychological and physical health disparities. *Basic and Applied Social Psychology, 35* (1), 75–87.

Chen, D., Jaenicke, E. C., & Volpe, R. J. (2016). Food environments and obesity: Household diet expenditure versus food deserts. *American Journal of Public Health, 106* (5), 881–888.

Childress, S. A. (1991). Reel "rape speech": Violent pornography and the politics of harm. *Law & Society Review, 25* (1), 177–214.

Chu, C. S. K., & Laidler, K. J. (2016). Becoming a male client of compensated dating. *Deviant Behaviour, 37* (1), 47–65.

Cimpric, A. (2010). *Children accused of witchcraft: An anthropological study of contemporary practices in Africa.* Dakar: UNICEF WCARA.

Clark, R. (2016). "Hope in a hashtag": The discursive activism of #WhyIStayed. *Feminist Media Studies, 16* (5), 788–804.

Clevenger, S. (2016). Mothers of sexual assault victims: How women "do mother" after their child has been sexually assaulted. *Feminist Criminology, 11* (3), 227–252.

Cloward, R. A., & Ohlin, L. E. (1960). *Delinquency and opportunity: A theory of delinquent gangs.* New York, NY: Free Press.

Cohen, A. J. (1955). *Delinquent boys.* New York, NY: Free Press.

Cohen, S. (1973). *Folk devils and moral panics.* London, UK: MacGibbons and Kee.

Complex Magazine (2011, June 22). The 25 funniest celebrity Twitter hacks. Retrieved from www.complex.com.

Conservative Party of Canada (2006). *Stand up for Canada: Conservative Party of Canada election platform 2006.* Retrieved from www.conservative.ca.

Coontz, S. (1992). *The way we never were: American families and the nostalgia trap.* New York, NY: Basis Books.

Correctional Services Program (2016). Youth correctional statistics in Canada, 2014/2015. *Juristat, 36* (1). Statistics Canada Catalogue No. 85-002-X. Ottawa, ON: Statistics Canada.

Couch, D., Thomas, S. L., Lewis, S., Blood, R. W., Holland, K., & Komesaroff, P. (2016). Obese people's perceptions of the thin ideal. *Social Science and Medicine, 148,* 60–70.

Covarrubias, I., & Han, M. (2011). Mental health stigma about serious mental illness among MSW students: Social contact and attitude. *Social Work, 56* (4), 317–325.

Coventry, P. A., Dickens, C., & Todd, C. (2014). How does mental-physical multimorbidity express itself in time and space? A phenomenological analysis of encounters with depression and chronic physical illness. *Social Science and Medicine, 118,* 108–118.

Cowan, D. E. (2003). *Bearing false witness? An introduction to the Christian countercult.* Santa Barbara, CA: Praeger.

Cromwell, P., & Thurman, Q. (2003). The devil made me do it: The use of neutralization by shoplifters. *Deviant Behavior, 24(6),* 1–16.

Cronin, T. A. (2001). Tattoos, piercings, and skin adornments. *Dermatology Nursing, 13* (5), 380–383.

Crowe, K. (2015). CRISPR gene-editing tool has scientists thrilled but nervous. *CBC News.* Retrieved from www.cbc.ca/news.

Cullen, F. T., & Agnew, R. (1998). *Criminological theory: Past to present.* Los Angeles, CA: Roxbury.

Das Gupta, T. (2000). Families of native people, immigrants, and people of colour. In N. Mandell & A. Duffy (Eds.), *Canadian families: Diversity, conflict, and change* (2nd ed., pp. 146–187). Toronto, ON: Nelson Thomson.

Daily Mail (2012, November 8). 'In Hollywood I'm obese ... I'm considered a fat actress': Jennifer Lawrence on why she'll never play Hunger Games. *MailOnline.* Retrieved from www.dailymail.co.uk.

Davidson, D. (2016). Introducing the tattoo project. In D. Davidson (Ed.), *The tattoo project: Commemorative tattoos, visual culture, and the digital archive* (pp. 1–17). Toronto, ON: Canadian Scholars' Press.

Davies, J. M. (2015). The criminalization of sexual commerce in Canada: Context and concepts for critical analysis. *The Canadian Journal of Human Sexuality, 24* (2), 78–91.

Davies, K. A. (1997). Voluntary exposure to pornography and men's attitudes toward feminism and rape. *Journal of Sex Research, 34* (2), 131–137.

Davies, L. (1994). In search of resistance and rebellion among high school drop-outs. *Canadian Journal of Sociology, 19* (3), 331–350.

Degher, D., & Hughes, G. (2003). The adoption and management of a "fat" identity. In P. A. Adler & P. Adler (Eds.), *Constructions of deviance: Social power, context, and interaction* (pp. 211–221). Belmont, CA: Wadsworth.

Delaney, T. (2005). *American street gangs.* Upper Saddle River, NJ: Prentice Hall.

DeLenardo, S., & Terrion, J. L. (2014). Suck it up: Opinion and attitudes about mental illness stigma and help-seeking behaviour of male varsity football players. *Canadian Journal of Community Mental Health, 33* (3), 43–56.

De Maio, F. (2010). *Health and social theory.* New York, NY: Palgrave Macmillan.

DeMello, M. (2016). Memories on the skin: A brief cultural history of tattooing. In D. Davidson (Ed.), *The tattoo project: Commemorative tattoos, visual culture, and the digital archive* (pp. 21–29). Toronto, ON: Canadian Scholars' Press.

D'Emilio, J., & Freedman, E. B. (1997). *Intimate matters: A history of sexuality in America* (2nd ed.). Chicago, IL: University of Chicago Press.

Dennis, A., & Martin, P. J. (2005). Symbolic interactionism and the concept of power. *The British Journal of Sociology, 56* (2), 191–213.

DePierre, J. A., Puhl, R. M., & Luedicke, J. (2014). Public perceptions of food addiction: A comparison with alcohol and tobacco. *Journal of Substance Use, 19* (2), 1–6.

Deshotels, T. H., & Forsyth, C. J. (2008). Sex rules: The edicts of income in exotic dancing. *Deviant Behavior, 29* (5), 484–500.

Deshotels, T. H., Tinney, M., & Forsyth, C. J. (2012). McSexy: Exotic dancing and institutional power. *Deviant Behavior, 33* (2), 140–148.

Desmond, R. J., & Carveth, R. (2007). The effects of advertising on children and adolescents: A meta-analysis. In R. Preiss, B. Gayle, N. Burrell, M. Allen, & J. Bryant (Eds.), *Mass media effects research: Advances through meta-analysis* (pp. 169–179). Mahwah, NJ: Lawrence Erlbaum.

Des Rosiers, N., & Bittle, S. (2004). Introduction. In the Law Commission of Canada (Ed.), *What is a crime? Defining criminal conduct in contemporary society* (pp. vii–xxv). Vancouver, BC: UBC Press.

deVries, D. A., Peter, J., de Graaf, H., & Nikken, P. (2016). Adolescents' social network site use, peer appearance-related feedback, and body dissatisfaction: Testing a mediation model. *Journal of Youth and Adolescence, 45,* 211–224.

Dewey, C. (2014, October 14). The only guide to Gamergate you will ever need to read. *The Washington Post.* Retrieved from www.washingtonpost.com.

Dickson, L. (2016, December 2). Teen granted new trial in 'sexting' case. *Times Colonist.* Retrieved from www.timescolonist.com.

Dickson, L., Dukes, R. L., Smith, H., & Strapko, N. (2015). To ink or not to ink: The meaning of tattoos among college students. *College Student Journal, 49* (1), 106–120.

Dieckmann, R., Boone, I., Brockmann, S. O., Hammerl, J. A., Kolb-Mäurer, A., Goebeler, M., … Al Dahouk, J. (2016). The risk of bacterial infection after tattooing. *Deutsches Arzteblatt International, 113,* 665–671.

Dobbs, R., Sawers, C., Thompson, F., Manyika, J., Woetzel, J., Child, P., ... Spatharou, A. (2014). *How the world could better fight obesity*. McKinsey & Company. Retrieved from www.mckinsey.com.

Doherty, B. (2014). Sensational Scientology! The Church of Scientology and Australia tabloid television. *Nova Religio, 17* (3), 38–63.

Doherty, T. (1988). *Teenagers & teenpics: The juvenilization of American movies in the 1950s*. Boston, MA: Unwin Hyman.

Donner, C. M., & Jennings, W. G. (2014). Low self-control and police deviance: Applying Gottfredson and Hirschi's general theory of crime to officer misconduct. *Journal of Quantitative Criminology, 7* (2), 201–211.

Downes, D., & Rock, P. (2011). *Understanding deviance* (6th ed.). New York, NY: Oxford University Press.

Dufur, M. J., Hoffman, J. P., Braudt, D. B., Parcel, T. L., & Spence, K. R. (2015). Examining the effects of family and school capital on delinquent behavior. *Deviant Behavior, 36* (7), 511–526.

Duguay, S. (2016). "He has a way gayer Facebook than I do": Investigating sexual identity disclosure and context collapse on a social networking site. *New Media and Society, 18* (6), 891–907.

Dukes, R. L. (2016a). Deviant ink: A meta-analysis of tattoos and drug use in general populations. *Deviant Behavior, 37* (6), 665–678.

Dukes, R. L. (2016b). Regret among tattooed adolescents. *The Social Science Journal, 53*, 455–458.

Durkheim, E. (1933). *The division of labor in society*. New York, NY: Free Press.

Durkheim, E. (1951). *Suicide*. New York, NY: Free Press.

Dyck, E. (2012). *Facing eugenics: Reproduction, sterilization, and the politics of choice*. Baltimore, MD: Johns Hopkins University Press.

Dye, H. (2016). Are there differences in gender, race, and age regarding body dissatisfaction? *Journal of Human Behavior in the Social Environment, 26* (6), 499–508.

Dyer, O. (2005). US survey shows extent of research misconduct. *British Medical Journal, 330*, 1465.

Eagle, D. E. (2011). Changing patterns of attendance at religious services in Canada, 1986–2008. *Journal for the Scientific Study of Religion, 50* (1), 187–200.

Eaton, W. W. (2001). *The sociology of mental disorders*. Westport, CT: Praeger Publishing.

Economou, M., Angelopoulous, E., Peppou, L. E., Souliotis, K., Tzavara, C., Kontoangelos, K., ... Stefanis, C. (2016). Enduring financial crisis in Greece: Prevalence and correlates of major depression and suicidality. *Social Psychiatry and Psychiatric Epidemiology, 51*, 1015–1024.

Eddy, M. (2015, February). Inside the dark web. *PC Magazine (Digital Edition)*. Retrieved from www.pcmagazine.com.

Edwards, A. R. (1988). *Regulation and repression: The study of social control*. Sydney, Australia: Allen & Unwin.

Egan, R. D. (2003). I'll be your fantasy girl, if you'll be my money man: Mapping desire, fantasy and power in two exotic dance clubs. *JPCS: Journal for the Psychoanalysis of Culture & Society, 8(1)*, 109–120.

Elan, P. (2016). 'My agents told me to stop eating'—the reality of body image in modelling. *The Guardian*. Retrieved from www.theguardian.com.

Elkind, P. (2015, June 25). Sony Pictures: Inside the hack of the century—Part 1. *Fortune*. Retrieved from www.fortune.com.

Elliot, D., Huizinga, D., & Ageton, S. (1985). *Explaining delinquency and substance use*. Beverly Hills, CA: Sage.

Ellis, A. D. (2015). A picture is worth one thousand words: Body art in the workplace. *Employee Responsibilities and Rights Journal, 27*, 101–113.

England, J. (2004). Disciplining subjectivity and space: Representation, film and its material effects. *Antipode, 36*, 295–321.

Entman, R. M. (1993). Framing: Toward clarification of a fractured paradigm. *Journal of Communication, 43* (4), 51–58.

Erickson, K. G., Crosnoe, R., & Dornbusch, S. M. (2000). A social process model of adolescent deviance: Combining social control and differential association perspectives. *Journal of Youth and Adolescence, 29* (4), 395–425.

Ericson, R. V., & Haggerty, K. D. (2001). Governing the young. In R. C. Smandych (Ed.), *Youth justice: History, legislation, and reform* (pp. 104–123). Toronto, ON: Harcourt.

Erikson, K. (1966). *Wayward Puritans*. New York, NY: Wiley.

Eriksen, K., & Kress, V. E. (2008). Gender and diagnosis: Struggles and suggestions for counselors. *Journal of Counseling and Development, 86* (2), 152–162.

Evangeline Middle School (2017). Home. Retrieved from www.ems.ednet.ns.ca.

Evans, M. (2017). L. Ron Hubbard's foray into the world of music. In S. A. Kent and S. Raine (Eds.), *Scientology in popular culture: Influences and struggles for legitimacy*. Santa Barbara, CA: Praeger.

Fanelli, D. (2009). How many scientists fabricate and falsify research? A systematic review and meta-analysis of survey data. *PLoS ONE, 4* (5), e5738.

Fanelli, D. (2014). We need more research on causes and consequences, as well as on solutions. *Addiction, 10,* 9–13

Fanelli, D., Costas, R., & Larivière, V. (2015). Misconduct policies, academic culture and career stage, not gender or pressure to publish, affect scientific integrity. *PLoS ONE, 10* (6), 1–18.

Fass, P. S. (1979). *The damned and the beautiful: American youth in the 1920s.* New York, NY: Oxford University Press.

Featherstone, R., & Deflam, M. (2003). Anomie and strain: Context and consequences of Merton's two theories. *Sociological Inquiry, 73* (4), 471–489.

Feinstein, Y. (2015). The thin line between "crazy" and "hero": Exploring the multiple statuses of US veterans in a work-therapy program. *Armed Forces and Society, 41* (1), 3–22.

Fekete, D. J. (2012, November 28). Commentary: New movie presents skewed view of bipolar disorder. *Edmonton Journal.* Retrieved from www.edmontonjournal.com.

Fiese, B. H., & Bost, K. K. (2016). Family ecologies and child risk for obesity: Focus on regulatory processes. *Family Relationships, 65* (1), 94–107.

Fischer, B., Ala-Leppilampi, K., Single, E., & Robins, A. (2003). Cannabis law reform in Canada: Is the "saga of promise, hesitation and retreat" coming to an end? *Canadian Journal of Criminology and Criminal Justice, 45* (3), 265–297.

Fischer, M. (2016). #Free_CeCe: The material convergence of social media activism. *Feminist Media Studies, 16* (5), 755–771.

Fischer, P., & Greitemeyer, T. (2006). Music and aggression: The impact of sexual-aggressive song lyrics on aggression-related thoughts, emotions, and behavior toward the same and the opposite sex. *Personality and Social Psychology Bulletin, 32,* 1165–1176.

Fitzgerald, I., & MacNaughton, W. (2016). *Knives and ink: Chefs and the stories behind their tattoos, with recipes.* New York: Bloomsbury USA.

Fleras, A., & Kunz, J. L. (2001). *Media and minorities: Representing diversity in multicultural Canada.* Toronto, ON: Thompson Educational Publishing.

Flynn, M. A., Park, S. Y., Morin, D. T., & Stana, A. (2015). Anything but real: Body idealization and objectification of MTV docusoap characters. *Sex Roles*, *72*, 173–182.

Foerschner, A. M. (2010). The history of mental illness: From skull drills to happy pills. *Inquiries Journal*, *2* (9), 1–4.

Force, W. R. (2009). Consumption styles and the fluid complexity of punk authenticity. *Symbolic Interactionism*, *32* (4), 289–309.

Ford, J. A., & Schroeder, R. D. (2009). Academic strain and non-medical use of prescription stimulants among college students. *Deviant Behavior: An Interdisciplinary Journal*, *30* (1), 26–53.

Fortunato, E. K., et al. (2014). Brand-specific alcohol consumption of flavored alcoholic beverages among underage youth in the United States. *American Journal of Drug and Alcohol Abuse*, *40* (1), 51–57.

Foss, K. A. (2014). (De)stigmatizing the silent epidemic: Representations of hearing loss in entertainment television. *Health Communication*, *29*, 888–900.

Foucault, M. (1980). *Power/knowledge: Selected interviews and other writings 1972–1977* (1st American ed.). C. Gordon, L. Marshall, J. Mepham, & K. Super (Trans.). New York, NY: Pantheon Books.

Foucault, M. (1995). *Discipline and punish: The birth of the prison* (2nd ed.). A. Sheridan, Trans. New York, NY: Vintage Books. (Original work published 1977.)

Foulks, E. F. (2004). Commentary: Racial biases in diagnosis and medication of mentally ill minorities in prison and communities. *Journal of the American Academy of Psychiatry and Law*, *32*, 34–35.

Fournier, S., & Crey, E. (1998). *Stolen from our embrace*. Berkeley, CA: Roundhouse Publishing.

Frailing, K., & Harper, D. W. (2010). The social construction of deviance, conflict and the criminalization of midwives, New Orleans: 1940s and 1950s. *Deviant Behavior*, *31* (8), 729–755.

Frances, A. (2013). *Saving normal: An insider's revolt against out of control psychiatric diagnosis—DSM-5, big pharma, and the medicalization of ordinary life*. William Morrow.

Freedhoff, Y. (2012, February 23). Disney's horrifying new interactive child obesity exhibit at Epcot. Retrieved from www.weightymatters.ca.

Freud, S. (1999). The social construction of normality. *Families in Society: The Journal of Contemporary Human Services*, *80* (4), 333–339.

Fuist, T. N. (2014). The dramatization of beliefs, values, and allegiances: Ideological performances among social movement groups and religious organizations. *Social Movement Studies*, *13* (4), 427–442.

Gabbidon, S. L. (2003). Racial profiling by store clerks and security personnel in retail establishments: An exploration of "shopping while black." *Journal of Contemporary Criminal Justice*, *19* (3), 345–364.

Gackenbach, J., & Snyder, T. (2012). *Play reality: How video games are changing everything*. Calgary, AB: Authors.

Galvin-White, C. M., & O'Neal, E. N. (2016). Lesbian police officers' interpersonal working relationships and sexuality disclosure: A qualitative study. *Feminist Criminology*, *11* (3), 253–284.

Gámez-Guadix, M., Orue, I., Smith, P. K., & Calvete, E. (2013). Longitudinal and reciprocal relations of cyberbullying with depression, substance use, and problematic Internet use among adolescents. *Journal of Adolescent Health*, *53*, 446–452.

Gardner, S. (2016). Children of God sex cult survivors come out of the shadows. *CBC News*. Retrieved from www.cbc.ca/news.

Gender Creative Kids Canada (n.d.). About GenderCreativeKids.ca. Retrieved from www.gendercreativekids.ca/.

Gibelman, M., & Gelman, S. R. (2005). Scientific misconduct in social welfare research: Preventive lessons from other fields. *Social Work Education, 24* (3), 275–295.

Gibson, M. F. (2015). Intersecting deviance: Social work, deviance, and the legacy of eugenics. *British Journal of Social Work, 45,* 313–330.

Giesbrecht, N. (2000). Roles of commercial interests in alcohol policies: Recent developments in North America. *Addiction, 95* (suppl. 4), S581–S595.

Giles-Gorniak, A. N., Vandehey, M. A., & Stiles, B. L. (2016). Understanding differences in mental health history and behavioral choices in a community sample of individuals with and without body modifications. *Deviant Behavior, 37* (8), 852–860.

Gili, M., Roca, M., Basu, S., McKee, M., & Stuckler, D. (2013). The mental health risks of economic crisis in Spain: Evidence from primary care centres 2006 and 2010. *European Journal of Public Health, 23,* 103–108.

Global Intellectual Property Center (2013). *Digital piracy costs global economy $75 billion.* US Chamber of Commerce. Retrieved from www.theglobalipcenter.com.

Glock, S., Beverborg, A. O. G., & Müller, B. C. N. (2016). Pre-service teachers' implicit and explicit attitudes toward obesity influence their judgments of students. *Social Psychology of Education, 19* (1), 97–115.

Godfrey, T. (2012, July 22). Strip clubs set to recruit high school students. *The Barrie Examiner.* Retrieved from www.thebarrieexaminer.com.

Goeij, M. C. M., Jacobs, M.A.M., van Nierop, P., van der Veeken-Vlassak, I.A.G., van de Mheen, D., Schoenmakers, T., ... Kunst, A.E. (2016). Impact of cross-sectoral alcohol policy on youth alcohol consumption. *Journal of Studies on Alcohol and Drugs, 77* (4), 595–605

Goffman, E. (1959). *The presentation of self in everyday life.* Garden City, NY: Doubleday-Anchor.

Goffman, E. (1961). *Asylums: Essays on the social situation of mental patients and other inmates.* Garden City, NY: Anchor Books.

Goffman, E. (1963). *Stigma: Notes on the management of spoiled identity.* Englewood Cliffs, NJ: Prentice Hall.

Goffman, E. (1979). *Gender advertisements.* New York, NY: Harper & Row.

Gomme, I. M. (1985). Predictors of status and criminal offences among male and female adolescents in an Ontario community. *Canadian Journal of Criminology, 27,* 157–159.

Goode, E. (1997). *Deviant behavior* (5th ed.). Upper Saddle River, NJ: Prentice Hall.

Goode, E., & Ben-Yehuda, N. (2009). *Moral panics: The social construction of deviance* (2nd ed.). New York, NY: Wiley Blackwell.

Goodstein, L. (2003, May 27). Seeing Islam as an evil faith, evangelicals seek converts. *New York Times.* Retrieved from www.nytimes.com.

Goodwin, J., & Tajjudin, I. (2016). "What do you think I am? Crazy?": The Joker and stigmatizing representations of mental ill-health. *The Journal of Popular Culture, 49* (2), 385–402.

Goring, C. (1919). *The English convict.* London, London, UK: H. M. Stationery Office.

Gottfredson, M. R., & Hirschi, T. (1990). *A general theory of crime.* Stanford, CT: Stanford University Press.

Government of Alberta (2015). *Tobacco and smoking reduction act*. Statutes of Alberta, 2005, Chapter T-3.8. Current as of June 1, 2015. Edmonton, AB: Author.

Government of Canada (2015). *Evaluation of retailers' behavior toward certain youth access-to-tobacco restrictions—2014*. Ottawa, ON: Author.

Grasmick, H. G., Tittle, C. R., Bursik, R. J., & Arneklev, B. J. (1993). Testing the core empirical implications of Gottfredson and Hirschi's general theory of crime. *Journal of Research in Crime and Delinquency, 30* (1), 47–54.

Greco, A. N. (1995). The first amendment, freedom of the press, and the issues of "harm": A conundrum for publishers. *Publishing Research Quarterly, 11* (4), 39–57.

Green, M. C., & Brock, T. C. (2000). The role of transportation in the persuasiveness of public narratives. *Journal of Personality and Social Psychology, 79* (5), 701–721.

Greenberg, A. (2014, September). Black markets evolved. *Wired*. Retrieved from www.wired.com.

Greenberg, B. S., Eastin, M., Hofschire, L., Lachlan, K., & Brownell, K. D. (2003). Portrayals of overweight and obese individuals on commercial television. *American Journal of Public Health, 93* (8), 1342–1348.

Greenberg, H., Grekul, J., & Nelson, R. (2016). Aboriginal youth crime in Canada. In J. A. Winterdyk and R. Smandych (Eds.), *Youth at risk and youth justice: A Canadian overview* (2nd ed.). Toronto, ON: OUP Canada.

Greer, C., & Jewkes, Y. (2005). Extremes of otherness: Media images of social exclusion. *Social Justice, 32* (1), 20–31.

Grekul, J. M. (2002). *The social construction of the feebleminded threat: Implementation of the Sexual Sterilization Act in Alberta, 1929–1972*. Unpublished doctoral dissertation, University of Alberta, Edmonton, AB.

Grekul, J., & LaBoucane-Benson, P. (2007). *An investigation into the formation and recruitment processes of Aboriginal gangs in Western Canada*. Ottawa, ON: Aboriginal Corrections Policy Unit, Public Safety Canada.

Grob, G. N. (1994). *The mad among us: A history of the care of America's mentally ill*. New York, NY: Free Press.

Ha, T. T. (2012, November 12). Denmark sheds its maligned fat tax. *Globe and Mail*. Retrieved from www.theglobeandmail.com.

Haas, S. M., Irr, M. E., Jennings, N. A., & Wagner, C. M. (2011). Communicating thin: A grounded model of online negative enabling support groups in the pro-anorexia movement. *New Media and Society, 13* (1), 40–57.

Hadden, J., & Bromley, D. (Eds.). (1995). *The handbook of cults and sects in America*. Greenwich, CT: JAI Press.

Haldane, J. B. S. (1927). "Science and technology as art-forms," in *Possible worlds and other essays*. London, UK: Chatto & Windus. Retrieved from www.bartleby.com.

Hall, G. S. (1904). *Adolescence* (Vol. I). Englewood Cliffs, NJ: Prentice Hall.

Hall, S. (2009). The work of representation. In Stuart Hall (Ed.), *Representation: Cultural representations and signifying practices* (pp. 1–11). Thousand Oaks, CA: Sage Publications.

Halushka, J. (2015). Work wisdom: Teaching former prisoners how to negotiate workplace interactions and perform a rehabilitated self. *Ethnography, 17* (1), 72–91.

Hamilton, S. N. (2014). Considering critical communication studies in Canada. In L. R. Shade (Ed.), *Mediascapes: New patterns in Canadian communication* (4th ed.). Toronto, ON: Nelson Education.

Harris, S. (2016, June 16). 'A shakedown against Canadians': Hollywood still telling Internet pirates to pay up. *CBC News*. Retrieved from www.cbc.ca/news.

Harris Interactive (2012). *One in five U.S. adults now has a tattoo.* Retrieved from www.prnewswire.com.

Harrison, M. L., Jones, S., & Sullivan, C. (2008). The gendered expressions of self-control: Manifestations of non-criminal deviance among females. *Deviant Behavior: An Interdisciplinary Journal, 29* (1), 18–42.

Harwell, D. (2014, October 17). More women play video games than boys, and other surprising facts lost in the mess of Gamergate. *The Washington Post*. Retrieved from www.washingtonpost.com.

Hawdon, J. E., Ryan, J., & Agnich, L. (2010). Crime as a source of social solidarity: A research note testing Durkheim's assertion. *Deviant Behavior, 31* (8), 679–703.

Hawkes, D., Senn, C. Y., & Thorn, C. (2004). Factors that influence attitudes toward women with tattoos. *Sex Roles, 50* (9/10), 593–604.

Hay, C., & Meldrum, R. (2010). Bullying, victimization, and adolescent self-harm: Testing hypotheses from general strain theory. *Journal of Youth and Adolescence, 39*, 446–459.

Hayden-Wade, H. A., Stein, R. I., Ghaderi, A., Saelens, B. E., Zabinski, M. F., & Wilfley, D. E. (2005). Prevalence, characteristics, and correlates of teasing experiences among overweight children vs. non-overweight peers. *Obesity Research, 13* (8), 1381–1392.

Hayle, S., Wortley, S., & Tanner, J. (2016). Race, street life, and policing: Implications for racial profiling. *Canadian Journal of Criminology and Criminal Justice, 58* (3), 322–353.

Health Canada (1999). *Trends in the health of Canadian children.* Ottawa, ON: Author.

Health Canada (2002). *A report on mental illness in Canada.* Ottawa, ON: Author.

Health Canada (2005). *2002 youth smoking survey: Technical report.* Ottawa, ON: Author.

Health Canada (2013). *Canadian tobacco, alcohol and drugs survey (CTADS).* Ottawa, ON: Author.

Heinonen, A. (2015). Neutralizing disciplinary violence: A typology of parents' use-of-violence accounts. *Victims and Offenders, 10* (3), 270–292.

Herdt, G. (1984). Ritualized homosexuality in the male cults of Melanesia, 1862–1982: An introduction. In G. Herdt (Ed.), *Ritualized homosexuality in Melanesia* (pp. 1–81). Berkeley, CA: University of California Press.

Hersch, P. (1998). *A tribe apart: A journey into the heart of American adolescence.* New York, NY: Ballantine Books.

Hervic, S. E., & Fasting, K. (2016). 'It is passable, I suppose'—Adult Norwegian men's notions of their own bodies. *International Review for the Sociology of Sport, 51* (7), 800–816.

Hess, A. (2016, May 25). Asian-American actors are fighting for visibility. They will not be ignored. *The New York Times*. Retrieved from www.nytimes.com.

Hesselman, F., Graf, V., Schmidt, M., & Reinhart, M. (2017). The visibility of scientific misconduct: A review of the literature on retracted journal articles. *Current Sociology [Online First]*. Retrieved from www.journals.sagepub.com.

Hicks, J. W. (2004). Ethnicity, race, and forensic psychiatry: Are we color blind? *Journal of the Amercian Academy of Psychiatry and Law, 32*, 21–33.

Hier, S. P. (2002). Raves, risks and the ecstasy panic: A case study of the subversive nature of moral regulation. *Canadian Journal of Sociology, 27* (1), 33–57.

Higgins, G. E., Wolfe, S. E., & Marcum, C. D. (2008). Digital piracy: An examination of three measurements of self-control. *Deviant Behavior, 29* (5), 440–460.

Hill, B. M., Ogletree, S. M., & McCrary, K. M. (2016). Body modifications in college students: Considering gender, self-esteem, body appreciation, and reasons for tattoos. *College Student Journal, 50* (2), 246–252.

Hinduja, S., & Higgins, G. E. (2011). Trends and patterns among music pirates. *Deviant Behavior, 32* (7), 563–588.

Hinduja, S., & Patchin, J. W. (2008). Cyberbullying: An exploratory analysis of factors related to offending. *Deviant Behavior, 29* (2), 129–156.

Hipes, C., Lucas, J., Phelan, J. C., & White, R. C. (2016). The stigma of mental illness in the labor market. *Social Science Research, 56,* 16–25.

Hirschi, T. C. (1969). *Causes of delinquency.* Berkeley, CA: University of California Press.

Holt, T. J., & Copes, H. (2010). Transferring subcultural knowledge online: Practices and beliefs of persistent digital pirates. *Deviant Behavior, 31* (7), 625–654.

Holt, T. J., & Turner, M. G. (2012). Examining risks and protective factors of on-line identity theft. *Deviant Behavior, 33* (4), 308–323.

Hope, T. L., & Chapple, C. L. (2005). Maternal characteristics, parenting, and adolescent sexual behavior: The role of self-control. *Deviant Behavior, 26* (1), 25–45.

Horowitz, K. R. (2013). The trouble with "queerness": Drag and the marking of two cultures. *Journal of Women in Culture and Society, 38* (2), 303–326.

Horowitz, M. (2014, July 4). The persecution of witches, 21st-century style. *The New York Times.* Retrieved from www.nytimes.com.

Hotton, A. E., Farrell, L. C., & Fudge, J. L. (2014). A threatening space? Stigmatization and the framing of autism in the news. *Communication Studies, 65* (2), 189–207.

Hotton, T., & Haans, D. (2004). Alcohol and drug use in early adolescence. *Health Reports, 15* (3), 9–19. Statistics Canada Catalogue No. 82003XIE. Ottawa, ON: Statistics Canada.

Hövermann, A., Groß, E. M., Zick, A., & Messner, S. F. (2015). Understanding the devaluation of vulnerable groups: A novel application of institutional anomie theory. *Social Science Research, 52,* 408–421.

Hruby, A., Manson, J.E., Qi, L., Malik, V.S., Rimm, R., Sun, Q., ... Hu, F.B. (2016). Determinants and causes of obesity. *American Journal of Public Health, 106* (9), 1656–1662.

Huaco, G. (1986). Ideology and general theory: The case of sociological functionalism. *Comparative Studies in Society and History, 28,* 34–54.

Huffington Post Canada (2016, April 9). Free People called out for cultural appropriation of Native clothing and symbols. Retrieved from www.huffingtonpost.ca.

Human Resources and Skills Development Canada (2012, July 4). Government of Canada takes action to protect temporary foreign workers. Canada News Centre. Retrieved from news.gc.ca.

Humphreys, A. (2012, March 26). Ontario Court of Appeal greenlights brothels, sweeps aside many of Canada's anti-prostitution laws. *National Post.* Retrieved from www.news.nationalpost.com.

Huncar, A. (2017, February 27). Hockey Edmonton warns parents that 'unacceptable' behaviour will not be tolerated. *CBC News.* Retrieved from www.cbc.ca/news.

Hundersmarck, S. F. (2015). Apprenticeship in drinking. *Applied Psychology in Criminal Justice, 11* (1), 40–51.

Hunt, A. (1998). The great masturbation panic and the discourses of moral regulation in nineteenth- and early twentieth-century Britain. *Journal of the History of Sexuality, 8* (4), 575–615.

Hunt, P. (2010). Are you kynd? Conformity and deviance within the jamband subculture. *Deviant Behavior, 31* (6), 521–551.

Hutterites.org (2017). Our beliefs. Retrieved from www.hutterites.org.

Interactive Advertising Bureau of Canada (2015). *Canada's media landscape.* Retrieved from www.iabcanada.com.

Ipsos-Reid (2012). *Socialogue: Hello, my virtual friend!* Retrieved from www.ipsos.ca.

Jack.org (2017). About. Retrieved from www.jack.org.

Jaimangal-Jones, D., Pritchard, A., & Morgan, N. (2015). Exploring dress, identity and performance in contemporary dance music culture. *Leisure Studies, 34* (5), 603–620.

Jankowski, M. S. (1991). *Islands in the street: Gangs and American urban society.* Berkeley, CA: University of California Press.

Janz, T. (2012). Current smoking trends. *Health at a Glance.* Statistics Canada Catalogue No. 82-624-X. Ottawa, ON: Statistics Canada.

Jenkins, P. (2000). *Mystics and messiahs: Cults and new religions in American history.* New York, NY: Oxford University Press.

Jhally, S. (Director). (2009). *Tough guise: Violence, media, and the crisis in masculinity.* Northampton, MA: Media Education Foundation.

Jiwani, Y. (2010). Race(ing) the nation: Media and minorities. In L. R. Shade (Ed.), *Mediascapes: New patterns in Canadian communication* (3rd ed.). Toronto, ON: Nelson Education.

Johnson, S. (2014, September 29). New research sheds light on daily ad exposures. *SJ Insights.* Retrieved from www.sjinsights.net.

Johnston, L. D., O'Malley, P. M., Bachman, J. G., Schelenberg, J. E., & Miech, R. A. (2016). *Monitoring the future national survey on drug use, 1975–2015: Volume 2. College students and adults ages 19–55.* Ann Arbor, MI: University of Michigan.

Jones, S., & Quisenberry, N. (2004). The general theory of crime: How general is it? *Deviant Behavior, 25* (5), 401–426.

Jordon, T. E. (1998). *Victorian child savers and their culture: A thematic evaluation* (Mellon Studies in Sociology, Vol. 19). Lewiston, NY: Edwin Mellon Press.

Joseph, J., & Baldwin, S. (2000). Four editorial proposals to improve social sciences research and publication. *International Journal of Risk & Safety in Medicine, 13,* 109–116.

Josephson, W. L. (1987). Television violence and children's aggression: Testing the priming, social script, and disinhibition predictions. *Journal of Personality and Social Psychology, 53* (5), 882–890.

Judd, A. (2015, January 21). 'We've been told to go die': Teen hockey ref speaks about parents' behaviour. *Global News.* Retrieved from www.globalnews.ca.

Judson, H. F. (2004). *The great betrayal: Fraud in science.* Orlando, FL: Harcourt.

Katz, J. (1999). From the film *Tough Guise,* produced by Sut Jhally. Available from the Media Education Foundation, www.mediaed.org.

Kaufman, J. M. (2009). Gendered responses to serious strain: The argument for a general strain theory of deviance. *Justice Quarterly, 26* (3), 410–444.

Kaufman, M. R. (2009). "It's just a fantasy for a couple of hours": Ethnography of a nude male show bar. *Deviant Behavior, 30* (5), 407–433.

Kearns, C. E., Schmidt, L. A., & Glantz, S. A. (2016). Sugar industry and coronary heart disease research: A historical analysis of internal industry documents. *JAMA Internal Medicine, 176* (11), 1680–1685.

Keeling, R. P. (2002). Binge drinking and the college environment. *Journal of American College Health, 50* (5), 197–201.

Keene, D. E., Cowan, S. K., & Castro-Baker, A. (2015). "When you're in a crisis like that, you don't want people to know": Mortgage strain, stigma, and mental health. *American Journal of Public Health, 105* (5), 1008–1012.

Keith, S., McClure, T. E., Vasquez, L. M., Reed, M. J., & May, D. C. (2015). How does gender identity affect the relationships between strain and negative emotions? *Sociological Spectrum, 35* (2), 179–206.

Kemmers, R., van der Waal, J., & Aupers, S. (2015). Becoming politically discontented: Anti-establishment careers of Dutch nonvoters and PVV voters. *Current Sociology, 64* (5), 757–774.

Kent, S. A. (1994). Lustful prophet: A psychosexual history of the Children of God's leader, David Berg. *Cultic Studies Journal, 11* (2), 135–188.

Kent, S. A. (2017). Scientology's recruitment policies targeting celebrities. In S. A. Kent and S. Raine (Eds.), *Scientology in popular culture: Influences and struggles for legitimacy*. Santa Barbara, CA: Praeger.

Kent, S. L., & Jacobs, D. (2004). Social divisions and coercive control in advanced societies: Law enforcement strength in eleven nations from 1975 to 1994. *Social Problems, 51* (3), 343–361.

Kerley, K. R., Copes, H., & Griffin, O. H. (2015). Middle-class motives for non-medical prescription stimulant use among college students. *Deviant Behavior, 36* (7), 589–603.

Kerley, K. R., Leban, L., Copes, H., Taylor, L., & Agnone, C. (2014). Methamphetamine using careers of white and black women. *Deviant Behavior, 35* (6), 477–495.

Kierstein, L., & Kjelskau, K. C. (2015). Tattoo as art, the drivers behind the fascination and the decision to become tattooed. *Current Problems in Dermatology, 48*, 37–40.

Kingori, P., & Gerrets, R. (2016). Morals, morale and motivations in data fabrication: Medical research fieldworkers' views and practices in two sub-Saharan African contexts. *Social Science and Medicine, 166*, 150–159.

Kinsey, A. (2006). In *Rand Lindsly's Quotations*. Retrieved from www .quotationspage.com.

Kinsman, G., & Gentile, P. (2009). *The Canadian war on queers: National security as sexual regulation*. Vancouver, BC: UBC Press.

Kirchgaesser, S. (2017). 'It is devastating': Abuse survivor quits Vatican child protection body. *The Guardian*. Retrieved from www.theguardian.com.

Kitsuse, J. I. (1980). Coming out all over: Deviants and the politics of social problems. *Social Problems, 28* (1), 1–12.

Klauer, (2005). *How the rich get thin*. New York, NY: St. Martin's Press.

Klein, J. L. & Tolson, D. (2015). Wrangling rumors of corruption: Institutional neutralization of the Jerry Sandusky scandal at Penn State University. *Journal of Human Behavior in the Social Environment, 25* (5), 477–486.

Kłonkowska, A. M., & Maj, A. (2015). "More-or-less body": The social perception of normativity of the body in Poland. *Filosofija Sociologija, 26* (2), 155–163.

Kluger, N. (2015). Epidemiology of tattoos in industrialized countries. *Current Problems in Dermatology, 48*, 6–20.

Koch, J. R., Roberts, A. E., Armstrong, M. L., & Owen, D. C. (2010). Body art, deviance, and American college students. *Social Science Journal, 47*, 151–161.

Koch, J. R., Roberts, A. E., Armstrong, M. L., & Owen, D. C. (2015). Tattoos, gender, and well-being among American college students. *The Social Science Journal, 52*, 536–541.

Koeppel, M. D. H., Bouffard, L. A., & Koeppel-Ullrich, E. R. H. (2015). Sexual orientation and substance use: The moderation of parental attachment. *Deviant Behavior, 36* (8), 657–673.

Kong, T. S. K. (2009). More than a sex machine: Accomplishing masculinity among Chinese male sex workers in the Hong Kong sex industry. *Deviant Behavior, 30* (8), 715–745.

Kornfield, D. S., & Titus, S. L. (2016). Stop ignoring misconduct. *Nature, 537,* 29–30.

Kosut, M. (2006). An ironic fad: The commodification and consumption of tattoos. *The Journal of Popular Culture, 39* (6), 1035–1048.

Krahé, B. (2014). Media violence use as a risk factor for aggressive behaviour in adolescence. *European Review of Social Psychology, 25* (1), 71–106.

Krashinsky, S. (2012, April 19). Canadian Club on the rocks? Far from it, thanks to *Mad Men. Globe and Mail.* Retrieved from www.theglobeandmail.com.

Kroska, A., & Harkness, S. K. (2006). Stigma sentiments and self-meanings: Exploring the modified labeling theory of mental illness. *Social Psychology Quarterly, 69* (4), 325–348.

Kubrin, C. E., Stucky, T. D., & Krohn, M. D. (2009). *Researching theories of crime and deviance.* New York, NY: Oxford University Press.

Kueneman, R., & Bowness, E. (2016). The social context of dispute settlement and the rise of law. In R. Linden (Ed.), *Criminology: A Canadian perspective* (8th ed.). Toronto, ON: Nelson Education.

Kühl, S. (2013). *For the betterment of the race: The rise and fall of the international movement for eugenics and racial hygiene.* New York, NY: Palgrave Macmillan.

Kuhns, E. (2003). *The habit: A history of the clothing of Catholic nuns.* New York, NY: Doubleday.

Kushner, D. (2015). The dark net. *Rolling Stone.* Retrieved from www.rollingstone.com.

Kwong, M. (2012). Tattoo culture making its mark on millennials. *CBC News.* Retrieved from www.cbc.ca/news.

The Lancet (2006, January 7). Editorial: Writing a new ending for a story of scientific fraud. Retrieved from www.thelancet.com.

Langone, M. D. (2015). Characteristics associated with cultic groups—revised. *ICSA Today, 6* (3), 10.

Larsen, K. (2017, February 27). Police called after confrontation between parents and teenage ref at pee wee hockey game. *CBC News.* Retrieved from www.cbc.ca/news.

Latner, J., & Stunkard, A. (2003). Stigmatization of obese children. *Nutrition Research Newsletter, 22* (4), 12.

Law, C., & Labre, M. P. (2002). Cultural standards of attractiveness: A thirty-year look at changes in male images in magazines. *Journalism & Mass Communication Quarterly, 79* (3), 697–711.

Lawson, R. (1995). Sect–state relations: Accounting for the differing trajectories of Seventh-day Adventists and Jehovah's Witnesses. *Sociology of Religion, 56* (4), 351–378.

Laycock, J. (2013). Where do they get these ideas? Changing ideas of cults in the mirror of popular culture. *Journal of the American Academy of Religion, 81* (1), 80–106.

Lazarsfeld, P. F. (1941). Remarks on administrative and critical communication research. *Studies in Philosophy and Social Science, 9* (1), 2–16.

Leader, K. (2016). "On the book of my body": Women, power, and "tattoo culture." *Feminist Formations, 28* (3), 174–195.

Lee, D. (n.d.). In *Rand Lindsly's Quotations.* Retrieved from www.quotationspage.com.

Lee, S. Guo, W., Toang, A., Mak, A. D. P., Wu, J., Ng, K. L., & Kwok, K. (2010). Evidence for the 2008 economic crisis exacerbating depression in Hong Kong. *Journal of Affective Disorders, 126*, 125–133.

Lemert, E. M. (1951). *Social pathology: A systematic approach to the study of sociopathic behavior.* New York, NY: McGraw-Hill.

Lengermann, P. M., & Niebrugge, G. (2007). *The women founders: Sociology and social theory, 1830–1930.* Long Grove, IL: Waveland Press.

Leon, J. S. (1977). The development of Canadian juvenile justice: A background for reform. *Osgoode Hall Law Journal, 15*, 71–106.

Levchak, P. J. (2015). Extending the anomie tradition: An assessment of the impact of trade measures on cross-national homicide rates. *Homicide Studies, 19* (4), 384–400.

Levine, M., & Maine, M. (2005). Eating disorders can be prevented. National Eating Disorders Association. Retrieved from www.nationaleatingdisorders.org.

Lewis, J., & Melton, J. G. (1994). *Sex, slander, and salvation: Investigating The Family/Children of God.* Stanford, CA: Center for Academic Publication.

Lewis, T. F., Milroy, J., Wyrick, D., Hebard, S. P., & Lamberson, K. A. (2017). Binge-drinking and non-binge-drinking student athletes: The role of proximal norms, negative expectancies, and selected sociodemographic variables. *Journal of Child and Adolescent Substance Abuse, 26* (2), 141–151.

Li, C. K. W., Holt, T. J., Bossler, A. M., & May, D. C. (2016). Examining the mediating effects of social learning on the low self-control–cyberbullying relationship in a youth sample. *Deviant Behavior, 37* (2), 1–13.

Li, Q. (2010). Cyberbullying in high schools: A study of students' behaviors and beliefs about this new phenomenon. *Journal of Aggression, 19*, 372–392.

Lianos, M., with Douglas, M. (2000). Dangerization and the end of deviance. *British Journal of Criminology, 40*, 261–278.

Liazos, A. (1972). The poverty of the sociology of deviance: Nuts, sluts, and perverts. *Social Problems, 20*, 102–120.

Lieberman, L. (2001). Reply. *Current Anthropology, 42* (1), 89–91.

Lilienfield, S. O., Lynn, S. J., & Lohr, J. M. (Eds.). (2015). *Science and pseudoscience in clinical psychology.* New York, NY: Guilford.

Link, B. G., Streuning, E., Cullen, F. T., Shrout, P. E., & Dohrenwend, B. P. (1989). A modified labeling theory approach to mental disorders: An empirical assessment. *American Sociological Review, 54* (3), 400–423.

Liska, A., & Reid, M. (1985). Ties to conventional institutions and delinquency. *American Sociological Review, 50*, 547–560.

Liu, C. M., & Lester, D. (2012). Body modification sites and abuse history. *Journal of Aggression, Maltreatment and Trauma, 21* (1), 19–30.

Löfgren-Mårtenson, L., & Månsson, S.-A. (2010). Lust, love, and life: A qualitative study of Swedish adolescents' perceptions and experiences with pornography. *Journal of Sex Research, 47* (6), 568–579.

Lombroso, C. (1911). *Crime, its causes and remedies.* Boston, MA: Little, Brown.

Longshore, D., Chang, E., Hsieh, S., & Messina, N. (2004). Self-control and social bonds: A combined control perspective on deviance. *Crime & Delinquency, 50* (4), 542–564.

MacEachern, S. (2006). Africanist archaeology and ancient IQ: Racial science and cultural evolution in the twenty-first century. *World Archaeology, 38* (1), 72–92.

Mackay, J. (2000). Global sex: Sexuality and sexual practices around the world. Paper presented at the 5th Congress of the European Federation of Sexology, June 29–July 2, 2000, Berlin.

MacKellar, C., & Bechtel, C. (2014). *The ethics of the new eugenics.* Oxford, UK: Berghahn Books.

MacLaurin, B., & Worthington, C. (2016). Street-involved youth in Canada. In J. Winterdyk and R. Smandych (Eds.), *Youth at risk and youth justice: A Canadian overview.* Toronto, ON: Oxford University Press Canada.

Macnamara, J. R. (2006). *Media and male identity: The making and remaking of men.* New York, NY: Palgrave MacMillan.

MacPhail, A., & Verdun-Jones, S. (2013). "Mental illness and the criminal justice system." Paper presented at *Re-Inventing Criminal Justice: The Fifth National Symposium.* Montreal, QC. January 2013.

Maggard, S. R., & Boylstein, C. (2014). Changing masks: Identity maintenance and the role of marijuana among a small circle of marijuana growers. *Deviant Behavior, 35* (8), 593–610.

Manca, T. (2017). Presentations of Scientology in prominent North American news series. In S. A. Kent and S. Raine (Eds.), *Scientology in popular culture: Influences and struggles for legitimacy.* Santa Barbara, CA: Praeger.

Mandell, N., & Momirov, J. (2000). Family histories. In N. Mandell & A. Duffy (Eds.), *Canadian families: Diversity, conflict, and change* (2nd ed., pp. 17–47). Toronto, ON: Nelson Thomson.

Markewich, C. (2016, October 20). Sask. First Nations facing 'state of crisis' after youth suicides. Retrieved from www.cbc.ca/news.

Marshall, B. L. (2006). The new virility: Viagra, male aging and sexual function. *Sexualities, 9* (3), 345–362.

Martin, J. (2014). *Drugs on the dark net: How cryptomarkets are transforming the global trade in illicit drugs.* New York: Palgrave MacMillan.

Martins, H. (1974). Time and theory in sociology. In J. Rex (Ed.), *Approaches to sociology.* London, UK: Routledge & Kegan Paul.

Marvasti, A. (2008). Being Middle Eastern American: Identity negotiation in the context of the war on terror. In E. J. Clarke (Ed.), *Deviant behavior: A text-reader in the sociology of deviance* (pp. 648–671). New York, NY: Worth.

Maugham, W. S. (1998). In *W. Somerset Maugham's Birthday: January 25, 1874.* Retrieved from www.quotationspage.com.

Mayers, L. B., & Chiffriller, S. H. (2008). Body art (body piercing and tattooing) among undergraduate university students: "Then and now." *Journal of Adolescent Health, 42,* 201–203.

McCaghy, C. H., Capron, T. A., & Jamieson, J. D. (2003). *Deviant behavior: Crime, conflict, and interest groups* (6th ed.). Boston, MA: Allyn & Bacon.

McCarthy, M. (2004). Lies, damn lies, and scientific research. *The Lancet, 364,* 1657–1658.

McCloud, S. (2007). From exotics to brainwashers: Portraying new religions in mass media. *Religion Compass, 1* (1), 214–228.

McCook, A., & Retraction Watch (2016). Whistleblower sues Duke, claims doctored data helped win $200 million in grants. *Science.* Retrieved from www.sciencemag.org.

McCormick, C. (2016). Youth deviance and the media: Mapping knowledge and limits to certainty. In J. A. Winterdyk and R. Smandych (Eds.), *Youth at risk and youth justice: A Canadian overview*

(2nd ed.). Toronto, ON: Oxford University Press.

McCue, D. (2016, April 18). For First Nations facing suicide crisis, the solution is rooted in the community. Retrieved from www.cbc.ca/news.

McGinty, E. E., Webster, D. W., & Barry, C. L. (2013). Effects of news media messages about mass shootings on attitudes toward person with serious mental illness and public support for gun policies. *American Journal of Psychiatry, 170*, 494–501.

McGinty, E. E., Webster, D. W., Jarlenski, M. & Barry, C. L. (2014). News media framing of serious mental illness and gun violence in the United States, 1997–2012. *American Journal of Public Health, 104* (3), 406–413.

McGoogan, C. (2017, February 6). Anonymous hacker knocks 20pc of dark web offline in campaign against child pornography. *The Telegraph.* Retrieved from www.telegraph.co.uk.

McGovern, C. M. (1985). *Masters of madness: Social origins of the American psychiatric profession.* Hanover, NH: University Press of New England.

McGuire, M. B. (2002). *Religion: The social context* (4th ed.). Belmont, CA: Wadsworth.

McKee, M. (2002). Substance use and social and economic transition: The need for evidence. *International Journal of Drug Policy, 13*, 453–459.

McKeen, S. (2002, March 24). An XXX-ray of our psyche: Basic instinct or debauchery? *Edmonton Journal*, D6.

McKibben, B. (2015). What Exxon knew about climate change. *New Yorker.* Retrieved from www.newyorker.com.

McIlroy, A. (2012, September 20). Home, sweet home gives hope to mentally ill. *Globe and Mail.* Retrieved from www.theglobeandmail.com.

McLorg, P. A., & Taub, D. E. (1987). Anorexia, bulimia, and developing a deviant identity. *Deviant Behavior: An Interdisciplinary Journal, 8* (2), 177–189.

Melendez, M. S., Lichtenstein, B., & Dolliver, M. J. (2016). Mothers of mass murderers: Exploring blame for the mothers of school shooters through an application of courtesy stigma to the Columbine and Newton tragedies. *Deviant Behavior, 37* (5), 525–536.

Mental Health Commission of Canada (2012). *Changing directions, changing lives: The mental health strategy for Canada: Executive summary.* Calgary, AB: Author

Mental Health Commission of Canada. (2013a). *Making the case for investing in mental health in Canada.* Ottawa, ON, and Calgary, AB: Author.

Mental Health Commission of Canada (2013b). *The mental health youth strategy for Canada: A youth perspective.* Ottawa, ON: Author.

Mental Health Commission of Canada (2013c). *The aspiring workforce: Employment and income for people with serious mental illness.* Ottawa, ON: Author.

Mental Health Commission of Canada (2013d). *Turning the key: Assessing housing and related supports for persons living with mental health problems and illness.* Ottawa, ON: Author.

Mental Health Commission of Canada (2015). *Informing the future: Mental health indicators for Canada.* Ottawa, ON: Author.

Mental Health Commission of Canada (2016a). *Mental health matters.* Retrieved from www.mentalhealthcommission.ca.

Mental Health Commission of Canada (2016b). *Mental Health Commission of Canada strategic plan, 2017–2022.* Ottawa, ON: Author.

Mental Health Commission of Canada (2016c). *The case for diversity: Building the case to improve mental health services for immigrant, refugee, ethnocultural and racialized populations.* Ottawa, ON: Author.

Menn, J. (2012, July 12). Can social media ever be made safe from sex predators? *Globe and Mail*. Retrieved from www.theglobeandmail.com.

Merriam-Webster (2017a). Deviant. *Merriam-Webster's Online Dictionary*. Retrieved from www.merriam-webster.com.

Merriam-Webster (2017b). Pornography. *Merriam-Webster's Online Dictionary*. Retrieved from www.merriam-webster.com.

Merriam-Webster (2017c). Science. *Merriam-Webster's Online Dictionary*. Retrieved from www.merriam-webster.com.

Merton, R. K. (1938). Social structure and anomie. *American Sociological Review, 3*, 672–682.

Merton, R. K. (1968). *Social theory and social structure*. New York, NY: Free Press.

Merton, R. K. (1973). *The sociology of science: Theoretical and empirical investigations*. Chicago, IL: University of Chicago Press.

Merton, R. K. (1995). Opportunity structure: The emergence, diffusion, and differentiation of a sociological concept, 1930s–1950s. In F. Adler and W. S. Laufer (Eds.), *The legacy of anomie theory* (pp. 3–78). New Brunswick, NJ: Transaction Publishers.

Messner, S. F., & Rosenfeld, R. (2013). *Crime and the American dream* (5th ed.). Belmont, CA: Wadsworth.

Mestemacher, R. A., & Roberti, J. W. (2004). Qualitative analysis of vocational choice: A collective case study of strippers. *Deviant Behavior, 25* (1), 43–65.

Milkie, M. A., Nomaguchi K. M., & Denny, K. E. (2015). Does the amount of time mothers spend with children or adolescents matter? *Journal of Marriage and Family, 77*, 355–372.

Miller, H. E., Thomas, S. L., Smith, K. M., & Robinson, P. (2015). Surveillance, responsibility, and control: An analysis of government and industry discourses about "problem" and "responsible" gambling. *Addiction Research and Theory, 24* (2), 163–176.

Miller, J. (1996). *Shingwauk's vision*. Toronto, ON: University of Toronto Press.

Milloy, J. S. (1999). *A national crime: The Canadian government and the residential school system, 1879–1986*. Winnipeg, MB: University of Manitoba Press.

Mond, J. M., Robertson-Smith, G., & Vetere, A. (2006). Stigma and eating disorders: Is there evidence of negative attitudes towards anorexia nervosa among women in the community? *Journal of Mental Health, 15* (5), 519–532.

Montgomery, K., & Oliver, A. L. (2009). Shifts in guidelines for ethical scientific conduct: How public and private organizations create and change norms of research integrity. *Social Studies of Science, 39* (1), 137–155.

Moon, B., Hays, K., & Blurton, D. (2009). General strain theory, key strains, and deviance. *Journal of Criminal Justice, 37*, 98–106.

Moon, D. (2008). Culture and the sociology of sexuality: It's only natural? *The Annals of the American Academy of Political and Social Science, 619* (1), 183–205.

Moon, D. (2012). Who am I and who are we? Conflicting narratives of collective selfhood in stigmatized groups. *American Journal of Sociology, 117* (5), 1336–1379.

Moore, K. E., Stuewig, J. B., & Tangney, J. P. (2016). The effect of stigma on criminal offenders' functioning: A longitudinal mediation model. *Deviant Behavior, 37* (2), 196–218.

Morrow, L. C. (2012). Cyclical role-playing and stigma: Exploring the challenges of stereotype performance among exotic dancers. *Deviant Behavior, 33* (5), 357–374.

Mosher, C. E. (2002). Impact of gender and problem severity upon intervention selection. *Sex Roles, 46* (3/4), 113–119.

Mosher, J. F. (2012). Joe Camel in a bottle: Diageo, the Smirnoff brand, and the transformation of the youth alcohol market. *American Journal of Public Health, 102* (1), 56–63

Mostert, M. P. (2002). Useless eaters: Disability as genocidal marker in Nazi Germany. *Journal of Special Education, 36* (3), 155–168.

Mrug, S., Madan, A., Cook, E. W., & Wright, R. A. (2015). Emotional and physiological desensitization to real-life and movie violence. *Journal of Youth and Adolescence, 44*, 1092–1108.

Mullaney, C. (2016). Reshaping time: Recommendations for suicide prevention in LGBT populations. *Journal of Homosexuality, 63* (3), 461–465.

Murphy, E. F. (1973 [1922]). *The Black Candle*. Toronto, ON: Coles Publishing.

Musambira, G. W., Raymond, L., & Hastings, S. O. (2016). A comparison of college students' perceptions of older and younger tattooed women. *Journal of Women and Aging, 28* (1), 9–23.

Nabors, L., Merianos, A., & Olsen, B. (2016). Perceptions of a child who was overweight or of average weight by African American children. *Child and Adolescent Social Work Journal, 33* (1), 47–53.

Nakash, O., & Saguy, T. (2015). Social identities of clients and therapists during the mental health intake predict diagnostic accuracy. *Social Psychological and Personality Science, 6* (6), 710–717

NAMBLA (n.d.). Homepage. Retrieved from www.nambla.org.

NAMBLA Controversy (n.d.). Let us first dispell the conservative myth on NAMBLA being supported by the gay community. Retrieved from www.network54.com.

Nanda, S. (2000). *Gender diversity: Crosscultural variations*. Chicago, IL: Waveland Press Inc.

National Eating Disorders Association. (2014). Home. Retrieved from nationaleatingdisorders.org.

Neal, L. S. (2008). "They're freaks!" The cult stereotype in fictional television shows, 1958–2008. *Nova Religio, 14* (3), 81–107.

Neighbors, H. W., Trierweiler, S. J., Ford, B. C., & Muroff, J. R. (2003). Racial differences in DSM diagnosis using a semi-structured instrument: The importance of clinical judgment in the diagnosis of African Americans. *Journal of Health and Social Behavior, 43*, 237–256.

Niebuhr, H. R. (1929). *The social sources of denominationalism*. Gloucester, MA: Peter Smith.

Nelson, A. (2010). *Gender in Canada* (4th ed.). Toronto, ON: Pearson Education.

Nelson, E. D., & Robinson, B. W. (2002). *Gender in Canada*. Toronto, ON: Prentice Hall.

Newhouse, D. (1998). Magic and joy: Traditional Aboriginal views of human sexuality. *Canadian Journal of Human Sexuality, 7* (2), 183–187.

Newman, A. W., Wright, S. W., Wrenn, K. D., & Bernard, A. (2005). Should physicians have facial piercings? *Journal of General Internal Medicine, 20* (3), 213–218.

Newman, G. (2008). *Comparative deviance: Perception and law in six cultures*. New Brunswick, NJ: Transaction Publishers.

Nietzsche, F. (2004 [1886]). *Beyond good and evil*. I. Johnston (Trans.). Retrieved from www.mala.bc.ca.

Nieuwoudt, J. E., Zhou, S., Coutts, R., Booker, R., Yoxall, J. & Booker, S. (2016). Evaluating the reliability and validity of the proposed muscle dysmorphia criteria. *International Journal of Sports and Exercise Psychology, 14* (3), 195–209.

Nofziger, S., & Callanan, V. J. (2016). Predicting suicidal tendencies among high risk youth with the general theory of crime. *Deviant Behavior, 37* (2), 167–183.

Norman, L. B., & Ford, J. A. (2015). Adolescent ecstasy use: A test of social bonds and social learning theory. *Deviant Behavior, 36* (7), 527–538.

Nylenna, M., & Simonsen, S. (2006). Scientific misconduct: A new approach to prevention. *The Lancet, 367,* 1882–1884.

O'Neil, L. (2016). White people with dreadlocks: Justin Bieber adds fuel to the cultural appropriation debate. *CBC News.* Retrieved from www.cbc.ca/news.

Ontario Consultants on Religious Tolerance (2004). Homepage. Retrieved from www.religioustolerance.org.

Opsal, T. (2012). 'Livin' on the straights': Identity, desistance, and work among women post-incarceration. *Sociological Inquiry, 82* (3), 378–403.

Orend, A., & Gagné, P. (2009). Corporate logo tattoos and the commodification of the Body. *Journal of Contemporary Ethnography, 38,* 493–517.

Oudshourn, J. (2015). *Trauma-informed youth justice in Canada: A new framework toward a kinder future.* Toronto, ON: Canadian Scholars' Press.

Owen, D. C., Armstrong, M. L., Koch, J. R., & Roberts, A. E. (2013). College students with body art: Well-being or higher risk behavior? *Journal of Psychosocial Nursing, 51,* 20–28.

Owen, P. R., & Laurel-Seller, E. (2000). Weight and shape ideals: Thin is dangerously in. *Journal of Applied Social Psychology, 30* (5), 979–990.

Owens, E. W., Behun, R. J., Manning, J. C., & Reid, R. C. (2012). The impact of Internet pornography on adolescents: A review of the research. *Sexual Addiction & Compulsivity: The Journal of Treatment and Prevention, 19* (1–2), 99–122.

Oxford Dictionaries (2017). Belief system. Retrieved from www.en.oxforddictionaries.com.

Ozanian, M. (2016, October 5). Confirmed: NFL losing millions of TV viewers because of national anthem protests. *Forbes Magazine.* Retrieved from www.forbes.com.

Palmer, S. J. (2011). *The new heretics of France: Minority religions, la republique, and the government-sponsored "war on sects."* Oxford, UK: Oxford University Press.

Parents Television Council (2017). Family guide to prime-time television. Retrieved from www.parentstv.org.

Parnaby, P. F., & Sacco, V. F. (2004). Fame and strain: The contributions of Mertonian deviance theory to an understanding of the relationship between celebrity and deviant behavior. *Deviant Behavior, 25* (1), 1–26.

Parrott, S., & Parrott, C. T. (2015). Law and disorder: The portrayal of mental illness in U.S. crime dramas. *Journal of Broadcasting and Electronic Media, 59* (4), 640–657.

Parsons, T. (1951). *The social system.* Glencoe, IL: Free Press.

Parsons, T., & Smelser, N. J. (1956). *Economy and society: A study in the integration of economic and social theory.* Glencoe, IL: Free Press.

Paton, N., & Figeac, J. (2015). Expressive violence: The performative effects of subversive participating media use. *Journal for Communication Studies, 8* (1), 231–256.

Patton, D. U., Lane, J., Leonard, P., Macbeth, J., & Smith-Lee, J. R. (2016). Gang violence on the digital street: Case study of a South Side Chicago gang member's Twitter communication. *New Media and Society.* Article first published online January 25, 2016.

Pearson, G. (1983). *Hooligan: A history of respectable fears.* London, UK: MacMillan Press.

Peck, R. L. (2001). What's new with ADHD? *Behavioral Health Management* (November/December), 26–29.

Pedersen, C. L., Champion, A. R., Hesse, C. L., & Lewis, B. J. (2015). A question of deviancy: Comparing exotic dancers and female university students. *Sexuality and Culture, 19*, 800–815.

Penrose, L. S. (1939). Mental disease and crime: Outline of a comparative study of European statistics. *British Journal of Medical Psychology, 18*, 1–15.

Perry, B. L. (2011). The labeling paradox: Stigma, the sick role, and social networks in mental illness. *Journal of Health and Social Behavior, 52* (4), 460–477.

Perry, B. L. (2014). Symptoms, stigma, or secondary social disruption: Three mechanisms of network discrepancies in severe mental illness. *Journal of Social and Personal Relationships, 31* (1), 32–53.

Pew Research Center (2017). *The changing global religious landscape.* Washington, DC: Author.

PFLAG Canada (n.d.). PFLAG Canada homepage. Retrieved from www .pflagcanada.ca.

Pfohl, S. (1994). *Images of deviance and social control: A sociological history.* New York, NY: McGraw-Hill.

Phil, R. (2014). Understanding the risk factors for substance abuse. In M. Leyton and S. Stewart (Eds.), *Substance abuse in Canada: Childhood and adolescent pathways to substance use disorders* (pp. 13-23). Ottawa, ON: Canadian Centre on Substance Abuse.

Pietrus, M. (2013). *Opening minds interim report.* Calgary, AB: Mental Health Commission of Canada.

Pinto, M. F. (2015). Tensions in agnotology: Normativity in the studies of commercially driven ignorance. *Social Studies of Science, 45* (2), 294–315.

Piquero, N. L., Tibbets, S. G., & Blankenship, M. B. (2005). Examining the role of differential association and techniques of neutralization in explaining corporate crime. *Deviant Behavior, 26* (2), 159–188.

Platt, A. M. (1977). *The child savers: The invention of delinquency.* Chicago, IL: University of Chicago Press.

Polansky, J. R., Titus, K., Atayeva, R., & Glantz, S. A. (2016). *Smoking in top-grossing US movies 2015.* Series: Tobacco Control Policy Making: United States. Retrieved from www.scholarship.org.

Pollard, J. (2016). Skinhead culture: The ideologies, mythologies, religions and conspiracy theories of racist skinheads. *Patterns of Prejudice, 50* (4–5), 398–419.

Popenoe, P., & Johnson, R. H. (1922). *Applied eugenics.* New York, NY: Macmillan.

Potts, A., & Tiefer, L. (Eds.). (2006). Introduction. *Sexualities, 9* (3), 267–272.

Powers, L. (April 13, 2016). Big business takes up role in fight against anti-LGBT laws in US. Retrieved from www.cbc .ca/news.

Pratt, T. C., Cullen, T. C., Sellers, C. S., Winfree, Jr., L. T., Madensen, T. D., Daigle, L. ... Gau, J. M. (2010). The empirical status of social learning theory: A meta-analysis. *Justice Quarterly, 27* (6), 765–802.

Price, V. D., Tewkesbury, D., & Powers, E. (1997). Switching trains of thought: The impact of news frames on readers' cognitive responses. *Communication Research, 24* (5), 481–506.

Proctor, R. (2011). *Golden holocaust: Origins of the cigarette catastrophe and the case for abolition.* Oakland, CA: University of California Press.

Pryor, J. B., & Reeder, G. D. (2011). HIV-related stigma. In J. C. Hall, B. J. Hall, and C. J. Cockerall (Eds.), *HIV/AIDS in the post-HAART era: Manifestations, treatment, and epidemiology* (pp. 790–806). Shelton, CT: PMPH-USA.

Public Health Agency of Canada (2010). *Curbing childhood obesity: a F/P/T framework for action to promote healthy weights*. Ottawa, ON: Author.

Public Health Agency of Canada (2011a). *Obesity in Canada*. Ottawa, ON: Author.

Public Health Agency of Canada (2011b). *Our health our future: A national dialogue on healthy weights: Dialogue report*. Ottawa, ON: Author.

Public Health Agency of Canada (2015). *Mental illness*. Retrieved from www .phac-aspc.gc.ca.

Public Safety Canada (n.d.). *Youth gang involvement: What are the risk factors?* Ottawa, ON: Author.

Public Safety Canada (2016). *Youth gangs in Canada: What do we know?* Ottawa, ON: Author.

Puhl, R., & Brownell, K. D. (2001). Bias, discrimination, and obesity. *Obesity Research, 9*, 788–805.

Puhl, R. M., & Heuer, C. A. (2009). The stigma of obesity: A review and update. *Obesity, 17*, 941–964.

Puhl, R. M., & Latner, J. (2007). Obesity, stigma, and the health of the nation's children. *Psychological Bulletin, 133*, 557–580.

Quaife, G. R. (1987). *Godly zeal and furious rage: The witch craze in early modern Europe*. New York, NY: St. Martin's Press.

Quinney, R. (1977). *The problem of crime: A critical introduction to criminology* (2nd ed.). New York, NY: Harper & Row.

Quisenberry, P. (2015). Texting and driving: Can it be explained by general strain theory? *American Journal of Criminal Justice, 40* (2), 303–316.

Raine, S. (2017). Colonizing terra incognita: L. Ron Hubbard, Scientology, and the quest for empire. In S. A. Kent and S. Raine (Eds.), *Scientology in popular culture: Influences and struggles for legitimacy*. Santa Barbara, CA: Praeger.

Razack, S. H. (2002). *Race, space, and the law: Unmapping a white settler society*. Toronto, ON: Between the Lines.

Reardon, S. (2015). US vaccine researcher sentenced to prison for fraud. *Nature, 523*, 7559.

reFOCUS (1998–2012). Singer's six conditions. Retrieved from www.refocus.org.

Regioli, R., & Hewitt, J. (1994). *Delinquency in society: A child-centered approach*. New York, NY: McGraw-Hill.

Reiner, R. (2013). Who governs? Democracy, plutocracy, science and prophecy in policing. *Criminology and Criminal Justice, 13* (2), 161–180.

Reitsma-Street, M. (1989–1990). More control than care: A critique of historical and contemporary laws for delinquency and neglect of children in Ontario. *Canadian Journal of Women and the Law, 3* (2), 510–530.

Research Alliance for Canadian Homeless, Housing, and Health (2010). *Housing vulnerability and health: Canada's hidden emergency*. Homeless Hub Report #2.

Restivo, E., & Lanier, M. (2005). Measuring the contextual effects and mitigating factors of labeling theory. *Justice Quarterly, 32* (1), 116–141.

Reyns, B. W., Henson, B., & Fisher, B. S. (2012). Stalking in the twilight zone: Extent of cyberstalking victimization and offending among college students. *Deviant Behavior, 33* (1), 1–25.

Rice, E., Petering, R., Rhoades, H., Winetrobe, H., Goldbach, J., Plant, A., ... Kordic, T. (2015). Cyberbullying perpetrators and victimization among middle school students. *American Journal of Public Health, 105* (3), e66–e72.

Richardson, J. T., Best, J., & Bromley, D. G. (1991). *The satanism scare*. New York, NY: Aldine de Gruyter.

Rifkin, M. (2011). *When did Indians become straight? Kinship, the history of sexuality, and native sovereignty*. New York, NY: Oxford University Press.

Ritzer, G. (2006). *McDonaldization: The reader* (2nd ed.). Thousand Oaks, CA: Pine Forge Press.

Ritzer, G., & Goodman, D. J. (2004). *Sociological theory* (6th ed.). New York, NY: McGraw-Hill.

Ritzer, G. & Stepnisky, J. (2014). *Sociological theory* (9th ed.). New York, NY: McGraw Hill.

Roberts, D. (2016). Using dramaturgy to better understand contemporary Western tattoos. *Sociology Compass, 10* (9), 795–801.

Roberts, D. (2015). Modified people: Indicator of a body modification subculture in a post-subculture world. *Sociology, 49* (6), 1096–1112.

Roberts, S. P., Siegel, M. B., DeJong, W., Ross, C. S., Naimi, T., Albers, A., ... Jerrigan, D. H. (2016). Brands matter: Major findings from the Alcohol Brand Research Among Underage Drinkers (ABRAND) project. *Addiction Research and Theory, 24* (1), 32–39.

Roberts, G., McCall, D., Stevens-Lavigne, A., Anderson, J., Paglia, A., Bollenbach, S., ... Gliksman, L. (2001). *Preventing substance use problems among young people: A compendium of best practices.* Ottawa, ON: Health Canada.

Robinson, C. M. (2008). Order in chaos: Security culture as anarchist resistance to the terrorist label. *Deviant Behavior: An Interdisciplinary Journal, 29* (3), 225–252.

Roscoe, W. (1998). *Changing ones: Third and fourth genders in native North America.* New York, NY: St. Martin's Press.

Rosenau, P. M. (1992). *Postmodernism and the social sciences.* Princeton, NJ: Princeton University Press.

Rosengren, C. (2015). Performing work: The drama of everyday working life. *Time & Society, 0* (0), 1–21.

Rosenhan, D. L. (1973). Being sane in insane places. *Science, 179,* 250–258.

Ross, W. (2014). Robbery on the Silk Road. *Newsweek.* Retrieved from www.newsweek.com.

Rothman, D. J. (1971). *The discovery of the asylum: Social order & disorder in the new republic.* Baltimore, MD: Johns Hopkins University Press.

Rubington, E., & Weinberg, M. S. (2002). *Deviance: The interactionist perspective* (8th ed.). Boston, MA: Allyn & Bacon.

Rubington, E., & Weinberg, M. S. (2008). *Deviance: The interactionist perspective* (10th ed.). Boston, MA: Pearson Education.

Sacco, V. F. (1992). *Deviance, conformity and control in Canadian society.* Toronto, ON: Prentice Hall.

Sagan, A. (2015). School dress codes 'demeaning' to both sexes. *CBC News.* Retrieved from www.cbc.ca/news.

Salvatore, C., & Taniguchi, T. A. (2012). Do social bonds matter for emerging adults? *Deviant Behavior, 33* (9), 738–756.

Sanders, C. (1989). *Customizing the body: The art and culture of tattooing.* Philadelphia, PA: Temple University Press.

Santoro, W. A., & Broidy, L. (2014). Gendered rioting: A general strain theoretical approach. *Social Forces, 93* (1), 329–354.

Sareen, J., Cox, B. J., Afifi, T. O., Yu, B. N., & Stein, M. B. (2005). Mental health service use in a nationally representative Canadian survey. *Canadian Journal of Psychiatry, 50* (12), 753–761.

Saxe, J. G. (1873). *The poems of John Godfrey Saxe.* Boston, MA: James R. Osgood and Company. Retrieved from rack1.ul.cs.cmu.edu.

Schaefer, B. P., Vito, A. G., Marcum, C. D., Higgins, G. E., & Ricketts, M. L. (2015). Examining adolescent cocaine use with social learning and self control theories. *Deviant Behavior, 36* (10), 823–833

Scheff, T. J. (1966). *Being mentally ill.* Chicago, IL: Aldine Publishing.

Schiele, K., & Venkatesh, A. (2016). Regaining control through reclamation: How consumption subcultures preserve meaning and group identity after commodification. *Consumption Markets and Culture, 5,* 427–450.

Schildkrout, E. (2004). Inscribing the body. *Annual Review of Anthropology, 33,* 319–344.

Schissel, B. (2001). Youth crime, moral panics, and the news: The conspiracy against the marginalized in Canada. In R. C. Smandych (Ed.), *Youth justice: History, legislation, and reform* (pp. 84–103). Toronto, ON: Harcourt.

Schreck, C., Stewart, E., & Fisher, B. (2006). Self-control, victimization, and their influence on risky lifestyles: A longitudinal analysis using panel data. *Journal of Quantitative Criminology, 22* (4), 319–340.

Schroeder, R. D., & Mowen, T. J. (2014). "You can't eat WHAT?" Managing the stigma of celiac disease. *Deviant Behavior, 35* (6), 456–474.

Schwadel, P. (2014). Are white evangelical Protestants lower class? A partial test of church-sect theory. *Social Science Research, 46,* 100–116.

Schwartz, M. B., Vartanian, L. R., Nosek, B. A., & Brownell, K. D. (2006). The influence of one's own body weight on implicit and explicit anti-fat bias. *Obesity, 14* (3), 440–447.

Scott, S., & Dawson, M. (2015). Rethinking asexuality: A symbolic interactionist account. *Sexualities, 18* (1/2), 3–19.

Scribner, R. A., et al. (2011). Alcohol prevention on college campuses: The moderating effect of the alcohol environment on the effectiveness of social norms marketing campaigns. *Journal of Studies on Alcohol and Drugs, 72* (2), 232–239.

Scull, M. T. (2015). The self-concept as a side bet: How stripping enhances the self-views of men who dance for women. *Deviant Behavior, 36* (1) 890–909.

Sefiha, O. (2012). Bike racing, neutralization and the social construction of performance-enhancing drugs. *Contemporary Drug Problems, 39,* 213–245.

Seib, C., Fischer, J., & Najman, J. (2009). The health of female sex workers from three industry sectors in Queensland, Australia. *Social Science and Medicine, 68,* 473–478.

Seldon, S., & Montagu, A. (1999). *Inheriting shame: The story of eugenics and racism in America.* New York, NY: Teachers College Press.

Sellin, T. (1938). *Culture conflict and crime.* New York, NY: Social Science Research Council.

Serup, J., Hutton, C. K., & Sepehri, M. (2015). Tattoo complaints and complications: Diagnosis and clinical spectrum. *Current Problems in Dermatology, 48,* 48–60.

Shade, L. R. (Ed.). (2014). *Mediascapes: New patterns in Canadian communication* (4th ed.). Toronto, ON: Nelson Education.

Shade, L. R., & Lithgow, M. (2014). Media ownership, public participation, and democracy in the Canadian media landscape. In L. R. Shade (Ed.), *Mediascapes: New Patterns in Canadian Communication.* Toronto, ON: Nelson.

Sharp, S. F., Terling-Watt, T. L., Atkins, L. A., & Gilliam, J. T. (2001). Purging behavior in a sample of college females: A research note on general strain theory and female deviance. *Deviant Behavior: An Interdisciplinary Journal, 22* (2), 171–188.

Shaw, G., & Raine, S. (2017). Remember the whole track? The hidden persuaders in Scientology art. In S. A. Kent and S. Raine (Eds.), *Scientology in popular culture: Influences and struggles for legitimacy.* Santa Barbara, CA: Praeger.

Shdaimah, C. S., & Leon, C. (2015). "First and foremost, they're survivors": Selective manipulation, resilience, and assertion among prostituted women. *Feminist Criminology, 10* (4), 326–347.

Shermer, M. (2001). *The borderlands of science: Where sense meets nonsense.* New York, NY: Oxford University Press.

Shields, M. (2005). The journey to quitting smoking. *Health Reports, 16* (3), 19–37. Statistics Canada Catalogue No. 82003XIE.

Shilling, C. (1993). *The body and social theory.* London, UK: Sage.

Shoenberger, N., Heckert, A., & Heckert, D. (2012). Techniques of neutralization theory and positive deviance. *Deviant Behavior, 33* (10), 774–791.

Shupe, A. D., & Bromley, D. G. (1995). The evolution of modern American anti-cult ideology. In T. Miller (Ed.), *America's alternative religions* (pp. 401–409). Albany, NY: State University Press.

Shute, N. (2000, October 2). Pushing pills on kids? *U S. News & World Report, 129* (13), 60.

Siegel, L. J., & McCormick, C. (2016). *Criminology in Canada: Theories, patterns, and typologies* (6th ed.). Toronto, ON: Nelson Education.

Silverstone, R. (2007). *Media and morality: On the rise of the Mediapolis.* Cambridge, UK: Polity Press.

Simply Reference (2017). Quotes. Retrieved from www.simplyreference.com.

Sinha, R., & Brotnow, L. (2014). A call to action. In M. Leyton and S. Stewart (Eds.), *Substance abuse in Canada: Childhood and adolescent pathways to substance use disorders* (pp. 84–88). Ottawa, ON: Canadian Centre on Substance Abuse.

Sloan, L., & Wahab, S. (2004). Four categories of women who work as topless dancers. *Sexuality & Culture, 8* (1), 18–43.

Smith, A. (2014). Indigenous feminists are too sexy for your heteropatriarchal settler colonialism. *African Journal of Criminology and Justice Studies, 8* (1), 89–103.

Smith, R. A. (2012). An experimental test of stigma communication content with a hypothetical disease alert. *Communication Monographs, 79* (4), 522–538.

Smith, R. A., & Hughes, D. (2014). Infectious disease stigmas: Maladaptive in modern society. *Communication Studies, 65* (2), 132–138.

Smokowski, P. R., Evans, C. B. R., & Cotter, K. L. (2014). The differential impact of episodic, chronic, and cumulative physical bullying and cyberbullying: The effects of victimization on the school experiences, social support, and the mental health of rural adolescents. *Violence and Victims, 29* (6), 1029–1046.

Sohrabi, H., & Farquharson, K. (2016). Social integration of Australian Muslims: A dramaturgical perspective. *Journal of Sociology, 52* (2), 387–402.

Spector, M. (1981). Beyond crime: Seven methods to control troublesome rascals. In L. Ross (Ed.), *Law and deviance* (pp. 127–148). Beverly Hills, CA: Sage Publications.

Spitzer, B. L., Henderson, K. A., & Zivian, M. T. (1999). Gender differences in population versus media body sizes: A comparison over four decades. *Sex Roles, 40,* 545–565.

Springhall, J. (1999). *Youth, popular culture and moral panics: Penny gaffs to gangsta rap, 1830–1997.* New York, NY: Palgrave Macmillan.

The Standing Senate Committee on Social Affairs, Science and Technology. (2006). *Out of the shadows at last: Transforming mental health, mental illness and addiction services in Canada.* Ottawa: Parliament of Canada.

Stark, C. A. (1997). Is pornography an action? The causal vs. the conceptual view of pornography's harm. *Social Theory & Practice, 23* (2), 277–306.

Stark, R., & Bainbridge, W. S. (1996). *A theory of religion.* New Brunswick, NJ: Rutgers University Press.

Statista (2016). *Advertising in Canada: Statista Dossier.* Retrieved from www.statista.com.

Statistics Canada (2013, May 8). 2011 National Household Survey: Immigration, place of birth, citizenship, ethnic origin, visible minorities, language and religion. *The Daily.*

Statistics Canada (2015). *Smoking, 2014.* Health Fact Sheet. Statistics Canada Catalogue No. 82-625-X. Ottawa, ON: Author.

Statistics Canada (2016a, September 28). Canada's crime rate: Two decades of decline. *Canadian Megatrends.* Statistics Canada Catalogue No. 11-630-X. Ottawa, ON: Author.

Statistics Canada (2016b, February 17). Youth crime in Canada, 2014. *The Daily.*

Statistics Canada (2016c). CANSIM Table 252-0092. Police-reported hate crime, by type of motivation, Canada. Accessed: January 28, 2017.

Statistics Canada (2016d). CANSIM Table 252-0052. Police-reported crime severity index, Canada, 2005–2015. Accessed: January 28, 2017.

Statistics Canada (2016e). CANSIM Table 105-0501. Health indicator profile, annual estimates, by age group and sex, Canada, provinces, territories, health regions (2013 boundaries) and peer groups. Accessed: March 1, 2017.

Steger, M. B. (2013). *Globalization: A very short introduction* (3rd ed.). New York, NY: Oxford University Press.

Steinmetz, K. F., & Tunnell, K. D. (2013). Under the pixelated Jolly Roger: A study of online pirates. *Deviant Behavior, 34* (1), 53–67.

Steeves, V. *Young Canadians in a Wired World: Phase III. Trends and Recommendations.* Ottawa, 2014 MediaSmarts.

Stone, M. M. (2014). "This could be a good avenue for you": Influential strategies in the hiring of exotic dancers. *Deviant Behavior, 35* (9), 727–741.

Stonebridge, C., & Sutherland, G. (2016). *Healthy brains at work: Estimating the impact of workplace mental health benefits and programs.* Ottawa, ON: The Conference Board of Canada.

Strike the Box (2017). *Strike the box: The Internet's first website dedicated to the art of firefighter tattoos.* Retrieved from www.strikethebox.com.

Stringer, K. L., & Baker, E. H. (2015). Stigma as a barrier to substance abuse treatment among those with unmet need: An analysis of parenthood and marital status. *Journal of Family Issues, 0* (0), 1–25.

Stronge, S., Greaves, L. M., Milojev, P., & Sibley, C. G. (2015). Facebook is linked to body dissatisfaction: Comparing users and non-users. *Sex Roles, 73,* 200–213.

Stuart, F. (2014). 'Cop wisdom' and the emerging cultural context of criminalized urban communities. Pulk Seminar, New York University, October 29, 2014.

Stuart, H., Arboleda-Flórez, J. & Santorius, N. (2012). *Paradigms lost: Fighting stigma and the lessons learned.* New York, NY: Oxford University Press.

Stylianou, S. (2002). Control attitudes toward drug use as a function of paternalistic and moralistic principles. *Journal of Drug Use, 32* (1), 119–152.

Sumner, W. G. (1906). *Folkways: A study of the sociological importance of usages, manners, mores, and morals.* Boston, MA: Ginn and Co.

Surowiecki, J. (2016). A big tobacco moment for the sugar industry. *New Yorker.* Retrieved from www.newyorker.com.

Sutherland, E. H. (1947). *Principles of criminology.* Philadelphia, PA: J. B. Lippincott.

Sutherland, N. (1976). *Children in English-Canadian society: Framing the twentieth-century consensus.* Toronto, ON: University of Toronto Press.

Swami, V., & Furnham, A. (2007). Unattractive, promiscuous and heavy drinkers: Perceptions of women with tattoos. *Body Image, 4*, 343–352.

Sykes, G., & Matza, D. (1957). Techniques of neutralization: A theory of delinquency. *American Sociological Review, 22*, 664–670.

Szasz, T. (1994). Mental illness is still a myth. *Society, 31* (4), 34–39.

Tannenbaum, F. (1938). *Crime and the community*. New York, NY: Ginn.

Tanner, J. (2001). *Teenage troubles: Youth and deviance in Canada* (2nd ed.). Toronto, ON: Nelson Thomson.

Tanner, J. (2015). *Teenage troubles: Youth and deviance in Canada* (4th ed.). Toronto, ON: Nelson Thomson.

Taylor, A. (2011). *Social media as a tool for inclusion*. Ottawa, ON: Human Resources and Skills Development Canada.

Taylor, H. (2016, February 5). The hacking economy: An inside look at what's driving the hacking economy. Retrieved from www.cnbc.com.

Taylor, N. L. (2011). Negotiating popular obesity discourses in adolescence. *Food, Culture and Society, 14* (4), 587–606.

Thio, A. (1983). *Deviant behavior* (2nd ed.). Boston, MA: Houghton Mifflin.

Thoits, P. A. (2011). Resisting the stigma of mental illness. *Social Psychology Quarterly, 74* (1), 6–28.

Thoits, P. A. (2016). "I'm not mentally ill": Identity deflection as a form of stigma resistance. *Journal of Health and Social Behavior, 57* (2), 135–151.

Thoits, P. A., & Link, B. G. (2016). Stigma resistance and well-being among people in treatment for psychosis. *Society and Mental Health, 6* (1), 1–20.

Thompson, J., Baird, P. A., & Downie, J. (2005, December 3). The Olivieri case: Context and significance. *Ecclectica*. Retrieved from www.ecclectica.ca.

Thomson Reuters (2016). Facebook reportedly builds censorship tool to re-enter China. Retrieved from www.cbc.ca/news.

Thornberry, T., Lizotte, A., Krohm, M., Farnworth, M., & Jang, S. (1991). Testing interactional theory: An examination of reciprocal causal relationships among family, school and delinquency. *Journal of Criminal Law and Criminology, 82* (1), 3–33.

Thyer, B. A., & Pignotti, M. (2016). The problem of pseudoscience in social work continuing education. *Journal of Social Work Education, 52* (2), 136–146.

Tiefer, L. (2006). The Viagra phenomenon. *Sexualities, 9* (3), 273–294.

Timming, A. R. (2015). Visible tattoos in the service sector: A new challenge to recruitment and selection. *Work, Employment and Society, 29* (1), 60–78.

Tittle, C. R., & Paternoster, R. (2000). *Social deviance and crime*. Los Angeles, CA: Roxbury.

Titus, S. L. (2014). Evaluating U.S. medical schools' efforts to educate faculty researchers on research integrity and research misconduct policies and procedures. *Accountability in Research, 21* (1), 9–25.

Totten, M. (2016). Street-involved youth in Canada. In J. A. Winterdyk and R. Smandych (Eds.), *Youth at risk and youth justice: A Canadian overview* (2nd ed.). Toronto, ON: OUP Canada.

Travers, R., Bauer, G., Pyne, J., Bradley K., for the Trans PULSE project; Gale, L., & Papadimitriou, M. (2012). Impacts of strong parental support from trans youth: A report prepared for Children's Aid Society of Toronto and Delisle Youth Services. *Trans Pulse*, 1–5.

Triplett, R., Payne, B., Collins, V. E., & Tapp, S. (2016). Does "violent" mean "bad"?

Individual definitions of violence. *Deviant Behavior, 37* (3), 332–351.

Tremblay, L., Lovsin, T., Zecevic, C., & Larivière, M. (2011). Perceptions of self in 3-5-year-old children: A preliminary investigation into the early emergence of body dissatisfaction. *Body Image, 8* (3), 287–292.

Truth and Reconciliation Commission (2015). *Truth and Reconciliation Commission of Canada: Calls to action.* Winnipeg, MB: Author.

Truth Tobacco Industry Documents (n.d.). *Marketing to youth.* Retrieved from www.industrydocumentslibrary.ucsf.edu/tobacco/

Tsoukala, A. (2008). Boundary-creating processes and the social construction of threat. *Alternatives, 33* (2), 137–152.

Turk, A. (1969). *Criminality and legal order.* Chicago, IL: Rand McNally.

Turner, J. H., & Maryanski, A. (1979). *Functionalism.* Menlo Park, CA: Benjamin/Cummings.

Tylka, T. L., & Calogero, R. M. (2011). Fiction, fashion, and function finale: An introduction and conclusion to the special issue on gendered body image. *Sex Roles, 65,* 447–460.

Tyyskä, V. (2014). *Long and winding road: Adolescents and youth in Canada today* (3rd ed.). Toronto, ON: Canadian Scholars' Press.

Ullman, S. R. (1997). *Sex seen: The emergence of modern sexuality in America.* Berkeley, CA: University of California Press.

UNESCO. (1997). *Universal declaration on the human genome and human rights.* Paris, FR: Author.

US Attorney's Office. (2012, June 26). Manhattan U.S. attorney and FBI assistant director-in-charge announce 24 arrests in eight countries as part of international cyber crime takedown. Retrieved from www.justice.gov.

US Bureau of Labor Statistics (2016). *American time use survey.* Retrieved from www.bls.gov/tus/.

US Department of State (2015). *International religious freedom report for 2015.* Retrieved from www.state.gov.

Vaidyanathan, B., Khalsa, S., & Ecklund, E. H. (2016). Gossip as social control: Informal sanctions on ethical violations in scientific workplaces. *Social Problems, 63,* 554–572.

Valverde, M. (1991). *The age of light, soap, and water: Moral reform in English Canada, 1885–1925.* Toronto, ON: McClelland & Stewart.

van der Meulen, E. (2011). Sex work and Canadian policy: Recommendations for labor legitimacy and social change. *Sex Research and Social Policy, 8,* 348–358.

Van Rassel, J. (2009, March 14). The evolution of Calgary's deadly gang war. *Calgary Herald.* Retrieved from www.calgaryherald.com.

Vartanian, L. R., Trewartha, T., & Vanman, E. J. (2016). Digust predicts prejudice and discrimination toward individuals with obesity. *Journal of Applied Social Psychology, 46* (6), 369–375.

Venkatesh, S. (2003). A note on social theory and the American street gang. In L. Kontos, D. Brotherton, and L. Barrios (Eds.), *Gangs and society: Alternative perspectives.* New York, NY: Columbia University Press.

Vines, M., & Linders, A. (2016). The dirty work of poker: Impression management and identity. *Deviant Behavior, 37* (9), 1064–1076.

Vold, G. (1958). *Theoretical criminology.* New York, NY: Oxford University Press.

Vowell, P. R., & Chen, J. (2004). Predicting academic misconduct: A comparative test of four sociological explanations. *Sociological Inquiry, 74,* 226–249.

Vuijst, F. (Director & Producer). (1995). *Onward Christian soldiers.* United States: Green Room Productions. Available from Filmakers Library, 124 East 40th Street, NY, NY 10016.

Wagner, A. C., McShane, K. E., Hart, T. A., & Margolese, S. (2016). A focus group qualitative study of HIV stigma in the Canadian healthcare system. *The Canadian Journal of Human Sexuality, 25* (1), 61–71.

Wahl, O. F. (2003). Depictions of mental illness in children's media. *Journal of Mental Health, 12* (3), 249–258.

Wai Ting Cheung, N., & Cheung, Y. W. (2010). Strain, self-control, and gender differences in delinquency among Chinese adolescents: Extending general strain theory. *Sociological Perspectives, 53* (3), 321–345.

Wallace, C., & Alt, R. (2001). Youth cultures under authoritarian regimes: The case of the Swings against the Nazis. *Youth and Society, 32* (3), 275–302.

Wang, J. L., Smailes, E., Sareen, J., Fick, G. H., Schmitz, N., & Patten, S. B. (2010). The prevalence of mental disorders in the working population over the period of global economic crisis. *Canadian Journal of Psychiatry, 55,* 598–605.

The Walrus (2015, April). Scientology attacks! Going to war with L. Ron Hubbard's disciples. Retrieved from http://thewalrus.ca/scientology-attacks/.

Warschburger, P. (2005). The unhappy obese child. *International Journal of Obesity, 29,* 127–129.

Weber, M. (1946). *Essays in sociology.* Translated and edited by H. H. Gerth and C. Wright Mills. New York, NY: Oxford University Press.

Wechsler, H., Lee, J. E., Kuo, M., Seibring, M., Nelson, M. S., & Lee, H. (2002). Trends in college binge drinking during a period of increased prevention efforts: Findings from four Harvard School of Public Health College alcohol student surveys: 1993–2001. *Journal of American College Health, 50* (5), 203–217.

Wechsler, H., & Nelson, T. F. (2008). What we have learned from the Harvard School of Public Health College alcohol study: Focusing attention on college student alcohol consumption and the environmental conditions that promote it. *Journal of Studies on Alcohol and Drugs, 69* (4), 481–490.

Wegs, R. (1999). Youth delinquency & "crime": The perception and the reality. *Journal of Social History, 32* (3). Retrieved from Expanded Academic ASAP database.

Weiler, B. (2007). Social Darwinism. *Blackwell Encyclopedia of Sociology.* Ritzer, George (ed). Blackwell Publishing, 2007. Blackwell Reference Online. Retrieved from http://www.blackwellreference.com.

Weimann, G. (2016). Going dark: Terrorism on the dark web. *Studies in Conflict and Terrorism, 39* (3), 195–206.

Weitzer, R. (2010). The mythology of prostitution: Advocacy research and public policy. *Sex Research and Social Policy, 7,* 15–29.

Weitzman, E. R., & Nelson, T. F. (2004). College student binge drinking and the "prevention paradox": Implications for prevention and harm reduction. *Journal of Drug Education, 34* (3), 247–266.

Wesely, J. K. (2003). "Where am I going to stop?" Exotic dancing, fluid body boundaries, and effects on identity. *Deviant Behavior, 24* (5), 483–503.

West, W. G. (1984). *Young offenders and the state: A Canadian perspective on delinquency.* Toronto, ON: Butterworths.

West, W. G. (1991). Towards a more socially informed understanding of Canadian delinquency legislation. In A. Leschied, P. Jaffe, & W. Willis (Eds.), *The Young Offenders Act: A revolution in Canadian juvenile justice.* Toronto, ON: University of Toronto Press.

Westlake, A. (2012). The view of tattoos in Japanese society. *Japan Daily Press.* Retrieved from www.japandailypress.com.

Weymouth, B. B., Buehler, C., Zhou, N., & Henson, R. A. (2016). A meta-analysis of parent-adolescent conflict: Disagreement, hostility and youth maladjustment. *Journal of Family Therapy and Review*, 8 (1), 95–112.

Wheeler, S. (1960). Sex offenses: A sociological critique. *Law and Contemporary Society*, 25 (Spring), 258–278.

White, R., Wyn, J., & Albanese, P. (2011). *Youth & Society: Exploring the Social Dynamics of Youth Experience* (Canadian Edition). Toronto, ON: Oxford University Press.

Whorton, J. (2001). The solitary vice. *The Western Journal of Medicine*, 175 (1).

Williams, S. (2016). #SayHerName: using digital activism to document violence against black women. *Feminist Media Studies*, 16 (5), 922–925.

Windecker, J. (1997). The prostitution of native women on the north coast of British Columbia. *British Columbia Historical News*, 30 (3), 29–33.

Wirtz, C., van der Pligt, J., & Doosje, B. (2016). Derogating obese individuals: The role of blame, contempt, and disgust. *Journal of Applied Social Psychology*, 46 (4), 216–228.

Wiseman, E. (2016, September 18). Gemma Arterton: 'It's easier to conform and shut up.' *The Guardian*. Retrieved from www.theguardian.com.

Withey, E. (2012, October 1). Tattoos offer parents permanent tributes to their children, says Edmonton artist. *Edmonton Journal*. Retrieved from www.edmonton-journal.com.

Wolff, N. (2007). The social construction of the costs of mental illness. *Evidence & Policy*, 3 (1), 67–78.

Wong, E. S. (2016). "The brains of a nation": The eugenicist roots of Canada's mental health field and the building of a white non-disabled nation. *Canadian Review of Social Policy*, 75, 1–29.

World Association for Sexual Health (2014). *Declaration of Sexual Rights*. Retrieved from http://www.worldsexology.org.

World Health Organization (2001). Costs of mental illness. *Fact Sheet No. 218*. Retrieved from www.who.int.

World Health Organization (2002). *Mental Health Global Action Programme*. Geneva: Author.

World Health Organization (2004). *WHO Constitution*. Retrieved from www.who.int.

World Health Organization (2011). *Mental health atlas*. Geneva: Author.

World Health Organization (2013). *Mental health action plan: 2013–2020*. Geneva: Author.

World Health Organization (2016). *Obesity and overweight: Fact sheet*. Geneva: Author.

Wroblewska, A. M. (1997). Androgenic anabolic steroids and body dysmorphia in young men. *Journal of Psychosomatic Research*, 42, 225–234.

Wu, Y., Lake, R., & Cao, L. (2015). Race, social bonds, and juvenile attitudes toward the police. *Justice Quarterly*, 32 (3), 445–470.

Yeun Thompson, B. (2015). *Covered in ink: Tattoos, women, and the politics of the body*. New York, NY: New York University Press.

Youngblut, S. (2012, January 4). Do these childhood obesity ads go too far? *Globe and Mail*. Retrieved from www.theglobeandmail.com.

Zeman, K., & Bressan, A. (2008). Factors associated with youth delinquency and victimization in Toronto, 2006. *Crime and Justice Research Paper Series*. Statistics Canada Catalogue No. 85561M, No. 14.

Index

youth, troubling and troubled 158
youth crime 159
see also date rape drugs
Dark Net 117–118
Date rape 135, 174
Deep Web. *See* Dark Net
Deinstitutionalization
  causes 237
  consequences, related
     factors 238–240
  criminality 240
    hydraulic relationship 240
  definition 237
  homelessness 239–240
Deviance dance
  body modification 203–204, 206
  body size 218–219, 222–224, 300
  critical theories 79, 90
  description 21, 300
  interactionist theories 70
  interpretive theories 77
  media, as a site of 109, 115–118,
    300
  mental illness 241–252, 300–301
  raves 21
  religion 259, 262, 267–268, 301
  science 301–302
  sexuality
    in contemporary North America 144,
     300
    exotic dancing 144, 147, 300
    historical views 144
    pornography 148–152, 300
    prostitution 153–155, 300
  youth 300
Deviancy amplification 261
Deviant career 76
Dictionary definitions
  of "deviant" 11, 18
  of "pornography" 150
  of "science" 274
Digital piracy 62, 111, 113–116
Disabilities
  human rights legislation 243
  identity management 73
  media 96, 116
  mental illness 232, 235
  Nazi government 197, 286
  physical appearance 195, 213

Discrimination paradigm, mental
  illness 241, 243–246
Disease paradigm, mental illness
  241–243
Disintegrative shaming 75
Dominant moral codes
  definition 14
  conflict theory 82
  influence of commercial enterprise 24,
    296
  influence of media 25, 94, 106, 110, 116,
    120, 296
  influence of politics 24, 296
  influence of power 14, 23, 82, 296
  influence of religion 24, 241, 257,
    296
  influence of science 24, 296
  postmodernism 88
  sexuality 123–125, 292
  social constructionism 115
Dramatization of evil 71, 76
Dramaturgy 73, 202–203
Drugs
  drug abuse and normative violation 11
  gangs 45, 164, 165
  homework drugs 47
  innovation 43
  mental illness 232, 237, 247
  objectivist view 292
  prevention and treatment programs
    179
  raves, deviance dance 21
  rebellion 44
  retreatism 44
  social control theories 63
  techniques of neutralization 53–54,
    56, 59
  theoretical integration 63
  usage
    contributing factors 178–179
    youth 172–174, 177–178
    reasons for use 178
  weight loss 215–216, 218
  see also date rape
  see also marijuana
  see also raves
  see also Viagra
DSM, critiques of 247–248
Dziekanski, Robert 9

public restrooms, use of 85
sexual cultures 128–129, 132, 137, 143
stigmatization 72
transgender persons 39, 85, 141, 246
General strain theory 46–47, 52
Generalized other 70, 202
Genetic science 287–288, 295, 302, 304–305
Globalization 16–17, 41, 51, 104
Group conflict theory 81

H

Hacking, computer 111–113, 116–118
Hashtag activism 82, 94, 106, 116, 219, 300
Hegemony 83, 94, 107
High-consensus deviance 13, 19, 113
Hippies 44, 195, 263
  see also Children of God
Homework drugs 47
Homicide
  absolutist view of deviance 11
  consequences of marijuana use, historical
      perceptions 7–8
  Manson family murders 261
  normative violation 11
  see also capital punishment
Homosexuality
  hate crimes 140
  in the *DSM* 247, 294
  Indigenous cultures 125–126
  legislation, changes in 139–140, 302, 304
  media 133, 141
  Nazi persecution 280
  same-sex marriage 10, 139
  sexual cultures, historical 124, 126, 132,
      297
  social construction 16, 19
  stigmatization 139, 140–141, 144
  Stonewall Inn uprising 139
  symbolic communication 69
Human rights policy 263, 266, 288, 303–306
Human trafficking 148

I

Iceberg theory 276–277, 295
Identity management 73–75, 203,
    241–243, 267, 293, 300
Ideology 49–50, 83, 99, 107, 130, 142

Impression management. *See* identity
    management
Indigenous peoples
  media framing 124–127
  mental health 246, 230–231
  physical activity 217
  sexuality 124–127
  youth 163, 165–166, 171, 230
  see also colonization
  see also cultural appropriation
  see also residential schooling
  see also Truth and Reconciliation
      Commission
Institutional anomie theory 43, 50, 52
Instrumental conditioning 57
Interactionist view of law 12–13
Interpretive theories
  body modification 202–207
  critiques of 77–78
  digital piracy 114
  gangs 164–166
  link to interactionism 68
  media research, critical 99
  mental illness 227, 234
  relationship to subjective views of
      deviance 67–68, 292
  scientific misconduct 278
  see also deviant career
  see also identity management
  see also labelling theories

J

Jamband subculture 54–55
Jazz, deviantization of 119
Joan of Arc 269
Juvenile Delinquents Act 170

K

King, Martin Luther, Jr. 44

L

Labelling theory 71–76, 78, 90, 106,
    114–115, 222, 234, 251
Latent functions 37
Left-handedness 5
Location of sex as deviant 142
Low-consensus deviance 13, 19, 113

M

Mandela, Nelson 44
Manifest functions 37
Marijuana
   The Black Candle 8, 94
     see also Murphy, Emily
   criminalization 8, 94
   deviant career 76
   debates over decriminalization 10, 19
   harmfulness 7–8
   usage
     relationship with tobacco use 177
     youth 161, 174, 177–178
Marxist theory 79–81, 86, 107, 164
Master status 72, 90, 197
Masturbation
   changing perceptions 142, 297
   perceptions of harm 6, 144
   social control 6–7
   stigmatization 142
Mechanical solidarity 40
Media
   administrative research 98–103, 108, 292
   advertising 99–101, 103, 110
   as a cause of deviance 110
   as a tool for deviance 111–115
   constructions of otherness 97
   critical research 98, 103–108, 109, 110, 292
   definition 94
   framing 104–107, 137, 294, 300
   ownership 107–108, 292
   power 14, 18, 25, 296
   sexuality 123, 132–133, 151, 154, 297
   usage 95–96
   violence 101–103
   see also alcohol
   see also body
   see also cults
   see also cyberbullying
   see also cybercrime
   see also deviance dance
   see also disabilities
   see also eating disorders
   see also gangs
   see also gender
   see also mental illness
   see also religion
   see also social typing

Mental illness
   costs 231–232, 293
     critique of cost-of-illness estimates 232
   definition 227
   historical views 236–237, 298
   Indigenous youth 230–231, 246
   LGBTQ persons 228, 230
   media portrayals 230, 233, 240
   Mental Health Commission of Canada (MHCC) 245
   Out of the Shadows at Last 245
   perceptions of 233–235
   prevalence 228–231, 293
   self-stigma 234
   stigmatization
     effects on recovery 234, 243
     positive effects of 242–243, 251
   total institutions 250
   see also deinstitutionalization
Middle-class measuring rod 47, 164
Midwifery 82
Modes of adaptation 43–44, 51, 229, 278
Moral entrepreneurs 23–25, 94, 132–133, 264, 296
Moral panics 110, 160–161, 163, 168, 190, 261
Mores 11–12
Murder. *See* homicide
Murphy, Emily 8, 94, 132
Muslims
   Crusades, the 259
   functionalist theories 41
   global religious affiliations 258
   identity/impression management 75, 267
   ISIS 24, 27
   media constructions of otherness 97
   religious typologies 256–258
   women 27
   see also countercult movement
   see also Quebec Charter of Values

N

Normality, definition 18
North American Man/Boy Love Association (NAMBLA) 137–138, 144
Nuns 8